Technology and Luxury Hospitality

The integration of pioneering information and communication technologies has transformed the hospitality sector. This groundbreaking book delves into the transformative power of cutting-edge technologies in the world of high-end travel and accommodation. As the digital revolution continues to reshape our lives, this book offers an exclusive look at how the hospitality industry is adapting and evolving to cater to the sophisticated tastes of the modern, tech-savvy traveller.

In this eye-opening exploration, readers will be taken on a journey through the latest innovations in artificial intelligence, blockchain, and the metaverse as they intersect with the world of luxury hospitality. From AI-driven concierge services and smart hotel rooms that cater to guests' every whim to the democratization of luxury experiences through blockchain-based loyalty programmes and the rise of virtual reality travel, this book reveals the extraordinary possibilities that lie ahead for the discerning traveller.

With insights from international experts, this edited collection provides a comprehensive and engaging overview of the current and future trends shaping the industry and will be valuable to scholars and postgraduate researchers across the hospitality sector, innovation, and luxury management.

Park Thaichon is Associate Professor of Marketing at the University of Southern Queensland and Adjunct Associate Professor of Marketing at the Griffith Asia Institute, Griffith University. Park's research, teaching, and consulting focus on digital marketing, AI, technology, relationship marketing, and consumer behaviour. He has been appointed to various leadership roles, for instance, in research, learning and teaching, student recruitment and agent engagements, and academic community service.

Pushan Kumar Dutta, Assistant Professor at Amity University Kolkata, Erasmus Mundus Post-doctorate, and ATL Mentor of Change, leverages over 12 years of interdisciplinary research across data mining, AI, sustainability, biomedical intelligent systems, and more, as evident through his 20 edited volumes with top publishers to advance critical conversations on industry 5.0 and machine ethics.

Pethuru Raj Chelliah is working as Chief Architect and Vice President in the Site Reliability Engineering (SRE) division of Reliance Jio Infocomm Ltd. (RJIL), Bangalore. He has worked with IBM Global Cloud Center of Excellence (CoE), Wipro Consulting Services (WCS), and Robert Bosch Corporate Research (CR). He has 17 years of IT industry experience and 8 years of research experience.

Sachin Gupta is Assistant Professor at Mohanlal Sukhadia University. Passionate about learning and academia, he continues advancing the field across research, writing, advisory boards, and teaching core subjects like corporate finance, strategy, economics, and entrepreneurship. Dr. Sachin Gupta has excelled across his robust academic journey, including earning his Ph.D., M.Phil., MBA in finance, master's in commerce, and B.Com. He further bolstered his finance credentials via an executive programme at XLRI Jamshedpur and certificate from IIM Indore.

Routledge Studies in Luxury Management

This series explores the luxury industry through an interdisciplinary lens, bringing together cutting-edge research to define and advance this growing field. Contributions to the series present original research from established and emerging scholars across the globe, offering a diverse range of empirical and critical perspectives on the luxury industry. Topics include, but are not limited to, marketing, brand management, sustainability, and supply chain management.

The Rise of Positive Luxury
Transformative Research Agenda for Well-being, Social Impact, and Sustainable Growth
Edited by Wided Batat

Made in Italy and the Luxury Market
Heritage, Sustainability and Innovation
Edited by Serena Rovai and Manuela De Carlo

Luxury Marketing, Sustainability and Technology
The Future of Luxury Management
Edited by Park Thaichon and Sara Quach

Managing Sustainable Luxury and Digitalization
Technology Trends and Ethical Challenges in the Swiss Luxury Watch Business
Mario D. Schultz and Peter Seele

Technology and Luxury Hospitality
AI, Blockchain and the Metaverse
Edited by Park Thaichon, Pushan Kumar Dutta, Pethuru Raj Chelliah and Sachin Gupta

For more information about this series, please visit: *www.routledge.com/Routledge-Studies-in-Luxury-Management/book-series/RSLM*

Technology and Luxury Hospitality

AI, Blockchain and the Metaverse

Edited by Park Thaichon, Pushan Kumar Dutta, Pethuru Raj Chelliah and Sachin Gupta

Routledge
Taylor & Francis Group
LONDON AND NEW YORK

First published 2024
by Routledge
4 Park Square, Milton Park, Abingdon, Oxon OX14 4RN

and by Routledge
605 Third Avenue, New York, NY 10158

Routledge is an imprint of the Taylor & Francis Group, an informa business

British Library Cataloguing-in-Publication Data
A catalogue record for this book is available from the British Library

ISBN: 978-1-032-78506-6 (hbk)
ISBN: 978-1-032-78507-3 (pbk)
ISBN: 978-1-003-48824-8 (ebk)

DOI: 10.4324/9781003488248

Typeset in Times New Roman
by Apex CoVantage, LLC

Contents

Contributors

Prof. K. Asha is an assistant professor in the Department of Artificial Intelligence and Machine Learning at Dayananda Sagar College of Engineering. Her areas of teaching are software engineering, cloud computing, database management system, and operating system.

Dr. Prashant H. Bhagat, Vice Principal, Chetanas Hazarimal Somani College of Commerce and Smt. Kusumtai Chaudhari, University of Mumbai, Mumbai, Maharashtra, India.

Namrata Chakraborty holds a master's degree in English literature and a post-graduate diploma degree in stress management and counseling. She has also pursued a B.Ed. and is committed to expanding one's horizons and to instilling critical thinking and effective communication skills in her students. She runs a self-owned initiative – Mindscape – and is dedicated to helping individuals navigate the complexities of the human mind and emotions through counselling. Ms. Chakrabortty believes in creating an engaging and inclusive classroom environment and is an advocate of mental health and body positivity.

She has published articles and book chapters in reputed journals and books (Scopus indexed). She has also participated in and presented papers in different national and international conferences.

Pratim Chatterjee is currently working as an assistant professor at the Amity School of Hospitality, Amity University, Kolkata, West Bengal. He is a graduate in hotel and hospitality administration from IHM, Bhubaneswar (NCHMCT&AN) and post-graduate in business management with specialization in marketing from ICFAI Business School. Mr. Chatterjee has qualified the UGC NET (Management) and is currently pursuing his Ph.D. in management from University of Engineering & Management, Kolkata. His areas of research interest include sustainability in hospitality and tourism, smart hospitality, tourist destination and hospitality, and tourism marketing policy. He has published research articles and book chapters in internationally reputed journals (Scopus & ESCI Index) as well as nationally reputed journals (*UGC Care Journal*). He has also participated in and presented papers at national and international conferences. Altogether, he has 14 years of working experience along with great desire for research and contribution to the society.

Dr. A. J. Frederick, Ph.D., M.B.A., UGC NET is Professor (Assistant) at Sam Higginbottom University of Agriculture, Technology and Sciences, Allahbad, Uttar Pradesh, India.

Dr. Vijay Prakash Gupta is an accomplished academician, educator, and leader at G.L.A. University in Mathura, India. Armed with a Ph.D., an M.B.A., a master's in economics, and UGC NET certification, Dr. Gupta serves as an associate professor at the Institute of Business Management. As Ph.D. coordinator for management, Dr. Gupta provides oversight of doctoral research. He coordinates the B.B.A. and B.Com. programmes and guides placement efforts for undergraduate students. Known for his analytical mind, communication strengths, and mentoring abilities, he assists students in developing their talents. Appointed to the University's Syllabus Design Committee for NEP 2020, Dr. Gupta helped reimagine the curriculum.

Dr. Princi Gupta is an assistant professor at JECRC University, Jaipur, with a Ph.D. in marketing and expertise in marketing and international business. She holds an M.B.A. from Amity University, Noida, and has numerous publications in national, international, UGC, and Scopus-indexed journals, along with a book on digital marketing. She has also supervised over 100 UG and PG research projects.

Zahid Hussain is a passionate student and young researcher from Pakistan, driven by his commitment to marketing, green marketing, social entrepreneurship, corporate social responsibility (CSR), and sustainable development. Currently pursuing a Master's degree in Marketing, Zahid has completed several courses in sustainability, social entrepreneurship, and CSR. Beyond academics, Zahid is actively involved in social entrepreneurship and community engagement initiatives. He co-founded a youth-led organization that promotes sustainable living practices and works towards building environmentally conscious society. Additionally, he volunteers with various non-profits focusing on issues such as ducationlleviation.

Piyush Kumar Jain, Research Scholar, Department of Business Policy and Administration, University of Mumbai, Mumbai, Maharashtra, India.

Dr. Vishal Jain is presently working as an associate professor at Department of Computer Science and Engineering, Sharda School of Engineering and Technology, Sharda University, Greater Noida, U. P. India. Before that, he worked for several years as an associate professor at Bharati Vidyapeeth's Institute of Computer Applications and Management (BVICAM), New Delhi. He has more than 14 years of experience in the academics. He obtained Ph.D. (CSE), M.Tech. (CSE), M.B.A. (HR), M.C.A., M.C.P., and C.C.N.A. degrees. He has authored more than 90 research papers in reputed conferences and journals, including Web of Science and Scopus. He has authored and edited more than 30 books with various reputed publishers, including Elsevier, Springer, Apple Academic Press, CRC, Taylor and Francis Group, Scrivener, Wiley, Emerald, NOVA Science, and IGI-Global. His research areas include information retrieval, semantic web, ontology engineering, data mining, ad hoc networks, and sensor networks. He received a Young Active Member Award for the year 2012–13 from the Computer Society of India, Best Faculty Award for the year 2017, and Best Researcher Award for the year 2019 from BVICAM, New Delhi.

Dr. Nirma Sadamali Jayawardena is an assistant professor in O P Jindal Global University, India. She completed a B.Sc. in business management (first-class honours) from NSBM Green University, Sri Lanka, and an MBA in international business from the University of Colombo, Sri Lanka. She completed her graduate diploma in business research and Ph.D. in marketing from Griffith University, Australia. Her research interests include consumer psychology, consumer social cognition, digital video advertising, and experimental research.

Dr. Malla Jogarao is a dedicated educator and administrator, shaping future generations at Indian Maritime University. Bringing over 10 years of higher education experience, he currently serves as an assistant professor, imparting his knowledge across management, law, and allied maritime domains. He has an M.Phil. in management. Dr. Jogarao actively enhances curriculum and pedagogy at IMU through research and faculty development initiatives. His student-centric teaching philosophy balances theoretical foundations and practical applications to equip graduates for long-term success.

Dr. Sebastian T. Joseph, triple gold medalist in history with a distinguished academic record. After topping multiple universities in Kerala for his B.A. and M.A., he received a State Merit Scholarship. His Ph.D. on forest history earned him a prestigious fellowship, and he recently received a British Council grant to visit England. A passionate educator, Dr. Joseph has introduced several innovative programmes at his college, edited the college journal, and co-created a signature film on the institution's history. He is a recognized expert on environmental history, regularly invited to speak at major conferences in India. With advanced qualifications in history and years of university teaching experience, Dr. Sebastian T. Joseph is an outstanding scholar and mentor guiding Ph.D. students on a range of historical research topics.

Dr. Rahul Joshi is has a doctorate in media studies and specializes in radio journalism and television production. Currently, he is working as an assistant professor at the Department of Journalism & Mass Communication, School of Media Studies & Humanities, Manav Rachna International Institute of Research & Studies, Faridabad.

Prof. Christian Kaunert is Professor of International Security at Dublin City University, Ireland. He is also Professor of Policing and Security as well as Director of the International Centre for Policing and Security at the University of South Wales. In addition, he is Jean Monnet Chair, Director of the Jean Monnet Centre of Excellence, and Director of the Jean Monnet Network on EU Counter-Terrorism (www.eucter.net). Previously, he served as Academic Director and Professor at the Institute for European Studies, Vrije Universiteit Brussels, Professor of International Politics, Head of Discipline in Politics, and the Director of the European Institute for Security and Justice, a Jean Monnet Centre for Excellence, at the University of Dundee. Prof. Kaunert has researched and taught in many international universities, such as University of Shandong, Jinan, China; IBEI Barcelona, Spain; Diplomatic Academy Yerevan, Armenia–United Nations Development Mission; University of Cairo, Egypt; Collegio Carlo Alberto, Turin, Italy; Ecole nationale d'administration Paris; European Institute of Public Administration Maastricht, Netherlands; European Studies Institute (ESI) at Moscow; University of Porto, Portugal, etc. He was previously a senior lecturer at the University of Dundee, Marie Curie Senior Research Fellow at the European University Institute Florence, and a senior lecturer in EU politics and international relations, University of Salford. Christian has been an invited expert for the European Institute for Public Administration (EIPA), the Counter-Terrorism Committee of the European Parliament, the European Union Institute for Security Studies (an agency of the EU), the United Nations Development Programme (UNDP), and the North Atlantic Treaty Organisation (NATO). Over his career, he has been awarded seven prestigious Marie Curie fellowships, four Jean Monnet chairs, and, finally, three Jean Monnet Centre of Excellence awards, as well as one Jean Monnet Network of Excellence EUCTER. Additionally, he was awarded a large Horizon 2020 research grant on terrorist radicalization processes – Mindb4Act. He is currently editor of the *Journal of Contemporary European Studies*, was also previously an elected member of the national (UK) Executive Committee of the University Association for Contemporary European Studies (UACES), and co-founded and co-led the special-interest section on the Area of Freedom, Security and Justice of the European Union Studies Association (EUSA). He has also previously been the editor of the *Journal of Contemporary European Research* (JCER), an executive committee member of the University Association for Contemporary European Studies (UACES), and an expert for the European Parliament. He is also on the editorial board of the journal *European Politics and Society* (EPS) and the *Journal of European Integration* (JEI). Prof. Kaunert holds a Ph.D. in international politics and an M.Sc. in European politics from the University of Wales Aberystwyth, a B.A. (Hons) European business from Dublin City University, ESB Reutlingen, and a B.A. (Hons) Open University.

Dr. Arman Khan with Ph.D. in Artificial Intelligence from the Putra Business School, Universiti Putra Malaysia, Malaysia. A marketing teacher at Shaheed Benazir Bhutto University, Pakistan from 2014 and teaching at graduate and post graduate level also driven to inspire students to pursue their academic and personal excellence. Provided well balanced educational and research experience, and exposure to extracurricular activities with a real-world perspective to learning. Dedicated partner to university programs and outreach events. He has published various articles in well-renowned journals. His research interests include Digital Marketing, Customer satisfaction, Customer Behavior, Marketing Mix, Visual Merchandising, Sustainable development goals, Neuromarketing etc. He is very keen to learn and work to explore new areas of Marketing.

Prof. Rajendra Khatik, Professor, School of Commerce and Business Studies, Jiwaji University, Gwalior, Madhya Pradesh, India.

Anoop Kumar, Ph.D. Scholar, Amity Business School, Amity University Madhya Pradesh, India.

Dr. Bhupendra Kumar completed his graduation and post-graduation from Chaudhary Charan Singh University, Meerut, U.P. and Ph.D. in computer science and engineering from Mewar University, Hapur. Presently, he is working as a professor in the Department of Computer Science and Applications, IIMT University, Meerut, U.P. He has teaching experience of 19 years. He is the reviewer member of some reputed journals. He has published several book chapters and research papers of national and international reputed journals.

Atul Kumar is working as an assistant professor in school of computer science and application, IIMT University, Meerut U.P India. His qualification is MCA., MTech.

Dr. Kamakshi Mehta is an associate professor at TAPMI School of Business, Manipal University Jaipur. An expert in management accounting and forensic audit, she has a Ph.D. in forensic audit along with C.A. and C.F.A. qualifications. With over 25 years of professional experience spanning accounting, auditing, and academics, Dr. Mehta currently teaches management accounting at TAPMI. She has previously taught finance and accounting courses at Amity University Haryana. Beyond academics, she has industry work experience in accounting and audit leadership roles at companies like Ujala Aquatech and Avj Group. Dr. Mehta also founded her own chartered accountancy firm, gaining hands-on expertise as a finance professional.

Udgam Mishra is an assistant professor at Tribhuvan University, Nepal. He completed his M.B.A. (finance and marketing) from Kurukshetra University, Haryana, India and his master's in philosophy (management) from Purbhanchal University, Nepal. He is a Ph.D. scholar, pursuing his Ph.D. in marketing from Purbhanchal University, Nepal. His areas of interest are consumer behaviour, digital marketing, and entrepreneurial marketing.

Dr. Archan Mitra brings interdisciplinary expertise in media, communication, and sustainability to his role as an assistant professor at Presidency University's School of Media Studies in Bangalore, India. An award-winning academic, he authored two books on media business and theory. Armed with a doctorate exploring environmental communications from Visva-Bharati Santiniketan, Dr. Mitra also obtained certifications in science communication, corporate training, social media analysis, and journalism. He previously assisted World Bank environmental capacity-building efforts in Southeast Asia and disaster mitigation research in Uttarakhand. An active researcher published in top emergency management and other reputable journals, Dr. Mitra has contributed to high-profile published reports on gender, witchcraft, and Himalayan policy. He is driven by a passion for elucidating the power and potential of strategic communication to advance sustainability. Through teaching and research, he equips future media professionals with the insight to drive dialogue and change.

Dr. Nurhafihz Noor is a lecturer in marketing at James Cook University Singapore. His research interests include services marketing and its intersections with technology, hospitality, well-being, and culture, including halal.

Rajneesh Panwar graduated and post-graduated in mathematics and computer application from Ch. Charan Singh University, Meerut (U.P.) and received his M. Tech. in computer science from Shobhit University, Meerut. Presently, he is working as an assistant professor in the School of Computer Science and Application IIMT University, Meerut, U.P. He qualified for GATE 2021 and UGC-NET June 2020 and December 2020. He has published several book chapters and research papers of national and international repute.

Dr. Anil Singh Parihar, Associate Professor, Department of Management, CDOE, Manipal University Jaipur, India.

Prof. (Dr.) Renu Pareek is Dean of Jaipur School of Business, JECRC University, with a Ph.D. in marketing. Her impressive contributions in national, international, UGC, and Scopus-indexed journals reflect her expertise. She actively engages in international conferences, fostering academic growth. Moreover, she has guided over 100 UG and PG research projects, nurturing the next generation of scholars at JECRC University.

Dr. B.C.M. Patnaik, Professor, KIIT School of Management, KIIT University, has 20 years of rich experience in educational research, content, and creative initiative at both postgraduate and undergraduate levels and the ability to handle core administration-related activities such as infrastructure, facility, human resources, training and development of staff members, and organizational behaviour and organization development. Dr. Patnaik possesses valuable insights, keen analysis, and a team approach to implement best practices and is adept at working in high-pressure environments with strict deadlines and multiple deliverables and introducing knowledge and assisting students in developing the skills necessary for success. As a faculty of accounts and finance, Dr. Patnaik has introduced students to the principles, processes, tools, and techniques that become the foundation of their ability to understand and take up challenges throughout their education and into their professional careers. Dr. Patnaik has expertise in planning, organizing, coordinating, and monitoring all types of curricular and co-curricular activities for the overall development of the personality of students. Dr. Patnaik is a devoted teacher, striving to help students change marginal grades into good grades and supporting colleagues and administration in facilitating each child's social and intellectual growth by creating an atmosphere of mutual respect and open communication. Dr. Patnaik has guided 15 Ph.D. scholars and six scholars and published more than 150 papers, including 34 papers in Scopus-indexed journals. Dr. Patnaik was awarded Best Faculty four times.

Prashasti Pritiprada is a director of HR in a reputed software product company named MUVI based in Bhubaneswar, Odisha. She has around 11 years of hands-on experience in various HR domains. Prior to this Ph.D. programme, she completed her master's in human resource management and finance from two different universities such as IIM Kozhikode and Utkal University, respectively, after graduation. She is a bachelor of technology in information technology from BPUT, Rourkela.

Namita Priya, is a Ph.D. scholar, KIIT University, a seasoned HR professional with 25 years of experience in the whole gamut of HR in various industries, and an alumnus of XISS and is currently working as dy. general manager – HR in an IT firm.

Dr. Roopashree Rao is an associate professor at Christ Deemed to be University, in the School of Business Management, Bengaluru. Her areas of interest include sustainability, strategic alliance, and applications of AI in management.

Dr. Ipseeta Satpathy is Senior Professor, KIIT School of Management, KIIT University, and has over 22 years of experience in teaching, research, and administration at KIIT University. She has authored six textbooks such as *Environment Management* and *Business Communication & Personality Development* published by Excel Books, New Delhi, *Transnational Marketing Strategy*, published by New Age International Publishers, *Organizational Communication*, published by Lap Lambert, Mauritius, and *Empowering Award Staff by Revamping Training System in Banks*, published by Lap Lambert, Germany. Dr. Satpathy has published more than 200 research papers in various refereed national and international journals, including journals in ABDC indexing, and conference proceedings and has more than 75 research papers in Scopus-indexed journals. Prof. Satpathy is a former visiting professor to Lynchburg College, Virginia, USA, and has attended/presented research papers in several international conferences including the International Conference on HRM & PD in the Digital Age in Singapore and Cambridge Business & Economics Conference, Cambridge University, UK. Some of her research papers have also won the Best Paper award, including one that was adjudged as the best paper by Emerald Group Publishing Ltd. Prof Satpathy is guiding several research scholars for the Ph.D. degree, and 22 of her scholars have been awarded Ph.D. degree by KIIT Deemed to be University, and she has also conducted a number of management development programmes. Dr. Satpathy has been awarded the prestigious Oxford Journal Distinguished Research Professor Award 2014 at Cambridge University, London. Dr. Satpathy was invited by the Charlton Business School University of Massachusetts, Dartmouth, USA, to address the faculty and the students. Prof Satpathy was invited by the Southampton University, UK, where she also addressed the faculty, students, and research scholars. Dr. Ipseeta Satpathy was awarded with the Times Power Women 2023 by the Times of India Group as an eminent academician in producing and upskilling quality professionals for today's workforce.

Dr. Kewal Krishan Sharma is a professor in computer science in IIMT University, Meerut, U.P, India. He did his Ph.D. in computer network. With this, he has an M.C.A., an M.B.A., and a law degree also. He did various certification courses also. He has an overall experience of around 33 years in academia, business, and industry. He wrote a number of research papers and books.

Dr. Smita Sharma, post-doctoral fellow, Department of Management Sciences, Indian Institute of Technology, Kanpur. Her areas of interest include sustainability, AI in management, and applications of AI in consumer behaviour.

Vikas Sharma completed his Graduation and Post Graduation from Chaudhary Charan Singh University, Meerut, U.P. Currently Pursuing his Ph.D. in Computer Science and Engineering from Govt. Recognized University. Presently, he is working as an Assistant Professor in the Department of Computer Science and Applications, IIMT University, Meerut, U.P. He has been awarded as Excellence in teaching award 2019. He is the reviewer member of some reputed journals. He has published several book chapters and research papers of national and international reputed journals.

Dr. Bhupinder Singh is working as a professor in Sharda School of Law, Sharda University Greater Noida, India, and is also an honourary professor in University of South Wales UK and Santo Tomas University Tunja, Colombia. He has three books, 90 paper publications, 159 paper presentations in international/national conferences and seminars, and has participated in more than 40 workshops/FDPs/QIPs, has developed 25 courses from international universities of repute, has organized more than 59 events with international and national academicians and industry people, has been editor-in-chief and co-editor in journals, and has developed new courses. He has given talks at international universities and been a resource person in international conferences such as in Nanyang Technological University Singapore, Tashkent State University of Law Uzbekistan, KIMEP University Kazakhstan, All'ah meh Tabatabi University Iran, the Iranian Association of International Criminal law, Iran and Hague Center for International Law and Investment, The Netherlands, Northumbria University Newcastle UK, Taylor's University Malaysia, AFM Krakow University Poland, European Institute for Research and Development Georgia, Business and Technology University Georgia, and Texas A&M University U.S., to name a few. His leadership, teaching, research, and industry experience is of 16 years and 3 months. His research interests are health law, criminal law, research methodology, and emerging multidisciplinary areas as blockchain technology, IoT, machine learning, artificial intelligence, genome editing, photovoltaic PV Glass, SDGs, and many more.

Dr. Umesh Solanki is an accomplished finance academic with over 15 years of experience spanning teaching, research, and administration. Currently, he teaches courses in finance, fintech, and infrastructure finance at TAPMI while coordinating IQAC and examination functions. Armed with a Ph.D. in financial management and C.F.A. certification, Dr. Solanki has made significant contributions in past academic roles as professor, HOD, dean, Ph.D. coordinator, and NAAC/NIRF coordinator. His expertise lies in designing finance curriculum and conducting management research. Beyond academics, he has industry exposure through finance domain training programmes. With his diverse skill set, Dr. Umesh Solanki brings holistic development and valuable administrative perspectives to TAPMI School of Business.

Dr. **Subbulakshmi Somu** is an associate professor at Dayananda Sagar College of Arts, Science and Commerce. Her areas of teaching are organizational behaviour, human resource management, artificial intelligence, and HR analytics.

Dr. **Ashley Tong** is a lecturer in accounting and finance at Curtin Singapore. Her research interests include behavioural corporate finance, economics behaviour and psychology, and corporate governance.

José Vargas-Hernández is a research professor at Brodward International University and at Tecnológico Superior de Jalisco, Unidad Zapopan, and worked before at University Center for Economic and Managerial Sciences, University of Guadalajara. He is a member of the National System of Researchers of Mexico. Professor Vargas-Hernández has a Ph.D. in public administration and a Ph.D. in organizational economics. He has been visiting scholar at Carleton University Canada, University of California Berkeley and Laurentian University, Canada. He holds a Ph.D. in economics, Keele University; Ph.D. in public administration, Columbia University; studies in organizational behaviour at Lancaster University; and has M.B.A.; published nine books and more than 600 papers in international journals and reviews (some translated to English, French, German, Portuguese, Farsi, Chinese, etc.) and more than 300 essays in national journals and reviews. He has obtained several international awards and recognitions. He also has experience in consultancy. His main research is in organizational economics and strategic management. He teaches for several doctoral programmes. He has won 15 international awards.

Dr. **Tarun Kumar Vashishth** is an active academician and researcher in the field of computer science with 21 years of experience. He earned Ph.D. mathematics degree specialized in operations research; served several academic positions such as HoD, Dy. Director, academic coordinator, member secretary of department research committee, assistant center superintendent and head examiner in university examinations. He is involved in academic development and scholarly activities. He is member of International Association of Engineers, the Society of Digital Information and Wireless Communications, Global Professors Welfare Association, International Association of Academic plus Corporate (IAAC), Computer Science Teachers Association, and Internet Society. His research interest includes cloud computing, artificial intelligence, machine learning and operations research. He has published more than 20 research articles, one book, and 10 chapters in edited books. He is contributing as a member of editorial and reviewers boards in conferences and various computer journals published by CRC Press, Taylor and Francis, Springer, IGI Global and other universities.

Dr. Aniruddh Vijay is an assistant professor with over seven years of academic teaching experience and additional industry expertise. He currently serves in the Department of Management Studies at J.C. Bose University of Science & Technology. Dr. Vijay recently obtained his Ph.D. in management from Dayalbagh Educational Institute, where his doctoral research explored green rural development and its connections to traditional knowledge systems. He also holds an M.Phil. in management, an M.B.A. in insurance and actuarial sciences, and a B.Com. with honours. His areas of research and teaching specialization cover a range of management subdisciplines, including rural development, sustainability, strategy, insurance, and actuarial science. Academic committees benefit from his cross-disciplinary perspective spanning both the science and business domains.

Dr. C. Vijai is working as an associate professor at the Department of Commerce and Business Administration, Vel Tech Rangarajan Dr. Sagunthala R&D Institute of Science and Technology–Chennai, India. He has authored four books and 86 research papers on commerce and management in various national and international journals of repute. He has presented several research papers in around 85 national and international seminars and conferences. He is on the International Editorial Advisory Board as a member of 50 international journals. He has reviewed more than 100 articles in international peer-reviewed journals. He received an ICSSR Doctoral Fellowship from the Indian Council of Social Science Research, the Ministry of Human Resource Development, and New Delhi. He received several outstanding awards for his academic achievements. He is the Most Promising Educator in Higher Education across India 2019, honoured by the Academic Council of uLektz India. His current research interests include green banking, fintech, mobile commerce, and blockchain technology in accounting.

Dr. Worakamol Wisetsri is an accomplished lecturer and researcher with a strong passion for advancing knowledge in the field of social sciences. In addition to her extensive teaching experience, she has actively engaged in research activities throughout her career. As an associate professor at King Mongkut's University of Technology North Bangkok, Dr. Wisetsri has made significant contributions to the academic community. She has served on various research paper committees and editor boards, including the *Social Sciences, IMRF and other International Journals*. Her commitment to research is evident through her participation in conferences and speaking engagements, such as the International Science Congress Thailand and International Conference on Recent Trends in Agriculture, Veterinary & Life Sciences.

Dr. Zahirah Zainol is a senior lecturer in marketing at Curtin Singapore. Her research interests include country of origin, consumer behaviour, artificial intelligence, and halal marketing.

1 Digital Trends in the Hospitality Industry

Exploring the Metaverse

Dr. C. Vijai and Dr. Worakamol Wisetsri

1. Introduction to the Metaverse

The "metaverse" is a term that refers to a virtual reality–based universe where users can engage in immersive and interactive experiences.[1] It is a concept that envisions a collective virtual shared space, combining elements of augmented reality, virtual reality, and the internet. In the metaverse, users can interact with each other and digital objects in real time, blurring the boundaries between the physical and digital worlds.[2]

The metaverse is often described as a three-dimensional, persistent virtual space that is accessible through various devices, such as virtual reality headsets, augmented reality glasses, or even traditional computer screens. It is not limited to a single platform or virtual world but encompasses a network of interconnected virtual spaces and platforms. Within the metaverse, users can explore virtual environments, create and customize avatars, interact with virtual objects, participate in virtual events, engage in social activities, and even conduct business transactions. The metaverse enables users to have unique and personalized experiences, offering opportunities for entertainment, education, socialization, commerce, and more.

The concept of the metaverse has gained increased attention in recent years as technology advancements, such as virtual reality, augmented reality, and blockchain, have brought us closer to realizing this vision. It represents a new paradigm in digital experiences, where users can transcend the limitations of physical space and engage in a vast, interconnected virtual world.[3–5] While the metaverse is still in its early stages and its full realization is a complex endeavour, it has the potential to revolutionize various industries and aspects of our lives. It offers a new frontier for creativity, collaboration, and innovation, transforming the way we work, learn, play, and connect with others. As the metaverse continues to evolve and expand, it raises important questions and considerations around privacy, security, ethics, and the governance of virtual spaces. Exploring the possibilities and challenges of the metaverse is a crucial step towards shaping its development and ensuring that it becomes an inclusive and beneficial environment for users worldwide.

DOI: 10.4324/9781003488248-1

2. Immersive Guest Experiences in the Metaverse

Immersive guest experiences in the metaverse refer to creating captivating and engaging virtual experiences for users within the metaverse. These experiences aim to provide users with a sense of presence, interactivity, and personalization.

2.1. Virtual Environments: Immersive guest experiences start with the design of virtual environments that captivate users' attention and stimulate their senses.[6] These environments can be virtual worlds, spaces, or themed experiences that users can explore and interact with.

2.2. Real-Time Interactivity: Immersive guest experiences in the metaverse involve real-time interactions with virtual objects, environments, and other users. Users can manipulate objects, solve puzzles, engage in virtual sports, or participate in collaborative activities, making their actions and decisions impactful within the virtual environment.

2.3. Personalization and Customization: Personalization is a crucial aspect of immersive guest experiences. Users can have the ability to create and customize their avatars, environments, and preferences to reflect their individuality. This enhances user engagement and a sense of ownership within the metaverse.

2.4. Social Interaction: Immersive guest experiences foster social interactions within the metaverse.[7] Users can engage with other participants, join virtual communities, and collaborate on projects or activities. Social interaction adds depth and richness to the overall experience, enabling users to connect and share experiences with others.

2.5. Multi-Sensory Engagement: Immersive guest experiences in the metaverse aim to engage multiple senses beyond just visuals and audio. Technologies like haptic feedback, spatial audio, and realistic simulations can provide users with a more immersive and sensorial experience, making them feel more present within the virtual environment.[8]

2.6. Storytelling and Narrative: Creating compelling narratives and storytelling within immersive guest experiences adds depth and context to the virtual environment. Users can engage in interactive narratives, quests, or story-driven experiences that unfold as they progress through the virtual environment, enhancing their emotional engagement and immersion.

2.7. Gamification Elements: Gamification techniques can be incorporated into immersive guest experiences to enhance user engagement and motivation. Leaderboards, achievements, rewards, and challenges can incentivize users to explore and engage more deeply with the metaverse experience.

2.8. Continuous Innovation and Updates: Immersive guest experiences in the metaverse should be dynamic and continuously updated to keep users engaged and coming back for more.[9] Regular updates, new content, and innovative features ensure that the experience remains fresh and exciting for users.

3. Virtual Meetings and Events in the Metaverse

Virtual meetings and events in the metaverse offer an exciting and immersive alternative to traditional in-person or online gatherings. They leverage the capabilities of virtual reality, augmented reality, and other immersive technologies to create engaging and interactive experiences for participants.[10]

3.1. Virtual Meeting Spaces: In the metaverse, participants can gather in virtual meeting spaces that simulate real-world venues or offer unique virtual environments. These spaces can range from conference halls and auditoriums to themed locations, customized environments, or virtual replicas of real-world locations.[11]

3.2. Avatars and Customization: Participants can represent themselves through avatars, which can be customized to reflect their appearance, preferences, and branding. Avatars provide a visual presence in the virtual meeting space, allowing for identification and social interaction with other participants.

3.3. Real-Time Interactions: Virtual meetings and events in the metaverse enable real-time interactions between participants. Users can engage in voice and text chat, express emotions through gestures or emojis, and collaborate on shared virtual whiteboards or documents. This fosters engagement, networking, and collaboration among participants.

3.4. Immersive Presentations and Content: Virtual meetings and events in the metaverse provide opportunities for immersive presentations and content delivery. Speakers can use virtual reality or augmented reality technologies to deliver captivating presentations, incorporating 3D visuals, interactive elements, and spatial audio. This enhances audience engagement and comprehension.

3.5. Networking and Socialization: The metaverse allows for networking and socialization within virtual meetings and events. Participants can explore the virtual environment, engage in one-on-one or group conversations, join virtual breakout rooms, or participate in interactive activities and games. Virtual social spaces facilitate casual interactions and foster connections among attendees.

3.6. Global Accessibility and Scalability: Virtual meetings and events in the metaverse overcome geographical limitations and enable global accessibility. Participants from anywhere in the world can join the event without the need for physical travel, reducing costs and expanding reach. Virtual environments can accommodate large numbers of participants simultaneously, ensuring scalability.

3.7. Enhanced Immersion and Engagement: The metaverse offers a high level of immersion and engagement, thanks to technologies like virtual reality and augmented reality. Users can feel a sense of presence within the virtual environment, increasing their focus and attention during meetings and events.[12]

4. Personalization and Avatars in the Metaverse

Personalization and avatars play a crucial role in the metaverse, allowing users to create unique digital representations of themselves and tailor their experiences within virtual environments.

4.1. Avatar Creation: In the metaverse, users can create digital avatars that represent their virtual presence. Avatars can be customized to reflect users' appearance, preferences, and identity. Users can choose attributes such as gender, body type, facial features, hairstyle, clothing, and accessories to create a personalized avatar that resonates with their individuality.

4.2. Self-Expression: Avatars provide a means for self-expression and creativity within the metaverse. Users can customize their avatars to reflect their personalities, interests, and aspirations. Avatars serve as a digital extension of oneself, allowing users to project their desired image or explore different identities within virtual environments.[13]

4.3. Virtual Identity: Avatars in the metaverse become an extension of a user's digital identity. They represent how users are perceived and interact with others within the virtual world. Avatars contribute to the social fabric of the metaverse, enabling users to engage in social interactions, form connections, and build relationships.[14]

4.4. Customization Options: The metaverse offers a wide range of customization options to personalize avatars. Users can select from a variety of appearances, clothing styles, accessories, and even virtual items or digital assets to enhance their avatars' uniqueness. This level of customization fosters a sense of ownership and connection to the virtual identity.[15]

4.5. Emotional Expression: Avatars in the metaverse allow users to express emotions and non-verbal cues within virtual environments. Through gestures, animations, and facial expressions, avatars can convey emotions, enhancing communication and fostering empathy among users.

4.6. Virtual Fashion and Commerce: Personalization and avatars contribute to the virtual fashion and commerce industry within the metaverse. Users can purchase or create virtual clothing, accessories, and cosmetic items to enhance their avatars' appearance. Virtual fashion brands and designers emerge, providing a marketplace for virtual goods and personalization options.[16]

4.7. Role-Playing and Immersion: Avatars enable users to immerse themselves in virtual roles and experiences. Users can adopt different personas, occupations, or roles within the metaverse, enhancing their immersion and allowing for role-playing activities, simulations, or virtual professions.[17–21]

5. Social Media Integration and Influencer Marketing in the Metaverse

Social media integration and influencer marketing play important roles in the metaverse, facilitating user engagement, brand promotion, and community building.

5.1. Cross-Platform Connectivity: Social media integration allows users to connect their metaverse experiences with their existing social media accounts. Users can share their metaverse activities, achievements, and virtual experiences with their social media followers, bridging the gap between the metaverse and the broader online social community.[22]

5.2. Social Sharing: Integration with social media platforms enables users to easily share their metaverse content, such as screenshots, videos, or live streams, on popular social media channels. This amplifies the reach and visibility of metaverse experiences and helps generate organic user-generated content that can attract new users and foster engagement.

5.3. Social Sign-In: Social media integration can facilitate a streamlined sign-in process within the metaverse. Users can log in using their social media accounts, eliminating the need for separate credentials. This simplifies the onboarding process and enhances user convenience and accessibility.

5.4. Social Features and Interactions: Social media integration can bring familiar social features into the metaverse, such as likes, comments, and sharing. These features encourage social interactions within virtual environments, allowing users to engage with each other's content and form connections.[23] Users can also follow, message, or tag each other using their social media profiles, extending the social experience beyond the metaverse.

6. Revenue Generation and Monetization Opportunities in the Metaverse

The metaverse offers various revenue generation and monetization opportunities for individuals, businesses, and platforms within virtual environments.

6.1. Virtual Goods and Assets: One of the primary revenue streams in the metaverse is the sale of virtual goods and assets. Users can purchase virtual clothing, accessories, digital artwork, virtual real estate, or other virtual items. These items can be sold directly by creators or through virtual marketplaces, providing a marketplace for buying and selling virtual goods.[24]

6.2. Virtual Currency and Microtransactions: Virtual currencies are commonly used within the metaverse to facilitate transactions. Users can purchase virtual currency with real money and then use it to buy virtual goods, access premium features, or participate in virtual experiences.[25] Microtransactions, such as small in-app purchases or upgrades, can generate revenue within virtual environments.

6.3. Virtual Real Estate and Property: Virtual real estate and property ownership present an opportunity for revenue generation in the metaverse. Users can purchase virtual land or properties within virtual worlds and monetize them through rental or lease agreements, hosting events, or creating virtual businesses within their virtual properties.

6.4. Virtual Events and Experiences: Hosting virtual events, conferences, or experiences within the metaverse can generate revenue through ticket sales or sponsorship deals. Brands can sponsor virtual events or experiences to reach a targeted audience within virtual environments.

6.5. Advertising and Sponsorships: Brands can leverage advertising opportunities within the metaverse to reach users and promote their products or services. This can include virtual billboards, branded locations, or product placements within virtual environments. Additionally, brands can sponsor virtual experiences, virtual influencers, or virtual events, creating revenue streams through brand partnerships.[26]

6.6. Virtual Services and Expertise: Users with specific skills or expertise can offer virtual services within the metaverse. This can include virtual consulting, virtual training, virtual performances, or virtual design services. Users can charge fees for their services, leveraging their expertise within the virtual environment.

6.7. Subscription and Membership Models: Platforms within the metaverse can adopt subscription or membership models, providing access to premium features, exclusive content, or enhanced experiences for a recurring fee. This model can offer ongoing revenue streams for platform owners or content creators.

6.8. Intellectual Property Licensing: Content creators can license their intellectual property, including virtual designs, artwork, or branded content, to others within the metaverse. This allows for the use of copyrighted materials in virtual environments in exchange for licensing fees or royalties.

6.9. Blockchain and Non-Fungible Tokens (NFTs): Blockchain technology and non-fungible tokens (NFTs) can facilitate unique ownership and scarcity within the metaverse. NFTs can be used to tokenize virtual assets, artwork, or collectibles, creating a market for buying, selling, and trading these unique digital items.[27–28]

7. Data Privacy and Security in the Metaverse

Data privacy and security are crucial considerations in the metaverse to ensure the protection and confidentiality of user information.

7.1. User Data Protection: Platforms and service providers within the metaverse must prioritize the protection of user data.[29] This includes implementing robust security measures to prevent unauthorized access, data breaches, or data loss. Encryption, secure authentication mechanisms, and regular security audits are essential for safeguarding user data.

7.2. Consent and Transparency: Users should have control and transparency over their personal data in the metaverse. Platforms should clearly communicate their data collection practices, obtain user consent for data processing, and provide options for users to manage their privacy settings. Users should be able to understand how their data is being used and make informed choices regarding its sharing or processing.[30]

7.3. Anonymity and Pseudonymity: The metaverse should provide users with options for anonymity or pseudonymity, allowing them to participate and interact without disclosing their real identities. This can protect users' privacy and prevent the unnecessary exposure of personal information.

7.4. Data Minimization: Platforms within the metaverse should practice data minimization, collecting only the necessary and relevant data for providing their services. By minimizing the collection and retention of personal data, platforms can reduce the risk of unauthorized access or misuse of user information.

7.5. User Control and Access: Users should have control over their personal data within the metaverse. This includes the ability to access, modify, delete, or export their data as required. Providing user-friendly interfaces and tools for managing personal data empowers users to exercise their privacy rights effectively.

7.6. Secure Transactions: As virtual commerce and transactions occur within the metaverse, it is crucial to ensure the security of financial transactions and sensitive information. Implementing secure payment gateways, encryption protocols, and fraud prevention measures is essential to protect users' financial data.

7.7. Cross-Platform Data Protection: The metaverse comprises multiple platforms, virtual worlds, and interconnected environments. Data protection measures should extend across these platforms to ensure consistent privacy and security practices. Collaboration and standardization efforts can help establish common principles and standards for data privacy and security within the metaverse ecosystem.[31]

8. Virtual Reality (VR) and Augmented Reality (AR) in Hospitality

Virtual reality (VR) and augmented reality (AR) technologies have transformative applications in the hospitality industry, enhancing guest experiences, improving operations, and driving innovation.[32]

8.1. Virtual Tours: VR enables hotels, resorts, and vacation rentals to provide immersive virtual tours of their properties. Potential guests can explore rooms, amenities, and common areas in a realistic and interactive way, helping them make informed decisions about bookings.

8.2. Virtual Reality Training: VR can be used for training hospitality staff, allowing them to practice various scenarios and improve their customer service skills. For example, employees can simulate check-in procedures, room service interactions, or emergency response situations in a virtual environment.

8.3. Virtual Concierge Services: AR can enhance the guest experience by providing virtual concierge services. Guests can use their mobile devices to access AR-powered applications that offer real-time information about nearby attractions, restaurants, and events or provide interactive maps and directions.

8.4. **Augmented Menus:** AR can be utilized in restaurants or bars to present interactive menus. By pointing their smartphones or tablets at the menu, guests can view images, descriptions, or even videos of the dishes, see allergen information, or receive recommendations based on their dietary preferences.
8.5. **Virtual Event Spaces:** VR can create virtual event spaces where conferences, weddings, or other events can take place. Attendees can join remotely and experience the event in a highly immersive way, interacting with other participants, accessing presentations, and networking virtually.
8.6. **VR-Based Entertainment:** Hotels and resorts can provide VR-based entertainment options to their guests. This could include VR gaming rooms, virtual reality arcades, or VR experiences tied to the destination's culture, history, or attractions.
8.7. **Design and Planning:** VR and AR can aid in the design and planning stages of hospitality properties. Architects, designers, and developers can create virtual mock-ups, allowing stakeholders to visualize and experience the spaces before construction begins. This can help optimize layouts, identify design flaws, and streamline decision-making.
8.8. **Virtual Event Attendance:** VR can enable remote attendees to virtually participate in events, such as conferences, trade shows, or weddings. Users can wear VR headsets to immerse themselves in the event, engage with virtual exhibitor booths, and interact with other attendees, providing a more engaging and inclusive experience.
8.9. **Language Translation and Cultural Education:** AR can assist guests in overcoming language barriers by providing real-time translation of signs, menus, or conversations.[33] Additionally, AR can offer cultural education by providing historical or cultural information about landmarks or attractions.

9. Sustainable Tourism and Reduced Travel Through the Metaverse

Sustainable tourism and reduced travel can be promoted using the metaverse, offering virtual alternatives to physical travel.

9.1. **Virtual Destination Experiences:** The metaverse allows users to explore virtual representations of real-world destinations. Users can experience the culture, history, and attractions of different places without the need for physical travel. This virtual exploration can reduce the environmental impact associated with transportation and the carbon emissions produced by travel.
9.2. **Virtual Tours and Exhibits:** Virtual reality technology enables immersive virtual tours and exhibits of natural wonders, museums, historical sites, and other attractions. Users can visit these destinations virtually, reducing the need for physical travel. This promotes sustainable tourism by minimizing the environmental footprint while still offering engaging experiences.
9.3. **Virtual Cultural Exchanges:** The metaverse facilitates virtual cultural exchanges, where people from different parts of the world can interact, learn, and share experiences. Through virtual platforms and shared virtual spaces,

individuals can engage in cross-cultural dialogue, fostering understanding and appreciation without the need for physical travel.

9.4. Virtual Events and Conferences: The metaverse enables virtual events, conferences, and trade shows, reducing the need for attendees to travel long distances. Participants can connect and engage in real time without the associated carbon emissions and travel expenses. This promotes sustainable business practices and reduces the environmental impact of large-scale gatherings.

9.5. Reduced Infrastructure Development: By embracing virtual alternatives in the metaverse, there may be reduced demand for building new infrastructure and accommodations to support physical tourism. This can help preserve natural landscapes, reduce habitat destruction, and protect sensitive ecosystems.

9.6. Education and Awareness: The metaverse can play a role in educating and raising awareness about sustainable tourism practices. Virtual experiences and simulations can showcase the impact of travel on the environment, highlighting sustainable alternatives and encouraging responsible travel choices.

9.7. Collaboration for Sustainability: The metaverse can be a platform for collaboration among stakeholders in the tourism industry, including businesses, governments, and NGOs, to develop and implement sustainable tourism initiatives. Virtual environments can facilitate discussions, knowledge sharing, and joint efforts towards sustainable practices and policies.[34]

10. Digital Skills and Training for the Metaverse

Digital skills and training are essential for individuals to effectively navigate and participate in the metaverse.

10.1. Virtual Reality (VR) and Augmented Reality (AR) Development: Acquiring skills in VR and AR development is crucial for creating immersive experiences within the metaverse. This includes learning programming languages, 3D modeling, spatial audio, and understanding the technical aspects of building virtual environments and augmented reality applications.

10.2. Virtual World Design: Digital skills related to virtual world design involve understanding user experience (UX) principles, graphic design, and interactive storytelling. Designers need to create intuitive and engaging virtual environments, incorporating elements such as navigation, interaction, and visual aesthetics to enhance user immersion and engagement.

10.3. Avatar Creation and Customization: Skills in avatar creation and customization involve 3D modeling, animation, and character design. Creating visually appealing and expressive avatars requires knowledge of digital art tools and techniques, rigging, and animation principles to bring avatars to life within the metaverse.

10.4. Social Media and Community Management: Social media skills are essential for community management within the metaverse. Community managers should understand how to engage with users, foster positive interactions, moderate content, and utilize social media platforms to promote virtual experiences, events, and content within the metaverse.

10.5. Digital Marketing and Branding: Skills in digital marketing and branding are crucial for promoting virtual experiences, events, and products within the metaverse. This includes knowledge of social media marketing, content creation, influencer marketing, analytics, and understanding how to create effective marketing strategies tailored to the metaverse audience.

10.6. Data Analytics and Insights: Digital skills related to data analytics and insights help individuals and businesses understand user behaviour, preferences, and engagement within the metaverse.[35] Analyzing data from user interactions and virtual environments can provide insights to optimize experiences, tailor content, and improve marketing strategies.

10.7. Ethical Considerations and Digital Citizenship: Skills related to ethical considerations and digital citizenship are important in the metaverse. Individuals need to understand issues such as privacy, security, online etiquette, and responsible use of virtual environments.[36] Being aware of ethical considerations ensures a positive and inclusive metaverse experience for all users.

10.8. Virtual Collaboration and Communication: Digital skills for virtual collaboration and communication involve using online collaboration tools and virtual meeting platforms and understanding effective communication practices within virtual environments. This includes skills in remote teamwork, effective communication, and utilizing virtual collaboration tools to facilitate productive interactions within the metaverse.[37]

10.9. Lifelong Learning and Adaptability: The metaverse is an evolving and dynamic environment, and individuals need to embrace a mindset of lifelong learning and adaptability.[38] Keeping up with emerging technologies, trends, and innovations within the metaverse requires continuous learning, exploring new tools, and staying updated with the latest developments.[39]

11. Recommendations for Business Practices: The Key to Success

In the dynamic landscape of today's business world, success is not simply a matter of chance. It is the result of deliberate and effective business practices that are consistently implemented.[40] Whether you are a seasoned entrepreneur or a budding start-up, certain fundamental principles can significantly impact your journey towards success. In this section, we will delve into some key business practices that can pave the way for sustainable growth and prosperity.[41]

11.1. Clear Vision and Mission

A clear and compelling vision serves as the North Star for any business. It outlines the purpose, direction, and long-term goals that guide decision-making. A well-defined mission, on the other hand, provides a roadmap for achieving that vision. [42] When these elements are communicated effectively and embraced by the entire team, they create a unified sense of purpose, aligning everyone towards a common goal.

11.2. Customer-Centric Focus

Customers are the lifeblood of any business. Understanding their needs, preferences, and pain points is paramount.[43] A customer-centric approach involves active listening, responsive communication, and a commitment to providing exceptional service. This not only builds customer loyalty but also fosters a positive reputation in the market.[44]

11.3. Continuous Learning and Adaptability

In a rapidly evolving business landscape, staying stagnant is a recipe for stagnation. Embrace a culture of continuous learning and adaptability. Stay abreast of industry trends, emerging technologies, and best practices. Be willing to pivot and adjust strategies in response to changing circumstances.[45]

11.4. Effective Leadership and Management

Strong leadership is the cornerstone of a successful business. Effective leaders set the tone, inspire their teams, and provide clear direction. They empower their employees, encourage collaboration, and foster an environment of trust and mutual respect. Moreover, adept management ensures that operational processes run smoothly, resources are utilized efficiently, and goals are met consistently.

11.5. Quality Products or Services

Delivering high-quality products or services is non-negotiable. It forms the foundation of customer satisfaction and loyalty.[46] Consistently meeting or exceeding customer expectations builds a reputation for reliability and excellence in the market.

11.6. Innovation and Creativity

Innovation is the engine that drives progress. Encourage a culture of creativity and problem-solving within your organization.[47] Foster an environment where employees feel empowered to suggest new ideas and solutions. This can lead to the development of innovative products, services, or processes that set you apart from competitors.

11.7. Foster a Strong Company Culture

A positive work environment is vital for attracting and retaining top talent. A healthy company culture is characterized by open communication, mutual trust, and a sense of belonging. It promotes teamwork, employee satisfaction, and overall productivity.[48]

11.8. Strategic Planning

A well-thought-out business plan is essential for providing direction and focus. It outlines your goals, target market, competition analysis, and marketing strategy. Regularly review and adjust this plan as needed to stay aligned with evolving business objectives.

11.9. Ethical and Responsible Practices

Integrity is the bedrock of sustainable business success. Act ethically in all interactions, whether with customers, employees, or partners. Treat employees fairly, consider the environmental impact of your operations, and uphold a strong sense of corporate social responsibility.[49] Success in business is not a one-size-fits-all proposition.[50] It is a dynamic and multifaceted journey that requires a commitment to excellence, continuous improvement, and ethical conduct. By embracing these key business practices, you can build a strong foundation for long-term success and make meaningful contributions to your industry and community. Remember, the pursuit of success is not just about reaching a destination but about maintaining a trajectory of growth and positive impact.[51]

12. Conclusion

The metaverse represents a transformative concept that is revolutionizing the way we interact, connect, and experience the digital world. It combines virtual reality, augmented reality, and the internet to create immersive and interactive virtual environments. The metaverse offers a wide range of applications across industries, including digital marketing, entertainment, education, tourism, and more. In digital marketing, the metaverse opens new opportunities for brands to engage with their audience, create immersive experiences, and leverage influencer marketing within virtual environments. The ability to personalize avatars and environments allows for targeted and customized marketing campaigns, enhancing user engagement and brand affinity. Furthermore, the metaverse offers advantages over traditional marketing methods by providing real-time interactivity, social interaction, and multi-sensory engagement. It allows for the creation of immersive guest experiences, virtual meetings, and events, transforming the way businesses connect with customers and stakeholders. However, as the metaverse continues to evolve, considerations for data privacy and security are crucial. Platforms and service providers must prioritize user data protection, consent, and transparency, ensuring that users have control over their personal information. Cross-platform data protection, ethical AI usage, and compliance with data protection regulations are essential for building trust within the metaverse ecosystem.

The metaverse also presents opportunities for sustainable tourism and reduced travel. Virtual destination experiences, virtual tours, and cultural exchanges within the metaverse offer alternatives to physical travel, reducing the environmental impact associated with tourism. Additionally, the metaverse allows for virtual events, conferences, and collaborations, minimizing the need for travel while still fostering global connections and knowledge sharing. To fully leverage the potential of the metaverse, individuals need to develop digital skills and undergo training in areas such as VR and AR development, virtual world design, avatar customization, digital marketing, data analytics, and ethical considerations. Lifelong learning and adaptability are key to staying updated with the latest advancements and trends within the metaverse. As the metaverse continues to evolve and expand, it will shape the future of digital experiences, communication, and interaction. Embracing the opportunities and challenges presented by the metaverse will pave the way for a digital-first future that is immersive, inclusive, and dynamic.

References

1. Chen, Z. (2023). Beyond reality: Examining the opportunities and challenges of cross-border integration between metaverse and hospitality industries. *Journal of Hospitality Marketing & Management*, 1–14.
2. Ampountolas, A., Menconi, G., & Shaw, G. (2024). Metaverse research propositions: Online intermediaries. *Tourism Economics*, *30*(1), 255–261.
3. EHL Insights (2023). *Digital transformation in hospitality industry: Key to customer service success*. Hospitality Insights by EHL. Available at: https://hospitalityinsights.ehl.edu/digital-transformation-facilitating-servitization [14th October 2023].
4. Kumar, S., Dhiraj, A., Shah, M. A., & Rani, D. (2023). Application of metaverse in the hospitality industry. In R. Bansal, S. Qalati, & A. Chakir (Eds.), *Influencer marketing applications within the metaverse* (pp. 178–194). IGI Global. https://doi.org/10.4018/978-1-6684-8898-0.ch011
5. Buhalis, D., Lin, M. S., & Leung, D. (2023). Metaverse as a driver for customer experience and value co-creation: Implications for hospitality and tourism management and marketing. *International Journal of Contemporary Hospitality Management*, *35*(2), 701–716. https://doi.org/10.1108/IJCHM-05-2022-0631
6. Buhalis, D., O'Connor, P., & Leung, R. (2023). Smart hospitality: From smart cities and smart tourism towards agile business ecosystems in networked destinations. *International Journal of Contemporary Hospitality Management*, *35*(1), 369–393. https://doi.org/10.1108/IJCHM-04-2022-0497
7. Papetti, C., Christofle, S., & Guerrier-Buisine, V. (2018). Digital tools: Their value and use for marketing purposes. In Sotiriadis, M. (Ed.), *The Emerald handbook of entrepreneurship in tourism, travel and hospitality: Skills for successful ventures* (pp. 277–295). Emerald Publishing Limited.
8. Choi, S., Yoon, K., Kim, M., Yoo, J., Lee, B., Song, I., & Woo, J. (2022). Building Korean DMZ metaverse using a web-based metaverse platform. *Applied Sciences, 12*(15), 7908.
9. Deale, C. S., Lee, S. H., & Bae, J. I. (2020). Making mentoring meaningful: Hospitality and tourism students' perceptions of mentoring. *Journal of Teaching in Travel & Tourism*, *20*(1), 1–22.
10. Tolkach, D., Chon, K. K., & Xiao, H. (2016). Asia Pacific tourism trends: Is the future ours to see? *Asia Pacific Journal of Tourism Research*, *21*(10), 1071–1084.
11. Sheresheva, M. Y., Savelyev, I. I., Nadzharyan, N. N., & Kudryavtsev, A. V. (2019, November). Digital platforms in hospitality business. In Bogoviz, A., Ragulina, Y.

(Eds.), *The international scientific and practical forum "Industry. Science. Competence. Integration"* (pp. 83–90). Springer International Publishing.
12. Du, H. et al. (2021). Optimal targeted advertising strategy for secure wireless edge metaverse. *GLOBECOM 2022–2022 IEEE Global Communications Conference,* 4346–4351.
13. Agwu, E. (2020). Contemporary management approaches to the global hospitality and tourism industry: Technology as a panacea for sector growth. In Abraham Pius, Husam H. Alharahsheh, Adenike A. Adesanmi (Eds.), *Contemporary management approaches to the global hospitality and tourism industry* (pp. 45–57). IGI Global.
14. Kumar, S., Dhiraj, A., & Hassan, S. C. C. (2023). Metaverse and cultural marketing in hospitality and tourism. In Amandeep Singh, Sandhir Sharma, Amrinder Singh, Murat Unanoglu, Sanjay Taneja (Eds.), *Cultural marketing and metaverse for consumer engagement* (pp. 224–233). IGI Global.
15. Singh, V., & Puri, D. (2021). An influence of digitalization and recent innovations on the hospitality and tourism sector. In Amandeep Singh (Ed.), *Big data analytics for improved accuracy, efficiency, and decision making in digital marketing* (pp. 150–161). IGI Global.
16. Kolobkova, V. A., Romanov, A. A., & Frolova, E. A. (2021). Digital technologies in the hotel industry: New prospects for sustainable development. *Socio-economic Systems: Paradigms for the Future*, 387–394.
17. Filimonau, V., Ashton, M., & Stankov, U. (2022). Virtual spaces as the future of consumption in tourism, hospitality and events. *Journal of Tourism Futures*. https://doi.org/10.1108/JTF-07-2022-0174
18. Gokou, H. et al. (2022). The hotel industry in the digital world. *Ekonomika*. ISSN: 2587-4713. https://doi.org/10.36962/ecs105/3/2022-266.
19. Gursoy, D., Malodia, S., & Dhir, A. (2022). The metaverse in the hospitality and tourism industry: An overview of current trends and future research directions. *Journal of Hospitality Marketing & Management, 31*(5), 527–534.
20. Han, Y., Niyato, D., Leung, C., Kim, D. I., Zhu, K., Feng, S., Shen, S. X., & Miao, C. (2022). A dynamic hierarchical framework for IoT-assisted metaverse synchronization. *arXiv preprint, arXiv:2203.03969.*
21. Dutta, P. K., Bose, M., Sinha, A., Bhardwaj, R., Ray, S., Roy, S., & Prakash, K. B. (2022). Challenges in metaverse in problem-based learning as a game-changing virtual-physical environment for personalized content development. *IET Conference Proceedings* (pp. 417–421). https://doi.org/10.1049/icp.2023.0641 IET Digital Library; https://digital-library.theiet.org/content/conferences/10.1049/icp.2023.0641
22. Muwandeniya, Kavindu & Eranda, Nuresh. (2022). Virtual Reality for Enhancing Customer Value in Sri Lankan Hospitality and Tourism Industry: Perspective of Industry Experts. *Sri Lanka Journal of Marketing*. 8. 64. 10.4038/sljmuok.v8i2.102.
23. Treiblmaier, H., & Önder, I. (2019). The impact of blockchain on the tourism industry: A theory-based research framework. In H. Treiblmaier, & R. Beck (Eds.), *Business transformation through blockchain*. Palgrave Macmillan. https://doi.org/10.1007/978-3-319-99058-3_1
24. Sarna, S., & Tyagi, A. (2023). Transforming the hospitality and tourism industry: A new paradigm shift of leadership approach. In Ahmet Baytok, Özcan Zorlu, Ali Avan, Engin Bayraktaroğlu (Eds.), *Leadership approaches in global hospitality and tourism* (p. 20). https://doi.org/10.4018/978-1-6684-6713-8.ch010
25. Schmidt, A. L. (2023). Changing the rules of the hotel business: The case of citizenM's digital business model disruption. In J. Marques, & R. P. Marques (Eds.), *Digital transformation of the hotel industry. Tourism, hospitality & event management*. Cham: Springer. https://doi.org/10.1007/978-3-031-31682-1_12
26. Olishevska, Y., & Kupach, T. (2022). Street art in the context of urban tourism development. *Journal of Geology, Geography and Geoecology, 31*(1), 120–132. https://doi.org/10.15421/112212.

27. Ivasciuc, I. S. (2020). Augmented reality and facial recognition technologies. Building bridges between the hospitality industry and tourists during pandemic. *Bulletin of the Transilvania University of Brasov. Series V: Economic Sciences*, 75–92.
28. Batinić, I. (2013). Current trends in hospitality industry. *Journal of Process Management and New Technologies*, *1*(4), 91–95.
29. Svitlana, T. (2021). Formation and development of the hospitality industry. УДК:338.48(477.42). *Black Sea Economic Studies*. https://doi.org/10.32843/bses.65-5
30. Marques, J., & Marques, R. P. (2023). Trends in the hospitality industry: A global perspective. In J. Marques, & R. P. Marques (Eds.), *Digital transformation of the hotel industry. Tourism, hospitality & event management*. Springer. https://doi.org/10.1007/978-3-031-31682-1_1
31. Bowen, J., & Whalen, E. (2017). Trends that are changing travel and tourism. *Worldwide Hospitality and Tourism Themes*, *9*(6), 592–602. https://doi.org/10.1108/WHATT-09-2017-0045
32. Jung, S. H., & Jeon, I. (2022). A study on the components of the Metaverse ecosystem. *Journal of Digital Convergence*, *20*(2), 163–174. https://doi.org/10.14400/JDC.2022.20.2.163.
33. Chon, K. S., & Olsen, M. D. (1988). An analysis of the trends in the hospitality industry through content analysis of industry publications. *Hospitality & Tourism Invitational Proceedings*, 55–67.
34. Kang, H. S., Nam, S. S., & Kim, H. T. (2022). A study on the hospitality industry and the metaverse. *한국엔터테인먼트산업학회논문지*, *16*(5), 143–153.
35. Konstantinova, S. (2019). Digital transformation in tourism. *KNOWLEDGE-International Journal*, *35*(1), 188–193.
36. Krylova, L. V., & Kulbida, A. A. (2022). Digital marketing in the hospitality industry. *Гостиничное дело*, (6), 1–5. https://doi.org/10.33920/igt-2-2206-05.
37. Zimbabwe. (2002). *Emotional intelligence and social capital for senior managers in the hospitality industry in Zimbabwe*. Available at: https://api.semanticscholar.org/CorpusID:204829773
38. Romanov, M. (2021). Priority technologies for the adoption of digitalised human resources management in hospitality industry. *SHS Web of Conferences*, *110*, 02011. https://doi.org/10.1051/shsconf/202111002011.
39. Yoon, I.-S., & Lee, H.-R. (2018). A study on the relative importance and priorities of internship factors in the hospitality industry by AHP. *International Journal of Tourism and Hospitality Research*. Available at: https://api.semanticscholar.org/CorpusID:169145324 [20th March 2024].
40. Nikopoulou, M., Kourouthanassis, P., Chasapi, G., Pateli, A. & Mylonas, N. (2023). Determinants of digital transformation in the hospitality industry: Technological, organizational, and environmental drivers. *Sustainability*, *15*(3), 2736. https://doi.org/10.3390/su15032736
41. Nataraja, C. T., & Mahesh, R. (2018). An overview of digital transformation initiatives in tourism, aviation and hospitality industry. *Journal of Emerging Technologies and Innovative Research*. Available at: https://api.semanticscholar.org/CorpusID:216847087
42. António, N., & Rita, P. (2021). COVID 19: The catalyst for digital transformation in the hospitality industry. *Tourism & Management Studies*, *17*(2), 41–46. https://doi.org/10.18089/tms.2021.17020441
43. Nurhikmah, S., & Sonny, S. (2020). Redesign promotion strategy of ABC senior living in west java to improve sales occupancy – A qualitative research. *Journal Muara Ilmu Ekonomi dan Bisnis*. *4*, 116. https://doi.org/10.24912/JMIEB.V4I1.7692
44. Oliinyk, O., Krasovskyi, S., Vasylenko, O., Prykhod'ko, K., Pliuta, O., & Tonkykh, O. (2022). Digitalization of business processes in the hospitality industry. *Economic Affairs*, *67*(4s), 725–733. https://doi.org/10.46852/0424-2513.4s.2022.6

45. Ndebele, P. (2019). *Understanding niche accommodation in tourism: The case of Couchsurfing hosts*. Dissertation submitted in partial fulfilment of the requirements for the degree Master of Commerce in Tourism Management. North-West University.
46. Peter, J. et al. (1998). Research and development in hospitality accounting and financial management. *International Journal of Hospitality Management, 17*, 161–182. https://doi.org/10.1016/S0278-4319(98)00013-9
47. Said, M. et al. (2002). The impact of strategic alliances on the hospitality and travel industry stakeholders quality of life. *Journal of Transnational Management Development, 8*, 157–170. https://doi.org/10.1300/J130V08N01_08.
48. Jain, P., Singh, R., Mishra, R., & Rana, N. P. (2023). Emerging dimensions of blockchain application in tourism and hospitality sector: A systematic literature review. *Journal of Hospitality Marketing & Management, 32*(4), 454–476. https://doi.org/10.1080/19368623.2023.2184440
49. Bhandari, R., & Sin, M. V. (2023). Optimizing digital marketing in hospitality industries. *Startupreneur Business Digital (SABDA Journal)*, *2*(1), 1–11. https://doi.org/10.33050/sabda.v2i1.263.
50. Bean, S. (1991). Technology trends in the hospitality industry. *The Bottomline*, *6*, 10–11. Available at: https://api.semanticscholar.org/CorpusID:166872097
51. Nozdreva, R., & Churakova, A. (2021). Digital tools in empirical marketing strategies of global hotel companies. In N. Konina (Ed.), *Digital strategies in a global market*. Palgrave Macmillan. https://doi.org/10.1007/978-3-030-58267-8_16

2 Exploring the Future of Luxury in Rural Tourism; Predicting Trends, Technologies, Opportunities and Challenges in the Digital Era

Dr. A. J. Frederick, Dr. Aniruddh Vijay, and Dr. Sebastian T. Joseph

Introduction

Luxury in present times has taken flight from skyscrapers, visiting high-end boutiques or being a member of elite clubs to the serenity of rural landscapes offering escape from the daily routine. Rural tourism is "a type of tourism activity in which the visitor's experience is related to a wide range of products generally linked to nature-based activities, agriculture, rural lifestyle/culture, angling and sightseeing" (*Rural Tourism | UNWTO*, n.d.). In other words, travellers and tourists who engage in any activity that belongs to rural area such as cherry plucking, sowing rice saplings, exploring in-hand experience of pottery making, enjoying food cooked on earthen fuels and fossils, etc. are examples of rural tourism. There has been a paradigm shift in the travel pattern of tourists, specifically after COVID-19 (Rousan et al., 2023).

Now, individuals who have royal blood, promotors of conglomerate business houses and recent high-net-worth individuals (HNIs) search for places that give them high-class facilities (Petroman, 2021) and extraordinary experiences in their vacations in remote and untouched rural areas that are free from pomp and show. Where they can freely engage in such activities and explore their innersoles. The advent of social media has boosted those in the tourism industry who focus on such individuals by showcasing their luxury brands on different social media platform (Thirumaran et al., 2021; Duong & Sung, 2021). A study by Xiang and Gretzel (2010) explored the scope of social media in tourism.

The worldwide rural tourism sector was moving towards the figure of 102.7 billion USD at the end of 2023. With an incremental CAGR of almost 7%, it is expected to cross the milestone of 175 billion USD in 2033 (*Rural Tourism Market – Size, Growth, Trends, Share | 2033*, n.d.)

Present Situation of Rural Tourism

Rural tourism is based upon rural villages. India has an edge, as a large part of its population resides in rural areas that have the potential of attracting tourists, and with the growing internet connectivity, tourists can never be off the grid. It is assumed by many researchers that in the present scenario, rural tourism carries

DOI: 10.4324/9781003488248-2

Table 2.1 Best Rural Tourism Villages Region-Wise 2022

Region	*Country*	*Village*
Asia-Pacific	China	Dazhai
	China	Jingzhu
	Vietnam	Thai Hai
	Korea	Pyeongsa-Ri
Africa	Ethiopia	Choke Mountains Ecovillage
	Morocco	Ksar Elkhorbat
	Morocco	Moulay Bouzerktoune
Europe	Romania	Rasinari
	Portugal	Castelo Novo
	Italy	Sauris Zahre
	Austria	Wagrain
Americas	Ecuador	Angochagua
	Colombia	Choachi
	Mexico	Creel
	Peru	Lamas
	Chile	Puqueldon
Middle East	Saudi Arabia	Alula Old Town
	Jordan	Umm Qais

Source: Villages – Best Tourism Villages, n.d.

greater prominence because tourists prefer less dense tourist destinations (Teare, 2023). The tourism sector was hit by COVID-19 at a wider level (Yeoman, 2023). The players have had to explore and take initiative for providing all the luxury in such rural destination, and we have already seen the success of Maldives (*Tourism in the Maldives Content*, n.d.), where it began with an unplanned 280 beds arranged for Italian tourists.

The beautiful beaches of Radhanagar in Andaman and the Nicobar Islands are listed as the best destinations for rural tourism in India, which also attracts tourists from all over world.

Table 2.1 showcases some of the Best Tourism Villages awardees by the United Nations World Tourism Organisation (UNTWO) in 2022. As present, 260 applications from more than 60 countries have been submitted for the present year. These villages offer their rural cuisines, engaging activities like feeding guinea pigs in Angochagua, Ecuador. The Dazhai village of China introduced the concept of green tourism with its sublime mountains, which are 76% covered in forests. Thai Hai village of Vietnam is serving as an ecological bank, safeguarding its cultural heritage. For tourists who enjoy water sports, Moulay Bouzerktoune is heaven.

The role of homestays in rural tourism is inevitable, as there is limited number of hotels available at such places, and forget about hotels offering luxury (*Homestay Tourism and the Commercialization of the Rural Home in Thailand: Asia Pacific Journal of Tourism Research: Vol 20, No 1*, n.d.). Therefore, homestays have an opportunity to convert to luxury homestays by offering services like fast internet connectivity, saunas, fresh water, massage therapy, sports activities, jungle safaris, etc. Thus, by offering such experiences, not only can the tourism flourish, but it will also contribute to the economic development of the country. So homestays will surely generate employment.

Trends of Rural Tourism

When we talk about modern couples who are working for long hours, sitting in front of a screen, stuck in traffic, these couples aspire for lodging in their vacation that can offer them facilities like a clear, starlit sky, the aroma of the fresh air, eco-friendly cottages and houseboats on back waters. In these lodging facilities, tourists want freshly cooked breakfasts served by the local people in their private lobby, far from the cacophony of day-to-day noise. Food freshly prepared from the kitchen gardens of homestays, salads and desserts prepared with organic vegetables and the flavours of locally grown spices all sum up the sense of luxury on rural tourism.

The stories and information about the untouched and still-to-be-explored places by the local staff create magic and give tourists an opportunity to connect themselves with the place. Local suppliers are the foundation of the concept of rural tourism, as they provide fresh, seasonable goods. They also promote and sustain the local market by reducing pollution caused by transportation and provide employment to the local people.

Rural tourism offers natural daylight and fresh air, which reduces the dependency upon high-energy-consuming devices and equipment. For instance, adding a mosquito net and sleeping in the fresh air on a terrace during homestays eliminates the cost of running an air conditioner. Homestays that are fully functional on renewable sources of energy are attracting more tourists as compared to the traditional ones. Solar and wind energy are playing a pivotal role in these rural destinations.

The clean water and sustainable sanitation systems of homestays reduce the chance of waterborne diseases, protect the eco-system and boost the process of sustainable development of villages.

Technologies Required in the Digital Era for Providing Luxury in Rural Tourism

Rural homestay and villages that aspire to attract more tourists, especially foreign tourists, must have the facilities of web-based applications for booking, mobile-based apps powered by local information and networks of local sightseeing places for attracting a global audience. People want to share their vacation escapes via social media, providing a way to showcase the serene beauty of such places.

When we discuss technology in rural tourism, we should also encompass virtual reality (VR) and augmented reality (AR), as they will give the experience of certain rural destinations for tourists who always have certain doubts about the place. AR-enabled tours can provide a glimpse of the local activities and sites of historical importance. Investment in the development of rural destinations and in providing such technology-driven offerings boosts private, public and voluntary sectors

(Nestorova, 2019; Garrod et al., 2006). And blockchain technology to provide secure and fair transactions is essential, especially in all booking and processes that involve cash management, leading to trust building and sense of ownership (Dokl et al., 2022).

Opportunities for Rural Tourism in the Digital Age

Stakeholders in the rural tourism sector should take advantage of digital platforms that will enable them to target a wider market by attracting visitors who are ready to spend for unique and offbeat experiences. There is a huge scope of data analytics to understand tourists' inclinations towards certain locations. Rural homestays can customize their offerings, too, in line with tourists' preferences, which will surely led to incremental service delight.

A viral web story of a remote areas of South Korea or snow-clad mountains of the Himalayas can be the cynosure for tourists, so online marketing can be surely a gamechanger.

A proper website showing the eco-tourism and sustainable and heritage culture of rural area attracts travellers who are environmentally conscious. Engaging the local community in rural tourism through social networking platforms and other forums provides employment and not only benefits the tourists but also the area, as it can open doors for technological education for the local people.

Therefore, it is important to leverage technological advancement, with a special reference to the sustainable development of rural tourism destinations.

Challenges for Rural Tourism in the Digital Era

Recent times have experienced multi-faceted developments in the developed and developing contexts, which has been reassured by the systematic literature review done by Rosalina et al. (2021) and Kausar and Nishikawa (2010). With emphasis on the issue of a skilled labour force, Mordue (2009) explained how the line between public and private places is getting thin due to the filmy tourism. For rural tourism development, a significant challenge is the limited internet connectivity in some rural areas, potentially deterring high-net-worth tourists (Zhu et al., 2022), which results in a digital divide. Securing visitors' personal information is another important issue, which can be a difficult job for rural destinations that lack expertise.

Inadequate digital infrastructure can also be another fear for tourists who require speedy internet. Rural homestays and villages must follow better marketing strategies based upon networking and word-of-mouth advertising from previous guests. Balancing the benefits of digital advancement in rural tourism with socio-ecological concerns is also a major challenge (Khartishvili et al., 2019).

Recommendations for Business Practices: The Key to Success

It is evident that the tourism sector has immense opportunities to grow further, which means it is a lucrative option for corporations to enter and gain maximum revenue from this sector. We recommend developing more effective marketing strategies, which should include marketing through social media platforms and digital advertising campaigns by way of audio-visual media. Corporations can also use the numerous blogs to communicate their offerings to tourists. Additionally, word of mouth from previous customers can also provide significant advantages to this sector. We recommend giving more emphasis to the homestay concept, as it gives tourists the feeling of finding a home away from home (Kataria et al., 2023). We also recommend that the Indian tourism industry adopt changes that are rapidly taking place in the environment due to the dynamic behaviour of this industry (Sujoodn et al., 2023).

References

Al Rousan, R., Siddiqui, S., Bano, N., & Sujood. (2023). Urban tourists' intention towards visiting national parks: An exertion of theory of planned behaviour and expectancy theory. *Journal of Hospitality and Tourism Insights*, Vol. ahead-of-print No. ahead-of-print. https://doi.org/10.1108/JHTI-11-2022-0549

Dokl, D., Rogelj, V., & Bogataj, D. (2022). Smart age-friendly villages: Literature review and research agenda. *IFAC-PapersOnLine*, *55*(10). https://doi.org/10.1016/j.ifacol.2022.09.459

Duong, V. C., & Sung, B. (2021). Examining the role of luxury elements on social media engagement. *Journal of Global Fashion Marketing*, *12*(2), 103–119. https://doi.org/10.1080/20932685.2020.1853585

Garrod, B., Wornell, R., & Youell, R. (2006). Re-conceptualising rural resources as countryside capital: The case of rural tourism. *Journal of Rural Studies*, *22*(1), 117–128. https://doi.org/10.1016/J.JRURSTUD.2005.08.001

Homestay Tourism and the Commercialization of the Rural Home in Thailand: Asia Pacific Journal of Tourism Research, *20*(1). (n.d.). Retrieved September 28, 2023, from www.tandfonline.com/doi/abs/10.1080/10941665.2013.852119

Kataria, P., Gupta, V. P., Kumar, S., & Gupta, R. (2023). Effect of collaborative consumption on sustainable homestay development: an empirical study. *Consumer Behavior in Tourism and Hospitality*, Vol. ahead-of-print No. ahead-of print. https://doi.org/10.1108/CBTH-12-2022-0206

Kausar, D. R., & Nishikawa, Y. (2010). Heritage tourism in rural areas: Challenges for improving socio-economic impacts. *Asia Pacific Journal of Tourism Research*, *15*(2), 195–213. https://doi.org/10.1080/10941661003629995

Khartishvili, L., Muhar, A., Dax, T., & Khelashvili, I. (2019). Rural tourism in Georgia in transition: Challenges for regional sustainability. *Sustainability (Switzerland)*, 11(2). https://doi.org/10.3390/su11020410

Mordue, T. (2009). Television, tourism, and rural life. *Journal of Travel Research*, *47*(3), 332–345. https://doi.org/10.1177/0047287508321203

Nestorova, P. (2019). Routledge handbook of human trafficking. *International Journal of Refugee Law*, *31*(1). https://doi.org/10.1093/ijrl/eez005

Petroman, C. (2021). *Types of luxury tourism consumers*, 312–320. www.mendeley.com/catalogue/debe108a-268c-306d-ba07-de72eebf3b94/

Rosalina, P. D., Dupre, K., & Wang, Y. (2021). Rural tourism: A systematic literature review on definitions and challenges. *Journal of Hospitality and Tourism Management*, *47*, 134–149. https://doi.org/10.1016/J.JHTM.2021.03.001

Rural Tourism | UNWTO. (n.d.). Retrieved September 28, 2023, from www.unwto.org/rural-tourism

Rural Tourism Market – Size, Growth, Trends, Share | 2033. (n.d.). Retrieved September 28, 2023, from www.futuremarketinsights.com/reports/rural-tourism-market

Sujood, Siddiqui, S., Bano, N., & Al Rousan, R. (2023). Understanding intention of Gen Z Indians to visit heritage sites by applying extended theory of planned behaviour: A sustainable approach. *Journal of Cultural Heritage Management and Sustainable Development*, Vol. ahead-of-print No. ahead-of-print. https://doi.org/10.1108/JCHMSD-03-2022-0039

Teare, R. E. (2023). Reflections on the theme issue outcomes: How could rural tourism provide better support for well-being and socio-economic development? *Worldwide Hospitality and Tourism Themes*, *15*(1), 94–98. https://doi.org/10.1108/WHATT-02-2023-173

Thirumaran, K., Jang, H., Pourabedin, Z., Wood, J., & Saura, J. R. (2021). The role of social media in the luxury tourism business: A research review and trajectory assessment. *Sustainability*, *13*(3), 1216. https://doi.org/10.3390/su13031216

Tourism in the Maldives Content. (n.d.). Retrieved March 20, 2024, from https://www.unwto.org/news/unwto-names-its-best-tourism-villages-2023

Villages – Best Tourism Villages. (n.d.). Retrieved September 28, 2023, from www.unwto.org/tourism-villages/en/villages/

Xiang, Z., & Gretzel, U. (2010). Role of social media in online travel information search. *Tourism Management*, *31*(2), 179–188. https://doi.org/10.1016/J.TOURMAN.2009.02.016

Yeoman, I. S. (2023). Editorial: Futureproofing: Ensuring tourism does not become obsolete. *Journal of Tourism Futures*, *9*(3), 302–303. https://doi.org/10.1108/JTF-09-2023-292

Zhu, Z., Ma, W., & Leng, C. (2022). ICT adoption and tourism consumption among rural residents in China. *Tourism Economics*, *28*(6), 1669–1675. https://doi.org/10.1177/13548166211000478

3 Transformative Technologies Changing the Hospitality Landscape

A Study of Digital Payment Systems in the Hospitality Industry

Dr. Anil Singh Parihar, Anoop Kumar, and Prof. Rajendra Khatik

1. Introduction

The hospitality industry is among the largest, most important, and oldest in the world. Indian hospitality has always been innovative, and this can be seen in the businesses that support the hospitality sector. The hotel industry, travel services, event planning, and transportation are the four main activities that make up the billion-dollar hospitality industry (Ali et al., 2021). The hospitality and tourism sectors are currently seen as major sources of income for the country, making them very significant. Therefore, to advance and enhance their national economies and quality of life, many countries compete for travellers' and tourists' attention. The structures, procedures, and practices of the hospitality and tourism industries have undergone a significant transformation because of technological advancements. These technological disruptions in this field led to cost reduction, improved operational efficiency, improved service quality, and improved customer experience.

The consumer's demand has changed paradigms from just a product to the experience surrounding the purchase due to the growing digitalization. At the start of the twenty-first century, there was a sizable shift in business strategy and management in favour of a cashless and digital payment system. India's payment system digitalization is a significant area of rising interest for all industries.

In the present scenario and in future, the ICT devices are the core of human life (Shaw, 2014). Telephones, smartphones, tablets, and other mobile devices have become integral parts of our daily lives. The socio-cultural structures in all spheres of life are changing because of these multipurpose devices (Shuib et al., 2015; Pimmer et al., 2016).

The industry must undergo digital transformation to adapt to the changing customer demands in the experience age and stay ahead of both established rivals and disruptive newcomers in a market that is rapidly changing (Lam & Law, 2019). Digital payments systems are critical for the growth of any industry and business. The terms had been assessed by various researchers in many ways. Our effort has been to investigate and analyze the impact of digital payments in customer satisfaction in the case of hospitality industry. Based on the area to be explored, our study has the following objectives and will try to answer the following questions.

DOI: 10.4324/9781003488248-3

1.1 Research Objectives

Technological application in the travel and hospitality industries improves service delivery convenience and business viability. At many tourist destinations, the option to pay with digital currencies for transactions at hotels, restaurants, and other tourism-related businesses has already been introduced (Susanto et al., 2022; Hameed et al., 2023). Quality is one of the most important components of business development in the service industry, such as tourism, because it positively correlates with profits, market share growth, and customer satisfaction. The quality of digital payment transaction usage services persuades visitors to come back to tourist destinations (Xia et al., 2018). Based on this discussion, we have the following objectives for this study:

a To explore the applicability of digital payments systems in the hospitality industry.
b To investigate the various factors affecting the technological acceptance.
c To analyze the impact of technological acceptance of digital payments systems on customer satisfaction in the field of hospitality industry usage.

1.2 Research Questions

a How is technological acceptance in terms of digital payments systems enablers affected by perceived mobility (PM), perceived word of mouth (POWM), and perceived ease of use (PEU)?
b How do various challenges such as lack of security, lack of trust, and lack of awareness affect the technological acceptance of digital payments systems by customers of hospitality businesses?
c How is customer satisfaction towards hospitality impacted by the usage of digital payment platforms?

2. Theoretical Background

2.1 Digital Payments in the Hospitality Industry

Hoteliers have had to defend their digital competitive positioning against not only other hotels but also other players and disruptors in the travel and lodging industries to meet evolving customer expectations, grow market share, and maintain profit margins (Lam & Law, 2019). Digital payments in tourist destinations are one of the trends in digitalization. This modification affects cash payments, the least secure form of payment, while digital payments are regarded as the safest (Almeida et al., 2019). A reality of service innovation is the growth of digital payments in tourist destinations. Digital transactions are thought to enhance the payment process in tourist destinations (Susanto et al., 2022). The hospitality sector has seen a massive transformation in payment technology in recent years. The push for quicker, more convenient, and more secure payment methods had started before the COVID pandemic, even though it was definitely a stimulus for many innovations and advancements (Gursoy & Chi, 2020; Jose, 2023). The objective of payments technology in the future is to streamline and ease the guest experience (Gupta et al., 2023). The hospitality sector also benefits from e-payments, as these come with faster transaction speed, secure transactions, ease of use, wide acceptability, and customer satisfaction, which also help the industry to maximize sales and generate more revenue (Suhaimi et al., 2022; Hameed et al., 2023). Businesses can benefit greatly from the adoption of artificial intelligence technology in payments systems in the hospitality sector. It will create opportunities to improve efficiency, cut expenses, and provide customers with individualized experiences.

2.2 Digital Payments Enablers

A digital payment system consists of the following three elements to provide any digital financial services (Raj et al., 2020):

a A digital transaction platform is a platform that accepts payments over the internet.
b Customers using the platform to send money as well as businesses using it to receive it
c A device such as a computer or smartphone that can be used to transact online

2.2.1 Perceived Mobility (PM)

Perceived mobility is a determinant used to assess a person's perception of the advantages they believe they have received in terms of time, space, and service access. Amberg et al. (2003) introduced the concept of perceived mobility in the domain of mobile payments. It is the feature of mobile that allows customers to access information, communication, and services independent of time and place (Mallat, 2009). It is a crucial antecedent in the arena of digital payments services (Huang et al., 2007. Zmijewska et al. (2004) argued that in case of there are not enough network coverage areas, the device discharges too fast, or there are not enough operators offering the service, this factor may not be satisfied. To study the perceived mobility, we have framed the following hypothesis:

H1: *Perceived mobility of digital payments enhances its technological acceptance among the customers of the hospitality industry.*

2.2.2 Positive Word of Mouth (PWM)

Word of mouth (WOM) has been acclaimed as one of the most significant resources of information diffusion (Jalilvand et al., 2011). Positive WOM tends to concentrate on the immediate results of customers' satisfaction or dissatisfaction with prior purchasing experiences (Brown, 2005). Kumar et al. (2021) found that researchers have identified WOM as a persuasive source of information. WOM is the interpersonal communication between consumers about goods and services. In the present scenario, this could be done by putting online reviews about the product or service, and any review of a product or business, whether favourable or unfavourable, that is published online and distributed to many people and institutions is referred to as this (Hennig-Thurau et al., 2004; Jalilvand et al., 2011).

$H_0$2: *Positive word of mouth of digital payments enhances its technological acceptance among the customers of the hospitality industry.*

2.2.3 Perceived Ease of Use (PEU)

Davis (1989) described it as the extent to which someone thinks using a certain system would be effortless. It has been considered for the technology acceptance model (TAM). The ease-of-use differences between cash transactions and digital payment systems have been studied by some researchers. Because it is user-friendly and secure, it is a benefit of digital payments. They also establish that perceived ease of use significantly boosts user satisfaction and encourages continued use of related technologies (Mahaboob Basha et al., 2020; Sinaga et al., 2021). Perceived usefulness includes control of one's own money, disintermediation, high speed of transfer, low cost of transfer, high transaction security, limited supply, international scope, lower merchant's cost, increased customer trust requirements, and higher price volatility (Folkinshteyn & Lennon, 2017). Considering perceived ease of use as an element of the study, we have framed the following hypothesis:

$H_0$3: *Perceived ease of use of digital payments enhances its technological acceptance among the customers of the hospitality industry.*

2.3 Challenges in Digital Payments

2.3.1 Lack of Security

The main concern for the user in adoption of digital payments is the security issues in these transactions. Their subjective likelihood that their personal information may not be accessed, stored, and manipulated by the outsiders is termed the perceived security (Denaputri & Usman, 2019; Ardiansah et al., 2020; Tahar et al., 2020). The requirement for multilateral security, or the security requirements of all users of an e-payment system, has been listed as one of the most significant challenges of mobile payments (Linck et al., 2006). E-payments can only be considered secret if each stage of the transaction process meets the needs and security expectations of the user. We try to analyze this as:

$H_0$4: Lack of s*ecurity does not significantly impact the technological acceptance of digital payments.*

2.3.2 Lack of Trust

Singh and Sirdeshmukh (2000) stated that the acceptance of a trustor's vulnerability, grounded in optimistic expectations of the trustee's behaviour, can be followed by a party's readiness to experience through action to a virtual party's role (Mayer et al., 1995; van der Heijden et al., 2003). It is an important asset for every business (Zhou, 2011) and especially becomes vital for tech-savvy enterprises (Lankton et al., 2015). De La et al. (2019) argued that with the widespread adoption of digital technology, trust in technology becomes the new challenge all together. The emergence of technological trust poses a new challenge to the industry, significantly influencing the rationale behind the selection of various payment methods or services/providers (Szumski, 2020). The trust and trust deficit level indicators can highlight the relation between the usage level and trust indicator. Based on this discussion, we have the following hypothesis:

$H_0$5: *Lack of trust does not significantly impact the technological acceptance of digital payments.*

2.3.3 Lack of Awareness

The term "technological awareness" describes how well a user is informed about new technology and develops a general understanding of what it entails (Dinev & Hu, 2007). It has been a significant element affecting digital payments. Lack of awareness is the degree to which users are unaware of the uses and advantages of the current digital payment services (Balakrishnan & Shuib, 2021; Oliveira, 2016; Al-Okaily et al., 2020). Customers' knowledge of a technology is thought to be a crucial factor influencing their intentions to use the technology, and as a result, knowledge serves as an antecedent in the formation of a user's attitude (Dinev & Hu, 2007). Lack of awareness could be due to not understanding how to use the digital payments platforms or not knowing what these can do for you. This may happen if the service provider has not advertised their product very well (Wushishi & Ogundiya, 2014). Hence, we assume that:

$H_0$6: *Lack of awareness does not significantly impact the technological acceptance of digital payments.*

2.4 Technology Acceptance (TA)

With the development and advancement of various technologies, specifically information and communication technologies (ICT) and their impact on users' private and professional lives, their technological acceptance has always been a prime concern for businesses (Davis, 1993; Davis & Venkatesh, 1996; Venkatesh et al., 2012; Marangunić & Granić, 2014). It is an interrelationship between the user's convenience, attitude, and intention towards the adoption and application of novel technologies, which have always been an area for researchers to explore (Davis, 1989; Chen & Chen, 2022; Lee et al., 2003).

2.4.1 Technological Acceptance and Customer Satisfaction

The term "customer satisfaction" was first used in business and marketing by Kotler (1999). According to Anwar (2017), the term "customer satisfaction" refers to a measurement of the services or goods delivered to meet the customer's expectations. Many new payment and transaction options known as "contactless payments" emerged with the advent of wireless and communication technology (Kongaut & Lis, 2017; See-To & Ngai, 2019) and are now being embraced by most industries, including travel and tourism (Park et al., 2022).

The tourism and travel industries use contactless payments because they enable travel businesses to process payments significantly faster, even when customers lack access to cash, credit, or debit cards. By saving time, it can also enhance the client experience and satisfaction. Hence, we assume that:

H7: *Technological acceptance of digital payments in the domain of the hospitality industry enhances customer satisfaction.*

3. Materials and Methods

This is an empirical study to investigate the impact of technological acceptance and usage of digital payments platforms by customers of hospitality businesses and their satisfaction. The variables were selected based on the thorough literature review on the various studies in this domain. There are two aspects of the study. First is the analysis of the technological acceptance of digital payments by the customer in the hospitality industry, and second is the analysis of customer satisfaction based on technology acceptance of digital payment systems by the customers. We have not considered the technological acceptance as a mediating variable in this study. PLS-SEM version 4.0.9.6 is used to analyze the data.

3.1 Sample Design

The G-Power software is used to calculate the sample size of this study. According to the variables of this study, G-Power suggested a sample of 146 respondents (Figure 3.1). This means that the sample size for this study must be greater than or equal to 146, whereas the sample of this study comprises 227 respondents.

3.2 Conceptual Model

Based on the comprehensive discussion on the proposed hypothesis, the conceptual model of this research study is given in Figure 3.2.

3.3 Questionnaire

The questionnaire is divided into two parts. Part I collects the demographic profile of the respondents like name, age group, gender, educational qualification, occupation, and marital status. Pat II covers the main questions of the study. A total of 38 items, based on the five-point Likert scale, ranging from strongly disagree – 1, disagree – 2, neutral – 3, agree – 4, and strongly agree – 5 were taken for the study. Table 3.1 presents the constructs and their reliability and validity.

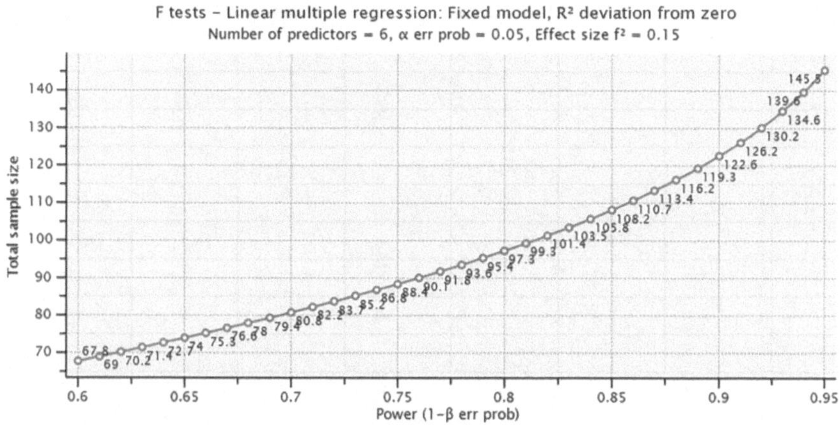

Figure 3.1 Sample size sufficiency using G-Power software

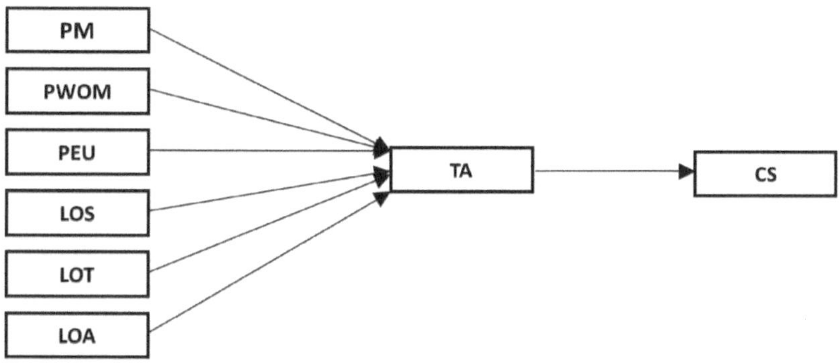

Figure 3.2 Conceptual model by author

4. Results and Discussion

In this study, the first-order constructs PM, PWOM, PEU, LOS, LOT, and LOA are considered to analyze their impact on TA. The next part covers the analysis of TA over CS in the hospitality industry. We have not considered TA as a mediating component in this study.

SEM is used for the empirical analysis and is based on two models. The first is a measurement model that verifies the reliability and validity of the data, and the second is a structural model that calculates the path coefficients and the correlation between variables, tests the hypothesis, and validates it.

4.1 Measurement Model

The outside model in SEM is used to measured reliability and validity, factor loading, and convergent validity of the constructs (Barclay et al., 1995). Composite

Table 3.1 Items for the Study and Their Reliability and Convergent Validity

Item No.	*Construct*	*Reference*	*Factor Loadings*	*Cronbach α*	*CR*	*AVE*
Perceived Mobility						
PM1	I can use digital payment whenever I want.	Kim et al., 2010	.754	.630	.802	.574
PM2	I believe digital payment can be used anywhere I like.		.753			
PM3	Digital payment is convenient because I always carry a mobile phone.		.766			
Perceived Word of Mouth						
PWOM1	If anyone asks me about digital payment, I will definitely recommend it.	Mehrad & Mohammadi, 2017	.826	.693	.815	.595
PWOM2	I will talk about digital payment to anyone quite positively.		.773			
PWOM3	I will talk about the strengths of the digital payment with people.		.712			
Technological Acceptance						
TA1	Using digital payment is fun.	Kim et al., 2010 & Oliveira et al., 2016	.798	.844	.883	.559
TA2	Using digital payment is enjoyable.		.769			
TA3	Using digital payment is entertaining.		.797			
TA4	I like to experiment with new technologies in payment system.		.691			
TA5	I believe digital payment is compatible with existing technologies.		.693			
TA6	I believe digital payment is compatible with my daily routine activities.		.729			
Perceived Ease of Use						
PEU1	I believe that digital payment is clear and understandable.	Gia-Shie & Pham Tan Tai, 2016; Mehrad & Mohammadi, 2017	.809	.861	.889	.535
PEU2	I think it is easy to use digital payment to do what I want it to do.		.714			

PEU3	Learning to use the digital payment is easy for me.		.689			
PEU4	It is easy for me to become skillful at using the digital payment.		.717			
PEU5	I find the digital payment easy to use.		.791			
PEU6	I find the digital payment procedure to be flexible to use.		.722			
PEU7	Digital payment is convenient because it is not complicated.		.667			
Lack of Security						
LOS1	I do not fear about spam or hacker invasions into digital payment system.	Kim et al., 2010; Slade et al., 2015; Oliveira et al., 2016	.799	.811	.875	.637
LOS2	I feel that digital payment system is secure.		.807			
LOS3	I believe that digital payment systems are trustworthy.		.783			
LOS4	I feel secure sending sensitive information across digital payment system.		.804			
Lack of Trust						
LOT1	I trust the information provided during the digital payment process.	Kim et al., 2010; Mehrad & Mohammadi, 2017	.715	.783	.858	.601
LOT2	I trust digital payment services.		.784			
LOT3	I trust the service providers to offer secure digital payment.		.768			
LOT4	I think digital payment service is reliable.		.831			
Lack of Awareness						
LOA1	I am using digital payment system easily and effectively.	Lwoga & Lwoga, 2017; Kim et al., 2010	.649	.772	.837	.510
LO2	I have sufficient knowledge to use digital payment services for financial transactions.		.764			
LOA3	I can use the digital payment services without detailed instruction on its use.		.663			

(Continued)

Table 3.1 (Continued)

Item No.	*Construct*	*Reference*	*Factor Loadings*	*Cronbach α*	*CR*	*AVE*
LOA4	I am aware about the digital payment process.		.643			
LOA5	In general, I am competent in using the digital payment services.		.833			
Customer Satisfaction						
CS1	Digital payment services have accelerated my regular activities.	Muhtasim, et al., 2022 & developed by author	.750	.855	.892	.581
CS2	Compared to conventional techniques, the digital payment is a time-saving system.		.722			
CS3	I feel comfortable while using digital payments services in hotels, restaurants, cab booking, movie ticket booking etc.		.796			
CS4	Digital payment services have improved the quality of my decision making for buying things or booking for hotels, movie tickets, event tickets etc.		.791			
CS5	Digital payment services are capable of providing benefits to individual for purchase of product/services.		.721			
CS6	I expect that in the near future majority of the people will be using digital payment services.		.788			

reliability and internal consistency were measured through Cronbach's alpha, construct validity was confirmed by factor loadings, and convergent validity was measured by AVE. Further, the discriminant validity is measured through the Fornell–Larcker criterion and the heterotrait-monotrait ratio of correlations (HTMT) criterion (Henseler et al., 2015).

4.1.1 Internal Consistency

It is primarily measured by Cronbach's alpha and composite reliability. Cronbach's alpha value between .60 and .70 is acceptable; a higher value indicates high composite reliability. In Table 3.1, values of Cronbach's alpha range from .630 to .859, indicating the internal consistency of data.

4.1.2 Indicator Reliability

It is the variance of items explained by that variable. Values of outer loadings of the items (questions) range from 0 to 1, the acceptable amount is .6, and higher would be better. Table 3.1 factor loading values range from .643 to .833, indicating the high indicator reliability.

4.1.3 Convergent and Content Validity

It measures the theoretical relationship between constructs. Convergent validity of the scale depends upon three factors. First, factor loading should be equal to or more than .60; second, composite reliability should be equal to or greater than .80; and third, AVE should be equal to or more than .50, as stated by Fornell and Larcker. In Table 3.1, all three measures are according to the standards.

4.1.3 Discriminant Validity

The discriminant validity of the constructs is based on the heterotrait-monotrait (HTMT) ratio, which is one of the most authentic methods. As per SMART PLS 4, if the HTMT value is below 0.90, discriminant validity has been established between two reflective constructs. Table 3.2 indicates the acceptance of discriminant validity.

4.2 Structural Model

This model represents the hypothesized relationship among variables. Path coefficients, whose values range from +1 to -1, show where the change occurred. A coefficient value that is closer to +1 indicates that there is a high positive impact or strong positive relationship, a value that is closer to -1 indicates a strong negative relationship, and a value that is closer to 0 indicates a weak relationship between the dependent and independent variables. T value and p value are the other values

Table 3.2 Discriminant Validity – Heterotrait-Monotrait (HTMT) Ratio

	LOA	*LOS*	*LOT*	*PEU*	*PM*	*PWOM*	*TA*
LOA							
LOS	0.697						
LOT	0.770	0.775					
PEU	0.852	0.509	0.638				
PM	0.627	0.509	0.522	0.718			
PWOM	0.733	0.580	0.626	0.746	0.779		
TA	0.808	0.669	0.729	0.775	0.712	0.768	
CS	–	–	–	–	–	–	0.645

Table 3.3 Path Coefficients and Effects

Hypothesis	*Standard Deviation*	*T statistics*	*P values*	*Decision*
H1: PM -> TA	0.053	2.199	0.028	Accepted
H2: PWOM -> TA	0.053	3.238	0.001	
H3: PEU -> TA	0.054	4.86	0.000	
H04: LOS -> TA	0.067	2.17	0.030	Rejected
H05: LOT -> TA	0.069	2.053	0.040	
H06: LOA -> TA	0.08	2.037	0.042	
H7: TA -> CS	0.051	10.822	0.000	Accepted

that need to be described in structural models. The significance of the relationship or impact between the variables is indicated by both values.

Table 3.3 presents path coefficients in the form of standard deviation, T statics, and p values. The p values for the hypothesis H1 to H3 are $p = 0.028$, $p = 0.001$, and $p = 0.000$, which indicates that our decision is supported. It means that perceived mobility, perceived word of mouth, and perceived ease of use enhance the technological acceptance of digital payments, and H7 ($p = 0.000$) signifies that customer satisfaction in the hospitality business is enhanced by the technological acceptance of digital payments systems. The hypothesis H_04 ($p = 0.030$), H_05 ($p = .040$), and H_06 ($p = .042$) indicates that these hypotheses, being null hypotheses, are rejected, and we can say that lack of security, lack of trust, and lack of awareness have a significant impact on technological acceptance of digital payments systems in the hospitality province. The results of PLS-SEM are mentioned in Figure 3.3.

5. Recommendations for Business Practices: The Key to Success

The digitalization of the payment system is a major turning point in the era of the faceless, paperless, cashless economy. These innovative technologies have gradually replaced the conventional one (Kristensen & Solvoll, 2019). Digital payment

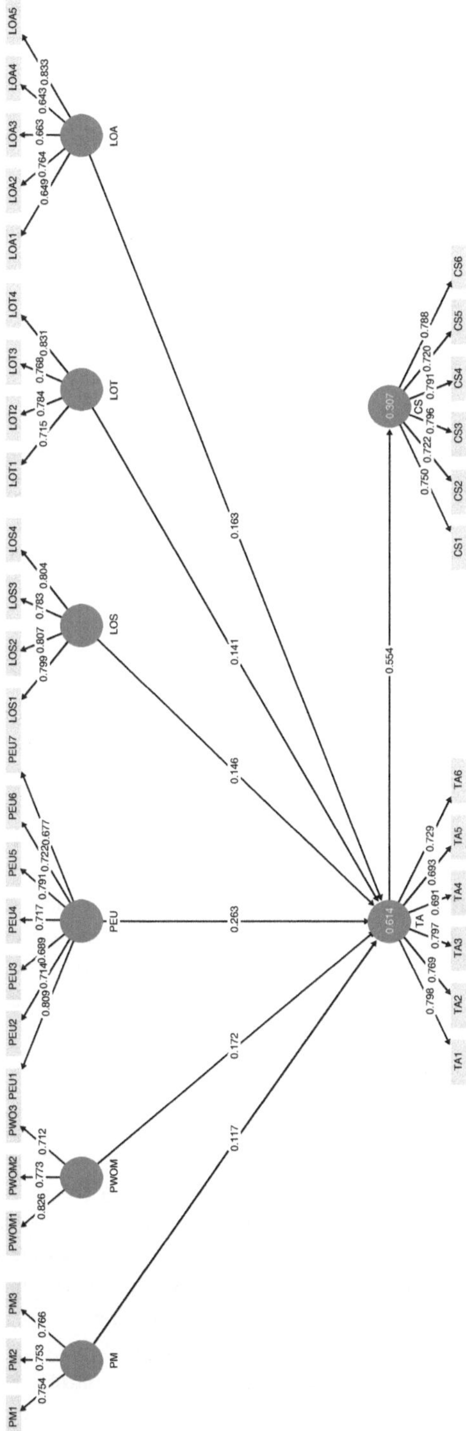

Figure 3.3 Results of PLS-SEM

methods are one of the most prominent trends in the hospitality sector. Whether via digital wallets or contactless cards, digital payments are commonplace these days and have had a particularly significant impact on the hospitality industry in recent years.

The payment system's digitalization will be a defining feature of the future cashless economy. With digital wallets, the day will hopefully come when a customer can leave their house without needing to carry a wallet. The acceptance of digital payments has grown as a result of new technological developments and the need for international trade (Shailza & Sarkar, 2019). The younger generation is more inclined to pay for digital services because they are more accustomed to doing so. Also, they value those services (Fletcher & Nielsen, 2016).

5.1 Applying Digital Payments Systems in the Hospitality Sector

The effectiveness, competitive edge, and prosperity of the hospitality industry are enhanced by new technologies (Nyheim et al., 2004; Spyridou, 2019; Gupta et al., 2023) because many people value travelling, particularly the younger generation, which enjoys utilizing new technologies. The digital payments services can be provided through many ways, such as:

- Debit cards – These cards save both time and effort by enabling customers to make quick payments for the services straight from their bank account.
- Net banking – Consumers can carry out a variety of financial transactions with the help of this electronic payment method, which is directly linked with their bank account.
- Unified payment interface (UPI) – It combines various banking features, seamless fund routing, and merchant payments into a single mobile application (of any participating bank).
- Mobile wallets – Carrying digital cash is possible with a mobile wallet. Customers can transfer money online to a mobile wallet or link to their credit card or debit card information on a mobile device to the application. They can make purchases using a smartphone, tablet, or smart watch in place of their physical plastic card.

5.2 Implementation of Digital Payments Systems in the Hospitality Industry

Since cash payments are difficult to trace, achieving transparency and accountability is more challenging. But on the other hand, digital payments promote accountability, tracking, and reduce the chance of theft; also, they may be more dependable. These can be easily implemented anywhere, anytime. Locations that offer digital payment services are regarded as smart tourist destinations because they can serve visitors more effectively (Rafdinal et al., 2021; Novianti et al., 2022). The effective use of digital payments by travellers is regarded as an enhancement to the services offered by tourist destinations. It is imperative that destination management companies consider incorporating local transaction services into the digital system. It is necessary to evaluate investments in digital payment technologies to improve the operational performance of businesses (Susanto et al., 2022). The way that payments are handled is rapidly changing, and hotels that choose their technology partners wisely will be able to adapt to the new environment, increase revenue, and provide a more seamless guest experience (Worrall, 2023).

6. Conclusion

Digital payments methods are among the most vital trends in the hospitality industry these days (Park et al., 2022). The travel and tourism industry has experienced a new boom in the booking and settlement of invoices through cashless methods due to the innovation of the digital and cashless economy generation in many ways.

Our findings reveal that the technological acceptance of digital payments plays a significant role in customer satisfaction in the realm of hospitality business. The digital payments methods are simple and easy to use (perceived ease of use), highly mobile – i.e. can be used from any device anywhere and anytime (perceived mobility) – and users are adopting them and also recommending them to others (perceived word of mouth). Apart from this, certain challenges are also associated with these payments systems. People still have concern over their security, they still don't trust them, and many of them are not aware about them. As a result of this, when people become more aware of the functions and capabilities of digital payment technology and find them to be secure and trustworthy, the more they will be inclined to make use of it.

The concept of digital payments systems has become one of the extremely evident developments in the hospitality sector. Though we have attempted to explore more into the influencing factors and provide a profound understanding, this study is not deprived of limitations. First, the study was conducted with a limited number for samples to provide the basic idea in this realm. We suggest conducting an enlarged survey to get the latest trends affecting the customers satisfaction in the hospitality industry while using digital payment platforms. Second, more variables may also be included and tested to get a better idea. Despite these limitations, this study has substantially contributed towards the better understanding of the subject. Stakeholders in this sector must be well versed in the nuances of technological development and must adopt them in their businesses.

References

Ali, B. J., Gardi, B., Othman, B. J., Ahmed, S. A., Ismael, N. B., Hamza, P. A., Aziz, H. M., Sabir, B. Y., & Anwar, G. (2021). Hotel service quality: The impact of service quality on customer satisfaction in hospitality. *International Journal of Engineering, Business and Management*, *5*(3), 14–28.

Almeida, F., Almeida, J. & Mota, M. (2019). Perceptions and trends of booking online payments in tourism. *Journal of Tourism and Services*, *10*(18), 1–15.

Al-Okaily, M., Lutfi, A., Alsaad, A., Taamneh, A., & Alsyouf, A. (2020). The determinants of digital payment systems' acceptance under cultural orientation differences: The case of uncertainty avoidance. *Technology in Society*, *63*, 101367. https://doi.org/10.1016/j.techsoc.2020.101367

Amberg, M., Hirschmeier, M., & Wehrmann, J. (2003). The compass acceptance model for the analysis and evaluation of mobile services. *International Journal for Mobile*

Communications (IJMC), Finland. www.wi3.uni-erlangen.de/forschung/publikation/PDF/IJMC.pdf

Anwar, K. (2017). Analyzing the conceptual model of service quality and its relationship with guests' satisfaction: A study of hotels in Erbil. *The International Journal of Accounting and Business Society*, *25*(2), 1–16.

Ardiansah, M., Chariri, A., Rahardja, S., & Udin, U. (2020). The effect of electronic payments security on e-commerce consumer perception: An extended model of technology acceptance. *Management Science Letters*, *10*(7), 1473–1480.

Balakrishnan, V., & Shuib, N. L. M. (2021). Drivers and inhibitors for digital payment adoption using the cashless society readiness-adoption model in Malaysia. *Technology in Society*, *65*, 101554. https://doi.org/10.1016/j.techsoc.2021.101554.

Barclay, D., Higgins, C., & Thompson, R. (1995). The partial least squares (PLS) approach to casual modelling: Personal computer adoption and use as an Illustration. *Technology Studies, Special Issue on Research Methodology*, *2*(2), 285–309.

Brown, T. J. (2005). Spreading the word: Investigating antecedents of consumers' positive word-of-mouth intentions and behaviors in a retailing context. *Journal of the Academy of Marketing Science*, *33*(2), 123–138. https://doi.org/10.1177/0092070304268417

Chen, X. and Chen, R. (2022), "Examining the influence of the performance of mobile devices on teaching quality based on the technological acceptance mode", *Library Hi Tech*, Vol. ahead-of-print No. ahead-of-print. https://doi.org/10.1108/LHT-12-2021-0489

Davis, F. D. (1989). Perceived usefulness, perceived ease of use, and user acceptance of information technology. *MIS Quarterly*, *13*(3), 319–340. https://doi.org/10.2307/249008

Davis, F. D. (1993). User acceptance of information technology: System characteristics, user perceptions and behavioral impacts. *International Journal of Man-Machine Studies*, *38*(3), 475–487. https://doi.org/10.1006/imms.1993.1022

Davis, F. D., & Venkatesh, V. (1996). A critical assessment of potential measurement biases in the technology acceptance model: Three experiments. *International Journal of Human-Computer Studies*, *45*(1), 19–45. https://doi.org/10.1006/ijhc.1996.0040

De La Pena, J., & Papadonikolaki, E. (2019) From relational to technological trust: How do the Internet of Things and Blockchain technology fit in? *Proceedings of the 2019 European Conference on Computing in Construction*, 415–424. https://doi.org/10.35490/EC3.2019.153.

Denaputri, A., & Usman, O. (2019). *Effect of perceived trust, perceived security, perceived usefulness and perceived ease of use on customers' intention to use mobile payment* https://ssrn.com/abstract=3511632 or http://dx.doi.org/10.2139/ssrn.3511632

Dinev, T., & Hu, Q. (2007). The centrality of awareness in the formation of user behavioral intention toward protective information technologies. *Journal of the Association for Information Systems*, *8*(7), 386–408. https://doi.org/10.17705/1jais.00133

Fletcher, R., & Nielsen, R. K. (2016, October 28). Paying for online news. *Digital Journalism*, *5*(9), 1173–1191. https://doi.org/10.1080/21670811.2016.1246373

Folkinshteyn, D., & Lennon, M. (2017). Braving bitcoin: A technology acceptance model (TAM) analysis. *Journal of Information Technology Case and Application Research*, *18*(4), 220–249.

Gia-Shie, L., & Pham, T. T. (2016). A study of factors affecting the intention to use mobile payment services in Vietnam. *Economics World*, *4*(6), 249–273. https://doi.org/10.17265/2328-7144/2016.06.001

Gupta, S. K., Tiwari, S., Hassan, A., & Gupta, P. (2023). Moderating effect of technologies into behavioural intensions of tourists toward use of mobile wallets for digital payments: TAM model perspective. *International Journal of Hospitality & Tourism Systems*, *16*(1).

Gursoy, D., & Chi, C. G. (2020). Effects of COVID-19 pandemic on hospitality industry: Review of the current situations and a research agenda. *Journal of Hospitality Marketing & Management*, *29*(5), 527–529. tandfonline. https://doi.org/10.1080/19368623.2020.1788231

Hameed, I., Akram, U., & Ashraf, A. (2023). Consumers' usage of mobile payment systems: An application of the innovation resistance and coping theory on the tourism sector. *Kybernetes*, ahead-of-print. https://doi.org/10.1108/K-03-2023-0495

Henseler, J., Ringle, C. M., & Sarstedt, M. (2015). A new criterion for assessing discriminant validity in variance-based structural equation modelling. *Journal of the Academy of Marketing Science*, *43*(1), 115–135. https://doi.org/10.1007/s11747-014-0403-8

Hennig-Thurau, T., Gwinner, K. P., Walsh, G., & Gremler, D. D. (2004). Electronic word-of-mouth via consumer-opinion platforms: What motivates consumers to articulate themselves on the Internet? *Journal of Interactive Marketing*, *18*(1), 38–52.

Huang, J., Lin, Y., & Chuang, S. (2007). Elucidating user behavior of mobile learning. *The Electronic Library*, *25*(5), 585–598. https://doi.org/10.1108/02640470710829569

Isaac, O., Abdullah, Z., Ramayah, T., Mutahar, A. M., & Alrajawy, I. (2016). *Perceived usefulness, perceived ease of use, perceived compatibility, and net benefits: An empirical study of internet usage among employees in Yemen*. The 7th International Conference on Postgraduate Education, Universiti Teknologi MARA (UiTM), Shah Alam, Malaysia, May 2017, 899–919.

Jalilvand, M. R., Esfahani, S. S., & Samiei, N. (2011). Electronic word-of-mouth: Challenges and opportunities. *Procedia Computer Science*, *3*(1), 42–46. https://doi.org/10.1016/j.procs.2010.12.008

Jose, S. (2023). Impact of demonetisation and pandemic on digital payments usage. *International Journal of Science and Research*, *12*(3).

Kim, C., Tao, W., Shin, N., & Kim, K. S. (2010). An empirical study of customers' perceptions of security and trust in e-payment systems. *Electronic Commerce Research and Applications*, *9*(1), 84–95. https://doi.org/10.1016/j.elerap.2009.04.014

Kongaut, C., & Lis, P. (2017). *Supply and demand sides of mobile payment: A comparative analysis of successful mobile payment adoption in developed and developing countries*. 28th European Regional Conference of the International Telecommunications Society (ITS): "Competition and Regulation in the Information Age", Passau, Germany, July 30–August 2, 2017, International Telecommunications Society (ITS), Passau.

Kotler, B. M. (1999). *Marketing for hospitality and tourism*, 2nd edn. Prentice Hall PTR. ISBN: 0130136980.

Kristensen, L.-B. K., & Solvoll, M. (2019). Digital payments for a digital generation. *Nordic Journal of Media Studies*, *1*(1), 125–136. https://doi.org/10.2478/njms-2019-0008

Kumar, S., Lim, W. M., Pandey, N., & Christopher Westland, J. (2021). 20 years of electronic commerce research. *Electronic Commerce Research*, *21*(1), 1–40. https://doi.org/10.1007/s10660-021-09464-1

Lam, C., & Law, R. (2019). Readiness of upscale and luxury-branded hotels for digital transformation. *International Journal of Hospitality Management*, *79*, 60–69. https://doi.org/10.1016/j.ijhm.2018.12.015

Lankton, N., McKnight, D. H., & Tripp, J. (2015). Technology, humanness, and trust: Rethinking trust in technology. *Journal of the Association for Information Systems*, *16*(10), 880–918. https://doi.org/10.17705/1jais.00411

Lee, Y., Kozar, K., & Larsen, K. (2003). The Technology Acceptance Model: Past, Present, and Future. *Communications of the Association for Information Systems*, *12* pp-pp. https://doi.org/10.17705/1CAIS.01250 https://aisel.aisnet.org/cais/vol12/iss1/50/

Linck, K., Pousttchi, K., & Wiedemann, D. G. (2006). Security issues in mobile payment from the customer viewpoint. In: Ljungberg, J. (Hrsg.) *Proceedings of the 14th European Conference on Information Systems (ECIS 2006)*. Göteborg, Schweden 2006, S.1–11.

Lwoga, E. T., & Lwoga, N. B. (2017). User acceptance of mobile payment: The effects of usercentric security, system characteristics and gender. *Electronic Journal of Information Systems in Developing Countries*, *81*(1), 1–24. https://doi.org/10.1002/j.1681-4835.2017.tb00595.x

Mahaboob Basha, A. M., Chenchu Reddy, P., Radha Krishna Murthy, G., Srivani, J. & Ankaiah, B. (2020). Moderating role of security and reliability on high customer satisfaction: Relationship among ease of use-content-service quality with respect to customer satisfaction in digital banking transactions. *International Journal of Advanced Science and Technology*, *29*(3), 6866–6876.

Mallat, N., Rossi, M., Tuunainen, V. K., & O€orni, A. (2009). The impact of use context on mobile services acceptance: The case of mobile ticketing. *Information & Management*, *46*(3), 190–195.

Marangunić, N., & Granić, A. (2014). Technology acceptance model: A literature review from 1986 to 2013. *Universal Access in the Information Society*, *14*(1), 81–95.

Mayer, R. C., Davis, J. H., & Schoorman, F. D. (1995). An integrative model of organizational trust. *Academy of Management Review*, *20*(3), 709–734.

Mehrad, D., & Mohammadi, S. (2017). Word of mouth impact on the adoption of mobile banking in Iran. *Telematics and Informatics*, *34*(7), 1351–1363. https://doi.org/10.1016/j.tele.2016.08.009

Muhtasim, D. A., Tan, S. Y., Hassan, M. A., Pavel, M. I., & Susmit, S. (2022). Customer satisfaction with digital wallet services: An analysis of security factors. *International Journal of Advanced Computer Science and Applications*, *13*, 195–206.

Nyheim, P., McFadden, F., & Connolly, D. (2004). *Technology strategies for the hotel industry*. Pearson Higher Ed.

Novianti, S., Susanto, E., & Rafdinal, W. (2022). Predicting tourists' behaviour towards smart tourism: The case in emerging smart destinations. *Journal of Tourism Sustainability*, *2*(1), 19–30.

Oliveira, T., Thomas, M., Baptista, G., & Campos, F. (2016). Mobile payment: Understanding the determinants of customer adoption and intention to recommend the technology. *Computers in Human Behavior*, *61*(2016), 404–414. https://doi.org/10.1016/j.chb.2016.03.030

Park, M. C., Manalili, I., Magtoto, T., Martinez, R., Solis, J., & Chua, C. (2022). Contactless payments in travel and tourism in Philippines: From a technological acceptance model. *American Journal of Economics and Business Innovation*, *1*(2), 23–33. https://doi.org/10.54536/ajebi.v1i2.264

Pimmer, C., Mateescu, M., & Gröhbiel, U. (2016). Mobile and ubiquitous learning in higher education settings. A systematic review of empirical studies. *Computers in Human Behavior*, *63*, 490–501. https://doi.org/10.1016/j.chb.2016.05.057

Rafdinal, W., Susanto, E., Novianti, S. & Juniarti, C. (2021). Is smart tourism technology important in predicting visiting tourism destination? Lessons From West Java, Indonesia. *Journal of Tourism Sustainability*, *1*(2), 102–115.

Raj, A., Jain, N., & Chauhan, S. S. (2020). Digital payments and its security. *Cybernomics*, *2*(2), 13–20.

See-To, E. W. K., & Ngai, E. W. T. (2019). An empirical study of payment technologies, the psychology of consumption, and spending behavior in a retailing context. *Information & Management*, *56*(3), 329–342. https://doi.org/10.1016/j.im.2018.07.007

Shailza, & Sarkar, M. P. (2019). Literature review on adoption of digital payment system. *Global Journal of Enterprise Information System*, *11*(3), 62–67.

Shaw, N. (2014). The mediating influence of trust in the adoption of the mobile wallet. *Journal of Retailing and Consumer Services*, *21*(4), 449–459. https://doi.org/10.1016/j.jretconser.2014.03.008

Shuib, L., Shamshirband, S., & Ismail, M. H. (2015). A review of mobile pervasive learning: Applications and issues. *Computers in Human Behavior*, *46*, 239–244. https://doi.org/10.1016/j.chb.2015.01.002

Sinaga, O. S., Marpaung, F. K., Dewi, R. S. & Sudirman, A. (2021). Kontribusi perceived usefulness, perceived ease of use dan perceived security Terhadap behavioral intention to use Aplikasi JAKET. *Insight Management Journal*, *1*(3), 86–94.

Singh, J., & Sirdeshmukh, D. (2000). Agency and trust mechanisms in consumer satisfaction and loyalty judgments. *Journal of the Academy of marketing Science*, *28*, 150–167.

Slade, E., Williams, M., Dwivedi, Y., & Piercy, N. (2015). Exploring consumer adoption of proximity mobile payments. *Journal of Strategic Marketing*, *23*(3), 209–223. https://doi.org/10.1080/0965254X.2014.914075

Spyridou, A. (2019). To cheat or not to cheat. *Journal of the International Academy for Case Studies*, *25*(2), 1–5.

Suhaimi, N. A. N., Nawi, N. M., & Kamarudin, W. N. B. W. (2022). Determining the use of cashless payment methods and the contributing factors: hotel guests' perspectives in Malaysia. *International Journal of Accounting*, *7*(41).

Susanto, E., Hendrayati, H., Rahtomo, R. W., & Prawira, M. F. A. (2022). Adoption of digital payments for travelers at tourism destinations. *African Journal of Hospitality, Tourism and Leisure*, *11*(2), 741–753.

Szumski, O. (2020). Technological trust from the perspective of digital payment. *Procedia Computer Science*, *176*, 3545–3554. https://doi.org/10.1016/j.procs.2020.09.032

Tahar, A., Riyadh, H. A., Sofyani, H., & Purnomo, W. E. (2020). Perceived ease of use, perceived usefulness, perceived security and intention to use e-filing: The role of technology readiness. *The Journal of Asian Finance, Economics and Business (JAFEB)*, *7*(9), 537–547.

van der Heijden, H., Verhagen, T., & Creemers, M. (2003). Understanding online purchase intentions: Contributions from technology and trust perspectives. *European Journal of Information Systems*, *12*(1), 41–48. https://doi.org/10.1057/palgrave.ejis.3000445

Venkatesh, V., Thong, J. Y. L., & Xu, X. (2012). Consumer acceptance and use of information technology: Extending the unified theory of acceptance and use of technology. *MIS Quarterly*, *36*(1), 157–178.

Worrall, F. (2023). *Hospitality upgrade*. www.hospitalityupgrade.com/_magazine/MagazineArticles/6_Trends_in_Payment_Technology.asp/

Wushishi, U. J., & Ogundiya, A. O. (2014). Mobile commerce and security issues. *International Journal of Scientific Research Engineering & Technology (IJSRET)*, *3*(4), 739–741. www.ijsret.org

Xia, M., Zhang, Y., & Zhang, C. (2018). A tam-based approach to explore the effect of online experience on destination image: A smartphone user's perspective. *Journal of Destination Marketing and Management*, *8*, 259–270.

Zhou, T. (2011). The effect of initial trust on user adoption of mobile payment. *Information Development*, *27*(4), 290–300. https://doi.org/10.1177/0266666911424075

Zmijewska, A., Lawrence, E., & Steele, R. (2004). Towards understanding of factors influencing user acceptance of mobile payment systems. *ICWI*, *2004*, 270–277

4 Digital Finance in the Hospitality Industry

Advancements, Challenges, and Opportunities

Kamakshi Mehta and Dr. Umesh Solanki

Introduction

In an epoch characterized by swift technological advancement, the hospitality sector emerges as a vanguard in adopting digital transformation. The use of advanced financial technologies has significantly transformed how organizations within the financial sector handle their operations, transactions, and client interactions. The integration of digital banking and hospitality has initiated a novel era characterized by enhanced efficiency, heightened security, and increased innovation. The progress of digital banking, encompassing contactless payments and loyalty programmes enabled by blockchain technology, has not only enhanced the efficiency of financial operations but also fundamentally transformed the concept of guest satisfaction.

Nevertheless, similar to any profound transformation, numerous problems arise. The hospitality sector faces the challenge of protecting sensitive financial information amidst increasing cyberrisks while also guaranteeing adherence to a constantly evolving regulatory environment. The issue of reconciling the desire for smooth digital experiences with the necessity for strong security measures is a crucial and intricate responsibility for individuals and groups involved in this domain.

This comprehensive review examines the crucial significance of digital finance in the hotel sector, scrutinizing recent progress, evaluating enduring obstacles, and revealing the multitude of prospects that await. By comprehending the complexities of this dynamic interaction, enterprises operating in the hospitality industry can not only adjust to the evolving environment but also establish themselves as pioneers of innovation, establishing a novel benchmark for financial prowess within the sector.

Review of Literature

According to Kapoor et al. (2022), the implementation of contactless payment methods and mobile wallet technologies has revolutionized payment procedures within the hotel industry. According to Ozturk et al. (2016), the implementation of this technological breakthrough has resulted in improved visitor experiences through the provision of better convenience and transactional efficiency. The utilization

DOI: 10.4324/9781003488248-4

of blockchain technology has garnered significant attention due to its capacity to potentially transform loyalty programmes and provide secure transactions (Srivastava et al., 2019). According to Casallas et al. (2020), the utilization of blockchain platforms enables the implementation of smart contracts, which, in turn, facilitates transparency and automation in financial activities. The utilization of sophisticated data analytics tools in the hotel industry allows firms to examine and interpret customer spending patterns and preferences, hence facilitating the provision of tailored offers and services (Rosário and Raimundo, 2021). As a consequence, there has been a notable rise in consumer satisfaction and loyalty. The integration of fintech startups and traditional hospitality facilities has resulted in the emergence of novel financial solutions, including the implementation of integrated payment systems and digital invoicing platforms (Gomber et al., 2018). The hospitality industry faces a growing vulnerability to cyberthreats, such as data breaches and financial fraud, due to its growing dependence on digital money (Vaidya, 2019). It is crucial to prioritize the implementation of strong cybersecurity measures to protect sensitive financial data. Businesses operating in the digital financial sector face issues in adhering to dynamic regulatory frameworks, which encompass data protection and payment processing standards (Kafi & Akter, 2023). The process of ensuring compliance necessitates continuous adaptation and attention. The implementation of sophisticated digital finance systems may result in substantial initial expenses, especially for smaller enterprises (Kim et al., 2006). Achieving equilibrium between investment allocation and anticipated returns is a pivotal factor to be taken into account. Ongoing progress in the field of digital banking is anticipated to augment guest experiences by facilitating smooth transactions, providing personalized services, and offering loyalty programmes (Shang & Chiu, 2022). According to Shrier (2016), the utilization of digital finance technologies in the hospitality industry allows firms to access international markets by providing a wide range of payment alternatives and facilitating currency conversions. As a result, these technologies contribute to the expansion of the client base for hospitality enterprises. According to Dutta et al. (2020), the utilization of blockchain technology in several domains such as guest reviews, identity verification, and supply chain management holds the potential to enhance trust and transparency within the sector.

The Objectives of This Study

This study aims to analyze the progress, obstacles, and potential prospects of digital financial technologies when used in the hotel sector. Specifically, it will focus on payment systems, blockchain, and data analytics, as well as new technologies such as artificial intelligence (AI) and the Internet of Things (IoT).

Analysis

This chapter offers a comprehensive examination of the progress made in digital finance within the hotel sector. The ongoing advancement of technology is significantly altering the landscape of financial transactions, leading to a notable transformation within the hospitality industry. This change is characterized by the use of digital payment systems, the integration of blockchain technology, and the implementation of inventive financial solutions. This research investigates the most recent developments and their effects on operational effectiveness, customer satisfaction, and the overall financial situation within the industry. The hospitality industry, well-known for its focus on guest happiness and operational effectiveness, is currently experiencing a period of significant change due to the introduction of digital financial technologies. This section provides an overview of the significant impact that improvements in digital finance have on transforming financial transactions, enhancing guest experiences, and optimizing business processes within the hospitality industry. This research investigates the widespread adoption of mobile payment systems and contactless transactions within the hospitality sector. The proliferation of smartphones has led to the utilization of technology by businesses to provide smooth and secure payment solutions, hence improving convenience for both customers and establishments. The incorporation of digital wallets represents a significant progression within the hotel industry. This section explores how digital wallet platforms enable expedited, enhanced security and customized payment experiences for customers. Case studies and best practices exemplify effective deployments across different types of establishments. The hospitality business has experienced a significant transformation in financial transactions due to the progress made in payment gateways and point-of-sale (POS) systems. This section examines the impact of contemporary payment processing technology on the efficiency of transactions, including the reduction of processing times and the enhancement of reconciliation processes.

The utilization of blockchain technology is demonstrating noteworthy progress in the reconfiguration of loyalty programmes within the hospitality industry. This section explores how blockchain-based platforms contribute to the improvement of transparency, security, and the exchange of loyalty points. These advancements ultimately result in the cultivation of stronger guest connections and increased brand loyalty. The utilization of data-driven financial insights enables the acquisition of vital knowledge about customer behaviour, spending patterns, and operational efficiencies, hence facilitating the process of making well-informed decisions. The hospitality industry is progressively embracing multi-currency solutions due to the phenomenon of globalization and the growing number of international visitors. This section evaluates the impact of digital finance technology on facilitating smooth cross-border transactions, resolving currency conversion difficulties, and enhancing the overall guest experience. This section focuses on the crucial significance of adhering to industry regulations and implementing strong security measures to ensure compliance in the realm of digital banking despite the various advantages it presents. This statement emphasizes the importance of implementing effective strategies to ensure the security of sensitive financial data and mitigate the risks posed by cyberthreats. This section presents a prospective analysis of the future of digital finance within the context of the hotel business. The text explores the discourse surrounding emerging technologies, prospective innovations, and strategic issues that firms must address to maintain competitiveness within an ever-evolving digital environment. This chapter highlights the significant influence that improvements in digital banking have on the hotel business. This statement emphasizes the significance of actively embracing digital finance technology to improve guest experiences, streamline operations, and maintain a leading position in industry advancements.

Challenges

This chapter critically examines the challenges faced by the hospitality industry in integrating digital finance technologies. The financial industry is currently facing several challenges as it navigates the shift toward digital payment systems, blockchain technology, and other novel financial solutions. This research endeavour aims to identify and examine the various problems associated with the implementation of digital finance in the hospitality industry. By doing so, it seeks to provide valuable insights into potential modifications and future views that can contribute to the effective integration of digital finance in this sector. The hospitality business, well known for its focus on guest happiness and operational effectiveness, is currently seeing a notable shift as it incorporates digital financial technologies. This section provides an overview of the significance and influence of digital finance in transforming financial transactions, guest experiences, and operational processes within the hospitality sector. A key obstacle in the implementation of digital finance in the hospitality industry pertains to ensuring adherence to regulatory requirements and maintaining robust security measures. This section explores the intricate terrain of adhering to financial regulations, encompassing aspects such as data protection, anti-money laundering, and payment card industry requirements. Additionally, the chapter delves into the necessity of implementing effective cybersecurity protocols to protect sensitive financial data. The adoption of digital finance is impeded by the considerable barrier presented by the intricacy of current technological infrastructure. This section explores the necessity of achieving a smooth integration between novel financial technologies and existing legacy systems. It delves into several concerns like interoperability, data migration, and compliance with current operational procedures. The resistance exhibited by employees and guests towards adopting digital banking is a significant obstacle to its deployment. This section examines the significance of thorough training programmes for both employees and guests to facilitate seamless adoption, with a specific emphasis on user-friendly interfaces, effective communication, and continuous support. The prioritization of accessibility and inclusion for all individuals is of utmost importance as the digital banking industry continues to evolve. This section examines the strategies that establishments might employ to cater to guests who may lack access to cell phones or digital payment methods, underscoring the importance of providing alternative payment solutions. The issue of gathering and managing guest data has grown increasingly sensitive due to the growing utilization of digital money. This section discusses the significance of transparent data-gathering procedures, acquiring appropriate consent, and implementing strong data privacy rules to uphold visitor trust and adhere to regulatory requirements. The financial outlay necessary to use digital finance technology can pose a substantial obstacle for certain establishments. This part provides an analysis of the financial ramifications, considering the expected return on investment, and presents techniques to optimize the advantages of integrating digital money. The effective deployment of digital finance in the hospitality industry heavily relies on imperative collaboration with vendors and partners. This section examines the difficulties associated with achieving alignment between technology providers, payment processors, and financial institutions by the goals of the organization. This section presents adaptive techniques and future-oriented viewpoints to effectively tackle the difficulties that have been identified. This chapter examines the possibilities of emerging technologies, industry collaborations, and creative business models to address challenges and facilitate the widespread adoption of digital finance within the hotel industry. This study highlights the importance of proactively tackling the problems associated with the integration of digital finance in the hotel industry. This statement highlights the significant impact that digital banking technology may have on improving guest experiences, streamlining operations, and positioning establishments as leaders in industry innovation.

The following discussion will explore potential future perspectives in the context of the given topic.

In the context of the ever-changing digital finance landscape, the hospitality industry is faced with the imperative of proactively anticipating forthcoming trends and adopting flexible tactics to maintain competitiveness and exploit nascent prospects. This section examines the prospective future outlook of digital finance in the hotel sector and provides adaptable tactics for stakeholders within the business. Future perspectives in digital finance include the integration of cutting-edge technologies such as artificial intelligence (AI), augmented reality (AR), and blockchain. Hospitality enterprises should allocate resources towards research and development endeavours to capitalize on these technologies to augment guest experiences, optimize transaction processes, and enhance operational efficiency. The potential trajectory of digital finance within the hospitality industry is in the effective utilization of data analytics and the implementation of artificial intelligence (AI) to facilitate personalized experiences. Organizations can utilize predictive analytics to anticipate the preferences of their guests, provide customized services, and generate unique experiences. This, in turn, can cultivate guest loyalty and advocacy. The utilization of blockchain technology holds the capacity to significantly transform financial transactions within the hotel sector. The use of a decentralized ledger for payments and contracts has the potential to improve transparency, mitigate fraudulent activities, and speed up reconciliation procedures. Consequently, this can foster confidence among various stakeholders involved in the process. The potential utilization of blockchain technologies in the development of loyalty programmes holds promise for granting guests comprehensive transparency and autonomy in managing their loyalty points. Smart contracts can automate the process of distributing rewards, thereby establishing a loyalty ecosystem that is characterized by enhanced efficiency and reliability. The integration of digital finance and IoT technology presents prospects for interconnected visitor experiences. The integration of smart room technology, automated check-in systems, and in-room payment solutions has the potential to enhance the visitor experience by offering a seamless and convenient service. Forthcoming adaptive solutions must prioritize the objective of guaranteeing accessibility for all patrons. It is recommended that establishments persist in providing alternate payment methods, assistive devices, and inclusive training to accommodate a wide array of customers. Engaging in partnerships with fintech start-ups can facilitate the acquisition of cutting-edge financial solutions tailored to address the unique requirements of the hotel sector. Partnerships have the potential to facilitate the creation of tailored payment solutions, integration of mobile wallets, and improvements to loyalty programmes. The ever-changing landscape of technology necessitates a constant evolution of cybersecurity measures to effectively mitigate emerging threats. It is recommended that establishments allocate resources toward the implementation of sophisticated cybersecurity solutions, regularly perform audits, and remain updated on new compliance standards to protect guest data and financial transactions. The importance of continuous personnel training and upskilling cannot be overstated in light of the advancing digital finance technologies. Employees must possess the requisite knowledge and abilities to effectively and confidently navigate and harness the potential of digital banking platforms. It is anticipated that forthcoming developments in the realm of digital finance will encompass a heightened emphasis on environmental, social, and governance (ESG) principles. Organizations can embrace sustainable and socially responsible financial practices, thereby integrating their operational strategies with overarching global sustainability objectives. By proactively considering these forthcoming viewpoints and employing flexible tactics, the hospitality sector can establish itself as a frontrunner in the effective incorporation of digital financial technologies. The adoption of these trends will not only optimize visitor experiences but also facilitate operational efficiency and ensure financial sustainability in an evolving digital landscape.

Conclusion

In summary, the incorporation of digital money within the hospitality sector signifies a significant transition towards enhanced effectiveness, heightened security, and increased ingenuity. The progressions in mobile payments, digital wallets, blockchain technology, and data analytics have brought about a significant transformation in the realm of financial transactions and visitor experiences. Nevertheless, the rapid progress in technology brings out a set of obstacles that must be addressed, such as ensuring adherence to regulations, safeguarding against cyberthreats, and promoting inclusion. To effectively overcome these issues, it is imperative for the sector to actively embrace flexible tactics that can adapt to changing circumstances. This entails adopting nascent technologies such as AI, blockchain, and the IoT while emphasizing the significance of data-driven personalization and loyalty initiatives. The enhancement of innovation can be facilitated through the establishment of partnerships with fintech startups and a deliberate emphasis on sustainability by adhering to ESG principles. It is of utmost importance for businesses to assign high priority to cybersecurity and compliance endeavours, allocating resources towards the implementation of comprehensive safeguards to safeguard sensitive financial information. In addition, it is crucial to prioritize accessibility for all guests and offer ongoing training for staff as integral components of an effective digital finance strategy. By proactively anticipating forthcoming trends and implementing adaptable strategies, the hospitality sector can establish itself as a leader in innovation, thereby establishing a novel benchmark for financial prowess. The adoption of digital finance not only improves the quality of guest experiences but also boosts operational efficiency, thereby facilitating the industry's progression towards a more sustainable and competitive future.

Practical Implications

The chapters' presentation of facts and ideas has significant practical consequences for stakeholders in the hospitality industry. Hospitality enterprises must give precedence to allocating resources towards the adoption and integration of cutting-edge technologies such as AI, blockchain, and the IoT. This includes endeavours in research and development aimed at harnessing modern technologies to improve guest experiences and optimize operational efficiency. Establishments must prioritize data-driven personalization as a means of anticipating visitor preferences and providing customized services. This phenomenon has the potential to result in heightened levels of guest pleasure, loyalty, and advocacy. Hospitality enterprises have the opportunity to consider the implementation of blockchain technology in loyalty programmes as a means to augment transparency and foster trust. Smart contracts can automate the process of distributing rewards, hence enhancing the efficiency of the loyalty ecosystem. The integration of IoT technology in the context of smart room features, automated check-ins, and in-room payment systems has the potential to offer visitors a streamlined and user-friendly experience. Establishments must persist in providing various payment options and guaranteeing the accessibility of their digital services to accommodate guests with varying needs. The implementation of this inclusive approach will effectively accommodate a wider range of customers. The establishment of collaborations with fintech start-ups has the potential to facilitate the creation of bespoke financial solutions that are specifically designed to cater to the unique requirements of the hospitality sector. The incorporation of integrated payment systems and digital invoicing platforms is a notable aspect. It is imperative to emphasize the significance of prioritizing cybersecurity. It is recommended that hospitality enterprises allocate resources towards the implementation of sophisticated cybersecurity measures, regularly perform audits, and be informed about emerging compliance standards to protect visitor information and financial transactions. Ensuring the provision of ongoing training and opportunities for upskilling to employees is essential in equipping them with the requisite knowledge and abilities to effectively navigate and harness the potential of digital finance platforms. Hospitality facilities can incorporate sustainable and socially responsible financial practices, so linking their operational strategies with overarching global sustainability objectives. This not only confers advantages to the natural surroundings but also augments the standing of the brand. Organizations must thoroughly evaluate the initial expenses associated with the adoption of sophisticated digital financial systems in comparison to the projected benefits. The careful evaluation of achieving equilibrium between investment and anticipated benefits is of utmost importance. By adopting these practical consequences, firms operating in the hospitality industry can successfully leverage the promise of digital finance technologies. This will not only improve the quality of guest experiences but also optimize operational efficiency and ensure long-term financial viability, establishing them as frontrunners in the constantly changing realm of digital transformation.

References

Casallas, J. A. T., Lovelle, J. M. C., & Molano, J. I. R. (2020). Smart contracts with blockchain in the public sector. *IJIMAI*, *6*(3), 63–72.

Dutta, P., Choi, T. M., Somani, S., & Butala, R. (2020). Blockchain technology in supply chain operations: Applications, challenges and research opportunities. *Transportation Research Part E: Logistics and Transportation Review*, *142*, 102067.

Gomber, P., Kauffman, R. J., Parker, C., & Weber, B. W. (2018). On the fintech revolution: Interpreting the forces of innovation, disruption, and transformation in financial services. *Journal of Management Information Systems*, *35*(1), 220–265.

Kafi, M. A., & Akter, N. (2023). Securing financial information in the digital realm: Case studies in cybersecurity for accounting data protection. *American Journal of Trade and Policy*, *10*(1), 15–26.

Kapoor, A., Sindwani, R., Goel, M., & Shankar, A. (2022). Mobile wallet adoption intention amid COVID-19 pandemic outbreak: A novel conceptual framework. *Computers & Industrial Engineering*, *172*, 108646.

Kim, P. H., Aldrich, H. E., & Keister, L. A. (2006). Access (not) denied: The impact of financial, human, and cultural capital on entrepreneurial entry in the United States. *Small Business Economics*, *27*, 5–22.

Ozturk, A. B., Bilgihan, A., Nusair, K., & Okumus, F. (2016). What keeps mobile hotel booking users loyal? Investigating the roles of self-efficacy, compatibility, perceived ease of use, and perceived convenience. *International Journal of Information Management*, *36*(6), 1350–1359.

Rosário, A., & Raimundo, R. (2021). Consumer marketing strategy and E-commerce in the last decade: A literature review. *Journal of Theoretical and Applied Electronic Commerce Research*, *16*(7), 3003–3024.

Shang, S. S., & Chiu, L. S. (2022). Leveraging smart technology for user experience personalization – a comparative case study of innovative payment systems. *Pacific Asia Journal of the Association for Information Systems*, *14*(1), 6.

Shrier, D. (2016). Mobile money & payments: Technology trends. In D. Shrier, G. Canale, & A. Pentland (Eds.), *Mobile money & payments technology trends*. Massachusetts Institute of Technology, pp. 2–27.

Srivastava, J. D., Kumar, N., & Bisht, H. (2019). Blockchain for loyalty rewards program management. *Journal of the Gujarat Research Society*, *21*(7), 92–100.

Vaidya, R. (2019). Cyber security breaches survey 2019. *Department for Digital, Culture, Media and Sport*, *66*.

5 Convergence of E-Banking and Hospitality in India

Exploring Opportunities and Challenges

Dr. Prashant H. Bhagat and Piyush Kumar Jain

1. Introduction

In recent years, the rapid growth of digital technology and the widespread adoption of online services have led to the convergence of various industries. One such notable convergence is between e-banking and the hospitality sector in India. E-banking, which encompasses online banking, mobile banking, and digital payment systems, has revolutionized the way financial transactions are conducted. Simultaneously, the hospitality industry has embraced digital transformation to enhance customer experiences and streamline operations.

1.1 Background

Traditionally, the banking and hospitality sectors have operated independently, serving distinct purposes. However, with the advancement of technology and the changing preferences of consumers, there has been a shift towards seamless integration between the two domains. The hospitality industry recognizes the value of incorporating e-banking services to offer convenience and flexibility to guests, while banks see the potential of targeting the travel and tourism market.

1.2 Research Objectives

The primary objectives of this chapter are as follows:

- To explore the convergence of e-banking and the hospitality industry in India.
- To identify the opportunities arising from the integration of e-banking services within the hospitality sector.
- To analyze the challenges faced by both industries in achieving successful convergence.
- To examine the impact of e-banking and hospitality convergence on customer experiences and satisfaction.
- To propose strategies for stakeholders to capitalize on the opportunities and mitigate challenges associated with this convergence.

DOI: 10.4324/9781003488248-5

1.3 Scope of the Study

This chapter focuses on the convergence of e-banking and the hospitality industry specifically within the context of India. It will delve into the current state and growth prospects of both sectors, with a particular emphasis on the digital transformation trends in the hospitality industry. The study will also explore successful case studies of e-banking integration in hotels and other hospitality establishments. However, the research will not cover other aspects of e-banking not directly related to the hospitality sector.

1.4 Research Methodology

To accomplish the research objectives, a comprehensive research methodology will be employed. The study will involve a combination of quantitative and qualitative approaches, including:

- **Extensive literature review:** Academic journals, books, reports, and online sources will be reviewed to gain insights into the convergence of e-banking and hospitality and to understand the opportunities and challenges in this context.
- **Data gathering:** Relevant data on e-banking adoption, hospitality industry trends, customer preferences, and technological advancements will be collected from reliable sources.
- **Interviews and surveys:** Stakeholders from the e-banking and hospitality sectors, including customers, bank representatives, hoteliers, and industry experts, will be interviewed or surveyed to gather firsthand insights and opinions.
- **Case studies:** Real-life case studies of successful convergence implementations in Indian hospitality establishments will be analyzed to understand best practices and lessons learned.

2. Overview of E-Banking and Hospitality Industries in India

2.1 E-Banking in India

E-banking, also known as electronic banking or online banking, refers to the provision of banking services and transactions through digital platforms such as the internet and mobile devices. In India, e-banking has witnessed significant growth and transformation over the past decade, driven by technological advancements, government initiatives, and increasing digital literacy among the population.

2.1.1 Growth and Trends

The growth of e-banking in India has been fueled by various factors, including the government's push for a cashless economy, the rise of smartphone usage, and the expansion of internet connectivity. As a result, the number of e-banking users has been steadily increasing.

Trends in e-banking include the rise of mobile banking applications, which allow customers to access their accounts, make transactions, and avail themselves of various banking services on their smartphones. Additionally, digital wallets and the Unified Payments Interface (UPI) have gained popularity as convenient and secure digital payment methods, enabling seamless fund transfers and payments (RBI 2021).

2.1.2 Digital Payment Systems

Digital payment systems have played a pivotal role in transforming the e-banking landscape in India. The introduction of various digital payment options has made financial transactions faster, more secure, and easily accessible to a wider audience. Some of the prominent digital payment systems in India include:

a **Unified Payments Interface (UPI):** Developed by the National Payments Corporation of India (NPCI), UPI allows instant and hassle-free fund transfers between bank accounts through mobile applications. UPI has seen remarkable adoption and has become the backbone of digital payments in India (NPCI 2021).
b **Mobile wallets:** Mobile wallets are applications that allow users to store money digitally and make payments for various goods and services. Companies like Paytm, Google Pay, and PhonePe have emerged as major players in the mobile wallet segment.
c **Internet banking:** Traditional Internet banking platforms provided by banks enable customers to perform various banking activities online, including checking account balances, paying bills, and transferring funds.
d **Aadhaar Enabled Payment System (AePS):** AePS leverages the Aadhaar biometric authentication system to facilitate financial transactions, especially in rural and remote areas where access to traditional banking services may be limited (PWC India 2021).

2.2 Hospitality Industry in India

The hospitality industry in India encompasses various sectors, including hotels, restaurants, travel, and tourism services. It plays a crucial role in India's economy, contributing significantly to employment generation and foreign exchange earnings.

2.2.1 Current State and Growth Prospects

India's hospitality industry has experienced steady growth, driven by rising disposable incomes, a burgeoning middle class, increasing domestic and international tourism, and government initiatives to promote the tourism sector. With India becoming a favoured destination for business and leisure travellers, the demand for hospitality services has seen a significant upswing (KPMG India 2021).

The growth prospects for the hospitality industry in India are promising, with an increasing number of domestic and international tourists, the development of infrastructure, and a growing trend towards experiential travel (IBEF 2021).

2.2.2 Digital Transformation in Hospitality

The hospitality industry in India has embraced digital transformation to enhance guest experiences, streamline operations, and stay competitive. The use of technology in the hospitality sector has resulted in several significant changes:

a **Online booking platforms:** The adoption of online booking platforms and travel aggregators has made it easier for travellers to find and book accommodation and travel services. This has enabled hotels to reach a broader audience and optimize their revenue management (PWC India 2021).
b **Mobile apps:** Hospitality establishments have developed mobile applications that offer seamless check-in and check-out processes, personalized services, and real-time communication with guests.
c **Contactless services:** In response to the COVID-19 pandemic, many hotels and restaurants have implemented contactless services, such as digital menus and mobile payments, to ensure a safe and hygienic environment for guests.
d **Data analytics and personalization:** The use of data analytics allows hotels to gather insights about guest preferences and behaviour, enabling them to offer personalized experiences and targeted marketing campaigns (Parikh 2021).

3. Convergence of E-Banking and Hospitality

3.1 Integration of Payment Solutions

The convergence of e-banking and the hospitality industry offers the opportunity to integrate various payment solutions seamlessly (Singh and Sharma 2020). By incorporating digital payment systems, such as mobile wallets and Unified Payments Interface (UPI), into the hospitality sector, guests can make cashless transactions for room bookings, dining, spa services, and other amenities. This integration not only enhances customer convenience but also streamlines the payment process for hotels and restaurants, reducing the reliance on traditional cash transactions and improving overall efficiency (Panda and Raut 2021).

3.2 Personalized Customer Experiences

The convergence of e-banking and hospitality allows for the collection and analysis of customer data to provide personalized experiences (Ayad 2020). By leveraging data analytics, hotels can gain insights into guest preferences, previous bookings, and spending behaviour. This information enables them to offer tailored services, such as personalized recommendations, room preferences, and exclusive offers, creating a more engaging and memorable experience for guests (Sharma and Thomas 2019).

3.3 Loyalty Programmes and Rewards

The convergence of e-banking and hospitality opens up new possibilities for loyalty programmes and rewards (Gupta and Dahiya 2019). Banks and hotels can collaborate to offer co-branded credit or debit cards that provide exclusive benefits, discounts, and reward points for hotel stays, dining, and other services. This symbiotic relationship enhances customer loyalty, drives repeat business, and fosters long-term partnerships between financial institutions and hospitality establishments (Chatterjee and Sharma 2020).

3.4 Streamlined Financial Management for Hospitality Businesses

E-banking integration streamlines financial management for hospitality businesses by automating various processes (Bhattacharya 2019). With features like online invoicing, automated expense tracking, and real-time financial reporting, hotels and restaurants can improve their financial efficiency, reduce manual errors, and make better data-driven decisions. Moreover, the integration of payment gateways simplifies the reconciliation process, providing a clear picture of revenue and cash flow (Gupta and Mahajan 2018).

4. Opportunities Arising From Convergence

4.1 Enhanced Guest Experience

The convergence of e-banking and the hospitality industry presents an opportunity to enhance the overall guest experience. By integrating digital payment solutions, guests can enjoy a seamless and hassle-free check-in and check-out process. Mobile apps can offer personalized services and recommendations based on guest preferences, such as room preferences, dining choices, and leisure activities (Dioko et al. 2021). The integration of payment and loyalty programmes enables guests to access exclusive rewards and benefits, fostering a sense of loyalty and satisfaction (Chan and Guillet 2020).

4.2 Increased Efficiency and Cost Savings

The convergence of e-banking and hospitality leads to increased efficiency and cost savings for both guests and hospitality businesses (Raza and Chang 2018). Digital payment systems streamline financial transactions, reducing the need for handling cash and associated security costs. Automation of processes, such as invoicing and expense tracking, optimizes operational efficiency and reduces manual errors. Moreover, the integration of e-banking services can lead to lower transaction fees and faster settlement times, benefiting both customers and businesses (Oh and Jeong 2020).

4.3 Data-Driven Decision-Making

The convergence of e-banking and hospitality generates a vast amount of data, which can be leveraged for data-driven decision-making (Kim et al. 2020). Hotels can analyze customer behaviour, booking patterns, and spending preferences to tailor marketing strategies and promotional offers. Data-driven insights also enable hotels to optimize pricing, inventory management, and resource allocation, leading to better revenue management and increased profitability (Niranjan and Sathish 2021).

4.4 Market Expansion and New Customer Segments

The convergence of e-banking and hospitality opens up opportunities for market expansion and targeting new customer segments (Juwaheer 2019). By collaborating with financial institutions, hotels can offer attractive packages and exclusive services to bank customers, thereby reaching a wider audience. Moreover, the integration of e-banking services can attract tech-savvy and digitally oriented customers who prefer cashless transactions and personalized experiences (Navale and Srivastava 2018).

5. Challenges of E-Banking and Hospitality Convergence

5.1 Data Security and Privacy Concerns

One of the primary challenges of e-banking and hospitality convergence is ensuring robust data security and privacy (Niranjan and Priya 2019). The integration of digital payment systems and customer data in the hospitality sector increases the risk of cyberattacks, data breaches, and unauthorized access to sensitive information. Both banks and hospitality establishments must implement stringent security measures, encryption protocols, and data access controls to safeguard customer data and maintain their trust (Agrawal and Bhattacharya 2020).

5.2 Regulatory Compliance and Legal Issues

The convergence of e-banking and hospitality introduces complex regulatory and legal challenges (RBI 2021). Both industries are subject to different regulations and compliance requirements, making it essential for them to align their practices and adhere to various financial and data protection laws. Failure to comply with these regulations can lead to fines, legal disputes, and reputational damage for both financial institutions and hospitality businesses (Dinçer 2021).

5.3 Customer Trust and Adoption

Building customer trust and promoting the adoption of e-banking services in the hospitality sector can be a challenge. Some customers may still prefer traditional payment methods and may be apprehensive about the security of digital transactions. Hospitality establishments need to educate their customers about the benefits of e-banking, reassure them about data security, and offer a seamless and user-friendly digital payment experience to encourage adoption (Kaur and Verma 2021).

5.4 Technological Infrastructure and Integration

Achieving seamless technological integration between e-banking and hospitality systems can pose challenges (Lai et al. 2019). Both industries may use different technology platforms, which may not be fully compatible. The implementation of integrated payment solutions, loyalty programmes, and data analytics systems requires robust and reliable technological infrastructure. The lack of interoperability can lead to operational inefficiencies and hinder the delivery of a unified and cohesive customer experience (Khanna and Deshmukh 2020).

6. Strategies for Successful Convergence

6.1 Collaboration and Partnerships

Collaboration and partnerships between e-banking institutions and hospitality establishments are essential for successful convergence (Bhusry and Singh 2020). Banks and financial institutions can collaborate with hotels and restaurants to offer co-branded credit or debit cards, loyalty programmes, and exclusive offers for customers. Such collaborations create a win-win situation, as banks gain access to a new customer base, and hotels can offer added benefits to their guests (Chaturvedi 2021).

6.2 Robust Cybersecurity Measures

To address data security and privacy concerns, robust cybersecurity measures are essential (NPCI 2021). Both banks and hospitality businesses should invest in state-of-the-art cybersecurity technologies and practices to protect customer data and financial transactions. Implementing end-to-end encryption, two-factor authentication, and regular security audits can help mitigate cyberthreats and safeguard sensitive information (Singh and Khan 2019).

6.3 Regulatory Alignment and Compliance

To ensure a smooth convergence, both e-banking and hospitality businesses must align with relevant regulations and comply with data protection laws (RBI 2020). This involves understanding and adhering to financial regulations, data privacy rules, and industry-specific guidelines. Regular monitoring of compliance and updating systems accordingly are critical to maintaining a secure and legally compliant ecosystem (MeitY 2021).

6.4 User Education and Awareness

User education and awareness play a vital role in encouraging the adoption of e-banking services in the hospitality sector (Thomas and Abhilasha 2018). Hospitality establishments should educate their customers about the benefits and safety of digital payment options, offering clear guidelines and tutorials on using e-banking features. User awareness campaigns can help dispel myths and misconceptions about e-banking, instilling confidence in customers to make cashless transactions (Mishra and Mahapatra 2020).

7. Case Studies of Successful Convergence Implementation

7.1 Case 1: Integration of E-Banking Services in Hotel Chains

Case Overview: A prominent hotel chain in India implemented the integration of e-banking services to enhance customer convenience and streamline financial transactions (Shah and Gupta 2019). The hotel chain collaborated with multiple banks to offer a seamless payment experience for guests, enabling them to make room bookings, pay for dining, and avail themselves of other services using various digital payment options (Tanwar and Dhawan 2020).

Implementation Details:

- **Integration of payment gateways:** The hotel chain integrated payment gateways into its website and mobile app, enabling guests to make secure and instant online payments for room reservations and other amenities.
- **Multiple payment options:** The e-banking integration allowed guests to choose from various payment options, such as credit/debit cards, net banking, mobile wallets, and UPI, catering to diverse customer preferences.
- **Loyalty programme tie-ins:** The hotel chain collaborated with banks to offer co-branded credit cards that provided exclusive benefits, reward points, and discounts on hotel stays and other services, fostering customer loyalty.

Results and Impact:

- **Enhanced guest experience:** The integration of e-banking services significantly improved the guest experience by offering seamless and convenient payment options, reducing the hassle of cash transactions.
- **Increased efficiency:** The streamlined payment process reduced check-in and check-out times, leading to improved operational efficiency and guest satisfaction.
- **Market expansion:** The collaboration with multiple banks and diverse payment options attracted new customers, including tech-savvy travellers who preferred cashless transactions.

7.2 Case 2: Mobile Banking Solutions for Travellers

Case Overview: A leading mobile banking provider in India collaborated with the travel and hospitality industry to offer innovative mobile banking solutions for travellers (Verma and Gupta 2019). The mobile banking app allowed travellers to access a range of financial services, such as currency conversion, fund transfers, and bill payments, during their trips (Khare and Bhatia 2020).

Implementation Details:

- **Travel-friendly features:** The mobile banking app offered travel-specific features, such as real-time currency exchange rates, localized language support, and location-based service recommendations.
- **Seamless integration:** The mobile banking app was integrated with various travel platforms, including flight booking websites, hotel booking platforms, and travel agencies, allowing travellers to make financial transactions directly from the app.
- **Enhanced security:** The mobile banking app employed robust security measures, including biometric authentication and transaction verification, to ensure secure financial transactions during travel.

Results and Impact:

- **Convenience for travellers:** The mobile banking app provides a one-stop solution for travellers' financial needs, eliminating the need to carry multiple cards and currencies.
- **Increased customer engagement:** The collaboration with the travel industry expanded the app's customer base and improved customer engagement with the mobile banking provider.
- **Data-driven insights:** The app's integration with travel platforms generated valuable data insights, enabling the provider to offer personalized services and promotions to travellers.

7.3 Case 3: Digital Wallets and Loyalty Programmes in the Hospitality Sector

Case overview: A renowned hospitality group in India implemented digital wallets and loyalty programmes to enhance guest experiences and foster customer loyalty (Gupta and Agarwal 2018). The digital wallet offered a secure and convenient payment option, while the loyalty programme provided exclusive rewards and benefits to frequent guests (Maheshwari and Jain 2019).

Implementation Details:

- **Digital wallet integration:** The hospitality group collaborated with a leading digital wallet provider to integrate their digital payment solution into their hotel booking platform and on-site payment systems.
- **Customized loyalty programme:** The loyalty programme was tailored to reward frequent guests with points for hotel stays, dining, spa services, and other on-site spending, with the option to redeem points for future bookings and discounts.
- **Personalized offers:** The digital wallet and loyalty programme data were leveraged to offer personalized offers and promotions to guests based on their preferences and past spending behaviour.

Results and Impact:

- **Improved customer loyalty:** The loyalty programme incentivized repeat bookings and increased customer retention, leading to higher guest loyalty and increased revenue from returning guests.
- **Simplified payments:** The integration of digital wallets reduced payment friction and expedited the check-out process for guests, resulting in enhanced customer satisfaction.
- **Data-driven marketing:** The data collected through the loyalty programme allowed the hospitality group to conduct targeted marketing campaigns, resulting in better customer engagement and increased bookings.

8. Future Trends and Outlook

8.1 Technological Advancements and Innovations

The convergence of e-banking and hospitality is likely to witness further technological advancements and innovations. Mobile banking apps and digital payment platforms are expected to evolve with improved security features, faster transaction processing, and enhanced user interfaces (Chen and Hu 2021). Artificial intelligence (AI) and machine learning will play a significant role in personalizing guest experiences, offering tailored services, and optimizing pricing and revenue management. Additionally, the integration of blockchain technology may bring more transparency and security to financial transactions in the hospitality sector (Gaur and Sankar 2020).

8.2 Changing Consumer Behaviour and Preferences

Consumer behaviour and preferences in the hospitality sector are continually evolving, driven by changing societal trends and technological advancements (Buhalis and Amaranggana 2015). The post-pandemic era is likely to witness an increased demand for contactless services, mobile-based experiences, and personalized interactions. Customers are expected to seek out environmentally sustainable and socially responsible practices in their hospitality choices. Hospitality establishments will need to adapt their offerings and services to cater to these evolving preferences and expectations (Dwyer and Kim 2003).

8.3 Potential Challenges and Opportunities

Challenges:

a **Security and privacy concerns:** As the convergence of e-banking and hospitality grows, the risk of data breaches and cyberthreats increases, necessitating stringent security measures and data protection protocols.

b **Competition and differentiation:** With the rise of e-banking integration in the hospitality sector, there may be increased competition among hotels and restaurants to offer unique and differentiated experiences to stand out in the market (Kim and DeCosta 2019).

Opportunities:

a **Enhanced guest experience:** The convergence of e-banking and hospitality presents an opportunity to create seamless and personalized guest experiences through mobile apps, loyalty programmes, and personalized services.

b **Market expansion:** By collaborating with financial institutions and offering innovative digital payment options, hospitality businesses can attract new customer segments and tap into the growing trend of cashless transactions (Altinay and Altinay 2017).

9. Conclusion

In conclusion, the convergence of e-banking and the hospitality industry in India presents a promising and transformative landscape for both sectors. The integration of digital payment systems, mobile apps, and loyalty programmes has the potential to revolutionize the guest experience, streamline financial transactions, and foster customer loyalty. The growth of e-banking in India, coupled with the increasing demand for personalized and contactless services in the hospitality sector, has paved the way for exciting opportunities and significant advancements.

However, this convergence also comes with its share of challenges. Ensuring data security and privacy, regulatory compliance, and building customer trust in digital payment solutions are critical areas that demand careful attention. The successful implementation of e-banking and hospitality convergence requires collaborative efforts, robust cybersecurity measures, regulatory alignment, and customer education.

Looking ahead, technological advancements, such as AI, blockchain, and data analytics, will continue to play a pivotal role in shaping the future of this convergence. By leveraging these technologies, the hospitality industry can offer personalized experiences, optimize pricing and resource management, and gain valuable insights into customer behaviour. Changing consumer behaviour and preferences will drive the need for continued adaptation and innovation in the sector to stay relevant and competitive.

In summary, the convergence of e-banking and hospitality in India holds immense potential for creating enhanced guest experiences, increasing efficiency, and tapping into new customer segments. By addressing challenges and embracing opportunities, the convergence can pave the way for a seamless and digitized future for the hospitality industry in India.

Bibliography

Agrawal, A., & Bhattacharya, S. (2020). Data Privacy and Security in the Hospitality Industry: A Review and Research Agenda. *International Journal of Hospitality Management*, 91, 102606.

Akbar, S., & Pathan, S. K. (2021). Customer Adoption of Mobile Banking in India: A Study on Demographic and Behavioral Factors. *Journal of Commerce and Accounting Research*, 10(1), 1–13.
Altinay, L., & Altinay, Z. (2017). Understanding the Complex Relationship Between Technology, Engagement and Experience in Hotels. *International Journal of Contemporary Hospitality Management*, 29(3), 907–929.
Ayad, A. (2020). Personalization of Hotel Services Using Big Data Analytics: An Empirical Study. *Journal of Hospitality Marketing & Management*, 29(3), 266–292.
Bhatia, S. (2019). Convergence of E-banking and Hospitality: Opportunities and Challenges. *International Journal of Business and Administration Research Review*, 2(11), 77–84.
Bhattacharya, S. (2019). E-Banking Solutions for Indian Hotels: A Case Study. *International Journal of Business and Administration Research Review*, 2(11), 100–105.
Bhusry, S., & Singh, N. (2020). Strategic Collaboration Between Banks and Hotels for E-Banking and E-Payments: A Case Study of India. *Journal of Advances in Management Research*, 17(5), 724–741.
Buhalis, D., & Amaranggana, A. (2015). Smart Tourism Destinations: Enabling Technologies and Data Empowerment. In: *The Wiley Blackwell Companion to Tourism*. John Wiley & Sons, Ltd.
Chan, E. S. W., & Guillet, B. D. (2020). Exploring the Impact of Mobile Technology on Hotel Guest Experiences. *International Journal of Hospitality Management*, 87, 102469.
Chatterjee, S., & Sharma, S. (2020). Co-branding of Credit Cards: A Win-Win Strategy for Banks and Hospitality Industry. *International Journal of Research in Management & Social Science*, 8(3), 145–156.
Chaturvedi, R. (2021). Impact of Digital Payment on Hospitality Services in India: A Study of UPI Payment Apps and Hotel Industry. *International Journal of Business and Administration Research Review*, 4(6), 7–13.
Chen, W., & Hu, Y. (2021). The Impact of AI in the Hospitality Industry: A Review and Research Agenda. *International Journal of Hospitality Management*, 94, 102868.
Datta, P. K., & Mitra, S. (2022). Application of Blockchain in Online Learning Findings in Higher Education Certification. In: *The Data-Driven Blockchain Ecosystem* (1st ed., pp. 9). CRC Press. eBook ISBN: 9781003269281.
Dinçer, H. (2021). E-Banking and Legal Challenges: A Comparative Review on India, the United States, and the European Union. *Journal of Money, Investment and Banking*, 42, 1–18.
Dioko, L. A., Zhang, H. Q., & Huang, S. (2021). The Role of Payment Apps in Enhancing Customer Experience in the Hospitality Industry. *Journal of Travel & Tourism Marketing*, 38(7), 926–939.
Dwyer, L., & Kim, C. (2003). Destination Competitiveness: Determinants and Indicators. *Current Issues in Tourism*, 6(5), 369–414.
Gaur, S. S., & Sankar, V. (2020). Gaur, S. S., & Sankar, V. (2020). Blockchain in the Hospitality Industry: A Review, Framework, and Future Research Directions. *International Journal of Hospitality Management*, 90, 102642.
Gupta, A., & Dahiya, R. (2019). Impact of Loyalty Programs on Customer Loyalty in the Indian Hotel Industry. *International Journal of Management Studies*, 6(3), 35–42.
Gupta, P., & Agarwal, A. (2018). Digital Wallets and Loyalty Programs in the Hospitality Industry: A Case Study of a Renowned Hotel Chain in India. *International Journal of Hospitality Management*, 74, 58–66.
Gupta, S., & Mahajan, P. (2018). Adoption of E-Banking and Its Impact on Financial Performance of Hotels: Evidence from India. *Asia Pacific Journal of Marketing & Management Review*, 7(5), 40–48.
IBEF. (2021). *Tourism & Hospitality Industry in India. India Brand Equity Foundation.* www.ibef.org/industry/tourism-hospitality.aspx
India Brand Equity Foundation (IBEF). (2021). *Tourism & Hospitality Industry in India.* www.ibef.org/industry/tourism-hospitality.aspx

Juwaheer, T. D. (2019). E-Banking and Its Impact on Tourism Development: A Conceptual Framework for Small Island States. *Journal of Tourism and Hospitality Management*, 7(4), 56–65.
Kaur, S., & Verma, A. (2021). Determinants of E-Banking Adoption in the Hospitality Industry: An Indian Perspective. *Journal of Internet Banking and Commerce*, 26(1), 1–17.
Khanna, M., & Deshmukh, S. G. (2020). Technological Challenges of E-Banking in India: A Critical Review. *International Journal of Business and Administration Research Review*, 3(7), 62–67.
Khare, A., & Bhatia, A. (2020). Impact of Mobile Banking Solutions on Travelers' Financial Behavior: A Study of India's Mobile Banking Industry. *Journal of Tourism and Hospitality Research*, 10(2), 84–94.
Kim, W. G., & DeCosta, P. (2019). Mobile Payment Strategies for Hotels: The Impact of User Adoption and Acceptance. *Journal of Travel & Tourism Marketing*, 36(1), 13–26.
Kim, W. G., Lee, H. G., & Singh, A. J. (2020). The Impact of Big Data Analytics on Hotel Firms' Performance: A Study of the US Hotel Industry. *International Journal of Hospitality Management*, 89, 102568.
KPMG India. (2021). *Indian Hospitality Sector: Poised for Growth*. https://assets.kpmg/content/dam/kpmg/in/pdf/2021/05/indian-hospitality-sector-poised-for-growth.pdf
Kumar, A., & Reddy, G. P. (2020). Impact of Digital Transformation in the Hospitality Industry: A Review. *International Journal of Scientific Research and Management*, 8(5), 318–323.
Lai, S., Cavusoglu, H., & Benbasat, I. (2019). The Impact of E-Banking Integration on E-Banking Capabilities and Firm Performance. *Information Systems Research*, 30(4), 1332–1352.
Maheshwari, A., & Jain, S. (2019). Impact of Digital Wallet Integration on Customer Loyalty in the Hospitality Sector: A Study of a Leading Hospitality Group in India. *Journal of Hospitality and Tourism Management*, 38, 71–78.
Ministry of Electronics and Information Technology (MeitY). (2021). *The Personal Data Protection Bill*. www.meity.gov.in/content/personal-data-protection-bill-2019
Mishra, S., & Mahapatra, S. S. (2020). E-Banking Awareness and Its Impact on Customer's Perception: An Indian Perspective. *International Journal of Financial Research*, 11(2), 197–212.
Navale, A., & Srivastava, V. (2018). Adoption of Mobile Payment Systems in the Indian Hospitality Industry. *Tourism Management Perspectives*, 28, 95–104.
Niranjan, T. T., & Priya, M. S. (2019). Cybersecurity Challenges and Solutions for E-Banking in India. *International Journal of Bank Marketing*, 37(6), 1396–1421.
Niranjan, T. T., & Sathish, P. (2021). Big Data Analytics in the Hospitality Industry: A Literature Review and Future Trends. *Journal of Revenue and Pricing Management*, 20(3), 246–263.
NPCI. (2021). *Unified Payments Interface (UPI)*. www.npci.org.in/product-overview/upi-product-overview
NPCI. (2021). *UPI Security*. www.npci.org.in/upi-security
Oh, H., & Jeong, M. (2020). Impact of Mobile Payment on Hotel Efficiency and Profitability. *Sustainability*, 12(11), 4450.
Panda, D., & Raut, R. D. (2021). Integration of Mobile Payment Systems in the Hospitality Industry: A Study on Customer Perception. *International Journal of Business and Administration Research Review*, 3(2), 43–49.
Parikh, S. (2021). Digital Transformation in the Indian Hospitality Industry: An Empirical Study. *Journal of Hotel and Business Management*, 10(3), 1–8.
PWC India. (2021). *Hotel Industry in India: A 2020 Perspective*. www.pwc.in/assets/pdfs/publications/2020/hotel-industry-in-india.pdf
PWC India. (2021). *Indian Mobile Wallet Market – The Billion-Dollar Industry*. www.pwc.in/assets/pdfs/publications/2021/indian-mobile-wallet-market-the-billion-dollar-industry.pdf

Raza, S. A., & Chang, V. (2018). A Framework for E-Banking Integration and Interoperability in Developing Economies: A Case Study of Pakistan. *Journal of Theoretical and Applied Electronic Commerce Research*, 13(3), 85–100.

RBI Annual Report. (2020–2021). *Reserve Bank of India*. www.rbi.org.in/Scripts/AnnualReportPublications.aspx?Id=1306

RBI Bulletin. (2021). *Digital Payment Trends in India. Reserve Bank of India*. https://rbidocs.rbi.org.in/rdocs/Bulletin/PDFs/71DT2021C6A1F0168F43D4BAAC6D43331A16B7A5E9.PDF

RBI. (2020). *Master Direction on Information Technology Framework for the NBFC Sector*. www.rbi.org.in/Scripts/BS_ViewMasDirections.aspx?id=11743

Reserve Bank of India (RBI). (2021). *Guidelines on Information Security, Electronic Banking, Technology Risk Management, and Cyber Frauds*. www.rbi.org.in/scripts/NotificationUser.aspx?Id=12026&Mode=0

Shah, S., & Gupta, R. (2019). E-Banking Integration in the Hospitality Industry: A Study of Hotel Chain's Digital Transformation. *International Journal of Hospitality Management*, 81, 61–69.

Sharma, S., & Thomas, T. (2019). Leveraging Big Data for Personalization in the Hospitality Industry: A Conceptual Framework. *Journal of Hospitality and Tourism Technology*, 10(4), 706–721.

Singh, R., & Sharma, R. (2020). Impact of Digital Payment Solutions on Hospitality Industry: A Study of Indian Hotel Industry. *International Journal of Research in Humanities, Arts, and Literature*, 8(4), 87–97.

Singh, V., & Khan, M. M. (2019). Cybersecurity Challenges and Solutions for E-Banking in India. *International Journal of Emerging Technologies and Innovative Research*, 6(5), 153–159.

Tanwar, R., & Dhawan, P. (2020). Impact of E-Banking on Hotel Industry in India: A Case Study of Hotel Chains. *Journal of Tourism and Hospitality Management*, 8(1), 23–32.

Thomas, R., & Abhilasha. (2018). Awareness and Acceptance of E-Banking among Customers of the Indian Banking Industry. *International Journal of Pure and Applied Mathematics*, 119(12), 501–513.

Verma, A., & Gupta, S. (2019). Mobile Banking Solutions for Travelers: A Case Study of a Leading Mobile Banking Provider in India. *Journal of Travel & Tourism Marketing*, 36(8), 1014–1026.

6 Convergence of the Metaverse and Luxury Hospitality as Avenues for Future Investigation

Agenda for Research, Practice, and Legal Outcomes

Dr. Bhupinder Singh and Prof. Christian Kaunert

1. Introduction

The convergence of the metaverse and luxury hospitality stands as a promising frontier, poised to reshape the landscape of both industries and potentially revolutionize the way individuals experience, engage with, and indulge in luxury. The metaverse, a multifaceted digital realm characterized by the integration of virtual and physical spaces, has captured the imagination of technologists, entrepreneurs, and creative visionaries alike. This immersive digital space, encompassing virtual reality (VR), augmented reality (AR), artificial intelligence (AI), and more, presents a unique opportunity for luxury hospitality to transcend traditional boundaries and offer unparalleled guest experiences (Buhalis et al., 2023). This convergence holds the potential to redefine not only the concept of luxury but also the strategies and avenues through which luxury hospitality establishments attract, engage, and retain their clientele.

It refers into the future investigation of this convergence, a multifaceted research agenda unfolds. At its core lies the exploration of how the metaverse can enhance guest experiences within the luxury hospitality realm. Virtual reality and augmented reality technologies can transport guests to exotic destinations, historic landmarks, or fantastical realms, allowing them to preview and customize their stays before setting foot on physical grounds. The personalization and customization potential of the metaverse become apparent as guests tailor their environments, from room decor to virtual butlers, culminating in bespoke luxury experiences that blur the boundaries between the real and the virtual (Barrera & Shah, 2023).

Virtual spa retreats and gourmet experiences can immerse guests in sensory delights, while virtual luxury retail introduces a new dimension of shopping where exclusivity meets accessibility. As with any convergence, legal implications and challenges loom large. Intellectual property rights in the virtual realm, ownership of virtual assets, jurisdictional complexities, and contractual disputes necessitate thorough examination to establish a robust legal framework that safeguards the interests of all stakeholders involved (Hadi et al., 2023). The convergence of the metaverse and luxury hospitality beckons with a sense of urgency.

DOI: 10.4324/9781003488248-6

1.1 Objectives of the Research

The primary objective of conducting comprehensive research on the convergence of the metaverse and luxury hospitality is to unravel the multifaceted dynamics that underlie this emerging intersection and to:

- provide a nuanced understanding of its implications for both industries and the broader socio-cultural landscape
- delve deep into the potential synergies, challenges, and transformative possibilities that arise as these two distinct realms coalesce, paving the way for novel avenues of investigation, innovation, and strategic planning
- meticulously analyze how the metaverse can enhance and reshape guest experiences within luxury hospitality
- illuminate the ways in which virtual reality, augmented reality, artificial intelligence, and other cutting-edge technologies can be harnessed to transcend conventional boundaries and deliver unparalleled levels of personalization and immersion
- address the ethical considerations inherent in this convergence, probing issues such as data privacy, consent, and the blurring of virtual and physical realities
- provide tangible insights that can guide luxury hospitality establishments in effectively integrating metaverse technologies into their offerings, from virtual property tours and events to spa experiences and retail endeavours
- identify and explore the intricate legal implications and challenges that this convergence presents, contributing to the development of a robust legal framework that safeguards the interests of all stakeholders involved
- foster a holistic and informed discourse, laying the groundwork for future advancements, innovative applications, and thoughtful considerations at the intersection of the metaverse and luxury hospitality

2. Movements of Recent Business Practices: Gap Analysis

The luxury hospitality industry has been greatly impacted by recent trends in business methods, demanding a thorough gap analysis to assure sustained success. The growing emphasis on sustainability and environmental friendliness is one significant trend. Luxury guests are demanding that expensive hotels and resorts implement green measures as they become more aware of their environmental impact. Numerous upscale hotels have noticed this trend and are making investments in eco-friendly technologies, energy efficiency, and sustainable sourcing. To find areas where more changes might be made to meet or surpass these increasing expectations, a critical gap analysis is necessary (Sestino & Amatulli, 2023).

Digital integration is another change in recent business methods in the luxury hospitality industry. Customers now anticipate seamless digital experiences, from mobile check-ins to smart room controls, as a result of the development of smart technology. Luxury hotels can do a gap analysis to determine how well their current digital infrastructure satisfies these expectations and where more investment is needed. It is crucial to ensure a seamless fusion of technology and the luxury experience. Also, luxury hospitality has changed as a result of the growth of experiential travel. Whether it's exclusive access to cultural events, tailored adventures, or private tours, guests are increasingly looking for distinctive, customized experiences. A thorough gap analysis can identify chances to develop more distinctive and memorable products, allowing the hotel to better match its services to the changing needs of affluent tourists (Koohang et al., 2023).

So a thorough gap analysis of current business practice trends is necessary to stay current and competitive in the luxury hospitality industry. Luxury hotels may better satisfy the needs of eco-conscious visitors, improve their digital capabilities, and deliver great, individualized experiences by filling these gaps, thereby ensuring their continued success in this rapidly changing market (Bafadhal & Hendrawan, 2023).

3. The Metaverse and Luxury Hospitality: An Overview

The metaverse and luxury hospitality constitutes a captivating juncture where the digital realm seamlessly intertwines with opulent experiences, fundamentally reshaping the paradigms of both industries. The metaverse, an intricate amalgamation of virtual and physical dimensions facilitated by emerging technologies such as virtual reality (VR), augmented reality (AR), blockchain, and artificial intelligence (AI), represents a dynamic, interconnected space that transcends traditional boundaries (Wongkitrungrueng & Suprawan, 2023).

It fosters an environment where individuals can engage, interact, and create within an expansive digital ecosystem, blurring the lines between the real and the virtual. In parallel, the domain of luxury hospitality has long epitomized refined indulgence, characterized by meticulous attention to detail, personalized service, and extraordinary sensory experiences. It encompasses a spectrum of high-end accommodations, upscale dining, wellness retreats, and exclusive events, all designed to cater to the discerning tastes and desires of affluent clientele.

However, this convergence is not without its challenges and complexities. Ethical considerations loom large, as the metaverse blurs distinctions between reality and simulation, raising questions about data privacy, informed consent, and the potential for psychological impacts. The metaverse also challenges traditional paradigms of ownership, as digital assets and virtual property gain significance, necessitating a reevaluation of legal frameworks and jurisdictional boundaries. Striking a delicate balance between technological innovation and ethical responsibility becomes pivotal as luxury hospitality navigates this uncharted territory (Koohang et al., 2023).

The concepts of metaverse and luxury hospitality represent a paradigm shift that intertwines digital innovation with timeless opulence, offering a gateway to hitherto unexplored dimensions of luxury experiences. This intriguing intersection beckons researchers, practitioners, and visionaries to embark on an exciting journey of exploration, innovation, and re-imagination. As both the metaverse and luxury hospitality continue to evolve in tandem, the potential for groundbreaking transformations and the creation of unparalleled indulgences beckons, promising a future where the boundaries between the tangible and the virtual dissolve, and a new era of luxury dawns (Ricci, 2022).

3.1 Definition and Characteristics of the Metaverse

"The metaverse is a vision of what many in the computer industry believe is the next iteration of the internet: a single, shared, immersive, persistent, 3D virtual space where humans experience life in ways they could not in the physical world."

The metaverse is a dynamic and immersive digital realm that represents the convergence of physical and virtual spaces, blurring the boundaries between the real world and digital experiences. It is a complex ecosystem facilitated by advanced technologies such as virtual reality (VR), augmented reality (AR), blockchain, and artificial intelligence (AI) (Kumar et al., 2023). As a concept, the metaverse is still evolving and can be interpreted in various ways, but several key defining characteristics set the stage for its understanding and exploration:

- a *The metaverse is a shared digital space that individuals can access, navigate, and interact with. It goes beyond individual virtual experiences and aims to create a collective digital environment where people can engage with each other, as well as with digital objects, environments, and data.*
- b *The metaverse is designed to provide immersive experiences that engage multiple senses, replicating aspects of the real world while enabling interactive engagement. Through VR and AR technologies, users can explore and manipulate digital spaces, objects, and avatars, fostering a sense of presence and embodiment.*
- c *Unlike traditional video games or virtual environments that reset or end after a session, the metaverse is characterized by persistence. Changes made within the metaverse persist over time, and interactions have lasting effects, contributing to a sense of continuity and evolution.*
- d *The metaverse thrives on user-generated content and creativity. Users have the ability to create, modify, and contribute to the digital landscape, whether it's building virtual structures, designing avatars, or scripting interactive experiences.*
- e *The metaverse is a network of interconnected spaces, platforms, and experiences. It aims to seamlessly connect different virtual worlds, applications, and services, allowing users to move between diverse environments without disruptions.*
- f *In many iterations of the metaverse, economic and social elements play a significant role. Virtual currencies, digital assets, and marketplaces exist within the metaverse, enabling transactions, trade, and ownership of virtual goods. Social interactions and communities also thrive, fostering connections and collaborations across geographical boundaries.*
- g *The metaverse is not confined to a single platform or device. It is accessible across various hardware, software, and networks, ensuring that users can engage with it from different entry points and devices.*

h *The metaverse is in a constant state of evolution. It adapts to technological advancements and user preferences, continually expanding its capabilities, features, and possibilities.*

3.2 Luxury Hospitality: Evolution and Current Landscape

The concept of "luxury hospitality" an embodiment of opulence, impeccable service, and refined experiences, has a rich and fascinating evolution that has shaped its current landscape. So, emerging from the grand hotels of the 19th century, where comfort and extravagance were paramount, luxury hospitality has traversed times and cultural shifts, continually redefining what it means to provide exceptional guest experiences (Lee & Jo, 2023).

The evolution of luxury hospitality can be traced through various eras, and the latter half of the 20th century witnessed a shift towards modernity and innovation. Luxury hotels embraced sleek design, cutting-edge amenities, and technological advancements. The rise of boutique hotels introduced a new concept of luxury, focusing on uniqueness, intimacy, and immersive environments (Wei, 2023). These developments marked the beginning of a more diversified luxury hospitality landscape, accommodating a range of preferences and tastes.

In recent years, the luxury hospitality sector has responded to changing consumer expectations and societal trends. Wellness and sustainability have emerged as integral aspects of the luxury experience, with spas, wellness retreats, and eco-friendly practices becoming central to many luxury establishments (Dwivedi et al., 2022). Also, a growing emphasis on authentic, local experiences has led to a reimagining of luxury hospitality, where guests are encouraged to connect with the local culture, cuisine, and communities.

Modern luxury hospitality is characterized by a fusion of tradition and innovation. While new entrants and disruptors redefine luxury by embracing technology, customization, and immersive storytelling, established luxury businesses preserve their history of elegant indulgence. The emergence of social media and digital platforms has also altered how luxury hospitality is promoted and enjoyed, allowing guests to share their adventures with a global audience and shaping the expectations of upcoming travellers. Luxury hospitality is at a crossroads as it confronts the convergence with the metaverse and is ready to rethink its offerings in ways that go beyond the physical world (Koohang et al., 2023). The metaverse creates opportunities for virtual interaction, exploration, and customization that can improve the current luxury experience by adding new and engaging digital tales.

3.3 Convergence of the Metaverse and Luxury Hospitality: Potential Synergies

The convergence of the metaverse and luxury hospitality heralds a new era of possibilities, unveiling a realm of potential synergies that promise to reshape the very foundations of how individuals perceive, access, and indulge in opulent experiences. This convergence signifies a harmonious blend of cutting-edge digital technologies and the quintessence of luxury, opening the doors to a landscape where the boundaries between the real and the virtual dissolve, paving the way for a reimagined luxury hospitality experience (Trunfio & Rossi, 2022).

These potential synergies have the ability to transcend the limitations of physical space and geographical constraints. The metaverse offers a virtual canvas upon which luxury hospitality establishments can craft immersive pre-stay experiences for guests. Virtual reality tours allow potential guests to step into elegant suites, explore lush landscapes, and indulge in the ambiance of a luxury hotel before setting foot on the premises. This virtual preview not only sparks anticipation but also provides an avenue for guests to customize their preferences and make informed choices, enhancing the personalization and tailor-made nature of luxury hospitality (Allam et al., 2022). This symbiosis between the metaverse and luxury hospitality sparks innovation, inviting stakeholders to push the boundaries of creativity and redefine the essence of luxury in the digital age.

The potential synergies are not without their challenges because ensuring data privacy, maintaining ethical standards, and balancing the immersive allure of the metaverse with responsible engagement are paramount considerations. Striking the delicate balance between technological advancement and safeguarding the trust and well-being of guests becomes a pivotal aspect of harnessing these synergies for the betterment of luxury hospitality (Wongkitrungrueng & Suprawan, 2023).

The convergence of the metaverse and luxury hospitality is akin to a symphony where technology harmonizes with elegance, innovation dances with tradition, and virtual landscapes merge with opulent environments (Alexander & Bellandi, 2022). This transformative convergence beckons the luxury hospitality industry to embrace a new dimension of indulgence, one that is intricately woven into the fabric of the metaverse, fostering an enchanting and immersive world of luxury experiences that transcend time, space, and imagination.

4. Enhancing Guest Experiences Through Virtual Reality (VR) and Augmented Reality (AR)

Enhancing guest experiences through the strategic integration of virtual reality (VR) and augmented reality (AR) technologies within hotels represents a transformative frontier that redefines the very essence of hospitality. The synthesis of these innovative technologies and the art of hospitality opens up a world of opportunities that may immerse visitors in gripping storylines, give them unparalleled degrees of personalization, and promote a closer bond between the actual world and the digital one (Bu et al., 2022).

Through the use of VR, which acts as a bridge to other dimensions, hotel guests are given the chance to discover locations, cultures, and experiences without being constrained by physical distance. Through VR, hotels can give visitors a sneak peek of their rooms and amenities prior to their arrival, letting them virtually explore opulent suites, take in panoramic views, and get a feel for public areas. This immersive experience not only raises expectations but also helps visitors make educated decisions, increasing their sense of ownership and involvement in their forthcoming trip (Cattaneo, 2023).

AR effortlessly incorporates digital aspects into the actual world, improving the visitor experience through real-time engagement. Hotels can offer interactive tours of historic sites using AR applications, complementing their visitors' investigation with relevant facts and engrossing tales. Restaurant menus can come to life as guests point their devices at dishes, revealing detailed descriptions, preparation methods, and even nutritional information. Moreover, AR can breathe new life into events, conferences, and meetings by overlaying informative content, dynamic visuals, and interactive elements onto the physical setting, fostering engagement and knowledge dissemination.

This personalization is a cornerstone of luxury hospitality, and VR and AR provide the tools to elevate this aspect to unprecedented heights. Through VR, guests can customize their virtual environments, adjusting lighting, decor, and ambiance to reflect their preferences. AR empowers guests to receive personalized recommendations and directions, guiding them to curated experiences and hidden gems within and outside the hotel. By understanding the power of personalization through these technologies, hotels can create bespoke experiences that resonate deeply with each guest, fostering a sense of exclusivity and tailor-made luxury (Sestino, & Amatulli, 2023).

4.1 Personalization and Customization in Virtual Luxury Hospitality

The idea of virtual luxury hospitality is the apex of guest-centric experiences, where cutting-edge technology blends with the skill of customizing each encounter to the person's tastes and needs. The sensation of exclusivity and indulgence that luxury hospitality aims to provide is amplified by this convergence, which also redefines how visitors interact with their surroundings. Because virtual luxury hospitality emphasizes personalization, each visitor must have a unique digital environment created for them.

Hotels may create virtual worlds that seamlessly match individual interests by using powerful data analytics and user profiling to acquire insights into guest preferences, prior actions, and even physiological responses. Imagine entering a virtual suite where the ambience, lighting, and furnishings change to reflect the visitor's preferred style, creating a sense of familiarity and comfort right away (Schmidt, 2023). By giving users the ability to actively alter their virtual experiences, customization expands on this idea. Visitors can participate in the creation of their virtual sanctuary by selecting the design of the furniture and artwork, altering the weather, and even customizing the background music. This degree of control not only improves immersion but also gives users the freedom to craft their own story, forging a strong emotional bond with the virtual setting.

The art of personalization and customization in virtual luxury hospitality necessitates a delicate balance. Striking the equilibrium between technology-driven personalization and human touch remains paramount, as the allure of luxury hospitality often lies in the authenticity and warmth of genuine interactions. Additionally, addressing data privacy concerns and ensuring that customization remains intuitive and user-friendly are crucial elements in realizing the full potential of this convergence. Through intricate design, data-driven insights, and innovative interfaces, hotels can sculpt virtual experiences that transcend traditional boundaries, fostering an intimate and enchanting environment where every guest becomes the protagonist of their own narrative (Kerim & Borrell, 2023). This convergence represents a paradigm shift, redefining luxury hospitality in a digital age where imagination knows no bounds.

4.2 Impact of the Metaverse on Destination Marketing and Branding

The emergence of the metaverse has had a profound impact on the landscape of destination marketing and branding, reshaping the strategies and narratives that underpin the allure of global locales. As this virtual realm blurs the lines between physical and digital experiences, it offers a dynamic canvas upon which destinations can craft immersive narratives, engage audiences in novel ways, and redefine the very essence of destination marketing.

With this influence comes the possibility of previously unheard-of participation and interaction. Destinations can engage potential guests in intriguing virtual adventures across the metaverse, bypassing more conventional forms of advertising. Traditional brochures and websites might find it difficult to create a sense of presence and excitement, but VR tours can transport people to famous monuments, busy streets, and magnificent landscapes (Yang & Mattila, 2016). Applications for AR can add historical details, tales, and contextual insights to real-world scenes, enhancing visitors' comprehension of and emotional connection to the place.

4.3 Role of AI and Machine Learning in Metaverse-Driven Luxury Hospitality

The dynamic and revolutionary function of AI and machine learning (ML) in the context of metaverse-driven luxury hospitality is altering how rich experiences are created, customized, and delivered in the digital sphere. Every aspect of the guest experience is improved by AI and ML technologies, from pre-stay excitement to post-visit interaction, adding a layer of intelligence that pushes the fusion of luxury and technology to unmatched new heights.

Virtual environments can dynamically adjust based on guest interactions and feedback, ensuring that the experience remains captivating and aligned with guest preferences. This responsiveness fosters a sense of agency and immersion, enabling guests to actively shape their digital narrative as they navigate through the metaverse. Striking a balance between technology-driven personalization and genuine human interactions is essential to preserve the authenticity and emotional resonance that luxury hospitality embodies.

Ensuring data privacy, transparency in algorithmic decision-making, and the opportunity for guests to control and customize their interactions are key pillars in upholding ethical standards. The role of AI and ML in metaverse-driven luxury hospitality is that of an enabler, an orchestrator of personalized enchantment that transcends the boundaries of the virtual and the real (Yang & Mattila,

2017). By harnessing the power of data-driven insights, predictive capabilities, and interactive intelligence, luxury establishments can curate digital experiences that resonate deeply with each guest, forging a harmonious fusion of technological innovation and the art of indulgence within the metaverse.

5. Virtual Property Tours and Pre-Stay Experiences in Luxury Hospitality

The advent of virtual property tours and pre-stay experiences represents a paradigmatic shift in how guests engage with and immerse themselves in the opulence of their upcoming accommodations. Gone are the days of relying solely on static photographs and glossy brochures to envision the splendor of a hotel or resort. Instead, cutting-edge technologies like VR and AR have revolutionized the art of anticipation, offering guests a captivating and interactive portal into the world of luxury they are about to embark upon. The virtual property tours stand as a pinnacle of innovation in this regard. No longer confined to mere visual snippets, these tours encapsulate a truly immersive experience that transports guests into meticulously crafted digital realms (Amatulli et al., 2021). The beauty stands not only in the lifelike visuals but in the agency afforded to guests to navigate and explore spaces at their own pace, fostering a sense of discovery akin to a physical visit.

The benefits of these experiences are manifold, because by offering guests the opportunity to virtually explore and engage with their chosen accommodations, luxury hospitality establishments enhance the level of anticipation, creating an emotional connection that bridges the gap between inspiration and arrival. This tangible sense of excitement translates into heightened guest satisfaction, as informed decision-making becomes a hallmark of the experience. Moreover, the personalization aspect empowers guests to curate their own journey, effectively embedding the spirit of luxury with a touch of exclusivity.

These virtual property tours and pre-stay experiences are a testament to the transformative power of technology within the realm of luxury hospitality. They transcend the boundaries of physical constraints, offering guests the chance to preview their opulent accommodations and immerse themselves in the lavishness that lies ahead. This fusion of innovation and indulgence epitomizes the era of anticipatory luxury, where every moment leading to the actual stay becomes an integral chapter of the overall guest narrative, elevating the journey from aspiration to experience (Bharwani & Mathews, 2023).

6. Legal Implications and Challenges: Convergence of the Metaverse and Luxury Hospitality as Avenues for Future Investigation

The convergence of the metaverse and luxury hospitality presents a captivating realm for future investigation because it introduces a plethora of intricate legal implications and challenges that necessitate thorough analysis and innovative solutions. This dynamic intersection between opulent experiences and immersive digital environments raises profound questions that require in-depth exploration to ensure a seamless and legally sound integration. Several avenues for future investigation emerge within this complex landscape in the metaverse and luxury hospitality.

With the metaverse operating within a digital ecosystem, cybersecurity becomes paramount. Investigating the legal obligations of luxury establishments to ensure the security of guest data, protect against cyberthreats, and mitigate the risks of unauthorized access or manipulation of virtual experiences is a critical area of exploration. The metaverse transcends geographical borders, leading to complex jurisdictional challenges. Future investigation could explore how luxury hospitality establishments navigate cross-border legal considerations, including tax implications, compliance with international laws, and resolving disputes that may arise when operating virtual experiences accessible to a global audience (Amatulli et al., 2022). The assimilation of immersive technology raises ethical questions about guest well-being, addiction, and digital dependence.

6.1 Data Privacy and Security Concerns in the Metaverse and Luxury Hospitality

The convergence of the metaverse and luxury hospitality has ushered in a new era of immersive experiences, where guests can seamlessly transition between physical and digital realms. However, this technological transformation also brings to the forefront a host of intricate data privacy and security concerns that demand rigorous examination. As luxury establishments craft intricate digital landscapes within the metaverse, safeguarding guest information and ensuring the sanctity of their personal data becomes a paramount consideration. The central challenge lies in navigating the delicate balance between customization and privacy.

While the metaverse allows for tailored and personalized experiences, the data required to achieve such levels of customization can be extensive (Back et al., 2022). Thus, researchers and industry stakeholders must delve into the legal and ethical dimensions of data collection, storage, and utilization. Investigating how luxury hospitality establishments can transparently communicate data usage practices to guests, obtain informed consent, and implement robust data protection mechanisms becomes an avenue of critical importance. Additionally, exploring the possibility of enabling guests to have control over the extent of personal data shared within the metaverse can empower them with a sense of agency over their digital interactions.

Besides, the metaverse introduces novel cybersecurity challenges that extend beyond the confines of traditional digital environments. As guests immerse themselves in digital spaces, the potential risks of data breaches, unauthorized access, or manipulation of virtual experiences become heightened. In-depth research into the legal obligations of luxury hospitality establishments to secure guest data within the metaverse is essential (Pereira et al., 2021). This may involve studying the applicability of existing cybersecurity frameworks, evaluating the efficacy of encryption technologies, and formulating strategies to promptly detect and respond to security incidents within virtual environments. Crossing borders within the metaverse amplifies data privacy concerns. With luxury hospitality establishments engaging with a global audience, data may traverse international jurisdictions, each governed by distinct regulatory frameworks. Investigating the legal complexities of cross-border data transfers, ensuring compliance with various data protection laws, and developing strategies to uphold consistent privacy standards across diverse geographies is an intricate avenue of exploration.

As the metaverse transforms the way guests engage with luxury hospitality, meticulous research into data privacy and security concerns emerges as a linchpin of responsible innovation. By probing these challenges from legal, ethical, and technological perspectives, the industry can cultivate a robust foundation that upholds guests' trust, ensures their digital well-being, and embraces the convergence of opulent experiences with the imperatives of privacy and security (Kwon et al., 2022).

6.2 Jurisdictional and Regulatory Challenges: The Metaverse and Luxury Hospitality

The convergence of the metaverse and luxury hospitality has unfurled a captivating digital landscape that transcends physical boundaries, but it also introduces a tapestry of complex jurisdictional and regulatory challenges that merit in-depth exploration. As guests traverse virtual realms within the metaverse to experience opulent hospitality, questions arise concerning the legal frameworks that govern these interactions across diverse geographical contexts. This novel intersection prompts a profound examination of how luxury establishments navigate legal landscapes that span multiple jurisdictions, each with its unique set of laws, regulations, and cultural sensitivities.

These challenges specify the need to harmonize cross-border operations within the metaverse with the legal intricacies of individual countries. Researchers and industry experts must investigate the application of existing international legal frameworks to virtual experiences, pondering how treaties, agreements, and conventions can extend to this digital domain. The establishment of clear guidelines for determining jurisdiction, defining legal responsibilities, and resolving disputes arising from metaverse-driven luxury interactions assumes paramount significance. This may entail charting a path for international cooperation and standardization in regulating digital cross-border activities to ensure consistent and equitable legal treatment (Bharwani & Mathews, 2021).

The diversity of regulatory environments further compounds these challenges. Different nations possess varying laws pertaining to data protection, consumer rights, intellectual property, and virtual transactions, among others. Comprehensive research is vital to understand how luxury hospitality establishments can navigate these regulatory mazes while delivering seamless and compliant virtual experiences (Aydin, 2020).

The exploring of mechanisms for ensuring that metaverse-driven activities adhere to a patchwork of national laws, avoiding conflicts and contradictions, becomes a compelling avenue for investigation. The cultural norms and ethical considerations introduce an additional layer of complexity. The metaverse may transcend borders, but the experiences it offers must be culturally sensitive and respectful of local customs. The in-depth exploration of how luxury establishments can adapt virtual offerings to align with cultural sensitivities while still providing opulent experiences is crucial. This could involve studying cultural variations in privacy expectations, preferences for virtual interactions, and the implications of cultural appropriation within immersive digital environments (Singh, 2023).

6.3 Contractual and Liability Issues in Virtual Luxury Hospitality

The fusion of virtual experiences with luxury hospitality ushers in a realm of opulence that transcends traditional boundaries, yet it also introduces a labyrinth of intricate contractual and liability considerations that warrant meticulous examination. As guests engage in immersive digital interactions within the metaverse, questions emerge surrounding the legal frameworks that underpin the agreements formed, the rights and responsibilities of both parties, and the mechanisms for resolving disputes within this captivating digital landscape.

The guest interactions within virtual luxury environments introduce complexities in attributing responsibility and allocating liability. The interactions may involve AI-driven virtual concierges, immersive events, and personalized experiences. In-depth research could delve into the legal mechanisms for ascertaining liability in scenarios where virtual entities, algorithms, or automated processes interact with guests, potentially giving rise to legal disputes. This includes probing issues related to agency, negligence, and the evolving standards of care within the metaverse. Also, the question of jurisdiction looms large in contractual and liability contexts. With the metaverse transcending physical borders, researchers must explore the legal challenges that arise when guests and luxury establishments operate in different legal jurisdictions. Investigating the efficacy of jurisdiction clauses, choice of law provisions, and mechanisms for cross-border dispute resolution is crucial in ensuring a coherent and equitable legal framework for virtual luxury hospitality. It also brings contractual and liability considerations to the forefront of legal inquiry (Aydin, 2020). By immersing guests in opulent digital realms, luxury establishments enter a new realm of legal complexity where traditional legal principles must be reevaluated.

Through comprehensive research, the industry can establish a robust foundation for forming contracts, delineating responsibilities, and addressing liability concerns within the metaverse. This proactive approach ensures that the allure of digital opulence is underpinned by a legal framework that upholds guest rights, safeguards industry integrity, and facilitates seamless and enriching virtual luxury experiences.

7. Recommendations for Business Practices: The Key to Success

Innovative possibilities for future growth must be investigated by forward-thinking businesses, because the business environment is constantly changing. The metaverse and the world of opulent hospitality are two such areas that have enormous potential. Businesses can position themselves for long-term success by embracing these new trends. The metaverse, a digital space where the real world and virtual worlds collide, presents innovative possibilities for marketing and customer involvement. Companies should invest in augmented reality and virtual reality technologies, build a strong online presence, and prioritize personalization and data protection if they want to succeed in this market. Luxury hospitality is also expanding as discerning travellers look for one-of-a-kind, unforgettable experiences. Success hinges on exemplary customer service, sustainability, creating distinctive experiences, flawless digital integration, and compelling storytelling in marketing. Businesses that explore these horizons, utilizing the metaverse and providing unmatched luxury in hospitality, are well positioned to steer a course toward enduring profitability in a constantly changing business environment (Nicola, 2023).

Businesses must embrace cutting-edge procedures if they want to succeed in the metaverse era, when the physical and digital worlds are merging. Investing in immersive technology like virtual and augmented reality to produce interactive experiences is part of embracing the metaverse. Engaging this population of digital natives requires a digital presence within the metaverse, complete with virtual storefronts and customer support. Customers must feel valued and protected in this new realm; thus, personalization and data security are crucial. Businesses must use technology effectively, adapt their offers to customer preferences, and place a high priority on security in order to prosper in the metaverse and secure their position in this nascent digital universe (Cheah & Shimul, 2023).

At the same time, the luxury hospitality industry presents a viable path for companies to go. The cornerstone of this industry, where customers want nothing less than excellence, is impeccable customer service. As more travellers look for ethical and environmentally beneficial solutions, investing in sustainability and eco-friendly practices is not only a moral decision but also a wise commercial decision. To differentiate yourself in this crowded market, you must offer guests one-of-a-kind, unforgettable experiences, from exclusive cultural events to custom vacations. Digital integration, such as smartphone apps and smart room controls, improves ease without sacrificing the luxury experience. Finally, in order to express the distinctive tales that make each guest's experience remarkable, marketing in the luxury hotel industry must rely on captivating storytelling. Businesses can succeed in the luxury hotel industry by using these strategies and providing visitors looking for more than just a place to rest with remarkable experiences (Jain et al., 2023).

8. Concluding Remarks

This chapter provides a comprehensive exploration of the convergence between the metaverse and luxury hospitality. By delving into a wide range of topics, from research agendas and practical applications to legal implications and future trends, the chapter aims to contribute valuable insights that can guide future investigations and foster a deeper understanding of this evolving intersection. As the metaverse continues to evolve and luxury hospitality adapts to technological advancements, this chapter serves as a foundation for researchers, practitioners, and legal experts to navigate this transformative landscape.

The convergence of the metaverse and luxury hospitality represents a captivating crossroads where innovation, opulence, and technological prowess intersect. This transformative journey has unveiled a landscape of possibilities that extend beyond the boundaries of traditional hospitality, ushering in a new era of immersive experiences, hyper-personalization, and boundless creativity. As this dynamic convergence continues to evolve, it presents a myriad of avenues for future investigation that promise to shape the trajectory of both industries.

9. Futuristic Approach

The future outlook for the convergence of the metaverse and luxury hospitality is one of limitless potential, as researchers, industry leaders, and innovators embark on a quest to unravel the intricate tapestry of legal, technological, ethical, and experiential dimensions. The exploration of data privacy, cybersecurity, ethical considerations, and the legal ramifications of virtual luxury experiences will guide the establishment of robust frameworks that ensure both innovation and responsibility.

The evolution of technologies such as virtual reality, augmented reality, artificial intelligence, and blockchain will continue to redefine the realm of opulence, offering guests unparalleled opportunities to indulge their senses, curate bespoke journeys, and create lasting memories within digital landscapes. The fusion of physical and digital realms, driven by seamless connectivity and personalization, will inspire a new breed of luxury experiences that transcend the confines of time and space. As we peer into the horizon, the convergence of the metaverse and luxury hospitality invites future investigation into uncharted territories, from the design of eco-friendly virtual spaces to the development of immersive cultural exchanges that celebrate diversity. The quest to harmonize cross-border operations, navigate jurisdictional complexities, and address evolving regulatory landscapes will shape a metaverse-driven luxury hospitality landscape that embodies integrity, inclusivity, and innovation.

References

Alexander, B., & Bellandi, N. (2022). Limited or limitless? Exploring the potential of NFTs on value creation in luxury fashion. *Fashion Practice*, *14*(3), 376–400.

Allam, Z., Sharifi, A., Bibri, S. E., Jones, D. S., & Krogstie, J. (2022). The metaverse as a virtual form of smart cities: Opportunities and challenges for environmental, economic, and social sustainability in urban futures. *Smart Cities*, *5*(3), 771–801.

Amatulli, C., De Angelis, M., & Stoppani, A. (2021). The appeal of sustainability in luxury hospitality: An investigation on the role of perceived integrity. *Tourism Management*, *83*, 104228.

Amatulli, C., Sestino, A., Peluso, A. M., & Guido, G. (2022). Luxury hospitality and the adoption of voice assistants: The role of openness to change and status consumption. In *The emerald handbook of luxury management for hospitality and tourism* (pp. 285–303). Emerald Publishing Limited.

Aydin, G. (2020). Social media engagement and organic post effectiveness: A roadmap for increasing the effectiveness of social media use in hospitality industry. *Journal of Hospitality Marketing & Management*, *29*(1), 1–21.

Back, K. J., Park, J. K., & LaTour, K. (2022). Luxury hospitality services: Editorial comment. *Cornell Hospitality Quarterly*, *63*(1), 4–4.

Bafadhal, A. S., & Hendrawan, M. R. (2023). Does virtual hotel shifting realities or just daydreaming? A wake-up call. *Digital Transformation of the Hotel Industry: Theories, Practices, and Global Challenges*, 37–64.

Barrera, K. G., & Shah, D. (2023). Marketing in the metaverse: Conceptual understanding, framework, and research agenda. *Journal of Business Research*, *155*, 113420.

Bharwani, S., & Mathews, D. (2021). Techno-business strategies for enhancing guest experience in luxury hotels: A managerial perspective. *Worldwide Hospitality and Tourism Themes*, *13*(2), 168–185.

Bharwani, S., & Mathews, D. (2023). Sustainable luxury: From an oxymoron to a tautology – the case of the Indian luxury hospitality industry. *Worldwide Hospitality and Tourism Themes*, *15*(3), 231–248.

Bu, X., Cherian, J., Han, H., Comite, U., Hernández-Perlines, F., & Ariza-Montes, A. (2022). Proposing employee level CSR as an enabler for economic performance: The role of work engagement and quality of work-life. *Sustainability*, *14*(3), 1354.

Buhalis, D., Leung, D., & Lin, M. (2023). Metaverse as a disruptive technology revolutionising tourism management and marketing. *Tourism Management*, *97*, 104724.

Cattaneo, E. (Ed.). (2023). *Managing luxury brands: A complete guide to contemporary luxury brand strategies*. Kogan Page Publishers.

Cheah, I., & Shimul, A. S. (2023). Marketing in the metaverse: Moving forward – what's next? *Journal of Global Scholars of Marketing Science*, *33*(1), 1–10.

Dwivedi, Y. K., Hughes, L., Baabdullah, A. M., Ribeiro-Navarrete, S., Giannakis, M., Al-Debei, M. M., & Wamba, S. F. (2022). Metaverse beyond the hype: Multidisciplinary perspectives on emerging challenges, opportunities, and agenda for research, practice and policy. *International Journal of Information Management*, *66*, 102542.

Hadi, R., Melumad, S., & Park, E. S. (2024). The metaverse: A new digital frontier for consumer behavior. *Journal of Consumer Psychology*, *34*(1), 142–166.

Jain, V., Wirtz, J., Salunke, P., Nunkoo, R., & Sharma, A. (2023). Luxury hospitality: A systematic literature review and research agenda. *International Journal of Hospitality Management*, *115*, 103597.

Kerim, P., & Borrell, M. (2023). The new frontier of co-creation: What are the drivers for consumers to engage in co-creation activities in the metaverse? Dissertation. https://urn.kb.se/resolve?urn=urn:nbn:se:mdh:diva-62734

Koohang, A., Nord, J. H., Ooi, K. B., Tan, G. W. H., Al-Emran, M., Aw, E. C. X., & Wong, L. W. (2023). Shaping the metaverse into reality: A holistic multidisciplinary understanding of opportunities, challenges, and avenues for future investigation. *Journal of Computer Information Systems*, *63*(3), 735–765.

Kumar, S., Dhiraj, A., & Hassan, S. C. C. (2023). Metaverse and cultural marketing in hospitality and tourism. In *Cultural Marketing and Metaverse for Consumer Engagement* (pp. 224–233). IGI Global.

Kwon, W., Lee, M., & Bowen, J. T. (2022). Exploring customers' luxury consumption in restaurants: A combined method of topic modeling and three-factor theory. *Cornell Hospitality Quarterly*, *63*(1), 66–77.

Lee, N., & Jo, M. (2023). Exploring problem-based learning curricula in the metaverse: The hospitality students' perspective. *Journal of Hospitality, Leisure, Sport & Tourism Education*, *32*, 100427.

Nicola, M. (2023). Gamification marketing in metaverse contexts: can the employment of immersive gamification experiences that leverage customer's creativity and sociality be a useful tool to influence customer engagement in metaverse applications? https://www.politesi.polimi.it/handle/10589/204154.

Pereira, V., Silva, G. M., & Dias, Á. (2021). Sustainability practices in hospitality: Case study of a luxury hotel in Arrábida Natural Park. *Sustainability*, *13*(6), 3164.

Ricci, C. M. (2022). From barter to virtual economy: Luxury and fashion markets' opportunities through metaverse and NFTs: Current and expected economic environment. https://tesi.luiss.it/35335/.

Schmidt, A. L. (2023). Changing the rules of the hotel business: The case of citizen M's digital business model disruption. In *Digital Transformation of the Hotel Industry: Theories, Practices, and Global Challenges* (pp. 233–246). Springer International Publishing.

Sestino, A., & Amatulli, C. (2023). The Issue of Integrating new technologies in luxury marketing: A literature review. In *New Technologies in Luxury Consumption: Evidences from Research and Implications for Marketing Strategies* (pp. 7–54). Springer Nature.

Singh, B. (2023). Blockchain technology in renovating healthcare: Legal and future perspectives. In *Revolutionizing Healthcare Through Artificial Intelligence and Internet of Things Applications* (pp. 177–186). IGI Global.

Trunfio, M., & Rossi, S. (2022, October). Advances in metaverse investigation: Streams of research and future agenda. In *Virtual Worlds* (Vol. 1, No. 2, pp. 103–129). MDPI.

Wei, W. (2024). A buzzword, a phase or the next chapter for the Internet? The status and possibilities of the metaverse for tourism. *Journal of Hospitality and Tourism Insights* (Vol. 7, No. 1, pp. 602–625). https://doi.org/10.1108/JHTI-11-2022-0568.

Wongkitrungrueng, A., & Suprawan, L. (2023). Metaverse meets branding: Examining consumer responses to immersive brand experiences. *International Journal of Human – Computer Interaction*, 1–20.

Yang, W., & Mattila, A. S. (2016). Why do we buy luxury experiences? Measuring value perceptions of luxury hospitality services. *International Journal of Contemporary Hospitality Management*, *28*(9), 1848–1867.

Yang, W., & Mattila, A. S. (2017). The impact of status seeking on consumers' word of mouth and product preference – a comparison between luxury hospitality services and luxury goods. *Journal of Hospitality & Tourism Research*, *41*(1), 3–22.

7 Fostering Women's Empowerment in Europe

Case Studies of Innovation in AI, Blockchain, and the Metaverse

Prashasti Pritiprada, Dr. Ipseeta Satpathy, Dr. B.C.M. Patnaik, and Dr. Park Thaichon

1. Introduction

There exists a significant distinction between the procedural comprehension of empowerment and the pragmatic forms of advocacy that necessitate the quantification and measurement of empowerment. The capacity to make choices encompasses three interconnected facets: resources (encompassing not just existing access but also expected claims to both tangible and intangible resources), agency (encompassing decision-making processes as well as less easily quantifiable instances of agency such as negotiation, manipulation, and deceit), and accomplishments (outcomes related to well-being). There is general agreement that the ideas of "process" and "agency" are crucial for women's empowerment. This helps us differentiate it from related concepts like gender equality. People have already made a lot of progress in creating frameworks that explain the different parts of empowerment, how it changes based on the situation, and the different ways to measure it. While no single framework is seen as the best, when we look at all of them together, they give us the basic tools we need to create a practical plan for measuring women's empowerment.

In real-world studies, many researchers from different fields have tried to measure different parts of women's empowerment. Sometimes, they focus on empowerment as the main result of their studying, and other times, they look at it as something that influences other outcomes. Collecting and analyzing data, especially at the level of individual people or households, has improved a lot recently. While these efforts still come with inherent limitations, they furnish us with valuable perspectives on how we can augment the assessment of women's empowerment in the times ahead. In this chapter, we explore the way development studies have looked at women's empowerment. We delve into the discussions and improvements that have happened regarding the idea of power during the latter part of the 20th century. Additionally, we contemplate how power dynamics could be explained and evaluated in the specific situation we are discussing.

The effects of blockchain on essential metaverse technologies compassing elements like the Internet of Things, immersive applications, digital twins, artificial intelligence, and big data can also be observed. In addition, noteworthy projects are

DOI: 10.4324/9781003488248-7

introduced to represent the concrete responsibility that is played by blockchain in the development of meta-version applications and services. As the narrative progresses, a set of constructive guidelines is presented, offering a pathway to steer forthcoming research, innovation, and development endeavours toward the effective utilization of blockchain in future meta-version undertakings.

2. Women in STEM and AI: Bridging the Gender Gap

A substantial portion of available job opportunities today fall within the realm of STEM fields, encompassing science, technology, engineering, and mathematics. In this context, domains associated with computer science and information and communication technology (ICT) are conspicuously sought after, both in Europe and on a global level. A 2018 report titled "Skills Forecast from the European Center for the Development of Vocational Training: Trends and Challenges to 2030," projects a notable 12.8% growth in demand for ICT professionals by the year 2030. However, there exists a striking gender disparity in these STEM domains, as revealed by data from the U.S. Census Bureau. While women comprise nearly half of the overall workforce, their representation in STEM fields is significantly lower, with only 27% of women working in these areas. This gender gap becomes even more pronounced when examining specific STEM subfields. Engineering has maintained a relatively stable but low representation of women, hovering around 10% since 2000. In contrast, computer science is witnessing a concerning trend, with only around 20% of women working in this field as of 2019. In other STEM disciplines such as social sciences, mathematics, physics, and life sciences, the gender balance appears more favourable, with women constituting between 40% and 60% of the workforce. However, the data concerning women in computer-related occupations is disconcerting, particularly given our trajectory towards a digitally driven society in which STEM professions will play an increasingly pivotal role, necessitating a more equitable gender distribution alongside men (Aksal, 2015).

In the year 2001, the National Science Foundation (NSF) initiated the ADVANCE Institutional Transformation (IT) programme with the aim of addressing gender disparities, not solely confined to STEM fields (Asubonteng et al., 2021) but encompassing the broader domain of higher education. This study draws upon insights from gender-focused organizations and specific instances at universities functioning as gender-aware entities. It examines the initiatives devised by ADVANCE institutions with the objective of promoting a fairer academic environment.

Considering the diverse ways in which biases can emerge within AI systems and the far-reaching consequences they can have on society, there is a growing debate about whether legal regulations should be established to ensure fair and non-discriminatory AI-based decision-making processes (Bear & Woolley, 2011). Nonetheless, these stipulations specifically target discrimination based on certain criteria and necessitate substantial evidence of unequal treatment rooted in a prohibited criterion, which can often pose challenges for substantiation. Conversely, concerning the regulation of data quality in decision-making, the General Data

Protection Regulation (GDPR) Article 5(1) underscores "the principle of data accuracy." However, this principle does not inherently preclude (Berman, 1997) the erroneous or disproportionate selection of data for AI-driven decisions.

Diverse leadership within the Information and Communication Technology (ICT) domain serves as a catalyst for driving digital innovation (Booth & Bennett, 2002), a fundamental force behind both digital and business transformations. This evolution necessitates human adaptation, aligning with business changes to secure long-term viability. It encompasses the intricate yet foundational facets of cultural shifts, fostering an inclusive mindset, and ensuring diversity's presence. These elements are of paramount importance in the establishment of a legacy and necessitate the guidance of inclusive digital ethics leadership. Our society is currently undergoing disruptive and transformative changes to keep pace with the rapid technological advancements in education, the labor market, culture, and governance. In this digital era, there is significant potential for heightened inclusivity and, potentially, the reduction or elimination of the gender leadership gap across various sectors, notably in industries like construction, IT, research and development, and academia, where women's representation remains insufficient.

3. Blockchain and Financial Inclusion for Women

a Blockchain applications advancing financial inclusion for women (Chang et al., 2020): The current buzz among fintech leaders centers around fintech (financial technology) and blockchain, which are making a significant impact on the financial sector. This chapter is more into the transformative effects of fintech and blockchain in finance and outlines the key features of these technologies. Furthermore, we explore the evolution of blockchain technology within the financial sector, shedding light on banks' motivations for exploring this technology and the hurdles they encounter. The growing importance of digital financial inclusion takes center stage in conversations concerning the extension of financial accessibility to marginalized communities (Da Silva et al., 2023). Fintech enterprises are harnessing AI technologies to streamline the integration of low-income individuals, women, young people, and small enterprises into the broader financial sphere. AI plays a pivotal role in areas such as risk management (Di Vaio et al., 2023), addressing information disparities, providing customer support through chatbots, and enhancing fraud detection and cybersecurity. By automating risk assessment and measurement through algorithms, AI enables previously excluded groups to access banking services.

b Blockchain-based microfinance platforms for underserved women entrepreneurs: Microfinance organizations encounter a hurdle in their investment decision-making processes (Dwivedi et al., 2022), primarily stemming from the restricted access to information concerning the attributes and objectives of microenterprises. In an extension of signaling theory, the narratives provided by microenterprises on microfinancing platforms serve as crucial signals for conveying valuable attributes and behavioural intentions to potential lenders. Numerous research outcomes (Gadekallu et al., 2022) indicate that microenterprises exhibiting attributes like independence, a strong competitive spirit, and a readiness for risk-taking tend to secure funding more readily and swiftly. In contrast, microenterprises placing importance on traits such as diligence, bravery, empathy, and affability are less likely to draw investment. Furthermore, when microenterprises employ communicative cues conveying initiative, conscientiousness, bravery, affability, or enthusiasm, it is linked to adverse effects on loan repayment.

c Ensuring data privacy and security in blockchain-based financial services: The financial and banking sector is increasingly adopting the concept of "open banking," which aims to enhance customer benefits by promoting data sharing and collaboration among financial institutions (García-Peñalvo & Kearney, 2016). However, this transition is encountering significant hurdles, particularly related to data privacy and ownership. Concerns regarding privacy and regulatory frameworks like the GDPR have made external data sharing a complex endeavour for institutions. Consequently, financial institutions and fintech companies are delving into the realm of technologies such as blockchain, frequently in tandem with artificial intelligence, cloud computing, big data, and the Internet of Things, with the aim of revamping their operational frameworks and offerings.

4. Navigating the Metaverse: Women's Participation and Creativity

a Unveiling opportunities for women in the emerging metaverse landscape: The rise of the metaverse has spurred significant academic discourse on its potential societal benefits and transformative potential. While it promises innovative interactions between virtual and physical realms, unlocking new opportunities and business models, its widespread adoption presents a host of governance, ethical, safety, security, behavioural, privacy, and accessibility challenges (George et al., 2021). This study goes beyond the initial excitement, offering valuable insights into the metaverse's advantages and challenges across various business and societal facets. While exploring how businesses can thrive in virtual spaces is crucial, there's an equally pressing need for research addressing ethical concerns, behavioural considerations, and the potential negative consequences, especially for vulnerable users (Gibert & Valls, 2022). The proposed research agenda outlines numerous avenues for in-depth academic exploration of the multifaceted aspects of the metaverse and its societal impact (Hacker, 2018).

b Women-led virtual reality content creation studios: The emergence of virtual reality (VR) technology holds significant potential, offering immersive experiences that bridge the gap between real and virtual worlds. While the adoption of VR in various industries led by women has been observed conceptually for decades, there's a need for theory-driven and evidence-based research to support its practical applications. Research in psychology has highlighted the concept of "presence" as a key factor in explaining VR's effectiveness in shaping attitudes and behaviours (Hunt et al., 2018). Presence is the sense of being transported to a virtual environment, and its contribution is pivotal to the achievement of successful VR encounters.

c Addressing inclusivity challenges and ensuring diverse representation in the metaverse: The metaverse, an immersive digital environment enabling human interactions through advanced technologies, is poised to reshape social interactions profoundly. Projections indicate that by 2026, a significant portion of the population will spend a substantial portion of their daily lives within the metaverse. This impending shift demands a comprehensive analysis of the diverse challenges and right set of circumstances that will shape the evolution of the metaverse. In order to gauge its societal impact regarding inclusivity (Huynh-The et al., 2023), diversity, equity, accessibility, and safety, an ethnographic study was conducted (Moss et al., 2015) in collaboration with industry experts. The study uncovered numerous research questions and informed the creation of best practices aimed at establishing an inclusive, accessible, and secure metaverse that places a premium on equity and diversity (Kabeer, 1999). These best practices serve as a fundamental framework for stimulating discussions, generating inquiries, and ultimately guiding the metaverse's design, positioning it as a complement to rather than a substitute for the physical world.

5. Closing the Gender Gap in Tech Leadership

a Exploring AI-powered talent management solutions (Ntoutsi et al., 2020) for achieving gender-balanced leadership: Persistent gender underrepresentation (Prügl & True, 2014) in STEM (science, technology, engineering, and mathematics) domains and the increasing importance (Kutty et al., 2020) of collaborative scientific initiatives have sparked an investigation into existing research examining the impact of gender diversity on team dynamics and productivity. Recent findings indicate a clear improvement in team collaboration when women are part of the team, primarily attributing this to their positive influence on group processes (Laguna-Sánchez et al., 2021). However, the effect of gender diversity on overall team performance is multifaceted, contingent upon various contextual variables. Acknowledging the pivotal role of collaboration in scientific endeavours (Malhotra et al., 2002), promoting greater participation of women in these domains holds the potential for substantial practical advantages in advancing science and technology.

b Machine learning models for identifying high-potential women leaders: Addressing the critical need for women's leadership development programmes (WLDPs) (Mhlanga, 2020) in higher education is needed to bridge the gender gap in executive positions. The underrepresentation of women in leadership roles, as evidenced by statistics from Fortune 500 companies and beyond (Miao et al., 2021), underscores the urgency of promoting women's leadership. As per a WLDP tailored for female undergraduate students and drawing from outcomes derived from three year-long courses held from 2017 to 2020, this initiative was crafted through collaborative efforts, engaging academic professionals, industry partners, managers, and leaders. This approach mirrors the tenets of open innovation (OI) (Misuraca, 2012; Morimoto et al., 2013).

c Promoting a culture of diversity and inclusion in tech organizations: Despite modest progress in gender and ethnic diversity (Shannon et al., 2019) on executive teams, companies with greater diversity continue to outperform their peers. Gender diversity alone boosts profitability and value creation, while ethnic and cultural diversity on executive teams correlates with industry-leading profitability (Mosedale, 2005). Conversely, companies that lag in diversity (Wang et al., 2020) face a financial penalty. Insights gleaned from leading organizations underscore the importance of inclusion and diversity (I&D) in attracting top-tier talent, enhancing customer-centricity (Tussyadiah et al., 2018), boosting employee contentment, strengthening decision-making processes, and ensuring the sustainability of business operations. The report outlines four imperatives for leveraging I&D for impact: commitment from leadership, alignment with growth strategy, a tailored initiative portfolio, and contextual relevance for maximum buy-in and impact. Ultimately, it encourages businesses to examine the case for I&D as a strategic driver of success.

6. The Future of Work: Upskilling and Reskilling Women

a Leveraging AI-powered e-learning platforms for women's skill development: Addressing the pressing issue of integrating artificial intelligence (AI) into education, particularly in developing countries, and its implications for sustainable development, explores how AI can enhance learning outcomes, with examples from countries like China, Uruguay, Brazil, South Africa, and Kenya, showcasing AI's potential for personalization, access, and data analytics in education systems.

b Employing blockchain-based credentials to validate women's skills enhancement efforts: Policymakers and private-sector collaborators increasingly recognize the need to leverage emerging technologies in addressing contemporary challenges. This chapter scrutinizes the prospective impact of blockchain technology on women and girls within humanitarian settings. A study done by Weber-Lewerenz and Vasiliu-Feltes (2022) gives insights derived from UN Women's exploration of blockchain technology and its inaugural gender-responsive pilot initiative targeting. In the absence of a deliberate commitment to these objectives, blockchain technology may inadvertently contribute to the further marginalization of women and girls.

c Fostering a culture of continuous learning in the digital age: The incorporation of information communication technologies (ICT) and the transition to tech-driven leadership and learning environments are integral components of educational strategies in developing countries. Embracing technological advancements like tablet PCs, mobile learning, and flipped classrooms has become a necessity for modern education standards and ensuring equal learning opportunities in primary and secondary schools. The successful implementation of these interactive learning settings relies on the awareness and preparedness within the education system, as well as the commitment of school principals to technological advancements. In today's digital age, both leadership and the learning environment play crucial roles in leveraging technology for learning, advancing leadership practices, and building networks that transcend geographical boundaries to reshape knowledge dissemination.

7. Policy Frameworks and Collaboration for Sustainable Change

a Government initiatives and regulatory frameworks supporting women in tech in Europe: Technology has played an integral role in the historical development of cities. In recent times, there has been a noticeable shift in the trajectory of smart city development, with a growing emphasis on sustainability through the utilization of information and communication technologies and other intelligent solutions. However, previous research has pointed out that many smart cities have not effectively integrated sustainable development goals into their strategies. Frequently, these initiatives prioritize achieving smart objectives over sustainability objectives.

b Public–private partnerships driving gender equality in tech innovation: Feminism's impact has notably expanded its reach into the corporate landscape, with concepts such as "gender equality is smart economics" endorsed by the World Bank and "womenomics," championed by *The Economist*, gaining prominence. While government initiatives to promote gender equality are firmly established, private corporations have emerged as new stakeholders in this arena (Zallio & Clarkson 2022). This article delves into the motivations and actions of businesses in collaboration with public partners to advance gender equality, analyzing how these endeavours align with existing power dynamics. It also examines their implications for feminist agendas, their perceived legitimacy, and their overall effectiveness. Through a feminist evaluation lens, the findings reveal a nuanced landscape, indicating that the heightened focus on gender equality in the corporate world and global economic governance is a reflection of changes occurring within states and corporations, set against the backdrop of global competition and restructuring.

c The role of academia, industry, and civil society in sustaining progress: The concept of "civil society" has gained widespread attention recently, with scholars emphasizing its role in shaping political, social, and economic outcomes. However, this prevailing notion is flawed, as it oversimplifies the idea that a vibrant civil society always strengthens democratic governance. This essay illustrates how a robust civil society contributed to undermining Weimar Germany, a critical democratic experiment of the 20th century. This analysis suggests that in certain situations, strong civil society engagement can have adverse effects on democratic stability. To better understand when civil society activities may take on oppositional or anti-democratic tendencies, it is crucial to ground analyses in real-world political contexts.

8. Challenges and Future Directions

a Addressing biases and disparities in AI, blockchain, and the metaverse: The emergence of the metaverse, exemplified by Meta Platforms' rebranding from Facebook, has garnered significant attention and investment across various sectors, including tech giants like Microsoft and Metaverse Group. This virtual realm, combining aspects of augmented reality, virtual reality, and blockchain technology, is rapidly evolving, with forecasts indicating substantial revenue growth, especially in the gaming industry. However, it's crucial to acknowledge that the development and utilization of these technologies, including AI and blockchain, may inherit biases and disparities that can have wide-ranging impacts on users. However, these AI systems are not immune to biases, and if left unaddressed, they can perpetuate discrimination and inequality within the metaverse. Furthermore, blockchain technology, while promising transparency and decentralization, has its own set of challenges related to biases and disparities. Issues like access to resources, control of decentralized networks, and disparities in participation can impact the equitable distribution of benefits from blockchain-based systems. This comprehensive survey seeks to not only explore AI's contributions and potential in various aspects of the metaverse but also to shed light on the biases and disparities that may arise within these technologies. It is crucial to confront these challenges and strive for a metaverse that prioritizes inclusivity and equity, ensuring that all users, regardless of their background or circumstances, can reap its benefits.

b Ensuring accessibility and digital literacy for all women: In Europe, the data highlights the multifaceted impact of emergency remote teaching during the pandemic on women, including professors and students from diverse backgrounds. They faced a range of challenges, such as increased workloads, limited interaction with peers, mental and physical health issues, digital technology proficiency issues, and the struggle to balance academic, professional, and household responsibilities. On a positive note, the embrace of digital technologies has empowered them to participate in a range of academic pursuits, including conferences, webinars, training sessions, and online courses, obviating the necessity for physical travel. These negative effects, particularly the burdens of excessive workloads, health concerns, and the challenge of balancing different responsibilities, were consistent. It is crucial to address the issue of inadequate infrastructure for effective digital literacy practices. Access to dependable internet connectivity and high-quality digital technologies is imperative, and it should not be contingent on individual financial means. It is crucial to ensure that both women and men enjoy equitable access to these resources throughout Europe.

c Anticipating the impact of future technological shifts on empowerment of women in Europe: In the European context, the emergence of youth as a distinct social entity empowered by digital technology has underscored their pivotal role in shaping the digital society, ushering in fresh behaviours and perspectives. However, a noticeable gap exists in acknowledging their active involvement in policymaking and decision-making processes, particularly in matters pertaining to the digital realm. This absence of representation and voice poses challenges in identifying and comprehending their specific requirements. Furthermore, the youth demographic is highly diverse, posing difficulties in effectively addressing their varied concerns. Additionally, some young individuals may exhibit hesitancy in participating in research endeavours. The project endeavours to create a platform that facilitates effective communication between youth and other stakeholders through innovative engagement methods. This will involve a dynamic research process comprising networking, dialogues, participatory research, and interpretation phases, all led by young individuals. The overarching objective of the project is to generate a wide range of outcomes, offer critical viewpoints, and provide insights that can inform policymaking and decision-making processes regarding the digital society's impact on children and young adults in European countries.

9. Recommendations for Business Practices: The Key to Success

Women's participation and leadership in these transformative technologies not only promote gender equality but also drive innovation and economic growth. To guide businesses in this endeavour, we present a comprehensive blueprint for success in empowering women in the fields of AI, blockchain, and the metaverse.

a **Champion Diversity and Inclusion:**
At the heart of promoting women's empowerment in these technology sectors lies a steadfast commitment to diversity and inclusion. Businesses should establish tangible diversity goals and implement strategies to achieve them. This encompasses setting targets for the recruitment, retention, and advancement of women in technology roles. Companies may even contemplate creating specialized positions or teams dedicated to diversity and inclusion, thus ensuring the realization of these objectives.

b **Implement Gender-Neutral Recruitment Practices:**
The adoption of gender-neutral recruitment practices is imperative for eradicating bias in the hiring process. Employing techniques such as blind screening of resumes and structured interviews helps evaluate candidates solely on their qualifications, skills, and experience, thus guaranteeing women equal opportunities for entry into the industry.

c **Foster Mentorship and Sponsorship Programmes:**
The creation of mentorship and sponsorship programmes is instrumental in supporting women's aspirations to excel in AI, blockchain, or the metaverse. These programmes pair seasoned professionals with women looking to advance in these fields, providing invaluable guidance, support, and access to influential networks, ultimately enabling women to shatter any glass ceilings.

d **Invest in Education and Training:**
Sustained investment in education and training is essential to ensure that women have access to the knowledge and skills demanded by these rapidly evolving sectors. Consider offering scholarships, workshops, and online courses that are tailored to AI, blockchain, and metaverse technologies. Collaborating with educational institutions can further bridge the skills gap and facilitate women's entry into these industries.

e **Ensure Equal Pay and Equal Opportunities:**
Ensuring pay equity for the same work is a fundamental aspect of women's empowerment. Businesses must conduct regular pay equity audits and make

necessary adjustments to compensation packages to eradicate wage disparities. Furthermore, equal opportunities for career advancement, leadership roles, and participation in high-impact projects must be extended to women.

f **Embrace Flexible Work Arrangements:**
Recognizing the significance of work–life balance, companies should offer flexible work arrangements such as remote work options, part-time schedules, and childcare support. These initiatives facilitate women in effectively balancing their professional and personal responsibilities, nurturing long-term commitment to the organization.

g **Cultivate a Supportive Work Environment:**
Promoting a workplace culture that actively combats discrimination, harassment, and bias is imperative. Create channels for reporting and addressing these issues and offer requisite training to foster a safe and inclusive environment. Encourage employees to embrace diversity and uphold the core values of the company.

h **Prioritize Transparency and Accountability:**
Regular monitoring and reporting on the progress of diversity and inclusion initiatives are vital. Transparency underscores a resolute commitment to the cause and holds organizations accountable for their efforts. Sharing diversity statistics, goals, and achievements with stakeholders, employees, and the public demonstrates the sincerity of these efforts.

i **Engage in Collaborative Partnerships:**
Collaboration with external organizations, non-governmental organizations (NGOs), and government initiatives focused on women's empowerment in technology is crucial. These partnerships can create new avenues for mentorship, education, and networking opportunities for women.

j **Demonstrate Leadership Commitment:**
The commitment of leadership is instrumental in the success of these initiatives. Business leaders should wholeheartedly champion the cause of women's empowerment in AI, blockchain, and the metaverse, thus displaying unwavering support and fostering a culture of diversity and inclusion from the highest echelons of the organization.

k **Celebrate and Showcase Success Stories:**
Celebrating and showcasing the accomplishments of women in these fields is inspiring. By highlighting successful women in AI, blockchain, and the metaverse, businesses can motivate the next generation of female talent and illustrate the immense potential for women to excel in these industries.

The blueprint for success involves adopting a holistic approach that encompasses recruitment, mentorship, education, and a supportive work culture. Embracing diversity and inclusion not only will lead to a more equitable workplace but also will drive innovation and success in these rapidly evolving fields. By implementing these recommendations, businesses can take a significant step towards realizing the full potential of women in technology and ensuring a brighter future for all.

10. Conclusion

Blockchain technology (BT), characterized by its distributed digital ledger system, offers secure and immutable data recording capabilities, originally conceptualized by Haber and Scott Scornetta in 1991. Beyond its technical dimensions, BT holds the transformative capacity to foster a more equitable and inclusive digital society. It achieves this by promoting democratic participation in financial services through transparency, accountability, efficiency, and security. By facilitating decentralization and anonymity, BT plays a pivotal role in promoting social inclusion and enhancing the living conditions of marginalized individuals, particularly by improving resource tracking and humanitarian functions. Government bodies and regulatory authorities recognize BT as a tool for advancing financial inclusion, a vital component in reducing global poverty and narrowing wealth disparities.

European countries, including France, the UK, Germany, Spain, Poland, Finland, Ireland, Luxembourg, the Netherlands, and the region of Flanders, engaged in forward-looking approaches to systematically evaluate potential pathways for research and innovation. The primary shared objective among these diverse approaches was to define research and innovation agendas that effectively address future needs by considering global challenges and national objectives, contributing to the broader goal of aligning research and innovation with the societal challenges outlined in the European Innovation Union Initiative. The confluence of two prominent trends within the contemporary business landscape is fundamentally reshaping the landscape of entrepreneurship theory and practice. The first of these trends underscores the ever-increasing attention being devoted to the pressing climate crisis, compelling societal actors to take on more expansive roles in the generation of environmental and social value. This urgency has been underscored by a myriad of stakeholders, ranging from formal governmental declarations of climate emergencies to high-profile media campaigns and authoritative scientific reports sounding the alarm on issues such as climate change and the loss of biodiversity. In response to this clarion call, businesses are embracing ambitious sustainability objectives, either voluntarily or in response to mounting pressures from investors and government entities.

The convergence of these dual imperatives – sustainability and digitalization – is manifesting across both the private and public sectors, yet systematic academic research on this intersection remains notably limited. The principal aim of this chapter is to catalyze a heightened scholarly and practical focus on entrepreneurial organizations actively engaged in digital sustainability initiatives. It underscores the imperative need to address the twin challenges of climate change and sustainable development through the innovative deployment of technological solutions and novel business models. In this context, "digital sustainability" refers to the range of activities undertaken by organizations that leverage technology to advance the goals of sustainable development.

References

Aksal, F. A. (2015). Are headmasters digital leaders in school culture? *Egitim ve Bilim*, 40(182).

Asubonteng, K. O., Ros-Tonen, M. A., Baud, I. S. A., & Pfeffer, K. (2021). Envisioning the future of mosaic landscapes: Actor perceptions in a mixed cocoa/oil-palm area in Ghana. *Environmental Management*, 68, 701–719.

Bear, J. B., & Woolley, A. W. (2011). The role of gender in team collaboration and performance. *Interdisciplinary Science Reviews*, 36(2), 146–153.

Berman, S. (1997). Civil society and the collapse of the Weimar Republic. *World Politics*, 49(3), 401–429.

Booth, C., & Bennett, C. (2002). Gender mainstreaming in the European Union: Towards a new conception and practice of equal opportunities? *European Journal of Women's Studies*, 9(4), 430–446.

Chang, V., Baudier, P., Zhang, H., Xu, Q., Zhang, J., & Arami, M. (2020). How Blockchain can impact financial services – the overview, challenges and recommendations from expert interviewees. *Technological Forecasting and Social Change*, 158, 120166.

Da Silva, C., Komesu, F., & Fluckiger, C. (2023). Digital literacy, remote teaching and access during COVID-19 pandemic: Impacts on postgraduate female in Brazilian Amazon. *Actualidades Investigativas en Educación*, 23(1), 279–311.

Di Vaio, A., Hassan, R., & Palladino, R. (2023). Blockchain technology and gender equality: A systematic literature review. *International Journal of Information Management*, 68, 102517.

Dwivedi, Y. K., Hughes, L., Baabdullah, A. M., Ribeiro-Navarrete, S., Giannakis, M., Al-Debei, M. M., . . . & Wamba, S. F. (2022). Metaverse beyond the hype: Multidisciplinary perspectives on emerging challenges, opportunities, and agenda for research, practice and policy. *International Journal of Information Management*, 66, 102542.

Gadekallu, T. R., Huynh-The, T., Wang, W., Yenduri, G., Ranaweera, P., Pham, Q. V., . . . & Liyanage, M. (2022). Blockchain for the metaverse: A review. arXiv preprint arXiv:2203.09738.

García-Peñalvo, F. J. & Kearney, N. A. (2016). Networked youth research for empowerment in digital society: The WYRED project. In *Proceedings of the Fourth International Conference on Technological Ecosystems for Enhancing Multiculturality* (TEEM '16) (pp. 3–9). Association for Computing Machinery, New York, NY, USA, https://doi.org/10.1145/3012430.3012489

George, G., Merrill, R. K., & Schillebeeckx, S. J. (2021). Digital sustainability and entrepreneurship: How digital innovations are helping tackle climate change and sustainable development. *Entrepreneurship Theory and Practice*, 45(5), 999–1027.

Gibert, K., & Valls, A. (2022). Building a territorial working group to reduce gender gap in the field of artificial intelligence. *Applied Sciences*, 12(6), 3129.

Hacker, P. (2018). Teaching fairness to artificial intelligence: Existing and novel strategies against algorithmic discrimination under EU law. *Common Market Law Review*, 55(4).

Hunt, V., Prince, S., Dixon-Fyle, S., & Yee, L. (2018). *Delivering Through Diversity* (Vol. 231, pp. 1–39). McKinsey & Company.

Huynh-The, T., Pham, Q. V., Pham, X. Q., Nguyen, T. T., Han, Z., & Kim, D. S. (2023). Artificial intelligence for the metaverse: A survey. *Engineering Applications of Artificial Intelligence*, 117, 105581.

Kabeer, N. (1999). Resources, agency, achievements: Reflections on the measurement of women's empowerment. *Development and Change*, 30(3), 435–464.

Kutty, A. A., Abdella, G. M., Kucukvar, M., Onat, N. C., & Bulu, M. (2020). A system thinking approach for harmonizing smart and sustainable city initiatives with United Nations sustainable development goals. *Sustainable Development*, 28(5), 1347–1365.

Laguna-Sánchez, P., Segovia-Pérez, M., Fuente-Cabrero, C. D. L., & Vargas-Pérez, A. M. (2021). A collaborative model for leadership education in high-potential university women students. *Journal of Open Innovation: Technology, Market, and Complexity*, 7(2), 138.

Malhotra, A., Schuler, S. R., & Boender, C. (2002, June). Measuring women's empowerment as a variable in international development. In *Background Paper Prepared for the World Bank Workshop on Poverty and Gender: New Perspectives* (Vol. 28, p. 58). The World Bank.

Mhlanga, D. (2020). Industry 4.0 in finance: the impact of artificial intelligence (ai) on digital financial inclusion. *International Journal of Financial Studies*, 8(3), 45.

Miao, F., Holmes, W., Huang, R., & Zhang, H. (2021). *AI and Education: A Guidance for Policymakers*. UNESCO Publishing.

Misuraca, G. (2012). Envisioning digital Europe 2030: Scenarios for ICT in future governance and policy modelling. *European Foresight Platform.–2012.–C*, 632012.

Morimoto, S. A., Zajicek, A. M., Hunt, V. H., & Lisnic, R. (2013). Beyond binders full of women: NSF ADVANCE and initiatives for institutional transformation. *Sociological Spectrum*, 33(5), 397–415.

Mosedale, S. (2005). Assessing women's empowerment: Towards a conceptual framework. *Journal of International Development*, 17(2), 243–257.

Moss, T. W., Neubaum, D. O., & Meyskens, M. (2015). The effect of virtuous and entrepreneurial orientations on microfinance lending and repayment: A signaling theory perspective. *Entrepreneurship Theory and Practice*, 39(1), 27–52.

Ntoutsi, E., Fafalios, P., Gadiraju, U., Iosifidis, V., Nejdl, W., Vidal, M. E., . . . & Staab, S. (2020). Bias in data-driven artificial intelligence systems – An introductory survey. *Wiley Interdisciplinary Reviews: Data Mining and Knowledge Discovery*, 10(3), e1356.

Prügl, E., & True, J. (2014). Equality means business? Governing gender through transnational public-private partnerships. *Review of International Political Economy*, 21(6), 1137–1169.

Shannon, G., Jansen, M., Williams, K., Cáceres, C., Motta, A., Odhiambo, A., . . . & Mannell, J. (2019). Gender equality in science, medicine, and global health: where are we at and why does it matter? *The Lancet*, 393(10171), 560–569.

Tussyadiah, I. P., Wang, D., Jung, T. H., & Tom Dieck, M. C. (2018). Virtual reality, presence, and attitude change: Empirical evidence from tourism. *Tourism Management*, 66, 140–154.

Wang, H., Ma, S., Dai, H. N., Imran, M., & Wang, T. (2020). Blockchain-based data privacy management with nudge theory in open banking. *Future Generation Computer Systems*, 110, 812–823.

Weber-Lewerenz, B., & Vasiliu-Feltes, I. (2022). Empowering digital innovation by diverse leadership in ICT – a roadmap to a better value system in computer algorithms. *Humanistic Management Journal*, 7(1), 117–134.

Zallio, M., & Clarkson, P. J. (2022). Designing the metaverse: A study on inclusion, diversity, equity, accessibility and safety for digital immersive environments. *Telematics and Informatics*, 75, 101909.

8 Leveraging Digital Transformation in Marketing of Home-Stay Businesses to Promote Tourism in the Hospitality Industry

Dr. Vijay Prakash Gupta

1.0 Introduction

In recent years, the global hospitality industry has witnessed a significant transformation due to the proliferation of digital technologies. The emergence of homestay businesses, facilitated by platforms like Airbnb and Vacation Rental by Owner (VRBO), has revolutionized the way travellers experience accommodations during their journeys. As the travel landscape continues to evolve, leveraging digital transformation in marketing homestay businesses has become crucial to promoting tourism in the hospitality industry.

Information provided by the UNWTO indicates that international tourist arrivals reached a remarkable 1.3 billion in 2019, with the travel and tourism sector contributing to over 10% of the global GDP. Additionally, the increasing preference for experiential travel has propelled the appeal of homestay businesses, as travellers actively seek authentic and immersive experiences.

The impact of digitalization on the hospitality sector cannot be ignored. A report by Statista indicates that in 2020, the online travel booking market size was valued at a staggering 817.2 billion U.S. dollars. This figure is expected to witness continued growth as more travellers rely on online platforms to search, book, and review accommodations, including homestays.

As traditional hotel chains and homestay hosts compete for tourists' attention, digital transformation has emerged as a game changer in marketing strategies. Social media platforms, search engines, and online travel agencies have created new avenues for targeting potential customers. According to a study by eMarketer, over 90% of millennials use social media to plan their trips, making it an indispensable tool for marketers.

Personalization is another critical aspect of modern marketing in the hospitality industry. Leveraging big data and artificial intelligence, homestay businesses can analyze customer preferences and behaviour, tailoring their offerings to meet specific needs. A study by Accenture reveals that 91% of consumers are more likely to shop with brands that offer personalized recommendations, highlighting the importance of data-driven marketing in attracting and retaining guests. In this dynamic landscape, the COVID-19 pandemic also played a significant role in accelerating digital adoption in the hospitality sector. Travel restrictions and safety concerns led

DOI: 10.4324/9781003488248-8

to an increased reliance on virtual experiences, online booking platforms, and contactless services. As the industry recovers, these digital transformations are likely to persist and shape the future of hospitality marketing.

In this context, this chapter explores the opportunities and challenges of leveraging digital transformation in marketing homestay businesses to promote tourism in the hospitality industry. We delve into the strategies and technologies that have proven effective in reaching and engaging modern travellers and how the convergence of digital marketing and personalized experiences can create a compelling competitive advantage for homestay hosts. Furthermore, we examine the impact of digital adoption in the industry and forecast the trends that will define the future of hospitality marketing.

2.0 Literature Review

Busulwa et al. (2022) offers a comprehensive exploration of the evolving relationship between digital transformation, digital business capabilities, and the competencies required of hospitality managers. Their proposed integrative framework bridges the gap between digital technology competencies and the broader set of skills essential for managing digital transformation in the hospitality and tourism sector. This research serves as a valuable resource for academia, industry professionals, and policymakers, emphasizing the need for continuous adaptation to the digital frontier in the pursuit of excellence in the field of hospitality management.

Kumar et al. (2023) underscores the profound changes brought about by digital transformation in the tourism sector and offers insights into the state of research in this field. By examining top-cited articles, publication trends, influential authors, and collaboration networks, the study provides a comprehensive overview of the current landscape while also directing attention to key areas for future exploration. This work contributes significantly to the understanding of digital transformation in the tourism sector, informing future research endeavours and guiding the industry toward a more digitally integrated future.

Rosário's study (2023) delves into the multifaceted relationship between security, challenges, and opportunities in the context of digital marketing. It underscores the urgency of addressing security concerns in a world in which customer data is increasingly stored digitally and simultaneously highlights the possibilities for improving security. By advocating proactive measures and ongoing vigilance, this study encourages businesses to navigate the digital marketing space with a heightened awareness of security while harnessing the potential for more robust data protection measures. It serves as a valuable resource for practitioners, scholars, and decision-makers alike, emphasizing the dynamic nature of security in the digital marketing realm and the critical need for continuous adaptation and innovation in this ever-evolving field.

The study "Marketing Strategy with Marketing Mix for Lake Toba Tourism Destination" by Kennedy et al. (2022) addresses the evolving tourism industry and the need for Lake Toba, an iconic Indonesian destination, to adapt to global competition. Employing the marketing mix theory, it aims to develop effective strategies focusing on product development, positioning, market analysis, and more. While the study holds value for local governments, tourism stakeholders, and communities, it is vital to recognize its limitations in addressing all industry complexities. The incorporation of the marketing mix framework in this context showcases an innovative approach to maintaining competitiveness in tourism.

Movements of Recent Business Practices

Digital Transformation Redefining Guest Experience: In 2022 and 2023, homestay businesses have increasingly leveraged digital transformation to provide personalized guest experiences. They utilize data analytics to understand guest preferences and offer tailored services. Airbnb, for example, uses machine learning algorithms to recommend accommodations based on user behaviour, significantly enhancing user satisfaction (Ifrach, 2015).

Virtual Tours and Augmented Reality: Homestay businesses are incorporating virtual tours and augmented reality (AR) experiences to showcase their properties. Travellers can now explore accommodations remotely before making bookings. Airbnb's "Online Experiences" allows users to participate in virtual activities, enhancing the booking process and guest expectations (Cenni and Vásquez, 2022).

Sustainability as a Marketing Tool: Sustainability practices have gained prominence in the marketing of homestay businesses. Travellers are increasingly conscious of environmental impact, and businesses are using sustainability initiatives to attract eco-conscious guests. For instance, organizations like Ecobnb promote eco-friendly stays, attracting travellers looking for sustainable (Arzoumanidis et al., 2022).

Influencer- and User-Generated Content: Marketing strategies have shifted towards user-generated content and influencer partnerships. Businesses encourage guests to share their experiences on social media, leveraging the authenticity and reach of influencer networks. Platforms like Instagram and TikTok play a pivotal role in showcasing homestay experiences to a broader audience.

Contactless Booking and Check-in: With the impact of the COVID-19 pandemic, contactless booking and check-in have become the norm. Digital transformation allows homestays to offer secure and seamless contactless experiences, such as keyless entry systems and digital check-ins, enhancing safety and convenience for guests (Curnes et al., 2023).

AI Chatbots for Customer Service: AI chatbots have become integral in managing customer inquiries and issues. Businesses like VRBO employ chatbots to provide instant responses to guest queries, improving customer service efficiency.

Blockchain for Trust and Transparency: Blockchain technology is being explored to enhance trust and transparency in the hospitality industry. Smart contracts and blockchain-based reviews can help prevent fraudulent listings and ensure accurate property descriptions, ultimately benefiting both hosts and guests (Skift, 2022).

2.1 Why We Need This Chapter

Based on the existing literature review and published date, this chapter is essential for several reasons. Firstly, it addresses the need for a more diverse range of sources and studies to identify gaps in the current literature related to digital transformation in the hospitality and tourism sector. By exploring underrepresented areas within the industry and incorporating a wider array of sources, it enhances the comprehensiveness of the review. Additionally, it recognizes the importance of geographical and cultural variations in digital transformation, emphasizing the need to understand how these trends differ across the globe, thereby providing a more inclusive perspective. Furthermore, the chapter delves into the temporal evolution of research in this field, investigating historical trends and shifts in research focus or methodology, which can reveal areas requiring more attention. It also highlights the need for interdisciplinary approaches to address the multifaceted nature of digital transformation, particularly in integrating technology and marketing strategies. The incorporation of qualitative and longitudinal studies addresses gaps in the understanding of long-term impacts, while exploring emerging technologies and trends fills a void in current literature that tends to focus on established technologies. Lastly, it promotes cross-sector comparisons to gain insights into unique challenges and opportunities specific to the hospitality and tourism industry in relation to digital transformation. In sum, this chapter strengthens the review by addressing these critical aspects and provides a more holistic view of the digital transformation landscape in the sector.

3.0 Overview of the Hospitality Industry

The hospitality industry is a vast and diverse sector that encompasses a range of businesses, including hotels, restaurants, resorts, homestays, cruise lines, airlines, and various other service providers. It plays a significant role in driving economic growth, generating employment, and contributing to the overall development of a country's tourism sector. Here, we provide an overview of the hospitality industry with a focus on India and other countries, supported by data, facts, and figures from reputable sources.

3.1 Hospitality Industry in India

India is known for its rich cultural heritage, diverse landscapes, and a wide array of tourist attractions, making it a popular destination for both domestic and international travellers. The hospitality industry in India has experienced remarkable growth over the years and has become a key contributor to the country's GDP.

According to the World Travel & Tourism Council (WTTC), the direct contribution of travel and tourism to India's GDP was INR 3,156.5 billion (approximately 6.7% of GDP) in 2020. This figure is projected to rise to INR 6,404.5 billion (approximately 8.3% of GDP) by 2030.

The hospitality sector in India is a major employment generator. As per a report by the Ministry of Tourism, the industry provided jobs to over 42 million people in 2019, accounting for approximately 8.1% of the total employment in the country.

The hotel industry is a significant segment within the hospitality sector. In 2019, the number of classified hotels in India was approximately more than two lakhs, offering a total of around 2.1 million rooms, as per data from the Indian Ministry of Tourism.

The COVID-19 pandemic severely impacted the hospitality industry in India, leading to a significant decline in tourist arrivals and revenue. However, the sector has shown signs of recovery as travel restrictions eased in subsequent years.

3.2 Hospitality Industry in Other Countries

The hospitality industry is a global phenomenon, with countries around the world experiencing varying degrees of growth and challenges in the sector.

United States: The United States is one of the leading countries in the global hospitality industry, with a robust infrastructure and a diverse range of accommodations and attractions.

In 2020, the travel and tourism industry directly contributed approximately 580.7 billion U.S. dollars to the U.S. GDP, accounting for 2.8% of the total GDP, as reported by the U.S. Bureau of Economic Analysis. The hotel industry in the U.S. is substantial, with around 56,000 properties and over 5 million guestrooms available, according to the American Hotel & Lodging Association.

The pandemic had a significant impact on the U.S. hospitality sector, leading to job losses and financial challenges. However, the industry has been witnessing a gradual recovery in subsequent years.

4.0 Concepts and Emergence of Homestay Businesses

Homestays have transformed the hospitality industry, offering travellers unique and personalized accommodation experiences in private homes or villas. This concept allows travellers to immerse themselves in local culture and explore off-the-beaten-path destinations. The idea of homestays gained popularity with the sharing economy and digital platforms.

Airbnb, founded in 2008, is a leading global homestay platform connecting millions of travellers with hosts worldwide. VRBO, founded in 1995, specializes in traditional vacation homes. Homestay.com, founded in 2013, focuses on authentic cultural experiences. Other players like Booking.com have also embraced homestays.

These platforms disrupted the traditional hotel industry, providing travellers with diverse and affordable options. Regional and niche players also cater to specific preferences. Homestays are now preferred by travellers seeking unique experiences and local interactions. The future of hospitality will be influenced by the ongoing growth and popularity of homestay businesses.

Homestays encompass a distinctive lodging option where tourists opt to reside with local families in their homes. This type of accommodation is marked by its affordability, informal ambiance, and immersive experience, even in the most secluded travel destinations. By choosing a homestay, travellers not only visit a place but also immerse themselves in the local lifestyle. A paramount element defining a homestay is the host, who plays a pivotal role in shaping the experience.

According to Richardson (2004), while the homestay industry might be relatively recent, the concept of travellers lodging with local families has historical roots. This trend gained traction thanks to homestays catering to international students studying abroad. These students discovered the benefits of residing with local families to gain genuine insights into the culture and lifestyle of their host country.

Richardson (2003) highlights that in Australia, this concept is particularly intertwined with international students. Additionally, homestays are favoured by language learners aiming to refine their language skills through immersion, as noted by Rivers (1998). In regions such as the United Kingdom, Ireland, and America, the homestay model shares similarities with the bed-and-breakfast arrangement, where hosts provide lodging in exchange for payment (Arneson, 2018).

According to the Cambridge Academic Content Dictionary, a bed-and-breakfast (B&B) is defined as a small hotel or private residence that rents out rooms and serves morning meals. Choudhary and Rai (2007) assert that B&Bs theoretically offer budget-friendly accommodations, typically comprising a bed-and-breakfast only. It is evident that the B&B model can be implemented within a private house or various other lodging types that provide rooms along with morning meals.

4.1 Homestays in India

The concept of homestays has gained recognition on an international scale, although in India, it remains relatively new, as pointed out by Sharat Dhall, the COO of Yatra's B2C division. According to sources, there exists hesitancy among people to either offer their homes to tourists or to choose homestays for their stay. This reveals a need for educating both hosts and guests about the homestay model (Banerjee, 2017). In a bid to promote this form of lodging, the Ministry of Tourism in India has been actively encouraging homestays while also urging states to make the concept more enticing (Sharma, 2016).

Key online travel agents like MakeMyTrip, Yatra, and Airbnb are playing a significant role in distributing homestay options. Collaborations between entities like the Maharashtra Tourism Development Corporation with Airbnb and the Odisha Tourism Development Corporation with Yatra, along with state tourism departments in Assam and Kumaun partnering with Rightstay of MakeMyTrip, highlight the concerted efforts to boost homestay popularity (Press Trust of India, 2017). Airbnb is also collaborating with organizations such as SEWA (Self-Employed Women's Association) in Gujarat, aiming to offer travellers an authentic rural experience while empowering SEWA members as micro-entrepreneurs (Johnson and Mehta, 2022).

In the Indian context, the terms "homestay" and "bed-and-breakfast (B&B)" are often used interchangeably (Choudhary and Rai, 2007). The government of India's Ministry of Tourism has laid down guidelines to categorize fully operational bed-and-breakfast/homestay facilities as "Incredible India Bed and Breakfast (IIB&B)/Homestay Establishments." The categorization varies based on the facilities offered and varies from state to state. Despite these efforts, a study by the Centre for Public Policy Research reveals that in Kochi, only a mere 20% of home-stays possess government recognition or classification. This might be attributed to the additional costs and administrative requirements associated with obtaining permits and covering commercial utility prices.

The trend of homestays in India has shown remarkable growth, with a 130-fold increase noted, from 17 homestays in 2004 to 2,281 registered homestays in 2016, according to a report by online travel community Holiday IQ (Dube and Sharma, 2018). Holiday IQ's 2014 report indicated that 72% of homestays were located in the southern region, with only 17% in the northern regions. Furthermore, 65% of homestays were available for INR 2,000 per night or less, while 31% ranged from INR 2,000 to 5,000 per night. The Mega Trends report by Holiday IQ in 2016 emphasized the significance of homestays within the Indian hospitality industry, particularly within the budget segment. However, the presence of homestays remains concentrated in specific regions, with Kerala and Karnataka being the leaders with 40% and 27% of homestays in India, respectively. Himachal Pradesh stands out in northern India, accounting for 10% of the total number of homestays. Notably, visitor satisfaction ratings in homestays exceed those in alternative lodgings in states like as Kerala, Karnataka, Maharashtra, and Himachal Pradesh, indicating a long-term trend.

4.2 Global Trends in Homestay Tourism

Within developing nations, tourism assumes the role of a catalyst for the growth of small-scale enterprises, which, in turn, contributes to the advancement of local communities (Honey, 1999). Presently, homestay tourism has garnered substantial acclaim as a rural community development initiative due to its inherent characteristics, fostering a sustainable model of tourism. Notably, countries such as Malaysia and Nepal often categorize homestay tourism under the umbrella term "rural tourism" (Yusnita et al., 2013; Ibrahim and Razzaq, 2010; Pham and Kayat, 2011).

In the context of India, the Kerala Homestay and Tourism Society has been instrumental in promoting rural and responsible tourism since 2008. This organization facilitates international homestay and rural tourism events, emphasizing the significance of rural homestays. Research endeavours in multiple countries, including Kenya, Malaysia, Nepal, and Thailand, have directed their focus toward rural homestays, signifying their importance in community-based tourism development.

4.3 Digital Adoption in Homestay Marketing

According to a survey by the American Hotel & Lodging Association, 93% of travellers reported using the internet for travel-related purposes, highlighting the importance of digital channels in reaching potential guests. In India, the rise of digitalization has significantly impacted the travel and hospitality sector. The Internet and Mobile Association of India (IAMAI) reported that the number of internet users in India reached over 624 million by the end of 2019, making it one of the largest online user bases in the world.

Homestay businesses have embraced digital platforms like Airbnb and VRBO, which have grown exponentially in popularity. Airbnb, for instance, had over 7 million listings worldwide in 2020, a testament to its digital transformation success.

- **Mobile Booking and Apps**

Mobile devices have become the primary means for travellers to search, book, and manage their trips. A report by eMarketer estimated that in 2021, 61.8% of digital travel researchers in the U.S. would do so via smartphones.

Homestay platforms have responded to this trend by developing user-friendly mobile apps that allow hosts to manage their listings and interact with guests on the go. These apps facilitate real-time communication, instant bookings, and seamless payment options.

- **Personalization and Data-Driven Marketing**

Data analytics and artificial intelligence have enabled homestay hosts to gather insights into travellers' preferences and behaviours, allowing them to personalize offerings accordingly. A study by Accenture revealed that 91% of consumers are more likely to shop with brands that provide personalized recommendations.

Homestay platforms use machine learning algorithms to recommend properties to potential guests based on their search history and past bookings, enhancing the user experience.

- **Social Media and Influencer Marketing**

Social media platforms have become powerful marketing tools for homestay businesses. Travellers often seek inspiration and recommendations from influencers and fellow travellers on platforms like Instagram, YouTube, and Facebook.

By collaborating with influencers, homestay hosts can showcase their properties to a broader audience and leverage the trust and authenticity that influencers bring to their recommendations.

- **Virtual Experiences and 360-Degree Tours**

During the COVID-19 pandemic, travel restrictions prompted homestay businesses to pivot their marketing strategies by offering virtual experiences and 360-degree property tours.

Virtual tours enable travellers to explore accommodations from the comfort of their homes, enhancing transparency and building trust before making a booking.

5.0 Importance of Tourism Promotion in the Hospitality Industry

Tourism promotion is vital for the hospitality industry. It helps attract travellers, boost business, and support local economies. Effective promotion showcases destinations, accommodations, and unique experiences to potential visitors. This generates interest, leads to bookings, and creates jobs in the hospitality sector. A well-promoted hospitality industry enhances tourism's economic impact, fostering growth and development in communities.

5.1 The Significance of Tourism Promotion in the Hospitality Industry

- **Attracting Travellers:** Tourism promotion helps draw the attention of potential travellers to different destinations and experiences offered by the hospitality industry.
- **Boosting Business:** Effective promotion leads to increased bookings and occupancy rates, which, in turn, boosts revenue for hotels, homestays, and other accommodations.
- **Supporting Local Economies:** A thriving hospitality industry creates job opportunities and stimulates economic growth in the communities where tourism flourishes.
- **Showcasing Destinations:** Promotion highlights the unique attractions and offerings of various destinations, encouraging tourists to explore new places.
- **Encouraging Cultural Exchange:** Tourism promotion fosters cultural exchange as travellers engage with local customs, traditions, and cuisines.
- **Creating Positive Image:** Promotional efforts create a positive image of a destination, making it more appealing and attracting repeat visitors.
- **Driving Investment:** A successful hospitality industry attracts investment in infrastructure and services, further enhancing the tourism experience.
- **Preserving Heritage:** Promotion of cultural sites and historical landmarks supports their preservation for future generations.
- **Stimulating Small Businesses:** Local restaurants, souvenir shops, and other small businesses benefit from increased tourist footfall, boosting their revenues.
- **Contribution to GDP:** The hospitality industry's growth through tourism promotion contributes significantly to the country's GDP and overall economic development.

6.0 Drivers/Motivations for the Hosts in Homestays

The drivers or motivations for hosts in homestays refer to the underlying reasons that prompt individuals or families to open their homes to travellers and offer accommodations. These motivations play a significant role in shaping the homestay experience for both hosts and guests. Several key factors drive hosts to engage in homestays:

Cultural Exchange and Interaction: Many hosts are motivated by a desire to share their local culture, traditions, and way of life with visitors. They see homestays as an opportunity to facilitate cross-cultural interactions, allowing guests to immerse themselves in the local community and gain authentic insights into the host culture.

Personal Connection: Hosts often find fulfillment in forming personal connections with travellers. By welcoming guests into their homes, hosts can establish meaningful relationships, share stories, and create lasting memories. This personal touch sets homestays apart from traditional accommodations.

Unique Experience: Homestays offer a distinct and personalized experience that can't be replicated in hotels or resorts. Hosts may be motivated by a desire to provide guests with a one-of-a-kind stay that highlights the local lifestyle, traditions, and hospitality.

Supplemental Income: Financial considerations are a significant driver for many hosts. Opening their homes to travellers can provide an additional source of income that can be used to cover household expenses, invest in property improvements, or pursue personal goals.

Utilization of Available Space: Hosts with extra rooms or spaces in their homes may choose to utilize these areas for homestays, making practical use of otherwise unused spaces. This can contribute to cost savings for both hosts and guests.

Entrepreneurship: Some hosts view homestays as a business opportunity. They may be motivated by the potential for growth and profit in the hospitality industry, especially as the demand for unique and authentic travel experiences continues to rise.

Social and Networking Opportunities: Engaging with travellers from diverse backgrounds can lead to networking opportunities for hosts. The connections formed during homestays can extend beyond the stays themselves, potentially opening doors to new friendships and professional relationships.

Promotion of Local Tourism: Hosts who are passionate about their local area may be motivated to contribute to local tourism by showcasing the unique attractions and experiences their region has to offer. This can have positive impacts on the overall tourism economy of the area.

Educational Benefits: Some hosts, particularly those with families, may view hosting as an educational experience for themselves and their children. Interacting with travellers from different cultures can broaden perspectives and enhance cultural awareness.

Overall, the motivations for hosts in homestays are diverse and multifaceted, reflecting a combination of personal, cultural, financial, and social factors. These motivations collectively contribute to the rich tapestry of homestay experiences that travellers around the world seek when looking for authentic and immersive accommodations.

7.0 Barriers/Challenges for the Hosts in Homestay Business

Barriers and challenges for hosts in the homestay business can present hurdles that impact their ability to provide successful and satisfying experiences for both themselves and their guests. These challenges can vary based on factors such as location, regulations, market demand, and personal circumstances. Some common barriers include:

Regulatory and Legal Constraints: Navigating local regulations, zoning laws, and licensing requirements for operating a homestay can be complex and time-consuming. Hosts may encounter obstacles in obtaining necessary permits or licenses to legally offer accommodations.

Compliance with Standards: Meeting safety, cleanliness, and hygiene standards set by authorities or platforms can be challenging for hosts. Maintaining a consistently high standard of accommodation is crucial, but it can also require additional investments of time and resources.

Privacy and Security Concerns: Hosts may have concerns about sharing their personal space with strangers, particularly when it comes to privacy and security. Finding a balance between welcoming guests and maintaining a sense of security within their own home can be challenging.

Guest Expectations: Managing guest expectations and providing a satisfactory experience requires effective communication and responsiveness. Hosts may find it challenging to anticipate and fulfill the diverse needs and preferences of guests.

Maintenance and Upkeep: Regular maintenance, repairs, and upkeep of the property can be demanding for hosts. Ensuring that the accommodations remain in good condition and addressing any issues promptly can be time-consuming and financially draining.

Competition and Market Saturation: As the popularity of homestays grows, hosts may face increasing competition in the market. Standing out among other options and attracting bookings can be challenging, especially in areas with a high number of homestays.

Marketing and Visibility: Effective marketing to reach potential guests is essential for success in the homestay business. Hosts may struggle to create a strong online presence, manage bookings, and handle customer inquiries.

Seasonal Fluctuations: Hosts may experience seasonal variations in demand, with peak and off-peak periods impacting their occupancy rates and income. Managing these fluctuations can be challenging, requiring flexibility and strategic planning.

Cultural and Language Differences: Interacting with guests from diverse cultural backgrounds and language barriers can pose challenges in communication, understanding needs, and ensuring guest satisfaction.

Guest Reviews and Ratings: Online reviews and ratings play a significant role in a homestay's reputation. Negative reviews or ratings can have a lasting impact on bookings and credibility, adding pressure for hosts to consistently deliver exceptional experiences.

Logistical Challenges: Coordinating check-ins, check-outs, cleaning schedules, and providing amenities can be logistically challenging, especially for hosts managing multiple properties or dealing with a high volume of guests.

Personal Commitment: Hosting requires a significant personal commitment in terms of time and energy. Balancing the demands of hosting with other responsibilities and personal life can be demanding.

While homestays offer unique opportunities, hosts must overcome these barriers to ensure the smooth and successful operation of their business. Effective planning, adaptation, and a commitment to guest satisfaction are essential in navigating these challenges and building a successful homestay venture.

8.0 Digital Marketing for Homestay Businesses

In today's dynamic hospitality industry, digital marketing has emerged as a game changer for homestay businesses. This approach harnesses online strategies and platforms to not only promote but also elevate the visibility of homestay accommodations. Digital marketing employs a wide array of techniques, aiming to attract potential guests, engage with them on a personal level, and ultimately convert their interest into actual bookings. With the contemporary traveller heavily relying on the internet to research and secure accommodations, a robust digital marketing strategy has become an essential cornerstone for the thriving success of homestay ventures.

At its essence, digital marketing empowers homestay businesses to showcase their distinct offerings effectively. Through optimized websites, engaging content creation, and enhanced user experiences, hosts can establish a compelling online presence that captures the essence and allure of their properties. The digital realm transcends geographical limitations, allowing potential guests worldwide to explore, evaluate, and contemplate various homestay options right from their screens. This empowers hosts to portray their homes in ways that resonate with the preferences and aspirations of their target audience, thereby facilitating an informed and personalized decision-making process.

Social media platforms serve as potent catalysts in bridging the gap between hosts and potential guests. Platforms like Facebook, Instagram, and X (formerly called Twitter) provide interactive avenues for engagement that traditional marketing methods could never offer. Leveraging these platforms, hosts share captivating visuals, intriguing stories, and insightful anecdotes that spark familiarity and curiosity among potential guests. This transformation of the transactional booking process into an interactive and dynamic relationship allows hosts to evolve from mere accommodation providers to storytellers, guides, and even companions on the traveller's journey.

In the competitive hospitality landscape, by harnessing the multifaceted tools and strategies provided by digital platforms, homestay businesses can carve out a distinct niche for themselves. Techniques such as search engine optimization (SEO), pay-per-click advertising, and content marketing empower hosts to rise above the noise and emerge as prominent contenders in a crowded market. As a result, potential guests are more likely to discover, engage with, and ultimately opt for the offerings of these distinct homestays, leading to increased bookings and occupancy rates.

9.0 Importance of Digital Marketing for Homestay Businesses

In the modern landscape of hospitality, digital marketing has emerged as a crucial tool for homestay businesses to thrive and succeed. Leveraging various online strategies and platforms, digital marketing offers a multitude of benefits that enhance visibility, engagement, and growth. Here, we explore the significance and advantages of digital marketing for homestay businesses:

1. **Expanded Reach:** Digital marketing enables homestay businesses to reach a global audience. With optimized websites, engaging content, and online booking platforms, hosts can attract potential guests from different corners of the world. This expanded reach translates into higher occupancy rates and increased bookings.
2. **Targeted Advertising:** Digital marketing allows hosts to target specific demographics and interests. Techniques like pay-per-click advertising and social media campaigns ensure that promotional efforts are directed towards individuals who are more likely to be interested in the homestay offerings.
3. **Cost-Effectiveness:** Traditional advertising methods can be expensive for small homestay businesses. Digital marketing offers cost-effective alternatives, such as social media marketing and email campaigns, allowing hosts to allocate their budgets more efficiently while achieving optimal results.
4. **Personalized Guest Experiences:** Digital marketing enables hosts to tailor their communication and offerings to match the preferences of their guests. Through personalized emails, customized promotions, and relevant content, hosts can create unique and memorable experiences for their guests.
5. **Enhanced Visibility:** With techniques like search engine optimization (SEO), homestay businesses can rank higher in search engine results, making it easier for potential guests to discover them when searching for accommodations in a specific location.
6. **Engagement and Interaction:** Social media platforms provide a direct avenue for hosts to engage and interact with potential and past guests. By sharing captivating visuals, stories, and insights, hosts can create meaningful connections that go beyond mere transactions.
7. **Online Reviews and Reputation:** Digital marketing allows hosts to manage their online reputation through reviews and ratings. Positive reviews can boost credibility and trust and ultimately drive more bookings.
8. **Data Analytics**: Digital marketing provides hosts with valuable insights through data analytics. By analyzing metrics like website traffic, click-through rates, and conversion rates, hosts can refine their strategies and make informed decisions.
9. **Flexibility and Agility:** Digital marketing strategies can be adjusted and adapted in real time based on performance. This agility allows hosts to respond to market changes and trends swiftly.
10. **Competing with Larger Establishments:** Digital marketing levels the playing field, allowing smaller homestay businesses to compete with larger hospitality

establishments. A strong online presence can help hosts stand out, irrespective of their size.

11 **Measurable Results:** Digital marketing efforts are measurable, providing hosts with clear data on the effectiveness of their campaigns. This allows hosts to track their return on investment and adjust strategies accordingly.

12 **Continuous Engagement:** Through regular updates, content sharing, and interactive posts, digital marketing ensures that hosts can maintain consistent engagement with their audience, keeping the brand and offerings fresh in the minds of potential guests.

The importance of digital marketing for homestay businesses cannot be overstated. It serves as a dynamic and essential tool that offers a range of benefits, from increased visibility and engagement to personalization and data-driven decision-making. By embracing digital marketing strategies, hosts can navigate the competitive landscape, connect with their audience on a deeper level, and pave the way for sustained growth and success in the hospitality industry.

10.0 Digital Transformation Trends in the Tourism Industry

Strategies for Modern Hospitality Industry Transformation/Trends	*Uses and Types of Digital Technology*
Guest Experience Enhancement	**Mobile Check-In/Check-Out:** Hotels like Marriott and Hilton offer mobile check-in and keyless room access through their mobile apps, improving guest convenience. **Virtual Concierge:** Chatbots and virtual assistants like IBM's Watson-powered "Connie" at Hilton help guests with inquiries and recommendations. **Personalized Recommendations:** AI-driven systems analyze guest preferences to suggest customized services and experiences.
Online Booking and Reservations	**Online Booking Platforms:** Platforms like Booking.com and Expedia enable easy reservations and comparisons across hotels. **Dynamic Pricing:** AI algorithms adjust room rates in real time based on demand, optimizing revenue.
Streamlined Operations	**Property Management Systems (PMS):** Systems like Opera by Oracle streamline front-desk, reservations, and billing processes. **Inventory Management:** Software tracks inventory levels in restaurants, bars, and stores, preventing stock-outs or overstocking. **Workflow Automation:** Tools automate tasks like housekeeping assignments, reducing manual errors.

(*Continued*)

(Continued)

Strategies for Modern Hospitality Industry Transformation/Trends	*Uses and Types of Digital Technology*
Marketing and Promotion	**Social Media Marketing:** Hotels use platforms like Instagram and Facebook to showcase amenities and engage with guests. **Email Campaigns:** Targeted email campaigns inform customers about promotions and events. **Influencer Collaborations:** Hotels collaborate with influencers for reviews and promotions.
Data Analytics and Insights	**Guest Behaviour Analysis:** Analyzing data helps hotels understand guest preferences and adapt services accordingly. **Demand Forecasting**: AI algorithms predict demand patterns to optimize inventory and staffing. **Competitor Analysis:** Monitoring competitor data helps in setting competitive pricing and strategies.
Contactless Services	**Mobile Payments:** Contactless payment methods like Apple Pay and Google Wallet expedite transactions. **QR Code Menus:** QR codes on tables allow customers to view menus on their devices, reducing physical contact. **Room Controls:** Guests control room amenities like lights and temperature through mobile apps.

Source: By author

11.0 Uses of Digital Marketing Transformation to Overcome Homestay Business Challenges

- **Regulatory and Legal Constraints:**
  Digital Education: Hosts can access online resources and platforms to understand local regulations and legal requirements for homestay operations. This digital knowledge empowers them to navigate the legal landscape more effectively.
- **Compliance with Standards:**
  Online Guides and Tutorials: Digital platforms can provide guides, tutorials, and checklists for hosts to understand and adhere to safety and cleanliness standards. These resources facilitate compliance and promote better guest experiences.
- **Privacy and Security Concerns:**
  Transparent Communication: Digital communication channels allow hosts to clearly communicate their privacy measures and security protocols to potential guests before they arrive. This transparency helps alleviate concerns and build trust.

- **Guest Expectations:**
  Online Booking Platforms: Digital platforms allow hosts to provide accurate and detailed descriptions of their accommodations, setting clear expectations for guests. High-quality images, virtual tours, and detailed amenities can showcase what guests can expect.
- **Maintenance and Upkeep:**
  Maintenance Scheduling Apps: Digital tools enable hosts to set up maintenance schedules and receive automated reminders for repairs and upkeep tasks. This helps hosts stay organized and ensures the property remains in good condition.
- **Competition and Market Saturation:**
  Online Presence: Effective digital marketing strategies, such as search engine optimization and social media campaigns, can help hosts stand out from competitors by increasing their visibility to potential guests.
- **Marketing and Visibility:**
  Social Media Engagement: Utilizing social media platforms allows hosts to engage directly with potential guests, share content, and respond to inquiries. This engagement enhances the host's online presence and fosters a sense of community.
- **Seasonal Fluctuations:**
  Dynamic Pricing Tools: Digital tools can analyze market trends and demand, allowing hosts to adjust pricing dynamically based on peak and off-peak periods, optimizing occupancy rates.
- **Cultural and Language Differences:**
  Translation Apps and Services: Digital translation tools facilitate effective communication between hosts and guests who may speak different languages, ensuring a smooth and comfortable stay.
- **Guest Reviews and Ratings:**
  Feedback Management: Digital platforms enable hosts to monitor guest reviews and ratings, allowing them to respond promptly to feedback and address concerns, enhancing their online reputation.
- **Logistical Challenges:**
  Booking Management Systems: Digital booking systems streamline check-ins, check-outs, and communication with guests. Automated processes reduce logistical challenges and ensure a smoother operation.
- **Personal Commitment:**
  Scheduling and Automation: Digital scheduling tools can help hosts manage their time more efficiently, allowing them to balance their personal commitments with the demands of hosting.

Incorporating digital transformation in marketing strategies equips hosts in the homestay business with the tools and resources needed to overcome various challenges. By leveraging technology, hosts can enhance guest experiences, streamline operations, improve communication, and ultimately create a more successful and rewarding homestay business.

12.0 Artificial Intelligence (AI) in Homestays

Artificial intelligence (AI) has revolutionized the hospitality industry, including the homestay sector, by offering innovative solutions that significantly enhance customer experiences. Through AI-powered technologies, homestay businesses can provide tailored and seamless services, creating a more personalized and enjoyable stay for their guests.

Personalized Recommendations: AI algorithms analyze guest preferences and behaviours to provide personalized recommendations for local attractions, activities, and dining options. This enhances the guest's experience by catering to their individual interests.

Smart Room Control: AI-enabled devices in homestays allow guests to control room settings like lighting, temperature, and entertainment systems through voice commands or mobile apps, enhancing convenience and comfort.

Efficient Booking Process: AI chatbots streamline the booking process, answering guest queries and guiding them through reservations 24/7, improving booking efficiency and guest satisfaction.

Predictive Analytics: AI analyzes historical data to predict demand patterns, helping hosts optimize pricing and availability for maximum occupancy and revenue.

Enhanced Safety and Security: AI-powered surveillance systems can monitor homestay premises for enhanced security, ensuring a safe environment for guests.

Natural Language Processing: AI-driven communication tools can translate languages and assist hosts in interacting with guests who speak different languages, bridging cultural gaps.

Virtual Assistants: AI-based virtual assistants can provide instant responses to guest queries, aiding in addressing concerns promptly and creating a smoother stay experience.

Personalized In-Room Services: AI-driven platforms can customize in-room services based on guest preferences, such as preferred amenities, room setup, and meal preferences.

Feedback Analysis: AI tools analyze guest feedback to identify trends and areas of improvement, enabling hosts to enhance their services continually.

Check-In and Check-Out Automation: AI-powered kiosks or mobile apps can facilitate quick and hassle-free check-in and check-out processes, minimizing wait times for guests.

13.0 Future of Digital Transformation in the Homestay Industry

The future of digital transformation in the hospitality industry is a landscape that seamlessly blends technology with guest comfort and satisfaction. Imagine a scenario in which travellers walk into a hotel, bypass the front desk, and enter their rooms using a digital key on their smartphones. As they explore the room, voice-activated devices adjust lighting, temperature, and entertainment according to their preferences. Throughout their stay, AI-powered chatbots answer questions promptly and efficiently, suggesting nearby attractions and restaurants based on past choices. Meanwhile, augmented reality guides them through immersive virtual tours of the destination's landmarks, enhancing their understanding and anticipation. In this future, data analytics provide valuable insights into guest preferences, enabling hotels to craft personalized experiences that feel tailored to each individual.

Consider also the impact on sustainability. IoT-enabled smart rooms monitor energy consumption, adjusting settings to conserve resources when rooms are unoccupied. Digital platforms allow guests to customize their stay, opting for reduced housekeeping services to minimize water and energy usage. Real-time data analysis informs hotels about areas where waste can be reduced and eco-friendly practices can be promoted. In this way, the digital transformation not only enhances guest experiences but also contributes to the industry's broader sustainability efforts.

The future of digital transformation in the homestay industry holds the promise of a more connected, personalized, and efficient guest journey. From contactless experiences to AI-driven personalization, every aspect of the guest experience is set to evolve. With the right balance of technology and human touch, the hospitality industry is poised for a new era where innovation enhances guest comfort and service excellence.

14.0 Forecasts for Homestay Marketing

The future of homestay marketing is set to transform significantly, driven by predictions that highlight the evolving hospitality landscape. An ongoing trend is the growth of online bookings. With the convenience of digital platforms, it's anticipated that homestay reservations will continue to dominate. Statista forecasts online travel booking revenue to hit $755 billion by 2023 (Statista).

A major innovation is the introduction of virtual reality (VR) tours as a method of showcasing properties. These VR tours, which are expected to become widespread, provide potential tourists with immersive experiences. The VR market is expected to be valued at $209.2 billion by 2022, demonstrating its growing importance in the sector.

Artificial intelligence (AI) is poised to reshape guest experiences through personalization. Deloitte predicts 73% of travellers will use AI to customize their journeys by 2021 (Deloitte). Social media's influence on bookings will remain strong. Around 75% of users on platforms like Instagram take action after being inspired by travel-related posts, indicating their ongoing impact (Omnicore Agency). Sustainability will gain traction, with 72% of travellers planning to choose eco-friendly accommodations by 2021 (Booking.com).

Voice assistants will enhance guest services, aligned with the projected $27.16 billion voice-recognition market by 2023 (Markets and Markets). Homestays will focus on offering authentic, hyper-local experiences, driven by 67% of global travellers preferring culturally rich stays (Skift).

Enhanced cleaning and safety measures will stay a priority, as 82% of travellers prioritize cleanliness when selecting accommodations (Booking.com). Overall, these insights underline the future of homestay marketing, showcasing the importance of technology, personalization, sustainability, and safety in catering to evolving traveller preferences.

15.0 Recommendations for Business Practices: The Key to Success

We will explore key recommendations for business practices that are essential for achieving success in the rapidly evolving landscape of homestay businesses, particularly in the context of promoting tourism in the hospitality industry through digital transformation. These recommendations serve as a practical blueprint to navigate the challenges and capitalize on the opportunities presented in the digital age.

Embrace Technology and Digital Transformation: The foundation of success in the modern hospitality industry lies in embracing digital transformation. Homestay businesses must invest in robust property management systems, online booking platforms, and websites that are user friendly and mobile responsive. These tools enhance customer experience, streamline operations, and facilitate efficient communication with guests. By leveraging technology, you can stay competitive and meet the ever-growing expectations of today's tech-savvy travellers.

Data-Driven Decision-Making: Harness the power of data analytics to make informed decisions. Collect and analyze data on guest preferences, booking patterns, and market trends. By understanding your guests better, you can tailor your offerings and marketing strategies to maximize customer satisfaction and revenue.

Personalization and Customer Engagement: Use the insights derived from data analytics to create personalized experiences for your guests. Tailor your marketing campaigns and services to meet the specific needs and preferences of individual guests. Engage with customers through social media, email marketing, and personalized offers to build lasting relationships and encourage repeat business.

Online Reputation Management: Your online reputation can make or break your homestay business. Encourage guests to leave reviews on popular platforms like TripAdvisor and Google. Address both positive and negative feedback promptly and professionally. A strong online reputation will attract new guests and reassure potential customers about the quality of your services.

Sustainability and Eco-Friendly Practices: As sustainability becomes a focal point in the hospitality industry, adopting eco-friendly practices is not just a trend but a necessity. Implement energy-efficient systems, reduce waste, and promote eco-friendly policies to attract environmentally conscious travellers and lower operational costs.

Continuous Learning and Training: Invest in the development of your staff through ongoing training and professional development programmes. Equip your team with the necessary skills and knowledge to provide exceptional service, handle digital tools, and adapt to changing industry trends. A well-trained staff is an invaluable asset to your business.

Collaborations and Partnerships: Forge partnerships with local businesses, travel agencies, and tourism boards. Collaborations can expand your reach and provide access to a broader customer base. Joint marketing efforts and package deals can be mutually beneficial and enhance the overall guest experience.

Regulatory Compliance and Ethical Practices: Stay up-to-date with local regulations and industry standards. Compliance ensures the safety and security of your guests and protects your business from legal issues. Additionally, ethical practices in all aspects of your operation, from employment to guest interactions, build trust and reputation.

Crisis Management and Contingency Planning: Prepare for unforeseen events by developing a comprehensive crisis management plan. This plan should cover scenarios such as natural disasters, global crises, and pandemics. Quick and effective responses during challenging times can make a significant difference in maintaining business continuity.

Focus on Feedback and Adaptation: Finally, remain open to feedback from both guests and your team. Continuous improvement is a core component of successful business practices. Be willing to adapt to changing circumstances, emerging technologies, and evolving guest expectations.

The recommendations for business practices outlined in this chapter serve as a roadmap for homestay businesses aiming to excel in the digital era and contribute to the promotion of tourism in the hospitality industry. By embracing digital transformation, emphasizing data-driven decision making, prioritizing customer engagement, and adhering to sustainable and ethical principles, you can position your business for long-term success. The journey towards success is ongoing, and a commitment to learning, adapting, and delivering exceptional guest experiences will set you on the path to achieving your goals in this dynamic and competitive industry.

16.0 Leverage the Power of Social Media

Develop a strong social media presence and encourage user-generated content to drive bookings and loyalty.

In summary, the future of business practices in hospitality and homestays revolves around technology, sustainability, personalization, trust, local experiences, and social media. Embracing these trends positions businesses for enduring success in this dynamic industry. Adapt and thrive in the evolving landscape.

17.0 Conclusion

- **Summary of Findings:** The findings of this study underscore the significance of embracing technological advancements in homestay marketing. The projected continued growth of online bookings reflects the convenience and accessibility offered by digital platforms. The integration of VR tours and AI-driven personalization enhances guest engagement and satisfaction. Social media's influential impact on decision-making remains steadfast, while the emphasis on sustainable practices and local experiences reflects changing traveller preferences.

- **Implications for Homestay Businesses:** These findings hold crucial implications for homestay businesses. Recognizing the transformative potential of digital marketing, VR, and AI is no longer a choice but a necessity. Focusing on sustainability, providing hyper-local experiences, and integrating voice assistants can set businesses apart and cater to guests seeking authenticity. Implementing thorough cleaning and safety protocols instills trust and confidence in a post-pandemic world. Homestay operators must embrace these implications to stand out in a competitive market and craft memorable, immersive guest experiences.
- **Recommendations for Future Marketing Strategies:** Drawing insights from this research, several recommendations emerge to shape effective future marketing strategies for homestay businesses. A strong emphasis on digital marketing campaigns and user-friendly websites is essential for captivating tech-savvy travellers. The integration of VR tours and AI personalization can elevate guest engagement. Harnessing the power of social media platforms can amplify brand visibility and attract potential guests. Prioritizing sustainability initiatives and offering culturally immersive experiences aligns with conscientious traveller trends. Finally, ensuring meticulous implementation of cleaning and safety protocols demonstrates a commitment to guest well-being. Embracing these recommendations positions homestay businesses for enduring success in an ever-evolving hospitality landscape.

In conclusion, this comprehensive exploration of the homestay industry's future unveils a landscape deeply influenced by digital transformation and evolving traveller preferences. The predictions and trends discussed emphasize the pivotal role of technology in reshaping marketing strategies and guest experiences. The convergence of online bookings, VR tours, AI, and social media underscores the dynamic nature of the hospitality sector.

Bibliography

Accenture (2019). *Personalization Pulse Check: The Key to B2B Customer Experience*. Retrieved from www.accenture.com/us-en/insights/consulting/sales-service-personalization-pulse-check.

Arneson, E. (2018, April 16). *The Ins and Outs of a Bed-and-Breakfast*. Retrieved April 20, 2018 from https://www.tripsavvy.com/what-is-a-bed-and-breakfast-310118.

Arzoumanidis, I., Petti, L., & Raggi, A. (2022). Online booking platforms: Towards making more sustainable choices. *Cleaner Production Letters*, 3, 100009.

Banerjee, J. (2017, June 24). The unique experiences of heritage hotels and homestays. *Forbes India*. Retrieved from www.forbesindia.com/article/recliner/the-unique experiences-of-heritage-hotels-and-homestays/47337/1.

Busulwa, R., Pickering, M., & Mao, I. (2022). Digital transformation and hospitality management competencies: Toward an integrative framework. *International Journal of Hospitality Management*, 102, 103132.

Cenni, I., & Vásquez, C. (2022). Early adopters' responses to a virtual tourism product: Airbnb's online experiences. *International Journal of Culture, Tourism and Hospitality Research*, 16(1), 121–137.

Choudhary, S., & Rai, R. (2007, November 29). Home in on homestays. *Business Today*. Retrieved from https://www.businesstoday.in/moneytoday/travel/home-in-onhomestays/story/6856.html.

Craig, D. (2017). *The Incredible Shrinking Hotel Industry*. Hospitality Net. Retrieved from www.hospitalitynet.org/opinion/4080555.html.

Curnes, A., Dirks, J., Hohn, C., Kreun, A., Royal, T., Zadalis, J. (2023). *Airbnb Strategic Audit Overview*. Undergraduate Honors Thesis. University of Nebraska-Lincoln. url: https://digitalcommons.unl.edu/honorstheses/627/.

Deloitte. (2020). *2020 Hospitality Industry Outlook*. Retrieved from https://www2.deloitte.com/us/en/insights/industry/hospitality-and-leisure/hospitality-industry-outlook.html.

Dube, A., & Sharma, R. A. (2018). Playing a homestay host: Drivers and barriers. *International Journal of Tourism and Travel*, 11(1 & 2), 60–66.

eMarketer. (2021, April). *Social Media Usage During the Travel Purchase Journey According to Travelers Worldwide*. Retrieved from www.emarketer.com/chart/244576/social-media-usage-during-travel-purchase-journey-according-travelers-worldwide-april-2021.

Honey, M. (1999). *Ecotourism and Sustainable Development: Who Owns Paradise?* Island Press.

Ibrahim, Y., & Razzaq, A. R. A. (2010). Homestay program and rural community development in Malaysia. *Journal of Ritsumeikan Social Sciences and Humanities*, 2(1), 7–24.

Ifrach, B. (2015). How Airbnb uses machine learning to detect host preferences. *Airbnb*. Retrieved from https://medium. com/airbnb-engineering/how-airbnb-uses-machine-learning-to-detect-host-preferences-18ce07 150fa3 [48].

Jain, B. (2017, June 13). Maharashtra tourism development corporation ties up with Airbnb to boost bookings. *Times of India*. Retrieved from https://timesofindia.indiatimes.com/city/mumbai/maharashtra-tourism-developmentcorporation-ties-up-with-airbnb-to-boost-bookings/articleshow/59130101.cms.

Johnson, A. G., & Mehta, B. (2022). Fostering the inclusion of women as entrepreneurs in the sharing economy through collaboration: A commons approach using the institutional analysis and development framework. *Journal of Sustainable Tourism*, 1–19.

Kennedy, P. S. J., Tobing, S. J. L., & Toruan, R. L. (2022). Marketing strategy with marketing mix for Lake Toba tourism destination. *Journal of Sustainable Tourism and Entrepreneurship (JoSTE)*, 3(3), 157–174.

Kumar, S., Kumar, V., Kumari Bhatt, I., Kumar, S., & Attri, K. (2023). Digital transformation in tourism sector: Trends and future perspectives from a bibliometric-content analysis. *Journal of Hospitality and Tourism Insights*, ahead-of-print. https://doi.org/10.1108/JHTI-10-2022-0472.

Pham, L., & Kayat, K. (2011). Residents' perceptions of tourism impact and their support for tourism development: The case study of Cuc Phuong National Park, Ninh Binh province, Vietnam. *European Journal of Tourism Research*, 4(2), 123–146.

Press Trust of India. (2017, January 6). Rightstay tie up to promote tourism. *Business Standard*. Retrieved from www.business-standard.com/article/pti-stories/assam-govt-make mytrip-s-rightstay-tie-up-to-promotetourism-117010600856_1.html.

Richardson, K. (2003, October). International education: The quality of homestay services. In *Presented at the 17th IDP Australian International Education Conference*, Melbourne.

Richardson, K. (2004, October 5–8). Homestay: Opening a world of opportunity. In *18th IDP Australian International Education Conference*, Sydney Convention Centre, Sydney, Australia.

Rivers, W. P. (1998). Is being there enough? The effects of homestay placements on language gain during study abroad. *Foreign Language Annals*, 31(4), 492–500.

Rosário, A. T. (2023). Security in digital marketing: Challenges and opportunities. *Confronting Security and Privacy Challenges in Digital Marketing*, 206–233.

Sharma, A. (2016, April 28). Government works to encourage home stays, promote tourism. *Economic Times*. Retrieved from http://economictimes.indiatimes.com/industry/services/travel/government-works-to-encouragehomestays-promote-tourism/articleshow/52016654.cms.

Singhal, M. (2017, March 25). Odisha tourism to promote homestay facilities. *Times of India*. Retrieved from https://timesofindia.indiatimes.com/city/bhubaneswar/odisha-tourism-to-promote-homestay-facilities/articleshow/57830148.cms.

Statista. (2022). *Vacation Rentals Market Size Worldwide from 2015 to 2023*. Retrieved from www.statista.com/statistics/1071374/vacation-rentals-market-size-worldwide/.

Yusnita, Y., Shaladdin, M. M., Aziz, A. W., & Ibrahim, Y. (2013). Rural tourism in Malaysia: A homestay program. *China-USA Business Review*, 12(3), 300–306.

Yusof, Y., Muda, M. S., Amin, W. A., & Ibrahim, Y. (2013). Rural tourism in Malaysia: A homestay program. *China-USA Business Review*, 12(3), 300–306.

Websites

www.airbnb.co.in/resources/hosting-homes/a/recommend-local-activities-with-this-simple-tool-477?locale=en&_set_bev_on_new_domain=1698634901_YmYxNmY0OWQ4MTg1.

https://ecobnb.com/.

www.gstcouncil.org/booking-com-2023-sustainable-travel-report/.

https://hellopartner.com/2022/09/12/is-user-generated-content-the-new-influencer-marketing/.

www.marketsandmarkets.com/Market-Reports/augmented-reality-virtual-reality-market-1185.html.

https://news.booking.com/en-us/bookingcom-reveals-how-travel-will-reset-itself-in-2021/.

www.omnicoreagency.com/instagram-statistics/.

www.phocuswire.com/why-the-hotel-ai-chatbot-is-a-must-have-for-data-collection.

https://skift.com/2022/12/22/how-blockchain-technology-is-disrupting-the-online-travel-agency-model/.

https://skift.com/2019/10/03/67-of-global-travelers-prefer-authentic-local-experiences-new-skift-research/.https://globalnews.booking.com/72-of-travelers-intend-to-make-more-sustainable-choices-in-2021-according-to-new-research-by-bookingcom/.

www.statista.com/statistics/226840/digital-travel-sales-worldwide/.

https://www2.deloitte.com/us/en/pages/consumer-business/articles/travel-hospitality-trends.html.

9 Assessment of Enablers for Adoption of Blockchain Technology in the Indian Hospitality Industry

Dr. Smita Sharma and
Dr. Roopashree Raghavendra Rao

1. Introduction

Blockchain technology has made a substantial contribution to many industry areas. The hospitality industry can also use this technology in various service dimensions of security, payments, and the hotel's overall experiential setting. A major tourist destination, India must quickly digitalise business processes and practices (Dash, 2023). Blockchain enables transparency across the value chain by tracking a product's origin, location, and history (Cozzio et al., 2023; Kizildag et al., 2020). Due to its effective features of transparency and disintermediation, blockchain technology can transform the tourism and hospitality industry. It has been effectively used in enhancing marketing capabilities in various industries (Doshi and Sandhane, 2022; Verma and Kaur, 2022) and has also been assessed positively by consumers for providing various benefits (Noonan and Doran, 2021). Studies have validated the role of blockchain in transforming the traditional tourism enterprise and recent tourism business concepts (Dhiraj et al., 2023). It has also been reported to enhance the sustainability performance of the tourism business (Chaudhuri et al., 2023). Due to these multifaceted applications, Indian hotels are moving towards incorporating blockchain technology in their processes and practices (Sharma et al., 2021). Blockchain implementation in the Indian hospitality sector is a relatively young and developing field (Önder and Gunter, 2022b; Ahmad and Samsudin, 2022). Most currently available research focuses on blockchain's advantages and prospective applications in the hospitality sector (Nuryyev et al., 2021). Hotels and other stakeholders will need research that provides clear adoption patterns and standards to implement blockchain effectively (Rajaguru, 2023). Thus, the present research analyses the major enablers for adopting blockchain as per the opinions of hospitality experts in the industry.

The research questions which this study attempts to answer are as follows:

RQ1. What are the enablers for incorporating blockchain technology in the Indian hospitality sector?

RQ2. What causal interactions exist among the enablers for incorporating blockchain technology in the Indian hospitality sector?

RQ3. How can the enablers of blockchain technology in the Indian hospitality industry be prioritised for adding value to the sector?

DOI: 10.4324/9781003488248-9

The study also performs a sensitivity analysis to verify the robustness of the results.

The study is organised as follows: Section 1 elucidates an introduction to blockchain technology in the hospitality sector. The review of the literature is covered in Section 2. The methodology for the study is depicted in Section 3. This is followed by Section 4, which provides insights into using blockchain technology in the hospitality sector. Section 5 provides results and discussion. This is further followed by Section 6, which sheds light on the various policy implications; Section 7, which provides the recommendations for business practices; Section 8, which concludes and suggests the future scope of the study; and Section 9, which lists the limitations.

2. Review of Literature

2.1 Scenario of Blockchain Technology in the Hospitality Sector

Reviewing the existing literature suggests that Hospitality 5.0 integrates technology into the hospitality domain (Gangwar and Reddy, 2023). These humanistic systems can fulfil the customer and employee requirements and expectations to a large extent (Wolfe, 2017; Ahmad and Samsudin, 2022; Puri et al., 2023). Blockchain is thus considered to disrupt and transform the current tourism and hospitality landscape (Lin et al., 2023). Studies have also highlighted the initiatives undertaken by the government of India to incorporate blockchain in various industries (Johari et al., 2021). Thus, the Indian hospitality industry can significantly benefit from blockchain technology (Khanna et al., 2020).

2.2 Enablers of Blockchain Technology in the Hospitality Industry

Various technologies based on blockchain have been known to create significant interventions in the hospitality industry. Certain services, such as smart contracts based on blockchain technology, have contributed to various applications like hotel reservations, car rentals, payment and reward management systems, etc. These applications gained a huge impetus during 2018–19, enabling time and transaction cost savings. Techniques like distributed ledger technologies (DLT) practice the concepts of cryptography for securing data and providing a unique signature, which, in turn, supports financial transactions to authorised users only; most importantly, it helps maintain the integrity of the transaction. Blockchain can also store transaction records to avoid money laundering, which helps avoid transaction breaches (Raj et al., 2023).

Some studies (Filimonau and Naumova, 2020a) attempt to close the existing knowledge gap in different industrial sectors spanning various markets by developing a framework. This encompasses blockchain technology involving the organisational, institutional, and technological challenges to enable appropriate solutions to the problems.

Various studies in China (Cheng, 2023) have validated that blockchain in hospitality can significantly impact the transparency, efficiency, and cost reduction of the various operations in the hospitality industry. Similar studies in Bangladesh

(Karim et al., 2023) on blockchain mobile payment in Bangladesh reveal that privacy, security, and customer satisfaction mediate the payment and loyalty intentions of customers.

Top management support has also been a major enabler in bringing about disruptive hotel changes (Sharma and Mathur, 2020). An attempt to study the benefits associated with adopting this technology and a discussion of the preliminary architecture, the functional details of the drivers, and the loopholes in the adoption are evaluated. Further, the identification of the gap in the literature and the further directions for evaluating the future application in the tourism and hospitality sector are also highlighted in a study by Marco et al. (2020) and Shao et al. (n.d.).

The issues faced by the operators in the hospitality sector are carried out by evaluating the various business models and the possibility of applying blockchain technology to enhance transparency, efficiency, and optimisation of the cost factor. The research highlights the various effects of the study on the sector and enumerates the possible upcoming avenues (Cheng, 2023). Studies have also revealed the application of blockchain technology to improve the efficiency in operation, revenue, security, and privacy issues in the hospitality industry and suggest a two-step research process (Khanna et al., 2020).

Blockchain technology is advocated as a solution to fill the gaps that are left unaddressed by the existing technology in areas like robustness, data storage, network latency, auditability, immutability, and traceability (Bodkhe et al., 2020a).

There have been around seventeen enablers extracted from the literature. As per the expert opinion, fifteen were retained for the final study. Table 9.1 reflects

Table 9.1 Criteria for Choosing the Important Enablers

S. No.	*Enablers of Sustainability Practices*	*Review of Literature Review (Y/N)*	*Opinion of Experts (Y/N)*	*Opinion Final (Y/N)*
1	Reduction in Cost	Y	N	Y
2	Traceability and Transparency	Y	Y	Y
3	Automation	Y	Y	Y
4	Disintermediation of the existing systems	Y	Y	Y
5	Government Regulations	Y	Y	N
6	Top Management Support	Y	Y	Y
7	Privacy	Y	Y	Y
8	Reduced System Complexity	Y	Y	Y
9	Trust	Y	Y	Y
10	Database security	Y	Y	Y
11	Immutability	Y	Y	Y
12	Decentralised Database	Y	Y	Y
13	Risk Aversion	Y	Y	Y
14	Collaborative communities	Y	N	N
15	Stakeholder Pressure	Y	Y	Y
16	Increased Service Efficiency	Y	N	N
17	Improved System Resilience	Y	N	N

Source: By authors

various criteria for selecting the enablers of adopting blockchain technology in the hospitality sector. Table 9.2 reflects the exhaustive summary of enablers used for our study. Two rounds of expert surveys were performed. One for finalising the enablers and the other to analyse the finalised enablers for cause-and-its effect relationships among them.

Table 9.2 Consolidation of the Important Enablers and the Corresponding Codes

Enabler Code	*Enablers*	*Details of the Enablers*	*References to Support the Enablers*
B1	Reduction in Cost	To sustain financially by optimising resource optimisation and striving for profitability.	(Sharma et al., 2021)
B2	Traceability and Transparency	This ensures the location, the involved supply chain functions, and the capacity to disseminate the same to all stakeholders.	(Cheng, 2023)
B3	Automation	To reduce cost and time, a mechanism to reduce the involvement of human-interface manual tasks, which is time-consuming.	(Sharma et al., 2021)
B4	Disintermediation of the Existing Systems	The propensity to enable direct association with the guests.	(Lin et al., 2023)
B5	Government Regulations	The regulations ensure a safe, reliable, and secure environment to succeed.	(Sharma et al. 2021)
B6	Top Management Support	The support to facilitate planning, reviewing, and providing adequate feedback to solve management problems.	(Sharma and Mathur, 2020)
B7	Stakeholder Pressure	The extent to which the organisations' decisions influence the stakeholders.	(Hsu and Leung 2022)
B8	Risk Aversion	The inclination to move away from the risks.	(Karim et al., 2023)
B9	Increased Service Efficiency	Optimisation of labor and time in the labor-intensive industry to achieve efficiency.	(Zhou et al., 2018)
B10	Decentralised Database	A database which does not have central data storage.	(Raj et al., 2023)

(*Continued*)

Table 9.2 (Continued)

Enabler Code	*Enablers*	*Details of the Enablers*	*References to Support the Enablers*
B11	Trust	The ability to attract and achieve maximum retention of customers.	(Salah et al., 2019)
B12	Database Security	Capability to prevent corruption, theft, and access to unauthorised sources.	(Raj et al., 2023)
B13	Collaborative Communities	The ability to facilitate teamwork and a collaborative culture.	(Salah et al., 2019)
B14	Reduced System Complexity	To facilitate adaptability of the systems involved.	(Agi, 2022)
B15	Improved System Resilience	Capability to adapt to the changing demands of the external environment.	(Bodkhe et al., 2019)

Source: By authors

2.3 Theory of Grey System and DEMATEL

2.3.1 Grey System Theory and DEMATEL

The decision-making trial and evaluation laboratory (DEMATEL) method has been used to handle complicated causal relationships among the variables through a combination of matrices or (and) graphs (Jeng and Tzeng, 2012). Earlier studies on DEMATEL have focussed on technology adoption in supply chains (Azar and Andalib Ardakani, 2014; Effendi et al., 2019). The use of DEMATEL, especially in the hospitality domain, has been naïve and still needs to be explored. The present study utilises the combination of grey theory and DEMATEL to evaluate causal relationships among the enablers of the adoption of blockchain technology in the Indian hospitality sector.

3. Methodology

The tool utilised for the study is GREY DEMATEL. This helps decision-makers understand the complicated relationships among the factors extracted from the literature. The study utilised a mix of various matrices and graphs as DEMATEL provides a set of complex relatabilities concerning the identified barriers. The DEMATEL methodology uses a smaller sample to identify the relationship between the causal variables. Azar and Andalib Ardakani (2014) introduced the grey systems theory to uncover the underlying causes as expressed using grey numbers.

It assists in decision-making and helps overcome imprecise human judgements. The modified CFCS (converting fuzzy values into crisp scores) technique can convert the grey values into crisp values. The present research thus utilises the grey theory and DEMATEL to explore the cause-and-effect interrelationships between the barriers to effective waste management. The steps followed for the grey DEMATEL approach follow Singh et al., 2023.

Step 1: To generate initial relation matrices.

Suppose the initial participant number is *d*, and the barrier is *v*. Use various linguistic assessment codes like NE, VLE, LE, ME, HE, and VHE. In that case, each expert *p* evaluates the strength of enablers as provided in Table 9.1. *The* expert opinions collected the first relation matrices.

Step 2: Enumerate the matrix for grey relation.

Conversion of the value of the integer into relative grey values using the following equation; $(\otimes z_{ij}^{t} = \underline{\otimes} z_{ij}^{t}, \overline{\otimes} z_{ij}^{t})$. (1) $where\ 1 \le t \le o; 1 \le i \le b; 1 \le j \le b$ and ($\underline{\otimes} z_{ij}^{k}$ and $\overline{\otimes} z_{ij}^{k}$) shows the upper and lower limit of the corresponding grey values applicable in the context of associated participant.

Step 3: Calculate the matrix for the average grey-relation.

The simple average grey relation matrix *can be evaluated* $\otimes \tilde{z}_{ij}$ from *d* matrices of grey relation $\otimes z_{ij}^{t}$ as shown in the following;

$$\otimes \tilde{z}_{ij} = \left(\frac{\sum_{k} \underline{\otimes} z_{ij}^{t}}{l}, \frac{\sum_{k} \overline{\otimes} z_{ij}^{t}}{l} \right). \tag{2}$$

Step 4: From the average grey-relation matrix, compute the crisp-relation matrix.

Generation of crisp values is performed using the CFCS-modified method; the crisp values can be obtained using the following steps (Dou et al., 2014):

i The final crisp value is then evaluated;

$$A_{ij}^{*} = \left(min \underline{\otimes} \tilde{z}_{ij} + \left(a_{ij} \times \Delta_{min}^{max} \right) \right), \tag{3}$$

$$\text{and } A = \left[a_{ij}^{*} \right]. \tag{4}$$

Step 5: Calculate the normalised direct crisp-relation matrix (V).

Enumerate the direct crisp-relation matrix (V) by computing M (Normalisation factor) and multiplying the crisp-relation matrix L with E.

$$M = \frac{1}{\max_{1 \le i \le m} \sum_{j=i}^{m} y_{ij}^{*}}, \tag{5}$$

$$\text{and } V = E \times L \tag{6}$$

Step 6: Assess the total relation-matrix F.
The total relation matrix (F) is shown in Equation (11);

$$F = M \times (F - M)^{-1}. \tag{7}$$

Where F indicates the identity matrix
Step 7: Compute the cause-and-effect parameters.
Compute the sum of various row (R_i) elements and columns (C_j) elements. For row (i) and column (j), the sum is computed from the total relation matrix (F), as mentioned under

$$R_i = \left[\sum_{j=1}^{m} F_{ij}\right] \forall \text{ i}, \tag{8}$$

$$C_j = \left[\sum_{i=1}^{m} F_{ij}\right] \forall \text{j}. \tag{9}$$

The sum $(R_i + C_j)$ gives the complete impact an individual barrier *i* has on remaining barriers. The net effect is provided by $(R_i - C_j)$ g, which also impacts other barriers.
Step 8: Finalise the threshold value and plot the digraph.
The threshold value is determined by evaluating the mean of the total relation matrix (F). The digraph is plotted from the data set of: (cap R sub i. plus cap C sub j), open paren cap R sub i. minus cap C sub j close paren ∀ i=j.

4. Utility of the Model Proposed

Technology integration has increased impetus in all service industry setups. With the governments focussing more on integrating change management and upgradation of present systems to incorporate technological interventions, industries need to rethink the processes undertaken to improve the overall service delivery experience in the hospitality industry. However, only some studies have addressed this part of the issue, concentrating on enablers of adopting blockchain technology in hospitality-sector products.

The present study initially identified seventeen enablers from the literature review, further scaled down to fifteen after expert opinion. For the second survey, six experts were approached, of which four agreed to be a part of the study. The details of the experts who were a part of the study are depicted in Table 9.4. These were further analysed for relationships between the cause and its effect using the grey DEMATEL technique. The pictorial representation of the methodology is depicted in Figure 9.1.

Four surveys were administered in person to the experts, and their responses were recorded on the incorporated linguistic scale (refer to Table 9.3). The details of the experts who were a part of the study are depicted in Table 9.4. These were further analysed for the relationship between the cause and its effect using this decision-making technique.

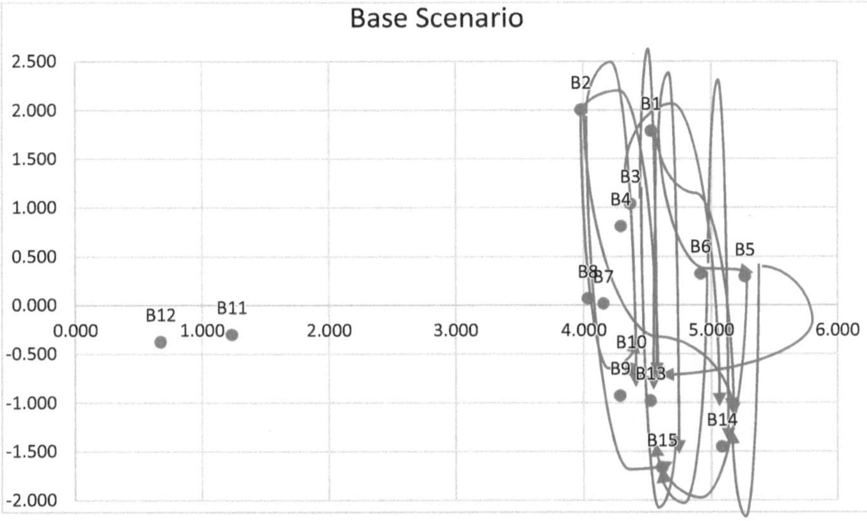

Figure 9.1 Diagraph reflecting the causal relations among the barriers

Source: By authors

Table 9.3 Linguistic Assessment Code and Corresponding Grey Values

Linguistic Assessment Code	*Associated Grey Values*
No effect (NE)	[0.0, 0.1]
Low effect (LE)	[0.1, 0.3]
Extremely low effect (VLE)	[0.2, 0.5]
Medium effect (ME)	[0.4, 0.7]
High effect (HE)	[0.6, 0.9]
Exceedingly high effect (VHE)	[0.9, 1.0]

Source: By authors

Table 9.4 Explanation of the contacted Experts

S. No.	*Expert*	*Total Work Experience (in years)*	*Designation of the Expert*
1	Industry	17	Hotel Manager
2	Industry	10	Hotel Manager
3	Academician	15	Associate Professor
4	Industry	4	Blockchain Project Manager

Source: By authors

Step 1: The responses provided by the experts were converted into a grey scale (Table 9.3). Using the 15 enablers, relation matrices of 15 × 15 have been generated. The different processes in analysing enablers using this decision-making technique are given in what follows.

Step 2: The values were initially captured on a linguistic scale ranging from No Effect to Very High Effect. The initial codes were then converted into grey values, and four matrices based on the expert responses were created using Equation (1).

Step 3: Initially, equal weightage was provided to all experts, which was later altered to different weights for different experts. Using Equation (2), the average grey relation matrix $\otimes\tilde{z}_{ij}$ is calculated, and the relevant matrix generated is denoted in Table 9.5.

Step 4: Using the steps of the modified CFCS technique, the crisp relation matrix was obtained. Equations (3), (4), (5), (6), (7), and (8) were utilised to generate the matrix, as shown in Table 9.6.

Step 5: The crisp relation matrix was normalised and obtained using Equations (9) and (10). The normalised matrix (M) is shown in Table 9.7.

Step 6: The Total relation matrix (B) was obtained using Equation (11). It is shown in Table 9.8.

Step 7: $R_i + C_j$ and $R_i - C_j$ were evaluated using Equations (12) and (13) ($R_i + C_j$ and $R_i - C_j$ value, denoted in Table 9.8). A total of six barriers, which are acknowledged as causal factor enablers $\left(\text{as } R_i - C_j > 0\right)$ and nine effect enablers $\left(\text{as } R_i - C_j < 0\right)$.

Step 8: The digraph was finally plotted using the dataset f $R_i + C_j$ and $R_i - the$ threshold value was calculated to reflect the digraph. Mean (μ) and standard deviation (σ) were obtained from the total relation matrix (B). The evaluation was done using a threshold value $\theta = \mu + 1.5\sigma$, i.e., $\theta = 0.133 + 1.50 \times 0.08 = 0.253$. The digraph is shown in Figure 9.2.

5. Discussion of Results

The proposed model was utilised in the Indian hospitality industry to understand the enablers for adopting blockchain technology in this sector. The present study utilised the grey systems theory and DEMATEL technique to determine the cause/effect interactions for the enablers of adopting blockchain technology in the hospitality sector. The results obtained have further been discussed under three subheadings: Ranking of individual enablers, classification of enablers as cause-and-effect groups, and third interaction effect for each enabler using grey theory. Based on the relative importance of values $R_i +, C_j$ the enablers were listed as **B1 > B2 > B3 > B5 > B6 > B4 > B7 > B8 > B10 > B14 > B13 > B9 >B15 > B11 > B12** (refer to Table 9.8). Thus, the factor of highest importance has been a cost reduction (B1). This is followed by traceability and transparency (B2), followed by automation (B3) and government regulations (B5). This is further led by top management support (B6). After that, these are followed by disintermediation of the existing system (B4), stakeholder pressure (B7), risk aversion (B8), decentralised database (B10),

Table 9.5 Average Relation Matrix

Barrier Code	*B1*	*B2*	*B3*	*B4*	*B5*	*B6*	*B7*	*B8*	*B9*	*B10*	*B11*	*B12*	*B13*	*B14*	*B15*
B1	0.00	0.83	0.83	0.83	0.83	0.60	0.78	0.38	0.45	0.68	0.18	0.15	0.78	0.75	0.83
	0.10	0.98	0.98	0.98	0.98	0.90	0.93	0.65	0.55	0.78	0.40	0.30	0.93	0.95	0.98
B2	0.00	0.00	0.45	0.45	0.38	0.30	0.45	0.25	0.45	0.38	0.05	0.20	0.45	0.45	0.38
	0.10	0.10	0.55	0.55	0.53	0.50	0.55	0.45	0.55	0.53	0.20	0.40	0.55	0.55	0.53
B3	0.00	0.05	0.00	0.90	0.63	0.83	0.75	0.70	0.75	0.90	0.25	0.00	0.90	0.75	0.75
	0.10	0.20	0.10	1.00	0.88	0.98	0.95	0.90	0.95	1.00	0.50	0.10	1.00	0.95	0.95
B4	0.03	0.13	0.18	0.00	0.53	0.60	0.60	0.40	0.45	0.55	0.28	0.10	0.55	0.60	0.53
	0.15	0.30	0.40	0.10	0.73	0.68	0.75	0.65	0.70	0.70	0.50	0.25	0.70	0.75	0.73
B5	0.45	0.40	0.38	0.33	0.00	0.83	0.83	0.83	0.68	0.78	0.15	0.00	0.75	0.90	0.60
	0.75	0.63	0.65	0.60	0.10	0.98	0.98	0.98	0.93	0.93	0.35	0.10	0.95	1.00	0.90
B6	0.70	0.03	0.33	0.28	0.68	0.00	0.83	0.63	0.90	0.90	0.25	0.00	0.83	0.65	0.75
	0.83	0.15	0.60	0.55	0.93	0.10	0.98	0.88	1.00	1.00	0.45	0.10	0.98	0.85	0.95
B7	0.03	0.10	0.10	0.20	0.25	0.20	0.00	0.45	0.45	0.20	0.00	0.20	0.45	0.45	0.45
	0.15	0.25	0.30	0.40	0.45	0.40	0.10	0.55	0.55	0.40	0.10	0.40	0.55	0.55	0.55
B8	0.73	0.18	0.05	0.08	0.60	0.18	0.03	0.00	0.83	0.70	0.20	0.00	0.70	0.70	0.75
	0.88	0.40	0.20	0.25	0.90	0.45	0.15	0.10	0.98	0.90	0.40	0.10	0.90	0.90	0.95
B9	0.25	0.15	0.30	0.33	0.30	0.35	0.08	0.10	0.00	0.10	0.30	0.10	0.63	0.90	0.55
	0.50	0.30	0.60	0.53	0.60	0.65	0.25	0.30	0.10	0.30	0.50	0.25	0.88	1.00	0.78
B10	0.18	0.15	0.40	0.20	0.45	0.25	0.15	0.10	0.60	0.03	0.35	0.05	0.75	0.83	0.58
	0.35	0.35	0.70	0.45	0.75	0.50	0.40	0.30	0.75	0.15	0.60	0.20	0.95	0.98	0.83
B11	0.13	0.00	0.10	0.03	0.18	0.13	0.00	0.03	0.00	0.03	0.15	0.35	0.30	0.25	0.20
	0.35	0.10	0.30	0.15	0.40	0.30	0.10	0.15	0.10	0.15	0.30	0.60	0.50	0.38	0.40
B12	0.00	0.00	0.00	0.00	0.00	0.00	0.00	0.00	0.00	0.00	0.05	0.30	0.00	0.00	0.00
	0.10	0.10	0.10	0.10	0.10	0.10	0.10	0.10	0.10	0.10	0.20	0.55	0.10	0.10	0.10
B13	0.53	0.18	0.25	0.13	0.30	0.35	0.15	0.25	0.35	0.63	0.03	0.00	0.00	0.90	0.60
	0.78	0.45	0.50	0.30	0.60	0.65	0.30	0.55	0.65	0.88	0.15	0.10	0.10	1.00	0.90
B14	0.20	0.20	0.40	0.18	0.50	0.45	0.25	0.40	0.35	0.35	0.05	0.68	0.00	0.03	0.75
	0.45	0.40	0.70	0.45	0.80	0.68	0.55	0.70	0.60	0.65	0.20	0.78	0.10	0.15	0.95
B15	0.08	0.15	0.18	0.30	0.28	0.55	0.35	0.10	0.03	0.25	0.00	0.00	0.18	0.45	0.00
	0.25	0.30	0.45	0.60	0.55	0.85	0.65	0.30	0.15	0.55	0.10	0.10	0.45	0.75	0.10

Table 9.6 Crisp Relation Matrix of the Enablers in Blockchain Technology in the Hospitality Sector

	B1	*B2*	*B3*	*B4*	*B5*	*B6*	*B7*	*B8*	*B9*	*B10*	*B11*	*B12*	*B13*	*B14*	*B15*
B1	0.097	0.148	0.208	0.225	**0.252**	0.246	0.237	0.194	0.245	0.254	0.077	0.053	**0.280**	**0.322**	**0.314**
B2	0.096	0.064	0.199	0.202	0.247	0.240	0.229	0.198	**0.268**	0.254	0.081	0.036	**0.272**	**0.311**	**0.296**
B3	0.090	0.065	0.099	0.189	0.224	0.236	0.205	0.197	0.242	0.242	0.075	0.033	0.256	**0.285**	**0.275**
B4	0.076	0.063	0.144	0.097	0.226	0.213	0.203	0.187	0.225	0.226	0.074	0.032	0.239	**0.278**	**0.265**
B5	0.145	0.109	0.152	0.150	0.161	0.230	0.214	0.209	0.243	0.240	0.064	0.034	0.255	**0.298**	**0.273**
B6	0.155	0.066	0.139	0.137	0.225	0.139	0.205	0.187	0.241	0.236	0.071	0.033	0.248	**0.269**	**0.269**
B7	0.074	0.069	0.097	0.129	0.173	0.147	0.094	0.172	0.209	0.168	0.050	0.018	0.211	0.242	0.230
B8	0.153	0.073	0.078	0.089	0.189	0.134	0.100	0.087	0.213	0.192	0.057	0.028	0.211	0.223	0.229
B9	0.099	0.056	0.103	0.107	0.139	0.136	0.098	0.086	0.096	0.107	0.045	0.034	0.175	0.212	0.186
B10	0.086	0.060	0.111	0.108	0.160	0.120	0.114	0.081	0.191	0.104	0.054	0.031	0.197	0.236	0.204
B11	0.030	0.017	0.023	0.030	0.034	0.033	0.020	0.018	0.023	0.024	0.012	0.085	0.046	0.037	0.035
B12	0.017	0.003	0.004	0.005	0.006	0.005	0.004	0.004	0.005	0.005	0.064	0.006	0.007	0.007	0.007
B13	0.117	0.065	0.102	0.087	0.141	0.140	0.102	0.111	0.148	0.173	0.043	0.024	0.109	0.221	0.200
B14	0.083	0.064	0.119	0.096	0.165	0.149	0.120	0.132	0.148	0.148	0.041	0.090	0.113	0.135	0.211
B15	0.058	0.052	0.084	0.104	0.128	0.159	0.127	0.087	0.096	0.128	0.026	0.018	0.121	0.178	0.109

Source: By authors

Table 9.7 Total Relation Matrix of Enablers in Blockchain Technology in the Hospitality Sector

	B1	*B2*	*B3*	*B4*	*B5*	*B6*	*B7*	*B8*	*B9*	*B10*	*B11*	*B12*	*B13*	*B14*	*B15*
B1	0.00	0.89	0.89	0.89	0.89	0.76	0.84	0.47	0.46	0.69	0.21	0.16	0.84	0.85	0.89
B2	0.00	0.00	0.90	0.87	0.78	0.83	0.90	0.62	0.90	0.83	0.30	0.00	0.87	0.87	0.83
B3	0.00	0.05	0.00	0.90	0.73	0.87	0.83	0.77	0.83	0.90	0.30	0.00	0.90	0.83	0.83
B4	0.03	0.14	0.29	0.00	0.85	0.82	0.89	0.75	0.76	0.84	0.33	0.00	0.84	0.89	0.85
B5	0.56	0.46	0.46	0.40	0.00	0.87	0.87	0.87	0.78	0.81	0.17	0.00	0.83	0.90	0.73
B6	0.72	0.03	0.40	0.34	0.78	0.00	0.87	0.73	0.90	0.90	0.28	0.00	0.87	0.72	0.83
B7	0.03	0.23	0.19	0.51	0.56	0.36	0.00	0.83	0.90	0.50	0.05	0.03	0.87	0.87	0.81
B8	0.78	0.21	0.06	0.09	0.76	0.23	0.03	0.00	0.89	0.79	0.23	0.00	0.79	0.79	0.85
B9	0.46	0.16	0.38	0.40	0.44	0.44	0.15	0.09	0.00	0.09	0.16	0.11	0.77	0.90	0.67
B10	0.16	0.18	0.52	0.35	0.58	0.18	0.27	0.09	0.89	0.00	0.23	0.06	0.89	0.89	0.74
B11	0.16	0.08	0.08	0.15	0.12	0.12	0.00	0.00	0.00	0.00	0.00	0.78	0.22	0.08	0.08
B12	0.13	0.00	0.00	0.00	0.00	0.00	0.00	0.00	0.00	0.00	0.61	0.00	0.00	0.00	0.00
B13	0.61	0.23	0.30	0.14	0.38	0.44	0.16	0.33	0.44	0.73	0.03	0.00	0.00	0.90	0.73
B14	0.26	0.24	0.53	0.24	0.65	0.54	0.35	0.53	0.44	0.47	0.06	0.71	0.00	0.03	0.87
B15	0.10	0.19	0.28	0.46	0.41	0.82	0.54	0.14	0.03	0.39	0.00	0.00	0.28	0.68	0.00

Source: By authors

reduced system complexity (B14), collaborative communities (B13), increased service efficiency (B9), improved system resilience (B15), trust (B11), and database security (B12).

The major causal enablers based on the $R_i - C_j$ values, which require the immediate attention of the government and policymakers, are cost reductions (B1). This is followed by traceability and transparency (B2), automation of the existing

Table 9.8 Cause/Effect Parameter for Enablers of Blockchain Technology in the Hospitality Industry

Barriers	*R*	*C*	$R_i + C_j$	$R_i - C_j$
B1	3.160	1.370	4.530	1.790
B2	2.993	0.987	3.980	2.006
B3	2.703	2.654	5.377	1.040
B4	2.550	2.741	5.290	0.809
B5	2.678	1.384	4.363	0.294
B6	2.620	1.297	3.917	0.323
B7	2.084	1.069	3.153	0.015
B8	2.050	2.982	5.032	0.069
B9	2.678	2.605	5.284	−0.927
B10	3.857	1.513	5.370	−0.656
B11	0.468	0.668	1.135	−0.300
B12	0.149	0.622	0.771	−0.374
B13	1.772	1.750	3.522	−0.978
B14	1.815	2.267	4.082	−1.452
B15	1.473	2.139	34.612	−1.666

Source: By authors

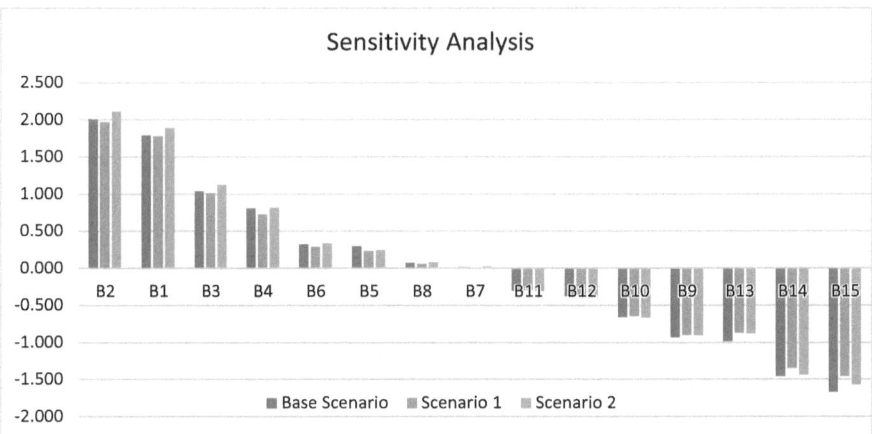

Figure 9.2 Sensitivity analysis

Source: By authors

system (B3), followed by government regulations (B5). This is further led by top management support (B6), disintermediation of existing system (B4), stakeholder pressure (B7), and risk aversion (B8).

The effect enabling variables based on the $R_i - C_j$ values are trusted (B11), database security (B12), decentralised database (B10), increased service efficiency (B9), reduced system complexity (B14), collaborative communities (B13), and improved system resilience (B15).

5.1 Comparison With Existing Literature

Various cause enablers are the factors which the government should lay prior emphasis on to enable the adoption of blockchain technology. The results suggest that cost reduction has been a major cause of the hospitality industry's adoption of blockchain technology. Similar results have been reported by Sharma et al. (2021) and Nijjer et al. (2023). Another major cause of the adoption of blockchain has been the increased transparency and traceability of records. The results are similar to those reported by Cheng (2023). This suggests a better reach of information among all stakeholders in the organisation. As revealed by the study, the next causal variable for adopting blockchain has been the automation of the existing systems. Similar results were reported in the study by Bodkhe et al., 2020b. The automation of the system primarily ensures that data availability is ensured for all levels of stakeholders. Various other studies have stressed the next element of disintermediation (Khanna et al., 2020), as it is a major enabling cause that may result in blockchain technology adoption. Similarly, top management support has been a major causal enabler for blockchain adoption. The results are similar to those reported in other studies (Yeung et al., 2022). Further government regulations have been instrumental in getting ground action (Filimonau and Naumova, 2020b). Blockchain has been known to mitigate the risk involved in everyday transactions in the hospitality industry. Similar results have been reported by Nuryyev et al. (2020) and Irannezhad and Mahadevan (2021).

The resultant effect enablers are the ones that have resulted from the various cause enablers.

Trust formation at various levels, especially at the consumer level, has been a major effect of this technology. Similar results have been reported by Karim et al. (2023).

This is followed by database security provided by the adoption of this technology. Studies have reported the feasibility of various dimensions of blockchain in various sectors of the tourism and hospitality sector (Williams, 2019). The third effect enabler is a decentralised database. Similar results have been reported by Raj et al. (2023). The next effect enabler of increased service efficiency has also been revealed in studies by Strebinger and Treiblmaier (2022). The system complexity is also thus reduced as the fifth effect enabler. The emergence of collaborative communities results from the data processing and decentralised administration of blockchain technology (Jain et al., 2023). Last, the seventh effect enabler is enhanced system resilience, which enhances the system's overall sustainability (Nijjer et al., 2023).

5.2 Validation of the Results by Sensitivity Analysis

The results reproduced have primarily been an output of the several rounds of discussions with the experts. Another group was formed, which resulted in the validation of the findings done previously. This included academicians, two senior hotel managers, and one blockchain project manager.

Table 9.9 The Various Weights Are Assigned to the Experts

	Expert 1	*Expert 2*	*Expert 3*	*Expert 4*
Scenario 1	0.50	0.50	0.25	0.25
Scenario 2	0.25	0.25	0.50	0.50

Source: By authors

Table 9.10 Cause and Effect Parameters

	Base Scenario	*Scenario 1*	*Scenario 2*
B1	2.006	1.967	2.108
B2	1.790	1.777	1.890
B3	1.040	1.013	1.124
B4	0.809	0.724	0.819
B5	0.323	0.287	0.334
B6	0.294	0.232	0.244
B7	0.069	0.060	0.077
B8	0.015	0.010	0.019
B9	−0.300	−0.290	−0.306
B10	−0.374	−0.363	−0.387
B11	−0.656	−0.642	−0.666
B12	−0.927	−0.897	−0.901
B13	−0.978	−0.868	−0.878
B14	−1.452	−1.345	−1.435
B15	−1.666	−1.456	−1.566

Source: By authors

The initial study assigned an equal weightage to all experts for the analysis. This may result in bias, as the experts' knowledge, experience, and sector vary. To further confirm the reliability of the study, sensitivity analysis was carried out. As depicted in Table 9.9, different weights were assigned to different experts in two scenarios to validate the study findings. The initial scenario provided different weightage to different experts. This was reversed in the second scenario. The procedure resulted in imparting different weights to different experts and analysing the results further (Table 9.10). The results suggest that the data is robust enough, and the findings are reliable (Figure 9.2).

6. Implications of the Study

The study has consequences for both management and policy. The current study investigates the various factors that facilitate blockchain adoption in the hospitality sector. There is a need for more scholarly studies on the use of grey DEMATEL to enable blockchain technology in the hospitality sector. A few studies have used the grey DEMATEL technique to analyse decision-making regarding blockchain in the hospitality sector; the research also fills a methodological gap in the literature.

The report is useful because it identifies the two key enhancers of cost reduction: transparency and traceability. This implies that hotels may naturally be inclined to invest in this technology. Furthermore, the study identifies database security and trust as important effect facilitators. The report suggests implementing blockchain because it can substantially influence businesses' security problems while fostering stakeholder trust.

7. Recommendations for Business Practices: The Key to Success

Blockchain technology can help hospitality businesses stand out and enhance customer experience. Using blockchain in the hospitality industry may result in various advantages, as provided in what follows:

7.1 **Guest data privacy and security:** Blockchain can be utilised to safely store and manage visitor data, including contact details, preferences, and booking history. The sensitive data may be protected by putting string encryption and access control methods in place.

7.2 **Streamlined payments and bookings:** Such a system may enable visitors to pay for accommodations and services using virtual currency or tokens. Smart contracts may be used for speedy and transparent transactions.

7.3 **Maintenance of supply chain resilience:** Blockchain may be used to trace the provenance and shelf life of the food items, linens, and toiletries used in the hotels. By tracking an item's journey from suppliers to consumers, its authenticity and safety may be ensured.

7.4 **Identity confirmation:** Implementing blockchain will lower the risk of fraud and enhance the guest experience by enabling secure identification and verification during check-ins and -outs.

7.5 **Loyalty programmes for visitors:** Blockchain-based loyalty programmes may help generate rewards for the customers for their visits and tokens for providing referrals. Tokens can also be used for extra services, discounts, or upgraded accommodations.

7.6 **Intelligent room management:** Blockchain can log all repairs and services done at the hotel property. Besides, the Internet of Things devices in the rooms may be integrated with blockchain to collect data regarding energy use and consumer use of various devices. This information can assist in reducing energy consumption and improve visitor satisfaction.

7.7 **Customer feedback management:** Visitors can provide feedback and evaluations on the blockchain, ensuring they cannot be tampered with.

7.8 **Working together with stakeholders:** Blockchain can further incorporate more coordination and data sharing between various service providers and may enhance trust among the various stakeholders.

7.9 **Effective marketing communication:** Hotels can even communicate their initiatives in their marketing communications. They can emphasise the security and openness of the blockchain-based technologies. It may also be used to inform visitors of the advantages and the reasons they should choose services.

Hence, carefully designing and carrying out the integration is essential, along with understanding the current customer demands and organisational objectives. Success in this field requires staying updated on the industry's recent advancements and best practices.

8. Conclusion and Future Research Scope

Many studies have yet to explore the application of grey DEMATEL in the hospitality sector in the past. Hence, the present study has revealed important insights for enabling the incorporation of blockchain in the hospitality industry. The main enablers are cost reduction transparency and traceability of data. The Indian government should thus focus on these causes to enable blockchain implementation in the hospitality sector. Further, the primary effect enablers have been the inclusion of more trust and database security. The hospitality industry can thus benefit from this, as it may lead to increased customer loyalty and enhanced visit intention. The government should encourage enterprises in tourism and hospitality to adopt blockchain technology. Certain implementations can ensure the trust among the hospitality stakeholders to adopt blockchain technology. Legislators can also implement programmes that increase knowledge of the technology and educate the industry and its associates, who can aid and put the policies into practice.

9. Limitations of the Study

The grey DEMATEL methodology has limitations, and the model relies heavily on the proficiency of the expert panel. Further studies can explore more contextual results based on the various hospitality chains incorporating blockchain and the benefits they have achieved through technology adoption.

References

Agi, M.A.N. 2022. "Understanding the Enablers of Blockchain Technology Adoption in Sustainable Supply Chains: A DEMATEL-Based Analysis." *IFAC-PapersOnLine* 55: 1962–1967. Elsevier B.V. https://doi.org/10.1016/j.ifacol.2022.09.686.

Ahmad, A.N., and N. Samsudin. 2022. *Blockchain Technology in Aviation, Tourism, and Hospitality: Theoretical and Practical Understanding. Digital Transformation in Aviation, Tourism and Hospitality in Southeast Asia*. https://doi.org/10.4324/9781003315179-6.

Azar, A., and D. Andalib Ardakani. 2014. "Application of Grey-Based DEMATEL Technique in Designing the Aggregate Green Supply Chain Management's Model." *Uncertain Supply Chain Management* 2 (3): 199–208. https://doi.org/10.5267/j.uscm.2014.3.001.

Bodkhe, U., P. Bhattacharya, S. Tanwar, S. Tyagi, N. Kumar, and M.S. Obaidat. 2019. "BloHosT: Blockchain Enabled Smart Tourism and Hospitality Management." In *CITS 2019 – Proceeding of the 2019 International Conference on Computer, Information and Telecommunication Systems*. https://doi.org/10.1109/CITS.2019.8862001.

Bodkhe, U., S. Tanwar, K. Parekh, P. Khanpara, S. Tyagi, N. Kumar, and M. Alazab. 2020a. "Blockchain for Industry 4.0: A Comprehensive Review." *IEEE Access* 8: 79764–79800. https://doi.org/10.1109/ACCESS.2020.2988579.

Bodkhe, U., S. Tanwar, K. Parekh, P. Khanpara, S. Tyagi, N. Kumar, and M. Alazab. 2020b. "Blockchain for Industry 4.0: A Comprehensive Review." *IEEE Access* 8: 79764–79800. https://doi.org/10.1109/ACCESS.2020.2988579.

Chaudhuri, R., S. Chatterjee, and D. Vrontis. 2023. "Adoption of Blockchain Technology in Hospitality and Tourism Industry and Sustainability Performance: Impact of Technological Turbulence and Senior Leadership Support." *EuroMed Journal of Business*. https://doi.org/10.1108/EMJB-04-2023-0128.

Cheng, R. 2023. "Assessing and Validating Tourism Business Model in Hospitality Industry: Role of Blockchain Platform." *Environmental Science and Pollution Research* 30 (23): 63704–63715. https://doi.org/10.1007/s11356-023-26832-6.

Cozzio, C., G. Viglia, L. Lemarie, and S. Cerutti. 2023. "Toward an Integration of Blockchain Technology in the Food Supply Chain." *Journal of Business Research* 162. https://doi.org/10.1016/j.jbusres.2023.113909.

Dash, S.P. 2023. *HR Digital Transformation: Blockchain for Business. Intelligent Systems Reference Library*. Vol. 237. https://doi.org/10.1007/978-3-031-22835-3_3.

Dhiraj, A., S. Kumar, D. Rani, S. Grima, and K. Sood. 2023. "Blockchain Payment Services in the Hospitality Sector: The Mediating Role of Data Security on Utilisation Efficiency of the Customer." *Data* 8 (8). https://doi.org/10.3390/data8080123.

Doshi, P., and R. Sandhane. 2022. "Enhancing Marketing Capabilities Using Blockchain." In *AIP Conference Proceedings*. Vol. 2519. https://doi.org/10.1063/5.0112355.

Effendi, U., C.F. Dewi, and S.A. Mustaniroh. 2019. "Evaluation of Supply Chain Performance with Green Supply Chain Management Approach (GSCM) Using SCOR and DEMATEL Method (Case Study of PG Krebet Baru Malang)." In *IOP Conference Series: Earth and Environmental Science*. Vol. 230. https://doi.org/10.1088/1755-1315/230/1/012065.

Filimonau, V., and E. Naumova. 2020a. "The Blockchain Technology and the Scope of Its Application in Hospitality Operations." *International Journal of Hospitality Management* 87. https://doi.org/10.1016/j.ijhm.2019.102383.

Filimonau, V., and E. Naumova. 2020b. "The Blockchain Technology and the Scope of Its Application in Hospitality Operations." *International Journal of Hospitality Management* 87. https://doi.org/10.1016/j.ijhm.2019.102383.

Gangwar, V.P., and D. Reddy. 2023. *Hospitality Industry 5.0: Emerging Trends in Guest Perception and Experiences. Opportunities and Challenges of Business 5.0 in Emerging Markets*. https://doi.org/10.4018/978-1-6684-6403-8.ch010.

Hsu, L., and R. Leung. 2022. "Examining Stakeholder Collaboration Intention with Blockchain OTA for Online Hotel Reservations: Case of Taiwan." *Asia-Pacific Journal of Innovation in Hospitality and Tourism* 11 (2): 127–153.

Irannezhad, E., and R. Mahadevan. 2021. "Is Blockchain Tourism's New Hope?" *Journal of Hospitality and Tourism Technology* 12 (1): 85–96. https://doi.org/10.1108/JHTT-02-2019-0039.

Jain, P., R.K. Singh, R. Mishra, and N.P. Rana. 2023. "Emerging Dimensions of Blockchain Application in Tourism and Hospitality Sector: A Systematic Literature Review." *Journal of Hospitality Marketing and Management* 32 (4): 454–476. https://doi.org/10.1080/19368623.2023.2184440.

Jeng, D.J.-F., and G.-H. Tzeng. 2012. "Social Influence on the Use of Clinical Decision Support Systems: Revisiting the Unified Theory of Acceptance and Use of Technology by the Fuzzy DEMATEL Technique." *Computers and Industrial Engineering* 62 (3): 819–828. https://doi.org/10.1016/j.cie.2011.12.016.

Johari, R., K. Gupta, and S. Jai. 2021. *MOLE: Multiparty Open Ledger Experiment, Concept and Simulation Using BlockChain Technology. Lecture Notes in Electrical Engineering*. Vol. 778. https://doi.org/10.1007/978-981-16-3067-5_42.

Karim, R.A., M.K. Rabiul, M. Ishrat, P. Promsivapallop, and S. Kawser. 2023. "Can Blockchain Payment Services Influence Customers' Loyalty Intention in the Hospitality Industry? A Mediation Assessment." *Administrative Sciences* 13 (3). https://doi.org/10.3390/admsci13030085.

Khanna, A., A. Sah, T. Choudhury, and P. Maheshwari. 2020. *Blockchain Technology for the Hospitality Industry. Lecture Notes in Business Information Processing*. Vol. 402. https://doi.org/10.1007/978-3-030-63396-7_7.

Kizildag, M., T. Dogru, T. Zhang, M.A. Mody, M. Altin, A.B. Ozturk, and O. Ozdemir. 2020. "Blockchain: A Paradigm Shift in Business Practices." *International Journal of Contemporary Hospitality Management* 32 (3): 953–975. https://doi.org/10.1108/IJCHM-12-2018-0958.

Lin, K.J., H. Ye, and R. Law. 2023. "Understanding the Development of Blockchain-Empowered Metaverse Tourism: An Institutional Perspective." *Information Technology and Tourism*. https://doi.org/10.1007/s40558-023-00262-z.

Marco, V., D.A. Cinzia, F. Rosario, and G.C. Elmo. 2020. "About on Organizational Impact on the Adoption of New Technologies in Tourism." In *Springer Proceedings in Business and Economics*, 247–256. https://doi.org/10.1007/978-3-030-36342-0_20.

Nijjer, S., J. Singh, P. Sharma, M. Malhotra, and R. Verma. 2023. *Unraveling a New Age of Travel in Blockchain-Based Metaverse. Lecture Notes in Networks and Systems*. Vol. 588. https://doi.org/10.1007/978-981-19-7982-8_47.

Noonan, J., and P. Doran. 2021. *Blockchain's Impact on Consumer's Perspective in the Luxury Fashion Industry: A Position Paper. Lecture Notes in Computer Science (Including Subseries Lecture Notes in Artificial Intelligence and Bioinformatics)*. Vol. 12896. LNCS. https://doi.org/10.1007/978-3-030-85447-8_49.

Nuryyev, G., A. Spyridou, S. Yeh, and C.-C. Lo. 2021. "Factors of Digital Payment Adoption in Hospitality Businesses: A Conceptual Approach." *European Journal of Tourism Research* 29.

Nuryyev, G., Y.-P. Wang, J. Achyldurdyyeva, B.-S. Jaw, Y.-S. Yeh, H.-T. Lin, and L.-F. Wu. 2020. "Blockchain Technology Adoption Behavior and Sustainability of the Business in Tourism and Hospitality SMEs: An Empirical Study." *Sustainability (Switzerland)* 12 (3). https://doi.org/10.3390/su12031256.

Önder, I., and U. Gunter. 2022a. "Blockchain: Is It the Future for the Tourism and Hospitality Industry?" *Tourism Economics* 28 (2): 291–299. https://doi.org/10.1177/1354816620961707.

Puri, V., S. Mondal, S. Das, and V.G. Vrana. 2023. "Blockchain Propels Tourism Industry – An Attempt to Explore Topics and Information in Smart Tourism Management through Text Mining and Machine Learning." *Informatics* 10 (1). https://doi.org/10.3390/informatics10010009.

Raj, A., A. Kumar, V. Sharma, S. Rani, and A.K. Shanu. 2023. "Enhancing Security Feature in Financial Transactions Using Multichain Based Blockchain Technology." In *4th International Conference on Intelligent Engineering and Management, ICIEM 2023*. https://doi.org/10.1109/ICIEM59379.2023.10166589.

Rajaguru, R. 2023. "Effects of Contemporary Technologies, Such as Blockchain and Artificial Intelligence (AI) in Enhancing Consumers' Trustworthiness of Online Reviews." *Journal of Hospitality Marketing and Management*. https://doi.org/10.1080/19368623.2023.2258522.

Salah, K., A. Alfalasi, and M. Alfalasi. 2019. "A Blockchain-Based System for Online Consumer Reviews." In *INFOCOM 2019 – IEEE Conference on Computer Communications Workshops, INFOCOM WKSHPS 2019*, 853–858. https://doi.org/10.1109/INFCOMW.2019.8845186.

Shao, J., M. Taisch, M. Ortega Mier, and E. D'avolio. 2014. "Application of the DEMATEL Method to Identify Relations among Barriers between Green Products and Consumers." In *17th European Roundtable on Sustainable Consumption and Production – ERSCP 2014*, 14–16 October 2014, Portoroz, Slovenia, 1029–1040.

Sharma, M., R. Sehrawat, T. Daim, and A. Shaygan. 2021. "Technology Assessment: Enabling Blockchain in Hospitality and Tourism Sectors." *Technological Forecasting and Social Change* 169. https://doi.org/10.1016/j.techfore.2021.120810.

Sharma, S., and N.D. Mathur. 2020. "An Assessment of Attitude towards Environment: A Study of Five Star Hotels in Rajasthan." *International Journal of Applied Management Science* 12 (2): 151–168. https://doi.org/10.1504/IJAMS.2020.106736.

Singh, G., Y. Daultani, R. Rajesh, and R. Sahu. 2023. "Modeling the Growth Barriers of Fresh Produce Supply Chain in the Indian Context." *Benchmarking* 30 (2): 653–677. https://doi.org/10.1108/BIJ-09-2021-0517.

Strebinger, A., and H. Treiblmaier. 2022. "Profiling Early Adopters of Blockchain-Based Hotel Booking Applications: Demographic, Psychographic, and Service-Related Factors." *Information Technology and Tourism* 24 (1). https://doi.org/10.1007/s40558-021-00219-0.

Verma, J., and J. Kaur. 2022. *Blockchain Technology: How Will It Impact the Marketing Domain? Developing Relationships, Personalization, and Data Herald in Marketing 5.0*. https://doi.org/10.4018/978-1-6684-4496-2.ch009.

Williams, P. 2019. "Can All Sectors of the Hospitality and Tourism Industry Be Influenced by the Innovation of Blockchain Technology?" *Worldwide Hospitality and Tourism Themes* 11 (2): 112–120. https://doi.org/10.1108/WHATT-11-2018-0077.

Wolfe, F. 2017. "Is Blockchain Technology Another Y2K for Hospitality?" *Hotel Management* 232 (11): 30.

Yeung, K.A., M. Gong, R. Naha, and A. Mahanti. 2022. "Analysis of Applying Blockchain Technology to Hospitality Operation." *Emerging Real-World Applications of Internet of Things*. https://doi.org/10.1201/9781003304203-6.

Zhou, H., Y. Niu, J. Liu, C. Zhang, L. Wei, and Y. Fang. 2018. *A Privacy-Preserving Networked Hospitality Service with the Bitcoin Blockchain. Lecture Notes in Computer Science (Including Subseries Lecture Notes in Artificial Intelligence and Lecture Notes in Bioinformatics)*. Vol. 10874. LNCS. https://doi.org/10.1007/978-3-319-94268-1_57.

10 Impact of AI in the Tourism Industry

A Double-Edged Sword

Dr. Rahul Joshi

1. Introduction

Significant shifts and transformations are now being seen in both demographics and industry. The global community is now seeing notable improvements in technology. The advancements are contributing to the development of nations and communities. Undoubtedly, the enhancement of quality of life and living conditions among individuals is also seen. The global demographic landscape has seen significant changes. The Generation Z cohort is emerging as a prominent demographic segment in the consumer market and the global labour force. The current need is to comprehend the requirements of individuals considering their distinctive attributes. Generation Z, sometimes referred to as digital natives, can access a vast array of knowledge about global affairs readily. According to Bhalla et al. [1], individuals exhibit high proficiency and comfort while using technology and automation. The increasing prevalence of technical developments in artificial intelligence and automation is becoming more apparent across several industries. Individuals are becoming more acquainted with its use, experiencing enhanced ease and improved manageability in their daily lives. One possible explanation might be the prevalence of highly educated cultures throughout Generation Z. It is noteworthy that human civilization operates based on emotions and sentiments.

The foundation of our connection with the natural world and other individuals is rooted in emotional experiences at the earliest stages. The service business also requires a human element to convey emotions to clients effectively. The presence of human beings has consistently been deemed essential in the hotel business [2]. The act of serving food with a smile or presenting it at the table has long been associated with the conveyance of emotions. The hotel sector has many divisions, including the kitchen department, front office, housekeeping, and food and beverage. These divisions rely on human resources to effectively carry out their operations seamlessly. Over time, the acceptance of artificial intelligence, robots, and automation has become widespread in the hotel business. According to Bowen and Morosan [3], it has been projected that around 25% of hospitality positions in the United States and over 50% of hospitality positions in Japan will be automated.

Notably, there exists first evidence of integrating artificial intelligence and robotics in several service sectors. The harmful effects resulting from the activities of the

DOI: 10.4324/9781003488248-10

hotel business were emphasized. Due to technological difficulties and operational inaccuracies, robotic waiters at Chinese restaurants were dismissed from their service duties. According to reports from other industrialized nations, it is widely observed that the proliferation of ground robots is associated with increased challenges and complications [4]. The hotel sector operates based on the fundamental principle of interpersonal interaction. The question at hand is the relevant matter. Introducing machines inside the realm of hospitality services has the potential to enhance service quality and overall customer experience. However, it remains to be seen to what extent these machines will effectively perform their designated functions. The issue of minimizing mistakes is a subject of concern. Furthermore, integrating automated systems in the hospitality industry, namely inside hotels, has become increasingly prevalent. According to Ivanov (2020), the hotel industry instils a sense of apprehension among its personnel around the possibility of losing their jobs [5]. The hotel business is transforming due to developments in technology. The use of artificial intelligence, robots, and automation as replacements or additions to the human labour force necessitates adapting operations, training staff, and addressing ethical concerns to maintain a high-quality guest experience.

It is worth noting that there is still a dearth of academic research on the impact of AI chatbots and virtual concierges on guest satisfaction. Nevertheless, it is encouraging to observe that leading hotel chains such as Marriott International and Hilton have embraced these technologies to enhance their clients' experience [6]. Incorporating automated services in the hotel sector presents many options facilitated by the ongoing progress of robots [7]. Automated artificial intelligence services have been implemented in many establishments, such as airports, bars, restaurants, and hotels [8]. The hotel business largely depends on AI technologies to provide exceptional-quality services and minimize direct contact between consumers and frontline personnel. Therefore, the service provision domain is shifting from being mostly human-centered to predominantly technology-centered. According to Fernandes and Oliveira (2021), there is a belief among some scholars that AI-powered systems have the potential to supplant traditional modes of engagement between customers and workers [9]. According to Aslam et al. (2022) argued, there is a growing trend in service sectors to include humanoid AI robots and chatbots as a means of replacing or supplementing human occupations. These technologies are being used as commercial services [10]. Nevertheless, other researches indicate that the substitution of human interactions is not feasible since empathy emerges as a prominent characteristic sought by customers in frontline services [11]. Using chatbots in the hotel industry yields several advantages and provides exceptional service quality. However, it is imperative to acknowledge that assessing customer views remains a crucial aspect that has yet to be explored comprehensively.

Singapore has installed temperature screening measures at hotel entrances to restore clients' faith. Korean hotels have recently introduced enhanced sanitary protocols and provided comprehensive training programmes to their staff members, thereby focusing on promoting health awareness. Hotels in Taiwan, China, and several other countries have implemented similar policies [12]. According to

Pillai et al. (2021), the Taiwanese hotel business had a decline of 29% in the stock market during one month of SARS [13].

The scholarly discourse around artificial intelligence and its implications for the hotel sector needs to adequately keep up with the rapid advancements in technology and business methodologies. There needs to be a significant improvement in analyzing the industry's most recent artificial intelligence implementations. In recent years, there has been a notable integration of various state-of-the-art artificial intelligence technologies within the sector. These solutions include various applications, including AI-driven guest services and sophisticated revenue management. Nevertheless, there is a need for more scientific literature that assesses the practical consequences and effects of these developments.

The current state of AI is marked by rapid progress in natural language processing, computer vision, and machine learning. The accessibility of AI solutions within the hotel sector has notably increased, accommodating enterprises of all sizes. The current process of development in technology brings out a range of possibilities and obstacles. However, it is observed that the academic literature often needs to thoroughly understand how companies are effectively using these advancing technologies and the possible consequences that may arise because of it. Artificial intelligence–powered recommendation systems, chatbots, and virtual concierges have emerged as indispensable tools for providing personalized services. Nevertheless, a significant void exists in the scholarly literature about the comprehensive examination of how these technologies transform guests' experiences, impact their decision-making processes, and influence levels of consumer satisfaction.

The existing research gaps within the literature and the significant advancements observed within the hospitality industry during 2022 and 2023 underscore the urgent requirement for a dedicated chapter. This chapter should not only investigate the most recent trends in artificial intelligence but also conduct a critical analysis of their practical implications, challenges, and consequences, specifically within the context of the hospitality industry. The inclusion of such a chapter would make a substantial contribution to our understanding of the dynamic changes occurring within the industry as well as provide valuable guidance for future research endeavours and corporate strategies.

2. Personal Touch in Tourism and Hospitality Industry

Incorporating the human touch into service delivery, especially within the context of the hospitality business, is an integral and indissoluble aspect. Previously, it was often seen as contributing to a company's competitive edge. However, in the hospitality and tourism industry, its importance is gradually being overshadowed by the emergence of technology and innovation. Technological developments are driven by minimizing labour expenses, mitigating human mistakes, and enhancing the efficiency of service provision. The hospitality sector encompasses a range of divisions, with higher-end establishments offering a more luxurious experience, while more basic accommodations focus on providing essential services for guests. It is noteworthy that, according to study findings, establishing emotionally captivating experiences within luxury accommodations necessitates interactions between hotel personnel and visitors. From an organizational perspective, the human resources department facilitates comprehensive experience offers to visitors, fostering a deeper emotional and personal connection between guests and hotel workers [14].

Artificial intelligence and automation within the hotel business might be regarded as disruptive innovations. According to the definition provided by Christensen et al. (2013), disruptive innovation refers to a concept within the field of business administration [15]. It involves the introduction of a novel invention that establishes a new market and value network, ultimately disrupting an established market and value network. As a result, this disruption displaces previously dominant businesses, products, and alliances within the market. Notably, the human resources inside firms, particularly in the hospitality industry, are seen as something other than tangible items or objects. These tools serve as guides and facilitate coordinating production and service activities. Numerous industries are currently undergoing significant changes, primarily driven by the processes of digitalization and automation. Nevertheless, the introduction of technological disruptions in human resources, which involve replacing human employees with robots and other machines, raises concerns about the potential erosion of the human touch element. The manifestation of this phenomenon is expected to be increasingly apparent in the form of disruption, whereby the human element plays a central role in the whole experience, especially within the hospitality sector [16].

The provision of personal contact and connection by personnel in the hospitality industry fosters the development of values such as compassion and kindness towards clients. The proliferation of technology-driven enterprises within the hospitality industry is seeing significant growth. Nevertheless, it is crucial to recognize that perceiving technology as a complete replacement for the human workforce may yield enduring consequences. Over time, the hotel business and its services evolve and transform to optimize productivity and reduce mistakes. Nevertheless, the conventional perspective of providing hospitality to consumers is rooted in the fundamental element of human interaction, which is considered the essence of the hospitality industry. Few scholars emphasized the need to evaluate the degree of human interaction and technology interventions in developing service experiences as perceived by consumers. Therefore, the trajectory of the hospitality industry is contingent upon achieving a harmonious equilibrium between operational efficiency, personalized service, and technological advancements [17].

3. Applications of AI in the Tourism Industry

Artificial Intelligence and automation have resulted in significant implications for the tourism industry across all domains. Within the hotel business, many technologies are used to augment client experiences, optimize operational processes, and boost overall efficiency. Artificial intelligence and automation in the tourism business are evident in many ways [18].

1. ***Customized guest experience:*** Artificial intelligence empowers hotels and restaurants to collect data about visitor preferences and behaviours, hence facilitating personalized services. Chatbots and virtual assistants can promptly address inquiries from guests, aid with making bookings, and give personalized suggestions according to individual interests.
2. ***Chatbots and virtual assistants:*** Chatbots manage regular client queries, reservations, and check-ins. They give rapid and precise replies, boosting customer satisfaction and saving staff time.
3. ***Robotic staff:*** The use of robotic staff has been seen in some locations where robots are being deployed to do various jobs, such as delivering room service, conducting cleaning operations, and even providing concierge services. These automated machines can operate continuously for a 24-hour period and demonstrate high proficiency in executing repeated tasks.
4. ***Predictive analytics:*** It involves using artificial intelligence systems to analyze consumer data to forecast trends and preferences. This facilitates the adaptation of services and offers to align with evolving needs.
5. ***Virtual reality and augmented reality:*** VR and AR have been shown to improve the travel experience by providing virtual tours of various locations, historical sites, and landmarks. Augmented reality applications can provide up-to-date information on various sites of interest to travellers in real time as they navigate their surroundings.
6. ***Revenue management:*** It uses artificial intelligence–powered pricing algorithms to dynamically modify hotel prices in response to various variables, including demand, competition pricing, and events. This strategy maximizes both income and occupancy rates.
7. ***Security and surveillance:*** Artificial intelligence technology in hotels and restaurants has facilitated security monitoring via AI-powered cameras and sensors. The use of facial recognition technology has the potential to improve visitor safety and optimize check-in procedures.
8. ***Language translation:*** It is an AI capability that may enhance communication with individuals who speak diverse languages. This is achieved via the provision of instantaneous translation services in real time.
9. ***Airport and travel hub automation:*** The use of AI-powered systems at airports and travel hubs has optimized several activities, including airport operations, security measures, and baggage handling. This integration has led to a reduction in wait times and an overall improvement in efficiency.
10. ***Sustainability and eco-tourism:*** Artificial intelligence has the potential to contribute significantly to monitoring and managing eco-tourism projects, wildlife conservation endeavours, and sustainable travel practices.
11. ***The analysis of feedback:*** Artificial intelligence methodologies are used to analyze customer assessments and feedback acquired from several platforms to extract significant insights on areas necessitating improvement.
12. ***Implementing check-in and check-out automation:*** Using self-check-in kiosks and mobile applications enables visitors to circumvent the traditional front-desk process, decreasing waiting periods and improving convenience.

4. AI and Implementation of Personalization Strategies Using Predictive Analysis

Predictive analysis is now used within the hospitality and tourism industry to anticipate and successfully address client demands and preferences proactively. Predictive analysis is a data-driven approach that involves collecting online data and subsequent use of algorithms and machine learning techniques to provide predictions about client preferences. These algorithms can examine previous data of customers to provide optimal bargains on sites that the customers choose. The use of advanced predictive analysis has the potential to enhance the accuracy and effectiveness of forecasting methodologies. The "Discover Your Aloha" campaign employed facial recognition software to assess clients' emotions when they interact with the videos on the Hawaii authority's website or app via their camera. The predictive analysis provided clients personalized offers and discounts using the data and feedback collected during video consumption and subsequent booking processes. Geolocation monitoring enables organizations to provide tailored and personalized offerings. Predicted analysis enables merchants to get insights into consumers' browsing and purchasing behaviours, allowing them to tailor adverts and communications according to predicted models strategically [19].

5. Virtual Assistance in Facilitating Travel Experiences

The use of sophisticated artificial intelligence and robotics is no longer limited to corporate entities seeking to implement automation. The current configuration of automation is designed to provide an enhanced customer experience via automated service delivery. For those who often engage in business-related travel, it is advantageous to adopt strategies for adequate preparation and organization to facilitate the seamless execution of each trip. The assistance and coordination provided by a travel assistant might be advantageous for professionals engaged in business-related travel [20]. Understanding the potential benefits of using a virtual travel assistant in enhancing one's business travel experience might facilitate selecting an appropriate solution that aligns with individual requirements.

The following describes eight advantages associated with the employment of a virtual travel assistant:

1 ***Time saving:*** A virtual travel assistant is responsible for doing many time-consuming duties, like researching airline options, making hotel reservations, and coordinating trip itineraries. To enhance the efficiency of an assistant's performance, it is advisable to provide them with pertinent information like trip dates, meeting schedules, and desired activities, such as partaking in a guided walking tour of a city. Subsequently, the travel assistant can meticulously organize all aspects of clients' itineraries and provide a comprehensive daily agenda encompassing all of the client's commitments. The details mentioned earlier include hotel, restaurant, and conference centre contact information, airline schedules, airport terminal designations, and opportunities for engaging in local

tourist activities. This approach facilitates optimizing time use via the efficient completion of work-related assignments.

2 ***Adhere to a certain budget:*** Virtual travel assistants have the knowledge and expertise to effectively locate affordable flight costs, hotel accommodations, and transportation services. The user may provide their allocated financial resources and a comprehensive set of personal choices, including preferred hotel facilities and favoured seating arrangements during air travel. Subsequently, the virtual travel assistant can locate and secure the most optimal choices that align with your financial constraints and specific requirements. Moreover, most virtual travel aides operate on an hourly basis, necessitating payment just for the duration of their services used. Due to their remote work arrangement, they may provide reduced costs compared to full-time or in-person assistants. This approach facilitates adherence to a designated budget and cost savings for individuals and their respective organizations while concurrently using the expertise and competencies of a qualified professional.
3 ***Reduced stress:*** Engaging in business travel, including several activities and intricate logistical considerations, might induce a state of stress. A virtual travel assistant has the potential to alleviate the anxieties associated with travel, enabling individuals to concentrate on their professional obligations. In the case of an unforeseen circumstance, such as the cancellation of a flight or a modification to one's schedule, individuals may find solace in the knowledge that their assistant is effectively handling the situation. Virtual travel assistants may also assist in misplacement or loss of personal belongings such as wallets, identity documents, or monetary resources. The service provider can provide digital copies of identification documents, communicate with the credit card issuer, and facilitate funds transfer to the designated account.
4 ***Ensuring prompt arrival and departure:*** Virtual travel assistants are responsible for coordinating and arranging travel itineraries to ensure punctual arrival at meetings and other significant engagements. Transportation may be scheduled, and contingency measures can be devised to accommodate driver or taxi arrival delays. A virtual travel assistant often has expertise in many travel firms, enabling them to comprehend those that provide expeditious and dependable service comprehensively. In addition, these specialists may provide a morning call service, scheduled alarm, or other forms of notice to guarantee punctuality and attendance at meetings.
5 ***Booking accommodations in a convenient location:*** Individuals may need more certainty over their expectations and accommodation options when embarking on a journey to an unfamiliar city or country. In order to aid in the selection of lodgings, a virtual travel assistant does thorough research to guarantee that the chosen lodging is situated in a secure and conveniently accessible location. Individual priorities also make reservations. For instance, if a flight is scheduled for the early hours of the day, an individual assisting may arrange accommodation near the airport.
6 ***Increase productivity:*** Virtual travel assistants can enhance one's productivity during trip endeavours by facilitating the management of travel arrangements,

financial matters, and administrative documentation. This allows individuals to allocate more time towards prioritizing essential responsibilities such as developing presentations or participating in conferences.

7 ***Customize trip:*** Virtual travel assistants can strategize and organize a travel itinerary that caters to an individual's requirements and preferences. For instance, if one wants to integrate a professional excursion with a recreational getaway, a virtual travel assistant can build a pragmatic schedule that effectively addresses both corporate objectives and leisurely pursuits. An assistant can coordinate travel plans for diverse individuals with differing financial constraints and personal preferences. This is advantageous when embarking on a journey with a cohort of professional acquaintances.

8 ***Provide expert advice:*** Virtual travel assistants have extensive knowledge in selecting popular accommodations, dining establishments, and attractions inside prominent urban areas. In addition, these individuals may own local solid networks and possess significant research proficiencies, enabling them to identify and explore noteworthy events, exclusive dining establishments, and local sights on their business travels. Virtual travel assistants often provide dependable guidance on the destination under consideration, reducing the need for extensive pre-trip study and allowing for a more immersive and pleasurable travel experience.

6. The Evolution of the Tourism Industry Amidst the Coronavirus Pandemic

The advent of COVID-19, a newly identified virus that originated in Wuhan, China, has resulted in a significant disruption not only to the tourist sector but also to worldwide business, causing it to reach an unprecedented standstill. To mitigate the widespread transmission of the disease, several governments implemented stringent measures, such as the closing of borders and airspace, the imposition of lockdowns, and a multitude of travel restrictions.

The following sections outline five key domains that are crucial in facilitating change:

1 ***Rapid advancement of digitalization:*** One of the most notable transformations related to the rapid advancement of digitalization is migrating tourist experiences to online platforms due to quarantine measures. This shift is accompanied by the anticipated expedited progress and use of virtual reality technology [21]. From a logical standpoint, the fall in in real life (IRL) tourism due to the impact of coronavirus has led to the emergence of online tourism as a viable alternative. An instance of this may be seen in the implementation of live virtual tours on YouTube by Tourism Australia, which serves as a platform for exhibiting notable landmarks inside the nation [22]. Virtual reality technology was used in Japan to experience the traditional beauty of cherry blossoms [23]. Specific online

experiences were integrated into video games, using a combination of games and virtual tourism [24]. This alteration enhances the need for incorporating digital technology solutions into the operational processes of tourist businesses and advocating for online tourism experiences via appropriate, unconventional distribution channels.

2. ***Corporate model adaptability:*** The second aspect of transition pertained to the business model adaptability shown by tourist enterprises. Business models varied based on the specific actor involved, such as tour operators, hotels, and restaurants. However, these actors used some adaptable value propositions to minimize the epidemic's adverse effects. For example, the hospitality industry, including hotels and other lodging establishments, saw significant decreases in demand and subsequently implemented strategies such as extended stays at discounted rates. During the first stages of the pandemic, individuals who had travelled internationally were provided with two-week isolation plans, sometimes accompanied by transportation arrangements that ensured adherence to social distancing measures upon arrival at the airport [25]. Furthermore, in response to the challenges posed by remote work, several establishments such as hotels, cafés, and karaoke bars have provided secluded work environments for those unable to carry out their professional duties from their residences.
3. ***Human resources:*** The global pandemic resulted in a significant loss of employment within the travel and tourism sector, affecting an estimated 75 million individuals globally [26]. Nevertheless, despite the downturn in the tourist industry, there was a noticeable labour shortage in many sectors, including online and retail shops [27]. The major notable transformation in the industry was the adoption of remote work practices. Hotels, travel agencies, and other entities within the tourist industry have implemented a policy to promote remote work for their office-based staff, except those who directly interact with customers. In contrast, the crisis adversely impacted several segments of the workforce. For instance, expatriates residing in Japan had difficulties due to travel restrictions, resulting in their inability to return to their home countries [28]. Furthermore, older employees saw a greater unemployment incidence than their counterparts in the middle stages of their careers [29]. The discrepancy has further emphasized the ethical dimensions of employment within the industrial sector and the vulnerability of safety provisions for workers in non-permanent positions. There was a significant focus on ensuring the health and safety of staff throughout the crisis.
4. ***Travel restrictions:*** The implementation of travel restrictions has significantly impacted tourism enterprises, as it has virtually brought the influx of tourists to a standstill. In due course, domestic travel has been reinstated, but with ongoing limitations on foreign and offshore travel. As an example, the Japan Tourism Agency has been proactively engaging in the promotion of domestic tourism via the implementation of various strategies, including the provision of discounts on travel items [30]. Thus, it is anticipated that air carriers will have ongoing challenges in the home market for a minimum of a few years and in the foreign

market for many years. This situation has the potential to significantly influence the state of international tourism soon.

5 ***Perception of risk and disaster management:*** The overarching subject matter that has been ascertained relates to the assessment of risk and the leadership of crises. The risk awareness and readiness levels among tourism enterprises were usually found to be poor. The tourist industry's significant dependence on the public sector for assistance, namely in government financing, assistance, economic stimuli, and policy actions that influence the sector, is mainly attributable to this factor. In addition to providing subsidies to enterprises and workers, the Japanese government allocated a substantial amount of ¥1.7 trillion (about $16 billion) towards promoting domestic tourism [31]. Additionally, the organization made a declaration on the creation of a novel framework aimed at offering loans to small and medium-sized enterprises (SMEs) with minimal interest rates and without the need for collateral. In addition to governmental entities, commercial players also provided financial assistance targeted at smaller enterprises.

7. AI and Machine Learning Technology Capturing Individual Presence

In previous decades, artificial intelligence and robotics were mainly used inside business contexts. However, in recent times, automation and improved technology have shown to be beneficial in assisting consumers in making more informed economic judgements. In the context of the Hospitality business, the implementation of chatbots, destination recommendations derived from client searches, and frequency technology can potentially introduce personal agents equipped with artificial intelligence capabilities. These agents would be capable of making judgements, such as providing reminders. The services provided include facilitating financial transactions, receiving tailored notifications on trip arrangements and cost reductions, and establishing a detailed schedule of activities. In addition, customers have begun using digital platforms to engage with chatbots in the capacity of frontline representatives to address and resolve their concerns.

Artificial intelligence is widely acknowledged as having the potential to revolutionize tourist paradigms and disrupt the conventional hotel industry. Technology facilitates the acquisition of precise and dependable information about travel. Individuals can personalize their hotel bookings, travel itineraries, and trip planning using internet platforms. According to Ruel and Njoku (2021), using AI technologies with well-defined roles can potentially enhance talent and talent management practices as a supporting system within the field of managing human resources [32]. Artificial intelligence can enhance client experiences, although it cannot entirely supplant the irreplaceable human touch. While using robots for automation in service quality is becoming more critical for organizations to achieve a competitive edge, there is scepticism over the impact on guest experiences and the delivery of personalized services [33].

Service encounters have a crucial role in shaping service experiences across all phases of the consuming process. To provide a positive customer experience, it is essential to prioritize staff engagement [34]. According to research findings, AI and automation have been shown to enhance process efficiency. However, lacking human touch and engagement may lead to subpar service quality experiences. One of the primary difficulties arising from using automation in hospitality organizations is the need to reconfigure existing structures and procedures. The factor mentioned would significantly affect several aspects, such as customer experience, customer happiness, employee engagement, retention, and productivity. Consequently, it is essential to balance using artificial intelligence and human resources [35, 36].

8. Disadvantages of the Adoption of Robotics by the Hospitality Industry

The use of robots within the hospitality sector has a multitude of advantages, although it has its drawbacks and obstacles [37]. Several drawbacks may be identified, including:

1 ***Probability of employment losses:*** One of the primary issues associated with implementing robotic automation pertains to its potential repercussions on employment opportunities for human employees. If a robot demonstrates superior speed and consistency in performance, concerns arise over the potential obsolescence of human involvement. Although it is comprehensible that these concerns exist, they need more factual accuracy.
2 ***Costs of initial investment:*** The determination of whether a corporation will invest in robotic automation or defer the decision to a later stage is often contingent upon overcoming this significant challenge. The use of this technology necessitates the construction of a thorough and all-encompassing business case. The potential gains may be significant and often materialize within a few time frames. Nevertheless, it is essential that the cash flow remains viable throughout this period, and the danger of jeopardizing the company's viability should not be taken lightly, especially if the returns are relatively small. However, it is essential to note that a repayment plan is typically provided in most cases, facilitating the affordability and management of financial obligations. The automation payback calculator, available for download, has a financing plan option to provide users with an understanding of its practical implications.
3 ***Hiring skilled personnel:*** Recently, organizations have encountered growing challenges in recruiting suitably skilled individuals to fill specialized roles within their organizational structures. The incorporation of automation introduces an additional dimension to this dilemma, as it necessitates the implementation of programming and the acquisition of operational expertise for the robots. This presents more prospects for current workers to get training and enhance their own repertoire of skills. An automation firm has the capability to

provide support throughout the initial installation and configuration phase, and with appropriate knowledge and training, personnel may acquire the skills necessary to effectively operate and maintain the robotic systems over an extended period.

9. Recommendations for Business Practices: The Key to Success

In the domain of artificial intelligence, adopting targeted business strategies can significantly bolster competitiveness and pave the way for success within the hospitality industry [38].

1 ***Ensuring strategic alignment with the business goals:*** First and foremost, it is crucial to ensure that organizational AI endeavours are in line with their overarching business objectives. Organizations must understand that AI can efficiently tackle complex issues within the hospitality industry, such as improving guest satisfaction, optimizing operational workflows, and increasing revenue. Organizations' AI plans should strive to aid and expedite the fulfilment of these goals.
2 ***The process of gathering and organizing data:*** The foundation of effective AI deployments is in the establishment and maintenance of resilient data collecting and management systems. The task at hand involves the collection and management of organized data on visitor preferences, booking trends, and operational key performance indicators. It is vital to ensure data quality and security to render it suitable for utilization in AI algorithms.
3 ***Personalization and guest experience enhancement:*** Incorporating AI technology can be a game changer for businesses looking to provide tailored experiences to their customers. By utilizing guest data, establishments can offer personalized suggestions on lodging, dining, and areas of interest [39]. Customization tactics have been shown to greatly improve guest satisfaction and foster customer allegiance.
4 ***Predictive analytics and demand forecasting:*** By leveraging the power of predictive analytics and AI algorithms, organizations can take control of their inventory management, pricing optimization, and demand estimation processes. With these powerful tools at their disposal, they can make data-driven decisions that maximize their occupancy rates and increase revenue. By analyzing historical data, organizations can gain valuable insights that enable them to fine-tune their operations and stay ahead of the competition [40]. With the help of predictive analytics, organizations can make informed decisions that help them to achieve their business goals and drive success.
5 ***Staff training and continuous monitoring and improvement:*** For organizations to effectively collaborate with AI systems, it is crucial to equip their employees with the necessary resources. Providing apt training to the staff allows efficient handling of guest interactions, utilizing AI tools, and troubleshooting AI-related issues. Consistent upgrades and monitoring of AI systems are also necessary. Regular evaluations of AI applications' performance help identify areas that require adjustments. By following these steps, organizations can ensure

that their AI solutions continue to meet both guest needs and their company objectives.

6 ***Cost-benefit analysis and data security and privacy:*** AI is expensive. Hence, it is critical to calculate the return on investment. As AI is growing, data security and visitor privacy needs cybersecurity safeguards to protect visitor information and guarantee compliance of data protection laws.
7 ***Integration and scalability:*** It is essential to ensure that the artificial intelligence systems implemented within the organization can seamlessly integrate with its current technological solutions. The company needs to opt for such AI solutions that can be customized and modified to meet new requirements.
8 ***Collaborate and partner with AI experts:*** The organization needs to build relationships with AI specialists, IT companies, or AI-focused startups to be on the leading edge of AI developments in the hotel industry. This will also foster access to cutting-edge AI technology and knowledge.
9 ***Ethical AI practices:*** When using AI, ethical issues need to be a priority. Make sure AI algorithms adhere to privacy laws and are impartial. In addition to keeping their visitors safe, ethical AI procedures also need to foster confidence and maintain a favourable reputation.

10. Conclusion

The field of artificial intelligence has significant promise. Organizations are increasingly moving away from automated solutions such as chatbots that rely on repetitive, rule-based processes. Instead, they are adopting intelligent cognitive agents that can analyze unstructured data, engage in interactions that resemble human conversation, and continuously learn and adapt. Integrating artificial intelligence and advanced analytics concepts in the travel and hospitality business enables personalized service, enhancing value and unique experiences for visitors. Artificial intelligence is revolutionizing the conventional perception of hotel services by enhancing operational efficiency, offering critical analytical perspectives, and optimizing guest experiences. The emergence of this phenomenon is driving a fresh surge of inventive, adaptable, and customer-focused approaches within the hospitality sector to enhance service excellence and foster the holistic development of the hotel business. Hotel visitors who lack knowledge or immediate intentions about artificial intelligence should gather and store data that may be converted into a competitive advantage. In due course, this accumulated data will evolve into a precious source of income. Undoubtedly, the integration of machine learning and human collaboration can enhance the quality of hospitality, transcending artificial intelligence from a simple term.

The use of artificial intelligence in the tourist industry offers several benefits, as it enhances the overall comfort and happiness of guests by facilitating their interaction with different hotel services. In the hospitality sector, our primary objective is to provide customers with the utmost comfort. Integrating artificial intelligence technology is expected to enhance consumer satisfaction and elevate their comfort levels. The advent of technology has introduced a wide range of smartphones that provide worldwide connectivity and enable individuals to initiate and operate diverse enterprises from the comfort of their homes. This phenomenon has left a substantial impact on the process of globalization. Considering the significant level of competitiveness and the need to promptly construct a substantial clientele, the tourism industry on a global scale will necessitate substantial advancements in technology in order to effectively cater to the escalating demand.

References

1. Bhalla, Rohan, Pinaz Tiwari, and Nimit Chowdhary. "Digital natives leading the world: paragons and values of Generation Z." *Generation Z Marketing and Management in Tourism and Hospitality: The Future of the Industry*. Springer International Publishing, 2021.3–23.
2. Solnet, David, et al. "Leveraging human touch in service interactions: lessons from hospitality." *Journal of Service Management* 30.3 (2019): 392–409.
3. Bowen, John, and Cristian Morosan. "Beware hospitality industry: the robots are coming." *Worldwide Hospitality and Tourism Themes* 10.6 (2018): 726–733.
4. Drexler, Nadine, and Viyella Beckman Lapré. "For better or for worse: shaping the hospitality industry through robotics and artificial intelligence." *Research in Hospitality Management* 9.2 (2019): 117–120.
5. Ivanov, Stanislav. "The impact of automation on tourism and hospitality jobs." *Information Technology & Tourism* 22 (2020): 205–215.
6. Štilić, Anđelka, Miloš Nicić, and Adis Puška. "Check-in to the future: exploring the impact of contemporary information technologies and artificial intelligence on the hotel industry." *Turističko poslovanje* 31 (2023).
7. Go, Hanyoung, Myunghwa Kang, and SeungBeum Chris Suh. "Machine learning of robots in tourism and hospitality: interactive technology acceptance model (iTAM)–cutting edge." *Tourism Review* 75.4 (2020): 625–636.
8. Buhalis, Dimitrios, and Emily Siaw Yen Cheng. "Exploring the use of chatbots in hotels: technology providers' perspective." *Information and Communication Technologies in Tourism 2020: Proceedings of the International Conference in Surrey, United Kingdom, January 08–10, 2020*. Springer International Publishing, 2020.
9. Fernandes, Teresa, and Elisabete Oliveira. "Understanding consumers' acceptance of automated technologies in service encounters: drivers of digital voice assistants' adoption." *Journal of Business Research* 122 (2021): 180–191.
10. Aslam, Wajeeha, et al. "Chatbots in the frontline: drivers of acceptance." *Kybernetes* ahead-of-print (2022).
11. Seyitoğlu, Faruk, and Stanislav Ivanov. "Service robots as a tool for physical distancing in tourism." *Current issues in tourism* 24.12 (2021): 1631–1634.
12. Kim, Jinkyung Jenny, and Heesup Han. "Saving the hotel industry: strategic response to the COVID-19 pandemic, hotel selection analysis, and customer retention." *International Journal of Hospitality Management* 102 (2022): 103163.
13. Pillai, Souji Gopalakrishna, et al. "COVID-19 and hospitality 5.0: redefining hospitality operations." *International Journal of Hospitality Management* 94 (2021): 102869.
14. Harkison, Tracy. "The importance of the human touch in the luxury accommodation sector." *Research in Hospitality Management* 7.1 (2017): 59–64.
15. Christensen, Clay, Michael E. Raynor, and Rory McDonald. *Disruptive Innovation*. Harvard Business Review, 2013.
16. Joshi, Basant P. "Disruptive innovation in hospitality human resource." *Journal of Tourism and Hospitality Education* 8.48 (2018): 1–29.
17. Kandampully, Jay, and David Solnet. "Competitive advantage through service in hospitality and tourism: a perspective article." *Tourism Review* 75.1 (2020): 247–251.

18. Popesku, Jovan. "Current applications of artificial intelligence in tourism and hospitality." *Sinteza 2019-International Scientific Conference on Information Technology and Data Related Research*. Singidunum University, 2019.
19. Garg, Vikas, and Richa Goel, eds. *Handbook of Research on Innovative Management Using AI in Industry 5.0*. IGI Global, 2021.
20. Pencarelli, Tonino. "The digital revolution in the travel and tourism industry." *Information Technology & Tourism* 22.3 (2020): 455–476.
21. Zwanka, Russell J., and Cheryl Buff. "COVID-19 generation: a conceptual framework of the consumer behavioral shifts to be caused by the COVID-19 pandemic." *Journal of International Consumer Marketing* 33.1 (2021): 58–67.
22. Lee, Hyun-Kyung, Soobin Park, and Yeonji Lee. "A proposal of virtual museum metaverse content for the MZ generation." *Digital Creativity* 33.2 (2022): 79–95.
23. Brozović, Danilo, and Hiroaki Saito. "The impacts of Covid-19 on the tourism sector: changes, adaptations and challenges." *Tourism: An International Interdisciplinary Journal* 70.3 (2022): 465–479.
24. ATSIZ, Ozan. "Virtual reality technology and physical distancing: a review on limiting human interaction in tourism." *Journal of Multidisciplinary Academic Tourism* 6.1 (2021): 27–35.
25. Shaw, Rajib, Yong-kyun Kim, and Jinling Hua. "Governance, technology and citizen behavior in pandemic: lessons from COVID-19 in East Asia." *Progress in Disaster Science* 6 (2020): 100090.
26. Bulin, Daniel, and Iulian-Petru Tenie. "Preliminary assessment of the COVID-19 pandemic impact on the tourism industry." *Global Economic Observer* 8.1 (2020): 41–46.
27. Weise, Karen. "Pushed by pandemic, Amazon goes on a hiring spree without equal." *The New York Times* 27 (2020).
28. Brozović, Danilo, and Hiroaki Saito. "The impacts of Covid-19 on the tourism sector: changes, adaptations and challenges." *Tourism: An International Interdisciplinary Journal* 70.3 (2022): 465–479.
29. Terrell, Kenneth. "Unemployment's toll on older workers is worst in half a century." *AARP*, October 21 (2020).
30. Tomura, Hajime. "Associations between components of household expenditures and the rate of change in the number of new confirmed cases of COVID-19 in Japan: time-series analysis." *PLoS One* 17.4 (2022): e0266963.
31. Hoshi, Takeo, Daiji Kawaguchi, and Kenichi Ueda. "Zombies, again? The COVID-19 business support programs in Japan." *Journal of Banking & Finance* 147 (2023): 106421.
32. Ruel, Huub, and Esther Njoku. "AI redefining the hospitality industry." *Journal of Tourism Futures* 7.1 (2021): 53–66.
33. Naumov, Nikola. "The impact of robots, artificial intelligence, and service automation on service quality and service experience in hospitality." *Robots, Artificial Intelligence, and Service Automation in Travel, Tourism and Hospitality*. Emerald Publishing Limited, 2019.123–133.
34. Nixon, Natalie W., and Alison Rieple. "Luxury redesigned: how the Ritz-Carlton uses experiential service design to position abundance in times of scarcity." *Design Management Journal* 5.1 (2010): 40–49.
35. Ivanov, S., and Webster, C. (2019). Conceptual framework of the use of robots, artificial intelligence and service automation in travel, tourism, and hospitality companies. *Robots. Artificial Intelligence and Service Automation in Travel, Tourism and Hospitality*. doi:10.1108/978-1-78756-687-320191001
36. Ruel, Huub, and Esther Njoku. "AI redefining the hospitality industry." *Journal of Tourism Futures* 7.1 (2021): 53–66.
37. Rasheed, Hafiz Muhammad Wasif, et al. "Exploring consumer-robot interaction in the hospitality sector: unpacking the reasons for adoption (or resistance) to artificial intelligence." *Technological Forecasting and Social Change* 192 (2023): 122555.

38. Buhalis, Dimitrios, Peter O'Connor, and Rosanna Leung. "Smart hospitality: from smart cities and smart tourism towards agile business ecosystems in networked destinations." *International Journal of Contemporary Hospitality Management* 35.1 (2023): 369–393.
39. Saini, Aarti, and Rohan Bhalla. "Artificial intelligence and automation: transforming the hospitality industry or threat to human touch." *Handbook of Research on Innovative Management Using AI in Industry 5.0*. IGI Global, 2022.88–97.
40. Gangwar, Veer P., and Deepika Reddy. "Hospitality Industry 5.0: emerging Trends in Guest Perception and Experiences." *Opportunities and Challenges of Business 5.0 in Emerging Markets* (2023): 185–211.

11 AI and IoT Applications in the Hospitality Industry

A Study of Their Potential in Transforming the Indian Online Travel Market by 2030

Dr. Archan Mitra and Dr. Vishal Jain

Introduction

1.1 Background

The hospitality industry is a pillar of the global economy, historically resilient and adaptive to ever-changing market conditions. According to a report by Statista (2021), the industry is projected to amass revenue exceeding $100,000 by the year 2030. Concurrently, emerging technologies like artificial intelligence (AI) and the Internet of Things (IoT) are experiencing exponential growth rates, with IDC (2020), Tractica (2019), and Globe Newswire (2021) reporting annual global spending on AI and IoT reaching into the hundreds of billions of dollars. The Indian market, a burgeoning economic powerhouse, has seen significant shifts in its hospitality sector, particularly in online travel arrangements comprising air travel, bus and train bookings, and hotel reservations. The World Travel and Tourism Council (WTTC) states that India's contribution to global tourism is expected to hit approximately $200 billion by 2028 (WTTC, 2020). With a teeming population that is increasingly tech savvy, India becomes a fertile ground for digital transformations driven by AI and IoT technologies (Smith, 2019). Moreover, the COVID-19 pandemic has been a game-changer. It accelerated the adoption of online platforms for travel planning, adding an urgency to the need for digital transformation in the hospitality industry (Johnson et al., 2021).

1.2 Statement of the Problem

Despite the promising numbers and the momentum in technology adoption, there is a glaring gap in research focusing on the Indian market. Existing studies predominantly analyze Western or global markets, leaving the unique challenges and opportunities in the Indian landscape largely unexplored (Patel & Sarker, 2018). This is concerning given the different consumer behaviours, market dynamics, and technological infrastructures in India compared to the Western world (Kumar, 2020).

DOI: 10.4324/9781003488248-11

1.3 Objective of the Study

The primary objective of this study is to investigate the specific applications and potential benefits of AI and IoT in India's online travel market. Specifically, the study aims to:

Identify how AI and IoT can enhance customer experiences in online travel bookings and hospitality services.

Examine the impact of these technologies on operational efficiency within the sector.

Evaluate how AI and IoT can support strategic decision-making in the hospitality industry in India.

Given India's expected massive contribution to global tourism and the corresponding potential for economic gains, understanding the transformative role of AI and IoT becomes critical (WTTC, 2020). Additionally, post-COVID-19, there is an increased emphasis on digital platforms and less physical contact, making technology not just an enhancer but a necessity (Johnson et al., 2021). This research, therefore, serves as a timely inquiry into how India can leverage these technologies for industry betterment. The study will focus on the Indian online travel market, considering the major segments such as air travel, buses, trains, and the hotel industry. However, it is essential to note the limitations: Accessibility of firsthand data may be constrained due to organizational unwillingness to share proprietary information. The fast-paced nature of technology means that findings may have a limited shelf-life.

Justification

The existing literature on the incorporation of artificial intelligence (AI) and Internet of Things (IoT) in the hospitality industry is extensive but primarily focuses on theoretical underpinnings or broad-scale impacts. A noticeable gap exists in research that pragmatically addresses how these technologies can be implemented into business practices, specifically in the context of the burgeoning Indian online travel market. While scholars like Singh and Kaur (2021) have explored the adoption of AI in customer service within the hospitality industry, they offer limited insights into a comprehensive range of business practices and the unique challenges and opportunities presented by the Indian market. Moreover, the literature generally overlooks the dynamism and rapid shifts in industry practices. The pivot towards digital transformation has been significantly accelerated in recent years – especially post-2020 – owing to the global pandemic situation (Gursoy et al., 2020). This acceleration has forced businesses to rethink and redesign their strategies at an unprecedented speed. For instance, in 2022, OYO Rooms, an Indian hospitality chain, leveraged AI to streamline its operational efficiency and customer relations, marking a significant shift from traditional practices (TechCrunch, 2022). Similarly, MakeMyTrip, a leading Indian online travel company, integrated IoT technologies into its platforms to offer real-time, personalized travel solutions in 2023 (Business Standard, 2023). These emerging trends in business practices underline the need for actionable recommendations grounded in rigorous research.

Therefore, this chapter is not only timely but also necessary. It serves to bridge the identified gaps in literature by offering pragmatic, actionable insights that are in step with the rapid technological advancements and shifts in business practices of 2022 and 2023. By doing so, the chapter stands to significantly contribute to both academic discourse and practical applications in the field of hospitality, particularly in the Indian online travel market.

Literature Review

2.1 Artificial Intelligence in Hospitality

AI has made significant strides in redefining customer service, operational efficiency, and even strategic decision-making within the hospitality industry. Numerous studies, such as the works of Kimes (2019), have delved into AI applications like chatbots for customer service, machine learning algorithms for optimizing room rates, and natural language processing tools for sentiment analysis (Kimes, 2019). However, Kim et al. (2020) have noted that the adoption of AI technologies is not without challenges, including ethical considerations surrounding data privacy and the need for substantial initial investment (Kim et al., 2020).

2.2 Internet of Things in Hospitality

Similar to AI, the IoT has also marked its territory in the hospitality sector. IoT technologies can be applied to various domains such as smart room systems, energy management, and even predictive maintenance of equipment (Brown, 2018). Li et al. (2021) carried out a case study on the impact of IoT on energy conservation in hotels, illustrating that IoT applications could lead to a 30% reduction in energy costs (Li et al., 2021). However, Chen (2019) argues that while IoT offers multiple avenues for innovation, the technology is still in its infancy in terms of security measures (Chen, 2019).

2.3 Digital Transformation in the Indian Travel Market

The Indian online travel market is ripe for digital transformation, especially considering the projected growth rates. Gupta and Kumar (2019) affirm that the Indian travel sector has made significant leaps in digital adoption but point out that the industry has been rather traditional in its approach (Gupta & Kumar, 2019). Sharma et al. (2020) provide a detailed analysis of the adoption of digital payment platforms in the Indian travel market, emphasizing that the key to digital transformation lies in aligning technology with customer preferences and cultural nuances (Sharma et al., 2020).

2.4 Theoretical Framework

The integration of AI and IoT in the hospitality industry can be best understood through the lens of the technology acceptance model (TAM) and the diffusion of innovations theory (Rogers, 2003; Davis, 1989). TAM, proposed by Davis (1989), postulates that perceived usefulness and perceived ease of use are fundamental in determining the acceptance of technology. The diffusion of innovations theory by Rogers (2003) offers insights into how, why, and at what rate new technologies are spread.

Methodology

3.1 Research Design

The research will employ a mixed-methods approach combining both qualitative and quantitative methods (Creswell & Plano Clark, 2017). This will allow the study to garner in-depth insights into the application of AI and IoT in the Indian online travel market while also producing statistically significant findings. The study will involve an exploratory sequential design, where qualitative data will be gathered first and the findings will be used to inform the quantitative phase (Yin, 2014).

3.2 Sample Selection

The sample for the qualitative phase will comprise key informants such as industry experts, executives, and technologists in the AI and IoT fields, drawn using purposive sampling (Palinkas et al., 2015). For the quantitative phase, a sample of end users will be selected using stratified random sampling to ensure representation across various segments such as air travel, trains, and hotels (Fowler, 2013).

3.3 Data Collection Methods

Qualitative data will be collected through semi-structured interviews and focus group discussions, to be transcribed and coded for analysis (Ritchie et al., 2014). The quantitative phase will involve the use of structured questionnaires, distributed both online and offline to gather primary data (Bryman, 2016). Secondary data will be collected from publicly available reports, academic journals, and organizational websites (Silva et al., 2018).

3.4 Data Analysis Techniques

For qualitative analysis, the study will employ thematic content analysis (Braun & Clarke, 2006). Coding and categorization of the data will be done using NVivo software (QSR International, 2018). Quantitative analysis will involve the use of statistical tools like SPSS to run descriptive and inferential statistical tests such as Chi-square and *t*-tests to draw insights (Field, 2013).

3.5 Ethical Considerations

All research activities will be conducted in compliance with the American Psychological Association (APA) ethical guidelines, ensuring informed consent, anonymity, and confidentiality of the participants (APA, 2017). Data will be stored securely to protect sensitive information, as mandated by GDPR guidelines for research (Krzysztofek, 2018).

Case Study

AI and IoT Application in the Hotel Industry

This introduction section's goals are to provide an overview of the current issue at hand and to set the stage for the rest of the chapter. Many people believe that AI and the IoT are two of the most influential technologies now available. These technologies have the potential to bring about enormous transformations in a variety of different fields. The hospitality industry is currently experiencing a large impact as a result of their operations, and it is anticipated that this impact will become much more pronounced in the years to come. In the current matter at hand, the hospitality industry is characterized by fierce rivalry, which compels hotels to continually look for ways to improve the overall quality of the experiences they provide for their guests while simultaneously lowering their operating costs. The use of AI and the IoT could be of assistance to hotels in achieving these goals. Both AI and the IoT have shown that they have the potential to be applied in a variety of ways to the hotel industry. For example AI has the potential to be used in a variety of applications. The introduction of personalized recommendations for restaurants, activities, and other attractions that are tailored to coincide with the guest's previous tastes can help to improve the overall experience that the guest has while staying at the hotel. Hotels could also automate various different administrative responsibilities, such as the check-in and check-out procedures, room service, and concierge services. The goal is to plan ahead for necessary maintenance and take preventative measures to reduce the likelihood of equipment faults. This task requires the identification of potential security threats, followed by an appropriate reaction. The IoT has the potential to be exploited for a variety of different applications, including collecting empirical data about the preferences and behaviours displayed by guests at an establishment.

Users are given the option to exercise control over these facilities thanks to a feature that gives them the capacity to handle a variety of smart gadgets that are contained within hotel rooms. These smart gadgets include, but are not limited to, the temperature, the lighting, and the entertainment system. Monitoring of security cameras and various other kinds of sensing equipment is a part of the current assignment.

The following is an account of what the study discovered. Hotels that have implemented technology such as AI and the IoT are experiencing a wide range of benefits, some of which include the following:

Enhanced satisfaction of the guests
An increase in profits and a decrease in expenses
Improved efficiency throughout all operations
The introduction of additional, more stringent safety protocols

This case study takes a closer look at Hotel Tonight, a major player in the field of internet hotel bookings, to analyze its business strategy and the techniques it employs. The purpose of this study is to present an academic examination of the business's operations, with a particular emphasis on the company's essential catering to the needs of spontaneous and last-minute travellers. The smartphone application known as Hotel Tonight makes it easier to reserve hotel rooms with a short amount of notice in advance. The programme makes use of AI in order to analyze data on demand and pricing in order to provide users with the best possible deals. In addition, Hotel Tonight is maximizing the potential of the IoT to boost the level of overall pleasure experienced by their customers. An illustration of this would be the capability of the programme to perform hotel check-in and check-out processes without the need for direct interaction with hotel staff. In addition, guests have the opportunity to use the programme to control the temperature of their room, make adjustments to the lighting, and take care of other responsibilities related to the accommodations they have been given.

The incorporation of AI and the IoT by Hotel Tonight has been demonstrated to be a fruitful attempt on multiple occasions. On the App Store, the programme has a rating of 4.5 stars despite having more than 10 million downloads, which is a testament to its popularity.

In conclusion, it is possible to deduce from the information presented earlier that the findings support the assertion that both AI and the IoT have the potential to bring about a sea change in the hospitality industry. Through the application of these technologies, hotels have the ability to improve the overall experience of their guests, reduce their operating costs, and increase their revenue.

The integration of technologies like artificial intelligence (AI) and the Internet of Things (IoT) into the hotel sector can yield significant benefits. The application of these innovative technologies enables the personalization of services, providing guests with greater convenience and enhanced enjoyment. Ultimately, this contributes to an overall improvement in the quality of the guest experience. This makes it possible to achieve an improvement in the visitor experience. The incorporation of technologies such as AI and the IoT has the potential to dramatically cut costs for hotels. This can be accomplished by automating a variety of jobs, accurately predicting the amount of maintenance that will be required, and improving overall operational efficiency. There is a possibility that the application of technologies such as AI and the IoT in the hotel business may result in an increase in revenue. These technologies make it possible for hotels to give consumers individualized recommendations, which streamlines the booking process and encourages customers to spend more money on a variety of additional services. Within the hospitality business, AI and the IoT have the potential to significantly improve operational efficiency and the overall quality of the experience provided to customers.

AI and IoT Application in Air Travel

This introduction section's goals are to provide an overview of the current issue at hand and to set the stage for the rest of the chapter. Both AI and the IoT are examples of important technological developments that have had a significant impact on modern civilization. The airline transportation industry is currently undergoing a substantial evolution as a result of their operations, and it is anticipated that this influence will continue to grow in the foreseeable future. The aviation industry is distinguished by the complexity and stringency of its requirements. Airlines are always looking for new ways to improve their operational efficiency, lower their operating costs, and boost the level of satisfaction experienced by their customers as a whole. There is a possibility that AI and the IoT will be of assistance to airlines in the process of accomplishing the goals outlined previously. There are a variety of ways in which AI and the IoT have the potential to be applied in the aviation industry. The use of artificial intelligence in a wide variety of fields is an example of an illustration of its application. The timetables and itineraries of flights are going to be optimized in order to achieve this goal. Airlines could also:

Plan ahead for necessary machine maintenance and take preventative measures to avoid unexpected breakdowns.

The current duty comprises identifying potential threats to security and coming up with a response to such dangers.

Provide individualized recommendations for the passengers, including options for food, entertainment, and additional amenities, to improve their overall experience.

The IoT has the potential to be exploited for a variety of different applications, including:

Collect empirical data concerning the performance of the aircraft, the behaviour of the passengers, and the predominant weather conditions.

The capability of managing sophisticated technology within airport and airplane environments, including lighting, temperature adjustment, and entertainment systems, among other functions.

The purpose of this study is to keep track of and locate expensive goods, such as luggage, in order to better understand their movements. The following is a rundown of what this inquiry discovered.

Airlines that have implemented technology such as AI and the IoT are reaping a variety of benefits, some of which include the following:

The cutting down on consumption of fuel and emissions, improved promptness in fulfilling deadlines, and cut down on costs connected with maintenance are potential benefits of adopting autonomous vehicles and automation technologies in the transportation and logistics industries. It has been observed that the deployment of additional security measures has a beneficial impact on the levels of happiness experienced by passengers. This case study focuses on the examination of SITA, a leading provider of IT and communication solutions for the aviation industry, to investigate the association between increased passenger safety and increased passenger satisfaction.

SITA is a well-known multinational information technology company with its headquarters in Switzerland. The company focuses on providing complete information technology solutions that are designed to meet the unique needs of the aviation industry. AI and the IoT are being utilized by SITA in order to develop a wide variety of groundbreaking solutions for the company's clientele.

As an illustration of this, SITA is now working on the creation of an AI-based system that has the power to anticipate maintenance needs and proactively prevent equipment faults. This system is intended to prevent equipment breakdowns. The data collected from the sensors that are put on airplanes are analyzed by the current system in order to proactively detect and identify any potential problems that may arise before they become apparent.

SITA is now working on developing a system that is based on the IoT and has the capability to monitor and detect the whereabouts of bags and other valuable assets. The current system makes use of radio frequency identification (RFID) tags in order to monitor the movement of assets across the airport grounds and aboard the aircraft.

In conclusion, it is possible to deduce from the discussion that has been presented thus far that the various factors taken together indicate that both AI and the IoT have the potential to bring about a sea change in the airline industry. By taking advantage of these technologies, airlines have the opportunity to improve their operational efficiency, lower their costs, and provide a better experience for their passengers overall.

AI and IoT Application in Bus and Train Travel

This opening section's primary objective is to give readers with a high-level summary of the subject matter that will be discussed further. AI and the IoT are two technologies that are commonly recognized as having the ability to significantly disrupt contemporary civilization due to their high levels of influence and substantial potential for revolution. The businesses of bus transportation and train transportation are currently experiencing a substantial evolution from their operations, and it is anticipated that this will continue into the foreseeable future. Public transportation systems around the world are grappling with a range of significant challenges. Aging infrastructure and equipment require costly maintenance and upgrades to ensure safe and reliable service. Funding shortfalls and budget constraints make it difficult to invest in necessary improvements and expansions. Increasing congestion and overcrowding, especially in urban areas, lead to longer commute times and uncomfortable conditions for passengers. Meeting accessibility goals to serve all community members, including those with disabilities, and sustainability targets to reduce environmental impact poses additional hurdles. Integrating new technologies like electric vehicles, mobile ticketing, and real-time tracking systems requires substantial resources for implementation. Attracting and retaining a skilled workforce of drivers, mechanics, and administrators is an ever-present obstacle. Finally, ensuring the safety and security of passengers and personnel remains a paramount concern amid evolving threats. Overcoming these multifaceted challenges will be essential for public transit agencies to fulfill their vital role in promoting mobility and connectivity. The following category is included in the list of challenges that public transportation systems are currently facing:

The problem of excessive congestion and the resulting delays are major sources of concern.

AI and the IoT have the potential to assist public transportation systems in efficiently handling these challenges and improving the overall experience for passengers. The schedules and routes of the buses and trains are going to be optimized in order to achieve this goal. The goal is to produce accurate predictions of future demand in order to then implement the necessary capacity changes.

The correct working and extended life of a variety of systems and pieces of equipment are dependent on the timely detection and resolution of any maintenance issues that may arise. The speed with which enterprises respond to these concerns determines the extent to which they can manage potential hazards, reduce downtime, and maximize operational efficiency.

The passenger experience can be improved by providing information that is up to date and by making personalized recommendations. The IoT has the potential to be put to work for a variety of different applications like collecting empirical data relevant to the functioning of cars, the behaviour of passengers, and the conditions of the traffic at the time.

The administration of smart devices in public transportation hubs like bus and train stations, as well as in vehicles, involves the regulation of a variety of functions. These include, but are not limited to, lighting systems, temperature controls, and information displays.

The purpose of this investigation is to keep track of and identify the whereabouts of different trains and buses across the country. The results of this investigation are going to be discussed in the following portion of this report. Systems of public transportation that make use of AI and the IoT are currently enjoying a wide range of benefits, which can be broken down into the following categories:

The reduction of both overcrowding and waiting times
Improved reliance and dependability

Expenses have been brought under control by the application of several tactics that cut down on costs. Additionally, improvements in levels of contentment among travellers have occurred as a direct consequence of initiatives made to improve the happiness of passengers. This case study takes a closer look at the Singapore Land Transport Authority (LTA) and the part it plays in the overall management of Singapore's land transportation system.

The LTA of Singapore is a government agency that is responsible with the oversight and administration of Singapore's land transport infrastructure. This responsibility includes the infrastructure's design, growth, and operation. In order to improve the efficiency and dependability of the public transportation system, the LTA is utilizing AI and the IoT. The LTA is implementing several AI strategies in order to improve the efficiency with which bus timetables and routes are optimized. The LTA is deploying technology that is based on AI in order to estimate demand and make modifications to capacity that are appropriate. This strategy has been beneficial in reducing the problems associated with overcrowding as well as delays.

The LTA is monitoring and determining the location of buses and trains through the use of technology that is based on the IoT. The aforementioned data is used for the goal of providing passengers with up-to-date information and efficiently allocating buses and trains to locations with the highest demand for transportation.

In conclusion, it is evident that AI and IoT have the potential to significantly transform the transportation industry, particularly in the bus and train sectors. The implementation of these technologies can enhance the overall user experience in public transit networks by alleviating crowding, reducing waiting times, improving reliability and dependability, controlling costs through efficient strategies, and increasing passenger satisfaction through targeted initiatives.

In general, the application of AI and the IoT has considerable promise in the enhancement of the efficiency and quality of public transportation systems, hence improving the entire experience for passengers. The usage of AI with the IoT, in addition to the aforementioned benefits, may also potentially include the following applications:

The goal is to come up with new and innovative services for passengers, such as on-demand transportation options and information that is updated in real time, and this will be accomplished by creating these services.

Encourage the use of environmentally friendly modes of transportation, such as cutting down on emissions and fuel use, and use this as an example.

In general, the integration of AI and the IoT holds promise for improving the effectiveness, dependability, and ease of bus and train transportation for all parties involved. This is because AI can learn from its own experience, and IoT connects physical objects to the internet.

Findings and Discussion

The use of AI and the IoT is being implemented in a variety of different ways to improve customers' experiences when travelling and using various modes of transportation. The fact that AI may be used in many different fields is an example of one of its applications. The application of AI makes it possible to obtain information on consumer preferences, which may then be used to provide individualized recommendations for a variety of travel-related services, such as flights, accommodations, dining alternatives, and other relevant activities.

The application of AI enables the analysis of data acquired from a wide variety of sensors and sources. This, in turn, makes it possible to facilitate the forecast of maintenance requirements by establishing the anticipated period at which equipment is projected to be in need of maintenance. It is possible that this strategy will reduce the number of operational interruptions and increase the reliability of the system. The application of AI in surveillance systems enables the identification of potential dangers through the monitoring of various sensing devices, including security cameras. The AI may then react to these recognized dangers by beginning relevant actions in response to them.

It is possible to use AI to improve the optimization of flight schedules, as well as bus and train routes, with the goal of lowering the number of delays and improving overall efficiency. The application of AI can make it easier to forecast the demand for travel and then make the necessary adjustments to capacity thereafter. This measure has the potential to improve both reliability and the situation with regard to overpopulation. The IoT has the potential to make it easier to collect data relevant to a variety of facets of vehicular operations, such as, but not limited to, vehicle performance, passenger behaviour, and existing traffic conditions. The aforementioned information can subsequently be put to use by AI systems in order to improve operational procedures and provide customers with a better overall experience.

To elaborate with an example, sensors connected to the IoT have the ability to track and record the exact geographical coordinates of trains and buses, which enables them to provide up-to-the-minute information regarding their locations. The aforementioned data can then be put to use to provide passengers with up-to-the-minute information and to route buses and trains to areas with the highest demand for those services. Sensors connected to the IoT have the potential to collect data relating to passenger behaviour, including the amount of time that passengers wait at bus stops or train stations. After the data have been collected, they can be used to improve the design of transportation infrastructure, which will ultimately result in an increase in convenience for passengers.

The combination of AI with the IoT holds the potential to improve the effectiveness, dependability, and convenience of travel and transportation for all parties involved. The following are some examples of how AI and the IoT are being used to make improvements in the realm of travel and transportation:

At this time, hotels are beginning to implement AI in order to improve the overall experience of their guests by providing individualized recommendations for local dining establishments, activities, and numerous attractions. These recommendations are honed to correspond with the specific preferences of the customer, which are gleaned from their previous actions and decisions. In the hospitality business, AI is currently being used to automate numerous processes, including check-in and check-out procedures, room service operations, and concierge services, among others. AI is being utilized by airlines to improve the effectiveness of aircraft schedules and routes, forecast maintenance needs, and detect and handle security issues. The application of AI is now being utilized in the field of personalizing the experience of passengers through the provision of recommendations relevant to a variety of services, including food, entertainment, and others.

The application of AI is currently being utilized in an effort to improve the effectiveness of transportation systems such as buses and trains. This comprises optimizing schedules and routes, projecting demand and adjusting capacity properly, identifying and correcting maintenance difficulties, and personalizing the passenger experience by providing real-time information and specific recommendations to each individual.

The aforementioned situations are merely illustrations of how AI and the IoT are being utilized to improve the experience of travelling and using various modes of transportation. As these technologies continue to improve, it is projected that in the not-too-distant future, there will be a rise in the number of applications that are both unique and transformative of existing paradigms.

Recommendations for Business Practices: The Key to Success

The effective integration of AI and IoT in the hospitality sector, specifically in the Indian online travel market, offers a strategic avenue for businesses to enhance customer satisfaction, optimize operational efficiency, and make informed decisions. However, the implementation of these technologies requires thoughtful strategy, operational design, and organizational alignment.

Adopt a Customer-Centric Approach

In the age of personalized experiences, AI can assist businesses in tailoring services to individual customer preferences through machine learning algorithms that analyze customer behaviour (Jiang et al., 2017). Companies should thus focus on developing and deploying AI algorithms that work cohesively across various customer touchpoints to enhance the overall user experience.

Data-Driven Operational Efficiency

IoT devices can generate a wealth of data that can be used to improve operations. Sensor-based systems in hotels, for example, can optimize energy use, thereby cutting costs and contributing to sustainability (Kar et al., 2019). Businesses should invest in IoT devices that can both reduce operational costs and contribute to environmental sustainability.

Interdisciplinary Teams for Strategic Decision-Making

The success of implementing AI and IoT is not solely a technological venture but a strategic one that necessitates input from various departments – from IT to marketing to human resources (Davenport & Ronanki, 2018). Companies would benefit from establishing interdisciplinary teams to ensure that the deployment of these technologies aligns with the organization's overall strategy.

Ethical and Compliance Measures

Given the amount of data being processed, businesses must put in place robust ethical and compliance measures to protect consumer privacy, in line with GDPR or other relevant local regulations (European Union, 2018).

Training and Development

Employees must be trained to work alongside AI and IoT systems to ensure seamless integration into existing operations. Investment in training programmes is essential for employee adaptation and overall organizational effectiveness (Chui et al., 2016).

Conclusion

The increasing integration of AI and the IoT in the hospitality industry presents a transformative opportunity, especially for the burgeoning Indian online travel market. The current study aims to contribute to a comprehensive understanding of how AI and IoT technologies can be effectively implemented in this context. The research brings into focus the applications and benefits of these technologies, including the enhancement of customer experiences, improving operational efficiency, and aiding strategic decision-making.

While the study is designed to provide an in-depth analysis of the subject, it is not without its limitations. The qualitative sample, although carefully selected, may not be fully representative of the broader industry. Similarly, the quantitative phase of the study may suffer from respondent bias or inadequate sample sizes (Bryman, 2016). Another notable limitation lies in the reliance on available secondary data, which might be dated or biased (Silva et al., 2018). Additionally, the study primarily focuses on the Indian online travel market, which may limit its generalizability to other geographical or cultural contexts (Creswell & Plano Clark, 2017).

Scope for Further Research

The study's findings are expected to spark further research in various directions. One viable avenue is to conduct a longitudinal study to assess the long-term impacts and sustainability of implementing AI and IoT in the hospitality industry. Future research could also explore the ethical dimensions surrounding these technologies, particularly in terms of data privacy and employment (Kim et al., 2020). Moreover, comparative studies focusing on different markets could be invaluable for global stakeholders.

References

APA. (2017). "Ethical principles of psychologists and code of conduct." *American psychologist 47, 12*(1992), 1597–1611.

Braun, V., & Clarke, V. (2006). Using thematic analysis in psychology. *Qualitative Research in Psychology, 3*(2), 77–101.

Brown, J. (2018). IoT in the hospitality industry. *Journal of Hospitality Management, 25*(1), 67–80.

Bryman, A. (2016). *Social research methods* (5th ed.). Oxford: Oxford University Press.

Business Standard. (2023). *MakeMyTrip integrates IOT for personalized travel experience*. Retrieved from Business Standard Website

Chen, S. (2019). Security challenges in the internet of things. *Journal of Cybersecurity, 8*(2), 111–129.

Chui, M., Manyika, J., & Miremadi, M. (2016). Where machines could replace humans-and where they can't (yet). *The McKinsey Quarterly,* 1–12.

Creswell, J. W., & Plano Clark, V. L. (2017). *Designing and conducting mixed methods research* (3rd ed.). Los Angeles: SAGE.

Davenport, T., & Ronanki, R. (2018). Artificial intelligence for the real world. *Harvard Business Review, 96*(1), 108–116.

Davis, F. D. (1989). Perceived Usefulness, perceived ease of use, and user acceptance of information technology. *MIS Quarterly, 13*(3), 319–340.

Field, A. (2013). *Discovering statistics using IBM SPSS statistics* (4th ed.). London: SAGE.

Fowler, F. J. (2013). *Survey research methods* (5th ed.). Los Angeles: SAGE.

Globe Newswire. (2021). *Internet of things market report*. Globe Newswire Research. https://www.globenewswire.com/news-release/2021/05/11/2226879/0/en/

Global-Industrial-Internet-of-Things-Market-Report-2021-2026-Combining-AI-with-Digital-Twins-Cloud-Robotics-and-Teleoperation-to-Drive-Substantial-Market-Opportunities-for-Systems-.html.

Godau, Ralph I. (2004). "Qualitative Data Analysis Software: NVivo." *Qualitative Research Journal*, 4 (2004): 77.

Gupta, S., & Kumar, R. (2019). Digital transformation in the Indian travel industry. *Tourism Management Perspectives, 10*(1), 25–31.

Gursoy, D., Lu, L., & Lu, S. (2020). Antecedents and outcomes of travelers' information-seeking behavior in the context of online reviews. *Journal of Travel Research, 59*(1), 16–30.

IDC. (2020). *Global AI market report*. International Data Corporation. https://www.mordorintelligence.com/industry-reports/global-artificial-intelligence-market.

Jiang, Z., Zhao, X., & Wang, X. (2017). The impacts of online hotel reviews on hotel room sales and room prices: A multi-level modeling approach with hierarchical functions. *International Journal of Hospitality Management, 62*, 247–258.

Johnson, L., Smith, A., & Kumar, R. (2021). Digital transformation in the age of COVID-19. *Journal of Hospitality and Tourism Technology, 10*(3), 350–364.

Kar, A. K., Ilavarasan, V., Gupta, M. P., Janssen, M., & Kothari, R. (2019). Moving beyond smart cities: Digital nations for social innovation & sustainability. *Information Systems Frontiers, 21*(3), 495–501.

Kim, Y., Lee, J., & Kim, M. (2020). Ethical concerns in artificial intelligence: A hospitality industry perspective. *Journal of Hospitality Ethics, 2*(1), 10–26.

Kimes, S. E. (2019). Artificial intelligence in the hospitality industry: Prospects and challenges. *Cornell Hospitality Quarterly, 60*(4), 351–365.

Krzysztofek, M. (2018). GDPR: General Data Protection Regulation (EU) 2016/679: Post-reform Personal Data Protection in the European Union. Kluwer Law International BV.

Kumar, S. (2020). Consumer behavior in online markets: A study of Indian context. *Journal of Digital Marketing, 6*(2), 21–35.

Li, X., Wang, D., & Liang, X. (2021). Energy conservation through IoT in hotels: A case study. *Journal of Sustainable Tourism, 12*(2), 205–222.

Palinkas, L. A., Horwitz, S. M., Green, C. A., Wisdom, J. P., Duan, N., & Hoagwood, K. (2015). Purposeful sampling for qualitative data collection and analysis in mixed method implementation research. *Administration and Policy in Mental Health, 42*(5), 533–544.

Patel, R., & Sarker, S. (2018). AI and hospitality: Global perspectives. *Journal of Information Systems, 15*(1), 55–72.

Ritchie, J., Lewis, J., Nicholls, C. M., & Ormston, R. (Eds.). (2014). *Qualitative research practice: A guide for social science students and researchers*. London: SAGE.

Rogers, E. M. (2003). *Diffusion of innovations* (5th ed.). New York: Free Press.

Sharma, P., Rangarajan, D., & Pauleen, D. (2020). Digital payment platforms and the future of Indian travel industry. *Journal of Asian Business Studies, 14*(3), 289–307.

Singh, R., & Kaur, P. (2021). AI in customer service: A review and research agenda. *Journal of Business Research, 129,* 800–817.

Smith, A. (2019). Technology adoption in emerging markets: The case of India. *Journal of Global Information Management, 4*(4), 25–40.

Silva Martins, Fellipe & Carneiro da Cunha, Julio & Serra, Fernando. (2018). Secondary Data in Research - Uses and Opportunities. *Revista Ibero-Americana de Estratégia. 17.* 01–04. 10.5585/ijsm.v17i4.2723.

Statista. (2021). "Global Market Size of the Hospitality Industry." *Statista*, www.statista.com/statistics/1247012/global-market-size-of-the-hospitality-industry/.

TechCrunch. (2022). *OYO rooms uses ai to transform hospitality industry*. Retrieved from TechCrunch Website

Tractica. (2019). *Market analysis on AI growth*. Tractica Research.

WTTC. (2020). "India Travel and Tourism Could Surpass Pre-Pandemic Levels by the End of 2022." WTTC, 20 Apr. 2022, https://cite.me/KTx9gyn.

Yin, R. K. (2014). *Case study research: Design and methods* (5th ed.). Los Angeles: SAGE.

12 AI-Enabled Guest Experience

Disrupting Hospitality Through Next-Generation AI Technologies

Dr. Princi Gupta and Prof. Renu Pareek

Introduction

In virtually all industries, there has been a considerable shift towards automation in the new millennium. Although this rise in robotic labour has increased efficiency, it has also raised questions about how workers would still be required in the age of labour automation (Jabeen, 2022). Given that inns and host–guest relationships have played a significant role in our shared cultural heritage, hospitality is one of the oldest professions in the world. We have worked to create a sense of home and comfort for others since thousands of years ago (Kong, 2023). The status quo has been to personalize customer experience and provide them with memorable and delightful service, a quality that all operations have strived to provide. In particular, the hospitality industry is facing increased hurdles due to the COVID-19 virus, and "anything that happens around the world may affect the business environment directly or indirectly." According to Buhalis and Leung (2018), "Proactive and reactive tactics enhance decision making and value co-creation and hence influence the competitiveness and profitability of firms. Guest satisfaction is the main priorities of hospitality services, which can be provided in both commercial and non-commercial settings. The customer's perspective might become the focal point of operations thanks to modern technology (Nannelli, 2023). The use of AI technologies can enhance consumer experiences while requiring less human labour overall. As a result, many hospitality organizations have increased their technological investments in recent years in order to enhance their revenue. One of the most significant, biggest, and fastest-growing industries in the world is the global hospitality and tourist sector. It accounts for about 10% of the global GDP and one out of every ten jobs globally, generating $7.6 trillion in revenue and employing 292 million people, with more employment anticipated to be generated in the upcoming years due to its anticipated stable growth. Hence, it is one of the most significant economic sectors and a market that is today quite competitive, and the hospitality industry is crucial (Mariani, 2021).

In 2022 and 2023, the global business landscape continued to witness significant shifts and innovations in response to emerging trends and challenges. The hospitality industry, for instance, adapted to the evolving needs and expectations of guests (Smith, 2023). AI-powered contactless services became a norm, with hotels

DOI: 10.4324/9781003488248-12

implementing mobile apps for seamless check-ins, room service requests, and concierge services, prioritizing guest safety and convenience. Personalization took center stage, with AI algorithms analyzing guest data to offer hyper-personalized experiences, such as curated in-room amenities based on past preferences. Sustainability initiatives also gained momentum, as AI was used to optimize energy consumption, reduce waste, and implement eco-friendly practices, reflecting the growing concern for environmental responsibility among travellers (Smith, 2022). Voice assistants and smart room integration continued to captivate tech-savvy guests, allowing them to control room settings and access information through voice commands. AI-driven customer feedback analysis helped hotels address concerns promptly, enhancing overall satisfaction. Collaborations with AI solution providers and startups led to innovative solutions for improved guest experiences. Data privacy and security remained priorities, with hotels investing in AI-based cybersecurity measures to protect guest data (Jones & Brown, 2023). Dynamic pricing and revenue management systems, driven by AI algorithms, optimized room rates based on demand and events, ensuring hotels maximized their revenue. These recent business practices underscore the industry's resilience and adaptability in embracing AI technologies to meet the ever-changing demands of guests and maintain a competitive edge in a dynamic business landscape (Miller, 2023).

Theoretical Background

AI in Next-Generation Hospitality: Overview, Adoption, and Impact

The hospitality sector has been increasingly embracing artificial intelligence (AI) technologies to enhance guest experiences, improve operational efficiency, and stay competitive in a rapidly evolving industry (Battour, 2023). The adoption of AI in hospitality has transformed various aspects of the guest journey, from booking and check-in processes to personalized recommendations and post-stay feedback analysis (Sharma, 2022). One of the key areas where AI is making a profound impact is in customer service. AI-powered chatbots and virtual assistants have become increasingly prevalent, serving as efficient and cost-effective solutions for handling routine inquiries, providing instant responses, and offering personalized recommendations to guests (Roy et al., 2020). These virtual assistants are available 24/7, ensuring guests receive timely assistance and information, which ultimately leads to enhanced customer satisfaction and loyalty. This data-driven approach empowers hotels to offer tailored services, personalized marketing campaigns, and customized offers, resulting in higher guest engagement and conversion rates (Limna, 2022).

AI is also proving instrumental in streamlining housekeeping and maintenance operations. Robotic devices equipped with AI algorithms are being deployed in hotels to autonomously navigate through corridors, deliver room service, and even perform basic cleaning tasks ((Roy et al., 2020). Virtual reality and augmented reality technologies are being utilized to provide immersive experiences to potential guests, allowing them to take virtual tours of hotel rooms and amenities before making a reservation, making the booking process more engaging and informed.

Biometric technologies, like facial recognition, are transforming the check-in process, offering a seamless and secure experience for guests (Limna, 2022). Facial recognition systems allow guests to access their rooms and other hotel facilities without the need for traditional key cards, streamlining the check-in process and improving overall security (Lee et al., 2021).

Furthermore, AI-driven sentiment analysis tools are being employed to monitor and analyze customer reviews and feedback across various platforms. This enables hotels to gain insights into guest sentiments, identify areas for improvement, and address any concerns promptly, thereby enhancing overall service quality and reputation. In the supply chain management domain, AI is optimizing inventory management processes, ensuring timely delivery of essential items and minimizing wastage (Lee et al., 2021). By accurately forecasting demand and adjusting inventory levels accordingly, hotels can maintain operational efficiency and cost-effectiveness. As AI technology continues to evolve, its integration in the hospitality sector is poised to further transform the industry (Ruel, 2021).

Virtual assistants and chatbots powered by AI have become integral parts of the customer service landscape, providing round-the-clock assistance to guests with tailored recommendations and instant responses to inquiries (Ruel, 2021). This not only enhances guest satisfaction but also frees up staff members to focus on more specialized tasks. Hotels can now adjust pricing dynamically in real time, ensuring maximum occupancy and profitability. AI-driven technologies have also made a significant impact on safety and security within the hospitality sector. With advanced surveillance systems and predictive maintenance algorithms, hotels can proactively identify potential security threats and maintain their facilities efficiently. This, in turn, fosters a sense of security and trust among guests (Lv, 2022).

Additionally, AI has revolutionized guest engagement through voice-activated systems and virtual concierges. Guests can now control various room features and access information using voice commands, providing a seamless and convenient experience. Virtual concierges assist guests with local recommendations, transportation details, and other personalized services, further elevating the overall guest experience. Data analytics powered by AI plays a crucial role in providing valuable insights into guest preferences and behaviours.

Although AI adoption has brought significant benefits to the hospitality sector, challenges remain (Doborjeh, 2022). The hospitality industry's adoption of AI continues to grow, driven by the desire to provide exceptional guest experiences, optimize operations, and stay competitive in an ever-evolving market. As AI technologies mature and new innovations emerge, the hospitality sector is poised to witness further transformative changes in the years to come (Lv, 2022).

The necessity for a dedicated chapter on AI-enabled guest experience in the hospitality sector is paramount, driven by the critical need to fill substantial gaps in the existing literature. Notably, the literature often overlooks the ethical dimensions of AI implementation, including data privacy and AI-driven decision-making, which demand comprehensive examination. Furthermore, the absence of longitudinal studies results in a limited understanding of how AI-enabled guest experiences evolve over time, emphasizing the importance of a chapter dedicated to exploring long-term impacts (Dwivedi et al., 2023). The COVID-19 pandemic has ushered in transformative changes in the industry, a dimension insufficiently explored in current literature. Smaller, independent establishments receive scant attention despite their significant presence in the sector, necessitating an investigation into how they leverage AI to stay competitive and enhance guest satisfaction. Lastly, the regional and cultural variations in AI adoption remain underexplored, underscoring the need for a dedicated chapter to elucidate how these factors influence AI integration and its impacts on guest experiences. Thus, this chapter is essential to bridge these substantial gaps and provide a more comprehensive understanding of the rapidly evolving landscape of AI in the hospitality industry (Mariani, 2023).

AI-Enhanced Guest Experience: A Relevance Assessment

In the ever-evolving landscape of the hospitality industry, providing exceptional guest experiences has become paramount for hotels and accommodations to stand out and thrive (Huang, 2022). With the advent of cutting-edge technologies, one of the most significant game changers in this domain is the integration of AI. AI-enabled guest experience has emerged as a transformative approach, redefining how guests interact with hospitality services. By leveraging AI technologies, hotels can personalize services, streamline operations, and create memorable stays for their guests like never before (Cain, 2019). AI-enabled guest experience refers to the strategic application of AI and related technologies to enhance and customize every aspect of a guest's journey in the hospitality industry (Pillai & Sivathanu, 2020).

The article discusses the relevance in context with AI-enabled guest experience, highlighting how next-generation AI technologies are disrupting the hospitality industry. The adoption of AI-enabled guest experience has a profound impact on the hospitality industry, revolutionizing how hotels and accommodations operate and interact with their guests (Li et al., 2021). Here's why AI-enabled guest experience is particularly relevant in the context of disrupting hospitality through next-generation AI technologies (Li, 2021).

- Efficiency and Automation: AI-powered chatbots, virtual assistants, and automated processes streamline guest interactions, reservation management, and check-ins, reducing wait times and enhancing operational efficiency (Limna, 2022). This frees up staff to focus on providing more personalized and high-touch services.
- Enhanced Services: Next-generation AI technologies, such as voice-activated interfaces and facial recognition, enable seamless and innovative guest services, ranging from in-room controls to frictionless check-ins.
- Revenue Growth: AI-driven pricing optimization and targeted marketing strategies can lead to increased revenue generation, ensuring competitive pricing while maximizing profitability (Chen, 2023).
- Competitive Advantage: Embracing AI-enabled guest experience allows hotels to differentiate themselves in a crowded market (KILIÇHAN, 2020). Properties that leverage AI effectively can attract tech-savvy guests and gain a competitive edge over traditional competitors.

AI Adoption Drivers and Hospitality Case Studies: Enhancing Guest Experiences

The hospitality sector is witnessing a rapid adoption of AI technologies, driven by several key factors that are reshaping the industry's landscape. One of the primary drivers is the quest for providing personalized guest experiences (Doborjeh, 2022). AI enables hotels to gather and analyze vast amounts of guest data, from preferences to past behaviours, allowing them to offer tailored recommendations and services that cater to individual preferences. This personalization creates a deeper connection with guests, fostering loyalty and advocacy (Chaturvedi, 2023).

Another critical driver is the pursuit of improved operational efficiency. By automating repetitive tasks and streamlining processes, AI frees up human resources, enabling staff to focus on delivering higher-touch and personalized services. This optimization of operations leads to cost savings, increased productivity, and enhanced guest satisfaction (Doborjeh, 2022).

Real-time guest support is also a significant factor propelling AI adoption. AI-powered chatbots and virtual assistants provide instant and accurate responses to guest inquiries and requests, 24/7. This round-the-clock availability ensures that guests receive timely assistance, making their stay more seamless and enjoyable (Battour, 2023).

AI's role in revenue management cannot be overlooked. AI algorithms analyze market trends and competitor rates to optimize pricing strategies in real time. This dynamic pricing approach allows hotels to maximize room revenue and capitalize on demand fluctuations.

Moreover, AI's data-driven decision-making capabilities empower hotels to make informed choices based on guest behaviour and market trends. By leveraging data insights, hotels can fine-tune marketing strategies, improve service offerings, and tailor experiences to meet guest expectations effectively (Jamaluddin, 2022). In the post-pandemic era, the importance of contactless solutions has surged, making AI-driven contactless technologies indispensable. From mobile check-ins to voice-activated interfaces, AI facilitates seamless and touchless interactions, prioritizing guest safety and convenience.

Lastly, as hotels seek to differentiate themselves in a competitive market, AI offers a distinct competitive advantage, attracting tech-savvy travellers seeking modern and personalized experiences (Koo, 2021). Hotels and accommodations that embrace AI technologies stand to benefit from improved guest experiences, enhanced operational efficiency, and a competitive edge in meeting the ever-changing demands of today's travellers (Koo, 2021).

Table 12.1 depicts how the hospitality industry has witnessed a paradigm shift with the integration of AI, revolutionizing guest experiences in numerous ways. AI-powered innovations have enabled hotels to deliver exceptional levels of personalization and efficiency, elevating guest satisfaction to unprecedented heights (Pillai & Sivathanu, 2020). One such case study is the implementation of AI-powered chatbots by Marriott International. These virtual assistants provide 24/7 support, allowing guests to make reservations, inquire about services, and receive personalized recommendations effortlessly. The natural language processing

Table 12.1 AI Case Studies in the Hospitality Industry

Case Study	*AI Implementation*	*Key Benefits*
Hilton Hotels – Connie	AI-powered robot concierge named Connie stationed at the front desk	Streamlined check-in, personalized guest assistance, improved engagement
Marriott International	AI-powered mobile app with chatbot integration	Reduced check-in times, personalized recommendations, enhanced guest convenience
Yotel – Yobot	AI-powered luggage storage and retrieval robot	Efficient luggage handling, unique guest experience
InterContinental Hotels Group	AI-driven personalization for loyalty programme members	Tailored room settings, personalized offers, increased guest loyalty
Wynn Las Vegas	AI-powered in-room assistants using Amazon's Alexa	Voice-activated room control, personalized stay experience

Source: By authors

capabilities of the chatbots ensure seamless interactions, reducing response times and alleviating the workload of hotel staff. Similarly, Wynn Las Vegas introduced AI in-room assistants, empowering guests to control various aspects of their stay through voice commands. This personalization extends beyond mere room control, as the AI system learns guest preferences over time and tailors its recommendations accordingly (Rosete et al., 2020). Moreover, AI-driven customer loyalty programmes, exemplified by Hilton Hotels & Resorts, analyze guest behaviour and preferences to deliver personalized offers and rewards, fostering customer engagement and loyalty. Additionally, AI-powered predictive analytics, as implemented by InterContinental Hotels Group (IHG), accurately forecast demand patterns, optimizing pricing, staffing, and inventory management for improved operational efficiency (Pillai & Sivathanu, 2020). These AI advancements also extend to immersive experiences like virtual tours offered by Four Seasons Hotels and Resorts, empowering guests to explore hotel facilities and amenities before booking. AccorHotels leverages AI algorithms to provide tailored recommendations for dining and activities, enhancing guest experiences and encouraging exploration of hotel offerings. These case studies collectively demonstrate how AI technologies are reshaping the hospitality landscape, forging deeper connections with guests, and propelling the industry towards new heights of excellence (Mariani, 2021).

Revolutionizing Guest Experience: The Transformative Impact of AI in Hospitality

The impact of AI on guest experience in the hospitality industry has been nothing short of revolutionary. AI technologies have fundamentally changed the way hotels and accommodations interact with their guests, ushering in an era of personalized and seamless experiences. Through advanced data analytics and machine learning algorithms, AI has enabled hotels to gain deep insights into guest preferences, behaviours, and needs, allowing them to offer highly personalized recommendations and services (Bulchand-Gidumal, 2022).

One of the most significant transformations has been the integration of AI-powered virtual assistants and chatbots. These intelligent systems provide instant and accurate responses to guest inquiries and requests, 24/7, ensuring that guests receive timely assistance and information at any time of the day (Nannelli, 2023). This round-the-clock availability enhances guest convenience and engagement, fostering a positive impression of the hotel's commitment to excellent guest service. AI allows guests to use mobile apps or self-service kiosks to complete the formalities without physical contact, ensuring both efficiency and guest safety. AI's predictive capabilities have also been instrumental in enhancing guest experiences. By analyzing historical data and guest behaviour, AI can anticipate guest needs and offer relevant services and amenities proactively (Chen, 2023). From personalized room settings upon arrival to pre-emptive suggestions for dining and activities, this level of attentiveness creates a sense of anticipation and delight among guests.

Furthermore, AI-driven revenue management systems optimize pricing strategies in real time, maximizing room revenue and profitability for hotels. The ability to offer dynamic pricing and personalized offers based on guest behaviour contributes to increased bookings and revenue generation. Beyond the stay experience, AI technologies continue to engage guests post-stay. Personalized follow-up communications, feedback requests, and loyalty rewards driven by AI create lasting connections with guests, encouraging repeat visits and fostering loyalty (Bhushan, 2021).

Overall, AI's transformative impact on guest experience in the hospitality industry is evident through its ability to deliver personalized, efficient, and contactless interactions. As AI technologies continue to evolve, hotels have an unprecedented opportunity to elevate guest satisfaction and loyalty, setting new standards for exceptional experiences in the ever-competitive hospitality landscape (Bulchand-Gidumal, 2022).

AI Drive: Disruptive Technologies Shaping Hospitality Industry for Seamless Guest Experiences

Table 12.2 presents a comprehensive overview of disruptive technologies that are shaping the hospitality industry, aiming to create seamless guest experiences.

These disruptive technologies are transforming the hospitality industry, leading to improved guest experiences, increased efficiency, and the adoption of sustainable practices. It lists various technologies, such as AI, Internet of Things (IoT), robotics and automation, augmented reality (AR), facial recognition, voice-activated interfaces, contactless technology, blockchain, big data and analytics, mobile apps and services, cloud computing, 5G connectivity, smart room technology, in-room entertainment, and green and sustainable technologies. Each technology has a description of its capabilities and the impact it has on hospitality, including enhanced guest experiences, improved operational efficiency, and alignment with sustainable practices.

Table 12.2 Disruptive Technologies in Hospitality: Shaping Seamless Guest Experiences

Disruptive Technology	*Description*	*Shaping Guest Experience*
Artificial Intelligence (AI)	AI-driven technologies offer personalized experiences, predictive analytics, chatbots, virtual assistants, and dynamic pricing.	Enhanced guest satisfaction, personalized services, and improved operational efficiency
Internet of Things (IoT)	IoT connects devices and amenities, enabling centralized control and automation of room settings, energy management, and guest services.	Seamless and connected guest experiences, improved energy efficiency
Robotics and Automation	Robots perform tasks like room service delivery, housekeeping, and concierge services, reducing labor and enhancing operational efficiency.	Streamlined operations, cost reduction, and improved service quality
Augmented Reality (AR)	AR technologies offer immersive experiences for guests, allowing them to virtually explore hotel facilities and destinations.	Powerful marketing tool, enhancing guest engagement
Facial Recognition	Facial recognition streamlines check-in and check-out processes, improving guest convenience and security.	Faster and secure check-in, enhanced guest experience
Voice-Activated Interfaces	Voice-activated technology allows guests to control room amenities and services, promoting hands-free and convenient interactions.	Enhanced guest convenience and accessibility
Contactless Technology	Contactless solutions like mobile check-in, digital keys, and mobile payments ensure a hygienic and seamless guest experience.	Hygienic and safe interactions, aligned with current health concerns
Blockchain	Blockchain enhances security, data management, and transparency in payment processing, loyalty programmes, and identity verification.	Secure and tamper-resistant transactions, improved loyalty programmes
Big Data and Analytics	Utilizing data analytics, hotels gain insights into guest behaviour, preferences, and operational performance.	Data-driven decision-making, personalized guest experiences
Mobile Apps and Services	Mobile apps offer guests easy access to hotel information, services, mobile check-in, and personalized experiences.	Improved guest engagement and seamless mobile-centric services
Cloud Computing	Cloud-based solutions streamline operations, improve scalability, and enhance data accessibility and security for hotels.	Improved operational efficiency, cost savings, and flexibility

(*Continued*)

Table 12.2 (Continued)

Disruptive Technology	*Description*	*Shaping Guest Experience*
5G Connectivity	The deployment of 5G networks improves internet connectivity, supporting faster guest Wi-Fi and seamless communication.	Faster and reliable connectivity, improved IoT performance
Smart Room Technology	AI-driven smart room systems enable guests to control various room features through mobile apps or voice commands.	Enhanced room customization and guest control
In-Room Entertainment	Integration of smart TVs, content streaming, and casting options enhance the in-room entertainment experience for guests.	Modern and immersive in-room entertainment options
Green and Sustainable Tech	Eco-friendly practices, such as energy-efficient lighting and water-saving systems, align hotels with sustainable trends.	Environmentally responsible operations, meeting guest expectations

Source: Compiled by authors

Next-Generation AI-Driven Guest Experience in Hospitality: Key Components

AI-driven guest experience in the hospitality industry involves the integration of various components and technologies that work together to create personalized and seamless interactions with guests. The key components of AI-driven guest experience in the hospitality industry include:

- Data Collection and Analysis: The foundation of AI-driven guest experience lies in data collection and analysis. Hotels gather data from various sources, such as guest profiles, past behaviours, preferences, and feedback (Jaiswal, 2020). This data is then analyzed using AI algorithms to gain insights into guest preferences and expectations.
- Personalization Engine: The personalization engine is a core component of AI-driven guest experience. It uses the insights from data analysis to create highly personalized recommendations and services for individual guests. This engine tailors room preferences, dining options, activities, and amenities to meet each guest's unique needs and preferences (Drexler & Lapré, 2019).
- AI-Powered Virtual Assistants and Chatbots: AI-driven virtual assistants and chatbots provide instant and accurate responses to guest inquiries and requests. They leverage natural language processing and machine learning to understand guest queries and offer personalized recommendations, enhancing guest engagement and convenience.
- Contactless Technologies: AI technologies enable contactless solutions in various aspects of the guest journey. From contactless check-in and check-out to

mobile room keys and voice-activated room control, these technologies minimize physical contact and enhance guest safety and convenience (Ivanov, 2020).

- Predictive Analytics: Predictive analytics is used to anticipate guest needs and behaviour based on historical data and guest interactions. This enables hotels to offer proactive and timely services, exceeding guest expectations and fostering a positive guest experience.
- Revenue Optimization: AI-driven revenue management systems analyze market trends, demand patterns, and competitor rates to optimize pricing strategies in real time. Dynamic pricing and personalized offers contribute to increased bookings and revenue generation (Qiu, 2022).
- Post-Stay Engagement: AI technologies facilitate post-stay engagement with guests. Personalized follow-up communications, feedback requests, and loyalty rewards ensure continued interaction with guests even after their stay, encouraging repeat visits and guest loyalty.
- AI-Enhanced Loyalty Programmes: AI is utilized to analyze guest behaviours and preferences, allowing hotels to create personalized loyalty rewards and incentives. This tailored approach increases guest engagement and participation in loyalty programmes.
- Sentiment Analysis: AI-powered sentiment analysis helps hotels gauge guest satisfaction and sentiment based on feedback and reviews. This information allows hotels to identify areas for improvement and address guest concerns promptly.
- AI-Powered Recommendations and Marketing: AI algorithms are used to deliver targeted marketing campaigns and personalized recommendations to guests. This ensures that guests receive relevant promotions and offerings that align with their preferences, driving conversions and guest loyalty (Saydam et al., 2022).

By integrating these components, the hospitality industry can deliver an AI-driven guest experience that is tailored, efficient, and memorable, setting new standards for personalized service and guest satisfaction (Chaturvedi, 2023).

Roadblocks: AI Advancements for Disruption in Hospitality

As AI advancements continue to disrupt the hospitality industry, several challenges and issues need to be addressed to ensure successful implementation and sustainable growth. Here are some of the key challenges:

- Data Privacy and Security: AI systems in the hospitality sector heavily rely on guest data, such as personal information and preferences. Ensuring the privacy and security of this data is critical to maintaining guest trust (Rasheed et al., 2023). Hotels must implement robust data protection measures, comply with relevant regulations (e.g., GDPR), and be transparent with guests about data collection and usage (El Hajal, 2020).
- Human–AI Collaboration: As AI becomes more prevalent, there might be concerns about the displacement of human workers in the hospitality industry.

Striking the right balance between AI automation and human touch is crucial. AI should complement human efforts rather than replace them, focusing on tasks that enhance guest experiences and operational efficiency.

- Trust and User Acceptance: Guests may be skeptical about interacting with AI-driven systems, especially in sensitive areas like personal assistance or decision-making. Building trust with users is essential, and businesses must ensure that AI systems are reliable, transparent, and responsive to user needs. Training staff and guests on how to use AI services effectively can also contribute to user acceptance.
- Integration and Infrastructure: Implementing AI technologies requires robust IT infrastructure and integration with existing hotel systems. This can be challenging, especially for older properties that might not have the necessary infrastructure to support AI advancements. Upgrading systems and ensuring seamless integration are crucial to leveraging AI effectively (Prentice et al., 2020).
- Data Quality and Availability: AI models heavily depend on high-quality data for training and decision-making. In the hospitality industry, data may be scattered across various platforms and systems, making it difficult to access, clean, and integrate into AI solutions. Hotels must invest in data management strategies to ensure data quality and accessibility (Nam, 2021).
- Cost and ROI: Implementing AI solutions can be expensive, particularly for smaller hospitality businesses. It's essential to carefully assess the return on investment (ROI) and long-term benefits of AI adoption to justify the costs involved (Cain, 2019).

AI-Enabled Guest Experience: Future Trends and Innovations

The future of AI-enabled guest experience in the hospitality industry promises exciting trends and innovations that will redefine how hotels interact with their guests. One of the most prominent trends is hyper-personalization, where AI algorithms will leverage guest data to deliver highly customized experiences. From personalized room settings to curated dining options and tailored activities, guests can expect a level of personalization that goes beyond their expectations (Al-Hyari et al., 2023).

Predictive service anticipation will be another game changer, as AI algorithms become more adept at understanding guest behaviours and preferences. Hotels will proactively anticipate guest needs throughout their stay, offering services and amenities before guests even make a request. This anticipatory approach will create a seamless and delightful experience, leaving guests feeling well cared for and valued.

Emotional AI and sentiment analysis are set to revolutionize guest interactions. AI-powered systems will be capable of recognizing and responding to guests' emotional states, enabling more empathetic and human-like interactions. Sentiment analysis will also allow hotels to gauge guest satisfaction in real time and respond promptly to any concerns, ensuring a positive and emotionally fulfilling stay (Mingotto, 2021).

AI will take loyalty programmes to new heights with AI-enhanced loyalty initiatives. Hotels will use AI-driven platforms to deliver personalized rewards, incentives, and exclusive experiences to loyalty programme members. This personalized approach will foster deeper guest loyalty and encourage repeat visits (Kong, 2023).

Furthermore, seamless multilingual support through AI-powered language translation will cater to the diverse needs of international travellers. AI-driven translation and natural language processing will enable hotels to provide instant and accurate communication in multiple languages, ensuring a smooth and enjoyable stay for guests from around the world.

AR experiences will enhance guest engagement and immersion. Hotels can leverage AR to offer interactive virtual tours, information overlays, and AR-enhanced in-room amenities, creating a novel and captivating experience for guests (Al-Hyari et al., 2023).

AI will also play a pivotal role in health and safety initiatives. AI-driven systems will support health protocols, ensuring guest safety and adherence to guidelines. Additionally, AI-enabled robots will become more prevalent, providing emotional engagement and support for guests, especially those travelling solo (Wang et al., 2022).

Finally, AI-powered sustainable initiatives will help hotels optimize resource usage, reduce waste, and promote eco-friendly practices, aligning with guests' increasing interest in environmentally conscious stays.

As these future trends and innovations take shape, AI's role in the hospitality industry will expand, revolutionizing guest experiences and setting new standards for personalized, efficient, and memorable stays (Pelet et al., 2019). Hotels that embrace these innovations will have a competitive edge in delivering exceptional guest experiences and fostering guest loyalty in the dynamic and evolving hospitality landscape.

Recommendations for Business Practices: The Key to Success

Achieving success in AI-enabled guest experience and disrupting the hospitality industry through next-generation AI technologies requires a well-defined blueprint for business practices. Here are key recommendations for achieving this goal:

First and foremost, businesses in the hospitality sector must adopt a data-driven approach. Understanding the guest journey is paramount. From booking to check-out, every touchpoint offers an opportunity to enhance the guest experience through AI. Begin by mapping this journey, identifying areas where AI can be seamlessly integrated to improve the overall guest experience.

One of the most crucial aspects of leveraging AI in the hospitality sector is the use of guest data for personalization. Gathering and analyzing guest data, such as preferences, behaviours, and feedback, is essential for tailoring services, recommendations, and promotions. By harnessing the power of AI, you can create unique and memorable experiences that resonate with your guests.

Implementing AI-powered chatbots and virtual assistants is another critical step. Chatbots also enable real-time communication and assistance, ensuring that guests' needs are met promptly, thus enhancing their overall satisfaction. To provide a truly personalized experience, develop AI algorithms that offer recommendations tailored to each guest's profile and historical data (Alam et al., 2023). These recommendations can range from room upgrades and dining options to local activities, creating a sense of exclusivity and luxury that guests will appreciate.

Voice assistants and smart room integration have become increasingly popular. They allow guests to control various room settings and request services through voice commands, contributing to a futuristic and convenient experience. By monitoring room equipment and predicting maintenance needs, you can proactively address issues, minimizing guest disruptions and improving operational efficiency. This predictive approach not only elevates the guest experience but also optimizes your resources.

In the age of data breaches and privacy concerns, it's imperative to invest in AI-driven security measures to protect guest data and privacy. Guest feedback is a valuable resource for continuous improvement. Implement sentiment analysis on guest feedback and reviews, using AI to identify areas for enhancement and addressing issues promptly. This data-driven approach ensures that your guest experience continually evolves in response to real-time feedback (Gangwar & Reddy, 2023). AI can also augment your staff's capabilities, enabling them to deliver high-touch services.

Furthermore, sustainability is a growing concern for travellers. Use AI to optimize energy consumption, reduce waste, and implement eco-friendly practices. Guests appreciate environmentally responsible practices, and AI technologies evolve rapidly, and staying updated on the latest advancements is crucial.

Incorporate user-friendly interfaces for your AI applications to enhance guest interaction. Ensure that AI systems are easy to use, even for those less familiar with technology (Gangwar & Reddy, 2023). This simplification will result in a more positive and seamless guest experience.

Building strong relationships in the AI ecosystem is equally important. Explore partnerships with AI solution providers, industry peers, and start-ups. Collaborative efforts can lead to faster innovation and give you a more competitive edge.

Define key performance indicators (KPIs) to evaluate the success of your AI-enabled guest experience initiatives. Regularly measure and analyze data to make data-driven improvements and ensure that your AI applications meet or exceed your guest satisfaction targets (Alam et al., 2023).

Finally, establish feedback loops with guests to gather insights about their AI-powered experiences and act on this feedback to fine-tune and improve your AI applications continually. This iterative process ensures that your AI-enabled guest experience remains dynamic and responsive to changing guest expectations (Wang & Uysal, 2024).

Conclusion

Findings: The findings of AI-enabled guest experience in the hospitality industry reveal a paradigm shift in the way hotels and accommodations interact with their guests. Through the adoption of next-generation AI technologies, hotels have successfully disrupted traditional guest service models, leading to a more personalized, efficient, and engaging guest experience. The implementation of AI-driven personalization has allowed hotels to cater to individual preferences and needs, fostering deeper guest satisfaction and loyalty. AI-powered chatbots and virtual assistants have significantly improved guest interactions, offering real-time assistance and reducing response times. Moreover, the integration of contactless technologies, facilitated by AI, has become a crucial aspect in ensuring guest safety and convenience, especially in the wake of the global pandemic. The ability of AI to anticipate guest needs and provide proactive services has further enhanced guest experiences, creating a sense of anticipation and delight. AI-driven loyalty programmes have been successful in boosting guest engagement and driving repeat visits through tailored rewards and incentives. These findings underscore the transformative impact of AI in reshaping the hospitality industry's approach to guest service and engagement (Gangwar & Reddy, 2023).

In conclusion, AI-enabled guest experience is a disruptive force in the hospitality industry, offering a powerful tool for hotels to stay ahead in an increasingly competitive landscape. The findings demonstrate that AI technologies have revolutionized guest interactions, empowering hotels to deliver personalized, efficient, and contactless experiences. By leveraging AI algorithms and data analytics, hotels can gain valuable insights into guest preferences and behaviours, elevating the level of personalization and anticipating guest needs (Wang & Uysal, 2024). The integration of AI-driven chatbots and virtual assistants has redefined guest communication, enhancing response times and guest convenience. Moreover, contactless technologies powered by AI have become an essential element in providing a safe and seamless stay experience for guests. The success of AI in disrupting the hospitality sector lies in striking the right balance between automation and human touch, ensuring that genuine connections and personalized service remain at the core of guest experiences. As AI technologies continue to evolve, hotels must remain agile and proactive in adopting next-generation solutions to meet and exceed guest expectations. Embracing AI-enabled guest experience will be the key to unlocking new opportunities for hotels to build guest loyalty, drive revenue growth, and position themselves as leaders in the ever-evolving hospitality landscape.

References

Alam, S. S., Masukujjaman, M., Mohamed Makhbul, Z. K., Helmi Ali, M., Ahmad, I., & Al Mamun, A. (2023). Experience, trust, eWOM engagement and usage intention of AI enabled services in hospitality and tourism industry: Moderating mediating analysis. *Journal of Quality Assurance in Hospitality & Tourism*, 1–29.

Al-Hyari, H. S. A., Al-Smadi, H. M., & Weshah, S. R. (2023). The impact of artificial intelligence (AI) on guest satisfaction in hotel management: An empirical study of luxury hotels. *Geo Journal of Tourism and Geosites*, *48*, 810–819.

Battour, M., Mady, K., Salaheldeen, M., Elsotouhy, M., Elbendary, I., & Boğan, E. (2023). AI-enabled technologies to assist Muslim tourists in Halal-friendly tourism. *Journal of Islamic Marketing*, *14*(5), 1291–1309.

Bhushan, S. (2021). The impact of artificial intelligence and machine learning on the global economy and its implications for the hospitality sector in India. *Worldwide Hospitality and Tourism Themes*, *13*(2), 252–259.

Buhalis, D., & Leung, R. (2018). Smart hospitality—Interconnectivity and interoperability towards an ecosystem. *International Journal of Hospitality Management, 71*, 41–50. ISSN 0278-4319. https://doi.org/10.1016/j.ijhm.2017.11.011

Bulchand-Gidumal, J. (2022). Impact of artificial intelligence in travel, tourism, and hospitality. In *Handbook of e-Tourism* (pp. 1943–1962). Cham: Springer International Publishing.

Cain, L. N., Thomas, J. H., & Alonso Jr, M. (2019). From sci-fi to sci-fact: The state of robotics and AI in the hospitality industry. *Journal of Hospitality and Tourism Technology, 10*(4), 624–650.

Chaturvedi, R., Verma, S., Ali, F., & Kumar, S. (2023). Reshaping tourist experience with AI-enabled technologies: A comprehensive review and future research agenda. *International Journal of Human – Computer Interaction*, 1–17.

Chen, Y., Hu, Y., Zhou, S., & Yang, S. (2023). Investigating the determinants of performance of artificial intelligence adoption in hospitality industry during COVID-19. *International Journal of Contemporary Hospitality Management, 35*(8), 2868–2889.

Doborjeh, Z., Hemmington, N., Doborjeh, M., & Kasabov, N. (2022). Artificial intelligence: A systematic review of methods and applications in hospitality and tourism. *International Journal of Contemporary Hospitality Management, 34*(3), 1154–1176.

Drexler, N., & Lapré, V. B. (2019). For better or for worse: Shaping the hospitality industry through robotics and artificial intelligence. *Research in Hospitality Management, 9*(2), 117–120.

Dwivedi, Y. K., Pandey, N., Currie, W., & Micu, A. (2023). Leveraging ChatGPT and other generative artificial intelligence (AI)-based applications in the hospitality and tourism industry: Practices, challenges and research agenda. *International Journal of Contemporary Hospitality Management, 36*(1), 1–12. https://doi.org/10.1108/IJCHM-05-2023-0686

El Hajal, G., & Rowson, B. (2020). The future of hospitality jobs. *Research in Hospitality Management, 10*(1), 55–61.

Gangwar, V. P., & Reddy, D. (2023). Hospitality Industry 5.0: Emerging Trends in Guest Perception and Experiences. *Opportunities and Challenges of Business 5.0 in Emerging Markets*, 185–211.

Huang, A., Chao, Y., de la Mora Velasco, E., Bilgihan, A., & Wei, W. (2022). When artificial intelligence meets the hospitality and tourism industry: An assessment framework to inform theory and management. *Journal of Hospitality and Tourism Insights, 5*(5), 1080–1100.

Ivanov, S. (2020). The impact of automation on tourism and hospitality jobs. *Information Technology & Tourism, 22*, 205–215.

Jabeen, F., Al Zaidi, S., & Al Dhaheri, M. H. (2022). Automation and artificial intelligence in hospitality and tourism. *Tourism Review, 77*(4), 1043–1061.

Jaiswal, G. (2020). A quantitative evaluation of customer marketing impact by artificial intelligence in hospitality industry. *Pranjana: The Journal of Management Awareness, 23*(2), 40–44.

Jamaluddin, Z., & Rahmat, A. K. (2022). Artificial intelligence technology in travel, tourism and hospitality: Current and future developments. In *Technology application in aviation, tourism and hospitality: Recent developments and emerging issues* (pp. 169–177). Singapore: Springer Nature Singapore.

Jones, M., & Brown, L. (2023). Hyper-personalization in the hospitality sector: An analysis of AI-driven guest experiences. *International Journal of Hospitality Management, 41*(1), 245–263.

Kiliçhan, R., & Yilmaz, M. (2020). Artificial intelligence and robotic technologies in tourism and hospitality industry. *Erciyes Üniversitesi Sosyal Bilimler Enstitüsü Dergisi, 50*, 353–380.

Kong, H., Wang, K., Qiu, X., Cheung, C., & Bu, N. (2023). 30 years of artificial intelligence (AI) research relating to the hospitality and tourism industry. *International Journal of Contemporary Hospitality Management, 35*(6), 2157–2177.

Koo, C., Xiang, Z., Gretzel, U., & Sigala, M. (2021). Artificial intelligence (AI) and robotics in travel, hospitality and leisure. *Electronic Markets, 31*, 473–476.

Lee, M., Kwon, W., & Back, K. J. (2021). Artificial intelligence for hospitality big data analytics: Developing a prediction model of restaurant review helpfulness for customer decision-making. *International Journal of Contemporary Hospitality Management, 33*(6), 2117–2136.

Li, M., Yin, D., Qiu, H., & Bai, B. (2021). A systematic review of AI technology-based service encounters: Implications for hospitality and tourism operations. *International Journal of Hospitality Management, 95*, 102930.

Limna, P. (2022). Artificial Intelligence (AI) in the hospitality industry: A review article. *International Journal of Computing Sciences Research, 6*, 1–12.

Lv, H., Shi, S., & Gursoy, D. (2022). A look back and a leap forward: A review and synthesis of big data and artificial intelligence literature in hospitality and tourism. *Journal of Hospitality Marketing & Management, 31*(2), 145–175.

Mariani, M., & Borghi, M. (2021). Customers' evaluation of mechanical artificial intelligence in hospitality services: A study using online reviews analytics. *International Journal of Contemporary Hospitality Management, 33*(11), 3956–3976.

Mariani, M., & Wirtz, J. (2023). A critical reflection on analytics and artificial intelligence based analytics in hospitality and tourism management research. *International Journal of Contemporary Hospitality Management, 35*(8), 2929–2943. https://doi.org/10.1108/IJCHM-08-2022-1006

Miller, S., & White, B. (2023). AI-driven customer feedback analysis in the hotel industry: A case study. *Hospitality Management Research, 32*(2), 189–206.

Mingotto, E., Montaguti, F., & Tamma, M. (2021). Challenges in re-designing operations and jobs to embody AI and robotics in services. Findings from a case in the hospitality industry. *Electronic Markets, 31*, 493–510.

Nam, K., Dutt, C. S., Chathoth, P., Daghfous, A., & Khan, M. S. (2021). The adoption of artificial intelligence and robotics in the hotel industry: Prospects and challenges. *Electronic Markets, 31*, 553–574.

Nannelli, M., Capone, F., & Lazzeretti, L. (2023). Artificial intelligence in hospitality and tourism. State of the art and future research avenues. *European Planning Studies*, 1–20.

Pelet, J. E., Lick, E., & Taieb, B. (2019). Internet of Things and Artificial Intelligence in the Hotel Industry: Which Opportunities and Threats for Sensory Marketing?. In: Martínez-López, F., Gázquez-Abad, J., Roggeveen, A. (eds) Advances in National Brand and Private Label Marketing. NB&PL 2019. *Springer Proceedings in Business and Economics*. Springer, Cham. https://doi.org/10.1007/978-3-030-18911-2_20.

Pillai, R., & Sivathanu, B. (2020). Adoption of AI-based chatbots for hospitality and tourism. *International Journal of Contemporary Hospitality Management, 32*(10), 3199–3226.

Prentice, C., Dominique Lopes, S., & Wang, X. (2020). The impact of artificial intelligence and employee service quality on customer satisfaction and loyalty. *Journal of Hospitality Marketing & Management, 29*(7), 739–756.

Qiu, H., Li, M., Bai, B., Wang, N., & Li, Y. (2022). The impact of AI-enabled service attributes on service hospitableness: The role of employee physical and psychological workload. *International Journal of Contemporary Hospitality Management, 34*(4), 1374–1398.

Rasheed, H. M. W., He, Y., Khizar, H. M. U., & Abbas, H. S. M. (2023). Exploring consumer-robot interaction in the hospitality sector: Unpacking the reasons for adoption (or resistance) to artificial intelligence. *Technological Forecasting and Social Change, 192*, 122555.

Rosete, A., Soares, B., Salvadorinho, J., Reis, J., & Amorim, M. (2020). Service robots in the hospitality industry: An exploratory literature review. In H. Nóvoa, M. Drăgoicea, & N. Kühl (Eds.), *Exploring service science. IESS 2020. Lecture notes in business information processing*, vol 377. Cham: Springer. https://doi.org/10.1007/978-3-030-38724-2_13

Roy, P., Ramaprasad, B. S., Chakraborty, M., Prabhu, N., & Rao, S. (2020). Customer acceptance of use of artificial intelligence in hospitality services: An Indian hospitality sector perspective. *Global Business Review*, 0972150920939753.

Ruel, H., & Njoku, E. (2021). AI redefining the hospitality industry. *Journal of Tourism Futures*, *7*(1), 53–66.

Saydam, M. B., Arici, H. E., & Koseoglu, M. A. (2022). How does the tourism and hospitality industry use artificial intelligence? A review of empirical studies and future research agenda. *Journal of Hospitality Marketing & Management*, *31*(8), 908–936.

Sharma, K., Dhir, S., & Ongsakul, V. (2022). Artificial intelligence and hospitality industry: Systematic review using TCCM and bibliometric analysis. *Journal for International Business and Entrepreneurship Development*, *14*(1), 48–71.

Smith, A. (2022). The role of AI in post-pandemic hospitality: A case study of contactless services. *Journal of Hospitality Technology*, 9(3), 112–128.

Smith, A., & Wang, Q. (2023). Data privacy and security measures in the hotel industry: An AI-driven approach. *Journal of Cybersecurity and Data Privacy*, *9*(1), 45–59.

Wang, H., Zhang, H., Chen, Z., Zhu, J., & Zhang, Y. (2022). Influence of artificial intelligence and robotics awareness on employee creativity in the hotel industry. *Frontiers in Psychology*, *13*, 834160.

Wang, Y.-C., & Uysal, M. (2024). Artificial intelligence-assisted mindfulness in tourism, hospitality, and events. *International Journal of Contemporary Hospitality Management*, *36*(4), 1262–1278. https://doi.org/10.1108/IJCHM-11-2022-1444

13 Enhancing Hospitality Service Quality With Artificial Intelligence

Nurhafihz Noor, Zahirah Zainol, and Ashley Tong

Chapter Introduction

The resurgence of the hospitality industry and the increasing use of artificial intelligence (AI) in service have resulted in new customer expectations and opportunities to enhance the quality of hospitality services. Accordingly, a clear understanding of these new service quality expectations and how best to design and implement these new technologies for the benefit of hospitality managers and consumers is key. This chapter provides theoretical and practical insights into how artificial intelligence service agents (AISA), such as chatbots and robots, in key hospitality sectors can provide excellent service quality and enhance customer relationships and well-being. The latest examples are illustrated to explore the application of AI within the hospitality industry, outlining the diverse prospects and obstacles that these advanced technologies offer to restaurant owners, hotel operators and other experts in the field.

Background

The hospitality industry continues to grow and contribute significantly to the service economy. Driven by factors such as the lifting of COVID-19 restrictions and an increase in leisure lifestyles, hospitality industry outperforming the technology and retail sectors after 2023 (Riaz 2023).

In several key sectors such as tourism, restaurants and hotels, consumers in the hospitality industry have traditionally been served by human service agents to meet their service needs. Some of these familiar human service agents include human tour guides, human waiters and human housekeeping personnel in hotels. However, increasingly, many of these services are performed by AISA, with consumers becoming more engaged (Fang, Han, and Chen 2023) and using AISA to get tour recommendations, book tables in restaurants and interact with room service (Chen et al. 2023). For example, Hilton has experimented with Connie, a robot concierge powered by IBM (IBM, 2016), to enhance customers' experience by personalizing tourism recommendations (Trejos, 2016). In a similar vein, generative AI is used in restaurants to develop personalized meal recommendations (Guszkowski 2023). Hi Arya, a food-tech company from India, has built a robotic tea maker

DOI: 10.4324/9781003488248-13

using AI and IoT technologies which enable users to create their own recipes from the mobile app and web interface (Collins et al. 2021). Mezli, the world's first fully automated restaurant, serves customers a complete menu of meals prepared by fully autonomous equipment (Van Hooijdonk 2023; CIB 2023). The movements of recent business practices have shown the significance of applying AISA in the hospitality industry.

AISA are adaptable AI-based agents that are human-like and that can improve their service performance in various service environments autonomously (Noor, Rao Hill, and Troshani 2022b). With advancements in AI and machine learning applications in service, there has been an increased use of AISA by service firms to facilitate mechanical and analytical service tasks, while emotional service tasks are carried out by both AISA and human service agents (Huang and Rust 2020). Mechanical tasks can come in the form of repetitive actions such as facilitating the guest's room booking, while analytical tasks may involve giving recommendations on the next preferred travel destination based on the traveller's profile. Emotional tasks may involve AISA in service activities that require more customer interaction and relationship management, such as managing customer feedback based on the overall trip experience or facilitating service recovery. These tasks can be performed by AISA in relatively more private settings where the consumer will engage AISA via their personal devices such as smartphones or smart speakers. In other instances, AISA may be accessed in more public contexts where AISA are being offered to the consumer in a specific service environment, such as autonomous tour buses that pick up commuters at designated stops and ply specific routes. In addition, AISA can be represented virtually or physically and meet a range of utilitarian or hedonic needs of consumers (Noor, Rao Hill, and Troshani 2022a). For instance, chatbots used in travel websites and mobile applications are virtual in representation and mainly offer utilitarian benefits to the consumer. On the other hand, robot tour guides for travellers are physical in representation and can offer both utilitarian and hedonic benefits to consumers with the integration of generative AI such as ChatGPT.

Continued interactions with traditional human service agents and AISA in the hospitality industry can result in consumers forming service perceptions and evaluating the services experienced. These attitudes can be positive or negative in nature (Kang, Koo, and Chung 2023), may differ based on the type of service performed by AISA in the hospitality setting (Alma Çallı et al. 2023) and, accordingly, lead to different degrees of acceptance among consumers (Ladeira, Perin, and Santini 2023). Responses can also be cognitive or affective, which can, in turn, result in behavioural outcomes. For instance, consumers may begin to form judgements on the perceived value of the hospitality service as well as express a level of customer satisfaction, which can then affect repurchasing intentions and overall loyalty (Hu, Kandampully, and Juwaheer 2009). One key concept that can play a vital role in impacting variables such as perceived value, customer satisfaction and customer loyalty is service quality (Cronin Jr, Brady, and Hult 2000). Accordingly, it is important to understand how AISA has affected service quality perceptions for hospitality managers to better design and implement AISA effectively.

Managing AI Service Quality in Hospitality

Service quality refers to the overall perception of excellence or superiority of the service as perceived by consumers (Zeithaml 1988). In the context of the hospitality industry, service quality evaluations are associated with the attitudes consumers form when experiencing the service of a specific hospitality sector. Accordingly, service managers may be concerned with the overall service quality of their specific service establishment, whereas tourism managers would be concerned with overseeing the service quality standards across key hospitality touchpoints, as travellers may form an overall judgement of the trip experience based on experiences across the entire travel journey.

In the past, as hospitality services were performed by humans, consumers would evaluate service performances in the context of human service agents. The seminal SERVQUAL scale was developed to answer the question of how consumers would perceive such human service performances. This resulted in the five dimensions of SERVQUAL, which are reliability (ability to perform the service task correctly), assurance (ability of human service agents to give confidence to consumers), tangibles (physical elements of the service environment including appearance), empathy (care and personalization given to consumers) and responsiveness (fast service when required) (Parasuraman, Zeithaml, and Berry 1988). While SERVQUAL was originally developed based on research conducted in the maintenance, banking, telephone, and finance service industries (Parasuraman, Zeithaml, and Berry 1988), the model has since been used to measure service quality across a wide variety of other service sectors (Ladhari 2009). In the hospitality industry, the five dimensions of SERVQUAL have been successful in explaining consumers' service quality expectations across sectors including restaurants (Lee and Hing 1995) and hotels (Hu, Kandampully, and Juwaheer 2009), with alternative measurement models continuing to support most of the five service quality dimensions (Stevens, Knutson, and Patton 1995).

However, service environments have changed from purely human-to-human service interactions to include other forms of service agents such as self-service technologies, websites and now AISA. Accordingly, the service environment and the nature of the service agent can affect how consumers evaluate the service quality of the hospitality service (Rust and Oliver 1994). This can be observed in the different service quality dimensions emerging in models developed for non-human service agents. For instance, while empathy was a key dimension for services performed by human service agents (Parasuraman, Zeithaml, and Berry 1988), consumers indicate that they value the design of service interfaces when services are performed by self-service technologies (Lin and Hsieh 2011). In the hospitality industry, this can come in the form of the attractiveness of the ticketing kiosk, which is operated by non-AI pre-programmed algorithms with a set of fixed rules and instructions based on the user's input. In the case of websites facilitating information and transaction services, consumers would also expect a level of privacy (Parasuraman, Zeithaml, and Malhotra 2005). Thus, while some service quality dimensions such as reliability appear consistently across different service environments, other dimensions are unique due to the nature of the service agent.

Accordingly, in the context of hospitality services performed by AISA, it is important to accurately measure service quality based on the set of dimensions that matter to consumers in such emerging AI-based service environments. With AISA performing services, consumers' overall expectations have changed, and consumers evaluate AISA service quality based on a unique combination of six dimensions. These dimensions are efficiency, security, availability, enjoyment, contact and anthropomorphism (Noor, Rao Hill, and Troshani 2022b):

- *Efficiency* – AISA's degree of reliability and ease of use and speed of AISA. Once again, reliability proves to be an important criterion for consumers in evaluating service quality.
- *Security* – The consumer's perception that AISA are safe to use and there is little risk associated with intrusion of privacy and personal data. This will continue to remain relevant as hospitality services attempt to further differentiate via greater personalization, in which a key trade-off is the customer's personal data.
- *Availability* – AISA is ready for use anytime, anywhere. This will become a greater expectation as services and devices become more integrated.
- *Enjoyment* – the degree to which using and interacting with AISA is enjoyable.
- *Contact* – The ability to access human service agents for assistance via AISA and reflects the valuable role human service agents continue to play in the AISA service environment.
- *Anthropomorphism* – AISA displays human-like attributes such as tangible features and intangible elements including personality. Anthropomorphism represents a new service quality dimension and reflects the emerging and changing service environments consumers experience with AISA.

By optimizing the design of AISA along these six dimensions, hospitality managers have greater certainty on the aspects of AISA that they need to focus on to achieve a high level of service quality. Close consultation with AISA developers as well as receiving feedback from consumers is crucial to ensuring that the design decisions are optimized for AISA service quality. In terms of tracking and benchmarking the performance of AISA, hospitality service managers can measure AISA service quality by using the 26-item AISAQUAL questionnaire, which can be administered to consumers who have interacted with services performed by AISA (Noor, Rao Hill, and Troshani 2022b). As several service tasks may still be performed with traditional service agents such as humans and non-AI self-service technologies, appropriate scales such as SERVQUAL (Parasuraman, Zeithaml, and Berry 1988) and SSTQUAL (Lin and Hsieh 2011) can be used in tandem to measure service quality based on the relevant service environments.

As established in this section, service quality in the hospitality industry is key for the firm's economic growth (Park and Jeong 2019). In the luxury hospitality sector as well, a careful understanding of service quality including the importance of customer interactions and the use of technology is vital for the continued success of the hospitality luxury brand (Lu et al. 2015). For hospitality services performed by AISA, the proper management of AISA service quality can increase the level of the perceived value of the service, customer satisfaction and customer loyalty (Noor, Rao Hill, and Troshani 2022b). How restaurants and hotels can implement AI to optimize services will be discussed in the concluding sections of this chapter.

Managing Well-Being and Relationships With AI

Beyond the bottom-line benefits that AISA can offer to the hospitality industry through service quality, it is important to understand how the use of AISA can affect consumers and their sense of well-being. In the literature, notwithstanding the importance of managing existing hospitality employees' well-being with the emergence of AISA (Xu et al. 2023), there continue to be important discussions on the need to understand the effects of service on the consumer's well-being to create more sustainable service ecosystems (Field et al. 2021). In terms of luxury hospitality services, this is in line with the responsibility luxury brands have in taking care of various stakeholders and their subjective well-being (Batat 2022).

Subjective well-being refers to consumers' overall evaluation of their lives and can come in the form of cognitive or affective evaluations (Diener 1984). Cognitive evaluations include people's judgements of their life satisfaction, while affective evaluations include levels of happiness (Diener et al. 1999). While services performed by human service agents can result in improvements in the consumer's subjective well-being due to human interactions and engagement with human service agents (Su, Swanson, and Chen 2016), it is important to understand if such social relationships can be replicated with AISA to create similar beneficial outcomes. Indeed, with continued interactions with AISA, consumers may begin to feel that they are forming relationships with AISA, despite the AISA not being able to truly feel for the consumer. One way to explain this phenomenon is by using the conceptualization of parasocial relationships (PSR).

PSR was initially used to refer to the illusionary social bond that the audience can form with performers, despite there not being any real reciprocation and attachment between audience members and the personas that are being portrayed (Horton and Wohl 1956). Like PSR effects that can grow between viewers and characters on television upon multiple viewings of a particular television show, PSR can also be developed between consumers and AISA because of several service interactions (Noor, Rao Hill, and Troshani 2022a). This is because AISA can be perceived as social beings due to their human-like attributes. PSR is driven due to the service quality dimensions of anthropomorphism and perceived enjoyment that consumers experience with AISA (Noor, Rao Hill, and Troshani 2022a). With anthropomorphism, AISA appear more human and relatable. With perceived enjoyment, interactions with PSR feel more human and intimate. PSR is further reinforced with AISA since AISA can sustain these interactions due to their AI-based capabilities.

Despite not being real relationships, the development of PSR between AISA and consumers should not be discounted, as consumers can form higher levels of subjective well-being due to increasing PSR (Noor, Rao Hill, and Troshani 2022a). Higher levels of PSR and subjective well-being can be activated with better AISA service quality through its dimensions of anthropomorphism and perceived enjoyment. Accordingly, affective responses such as PSR and happiness can be increased when AISA are designed to be more physical in representation and can serve consumers with more hedonic benefits (Noor, Rao Hill, and Troshani 2022a). Overall, these are opportunities for the hospitality industry to promote AISA in their services due to their benefits for PSR and subjective well-being. Consumers too can be part of the process of personalizing AISA for more social experiences. Examples of these initiatives to the key hospitality sectors of restaurants and hotels will be discussed in the subsequent sections of this chapter.

AI-Restaurant Service Quality and Relationship Management in Practice

A Closer Look at AI in the Food Service and Restaurant Industry

As established earlier in the chapter, the rise of AI in the food service and restaurant industry has shown a positive impact on both business outcomes and customer satisfaction. In a labour-intensive industry, AI can be used to automate and delegate tasks in the front end of the business to the back-end processes. Tasks such as reservations, order taking, inventory management and marketing efforts can be done with the help of AI tools, hence allowing the staff to focus on providing quality customer service interactions.

More and more businesses are investing in these AI automation tools to improve the whole dining experience, with customers preferring contactless payment processing and user-friendly service. In a survey by Forrester conducted in 2019, 69% of companies reported that operating costs were reduced after implementing AI automation and chatbots. 62% of companies reported increased employee productivity (Linthwaite 2019). According to Arizton (2023), the global self-service kiosk market size was valued at USD26.45 billion in 2022 and is estimated to reach USD43.65 billion by 2028, expanding at a CAGR of 8.71%.

Specific Benefits of AI to Restaurant Services

Restaurants can use AI technology to enhance consumers' dining experience and ease the brand's service journey (Srivastava 2022). Specifically, AI technology improves businesses' operations by:

- *Streamlining operations* – AI can predict waiting times, guest count and reservations based on past data and inform staff of upcoming surges or downtime.
- *Increasing efficiency* – Automated self-service kiosks can send the menu and any special requests directly and accurately to the kitchen to minimize wait times.
- *Utilizing predictive maintenance* – AI-driven predictive maintenance systems can provide real-time equipment data and continuously monitor the performance of the kitchen equipment such as energy consumption, temperature, and pressure. The AI systems will notify when it's time to be sent for servicing or repairs.

- *Automating inventory management* – Using historical sales data, AI systems can help restaurants forecast demand and create a precise inventory list based on patterns and trends from consumers' preferences, seasonal orders and popular dishes.

In fast food restaurants, AI technology can enhance consumers' dining experience by making restaurant visits more consistent and predictable, improving the speed of service and order accuracy, minimizing human interaction and letting staff focus on other tasks.

AI Enhancing Customer Experience

The use of AI can be integrated into various points of the business process and customer service journey. AI technology is used for the customer-facing process like AI phone answering when placing reservations, voice ordering to minimize waiting time, self-serve options and kiosks that can personalize customer experience using conversational AI and facial recognition. AI technology essentially can be used to elevate customers' dining experience by simplifying and personalizing customer interactions without compromising on the quality of customer service (Sweeney n.d.).

Restaurants can use AI technology to enhance their inventory, purchasing and delivery processes, which can lead to a reduction in food waste and promote sustainability. Smarter staff scheduling can also be implemented to optimize productivity and ensure proper staff allotments during critical periods. Data-based insights and predictions allow the business to utilize resources efficiently based on previous sales data collected by the AI program. Automated marketing and remarketing can help businesses target new consumers and remarket to previous ones more effectively. Industry leaders such as McDonald's, Wendy's, Nestle and Mastercard are making sizable investments in fitting AI systems and AI humanoids into their business processes (Nestlé 2014). The food service and restaurant industry will be seeing plenty of widespread adoption of this new technology (Sweeney n.d.).

Examples of AISA in the Restaurant Industry

Mugaritz

Chef Andoni Luis Aduriz, along with François Chartier and the SONY AI Gastronomy Team, has collaborated on a molecular gastronomy AI programme that utilizes machine learning algorithms to generate innovative combinations of flavours and textures. Chef Aduriz has incorporated pine needles into dishes to add a flavour of smokiness to the dish and used soil as a seasoning (Mugaritz 2023; Chartier n.d.).

CloudChef

Californian start-up CloudChef has developed a software programme that uses AI to cook a dish precisely with cameras and sensors placed near the cooking hob.

Every aspect of the cooking process can be measured and transcribed into the AI program, following a highly detailed recipe. Cooking processes such as cutting, portion control, the thickness of the sauce and the degree of food caramelization can be monitored and managed by the program. Such AI programmes allow chefs to monetize their secret recipes and cooking practices to other external sources (Travel and Leisure 2023).

Miso Robotics

Another Californian start-up, Miso Robotics, has developed an AI kitchen assistant, Flippy. Flippy assists with prepping, grilling, frying and plating. Like CloudChef, Flippy uses sensors and cameras to prepare and monitor the cooking processes. The limited processes of Flippy could help fast food restaurants solve the issue of high employee turnover and low retention rates. Cali Group, the team managing the fast-food chain CaliBurger, announced a partnership with Miso Robotics to bring Flippy's expertise into their Pasadena, California branch by 2019 with goals to expand to 50 locations worldwide (Sennaar 2019).

Pepper

Japanese technology firm Softbank has collaborated with Mastercard to develop an AI-driven humanoid robot named Pepper. Pepper is a robot waiter that is equipped to process customers' orders, upsell recommendations and enable customers to make contactless payment using their Mastercard account on the robot's screen tablet. Pepper was seen working at Pizza Hut in Asia in 2016 (Sennaar 2019; McEleny 2016).

Halla

The Los Angeles-based company Halla is a personalized restaurant and dining search engine. Halla claims to make food delivery more convenient by integrating several food delivery applications into one system (Sennaar 2019).

Domino's

In 2017, Domino's announced an enhanced feature of its Facebook Messenger that included the use of a chatbot, named Dom, during the Super Bowl. Dom allowed consumers to order pizza by typing the word 'pizza' on the Facebook Messenger application. Subsequently, customers were able to order wings and salads using Dom. In an attempt first of its kind, Domino's has partnered with Flirtey, a drone company, to deliver pizza to a customer in Whangaparaoa, New Zealand. Although the flying drone attempt was a conceptual one, Domino's has plans to use wheeled robots to deliver pizza within a one-mile radius in Germany and the Netherlands (Walker 2019).

Mezli

Mezli is the world's first fully automated restaurant, started in San Francisco by a team of engineers from Stanford. Robots will serve customers a complete menu of meals prepared by fully autonomous equipment. The unique selling proposition of Mezli is to sell healthy, affordable and convenient food without social interaction. This makes the business model cheaper to run compared to traditional restaurants. The engineers partnered with Michelin star Chef Eric Minnich to create more than 60,000 variations of the menu items (Van Hooijdonk 2023; CIB 2023).

McDonald's

McDonald's has opened a new highly automated test restaurant in Texas equipped with conveyor belts, a self-service kiosk, and drive-thru express lanes. The ban on indoor dining and social interactions during the COVID-19 pandemic led McDonald's to review its customer service journey. Aiming at reducing in-person interaction, McDonald's CEO Chris Kempczinski in November 2020 announced that customers will receive more services through their digital devices. The future of fast food, according to McDonald's, is focused on innovative customer experience, increased order speed and accuracy to make the service more enjoyable for the consumer (Houser 2023).

Donatos Pizza

Appetronix has entered into an exclusive agreement with Donatos Pizza and its affiliate companies, Agápe Automation and the Grote Company, to launch a fully autonomous pizza vending machine. This innovative partnership will lead to the development of a standalone, fully autonomous restaurant in Columbus, Ohio. The fully autonomous restaurant developed by Appetronix for Donatos will enable a seamless and efficient dining experience for customers from start to finish (PR News Wire 2023).

AI-Hotel Service Quality and Relationship Management in Practice

A Closer Look at AI in the Hotel Industry

AI is becoming increasingly prevalent across various sectors of the economy, including the travel and hospitality industry. AI-powered tools and services can enhance the guest experience while simultaneously optimizing operations, reducing costs and saving time for hotel operators. While AI cannot entirely replace the human touch in the hospitality sector, it can proficiently handle many tasks that have traditionally been the domain of human staff, at any time of the day. These tasks include a wide range of functions, from handling hotel bookings, streamlining pre-arrival processes, offering personalized recommendations and facilitating check-in and check-out procedures to analyzing customer feedback. The potential of AI is virtually limitless.

According to research by HubSpot, business professionals report that AI can help them understand their customers better and improve the overall customer experience (Santiago 2023). Ultimately, hotels that integrate AI into their operations can provide superior service to their guests, resulting in heightened customer satisfaction and increased loyalty. According to data from Statista (2023), the current market capitalization of AI is nearing 100 billion U.S. dollars and is projected to surge to approximately $2 trillion by 2030.

Specific Benefits of AI to Hotel Services

With the introduction of AI and digitization in the hospitality industry, AI can improve hotel operations in many ways, making them more efficient and effective:

- *Automating repetitive tasks* – AI can automate online reservations and contactless check-ins, freeing up staff to concentrate on offering personalized guest experiences (Wadhwa 2023). Many administrative tasks can be automated to reduce human error and increase operational efficiency.
- *Enhancing customer service* – Chatbots and virtual assistants can assist guests with booking reservations, addressing inquiries and providing recommendations (Hollander 2023).
- *Improving housekeeping room assignments and maintenance* – Sensors and cameras can be used to oversee and regulate the temperature, lighting and security of guest rooms and improve energy efficiency through smart building systems.
- *Optimizing pricing and revenue management* – Via data analysis and predictive modelling, AI-driven algorithms are used to optimize pricing and availability in real time. It helps hotels maximize revenue by adjusting rates based on demand, seasonality and other factors. It ensures that rooms are neither underpriced nor overpriced, leading to increased profitability.
- *Analyzing customer feedback* – AI can be used to analyze feedback from various sources, such as social media, review websites and guest surveys. This helps hotels identify areas for improvement and respond to customer concerns promptly, ultimately improving guest satisfaction.
- *Utilizing predictive maintenance* – AI-driven predictive maintenance can monitor the condition of equipment and infrastructure within a hotel. By analyzing data from sensors, AI can predict when maintenance is needed, reducing downtime and operational disruptions (OTA Insight 2023).
- *Optimizing energy consumption* – In hotels, adjustments can be made to heating, cooling and lighting based on occupancy and weather conditions. This not only reduces operational costs but also contributes to sustainability efforts.
- *Refining overall efficiency* – Hotel operations can be improved by applying AI for forecasting demand, inventory management and logistics optimization (Hollander 2023).

AI Enhancing Guest Experience

The hospitality industry is all about delivering the utmost customer service. With the rise of AI, hotels now have new tools to help them enhance guest experience via several methods.

Some hotels are experimenting with robots for tasks like room service delivery, luggage handling and even cleaning. For instance, Hilton Hotels' First Robot Concierge, Connie, can provide tourist information to guests who interact with it (Revfine 2021). Henn na Hotel in Japan has nearly every role in the hotel fulfilled by an AI-powered robot (Revfine 2021). Chatbots and virtual assistants powered by AI can interact with guests in real time and offer personalized suggestions and support. They can handle a wide range of guest inquiries, such as booking inquiries, room service requests and even concierge services. AI-powered systems provide 24/7 support and communicate in multiple languages.

AI is also used to gather and analyze guest data to offer highly personalized experiences. This includes customized room preferences and restaurant recommendations drawing from their preferences, demographics and past interactions (Wadhwa 2023). For example, The Cosmopolitan of Las Vegas has a robot named Rose (Resident Mischief-Maker & Digital Concierge) that guests can text for anything from dinner suggestions to fresh towels (Revfine 2021). With virtual reality and augmented reality, smart room technology provides guests with immersive experiences, including virtual tours, virtual room selection and access to virtual events. Technology like in-room voice assistants can fill guests in on the weather or today's news, monitor room temperatures and more (ROH 2023).

AI can also facilitate automated check-ins and check-outs, quickening the process for guests and leading to a greater first impression and novel experience (Hospitality Net 2022). It also enables guests to settle their bills directly from their mobile devices or voice commands, with the receipt sent to them via email or text message (Revfine 2021). In addition, AI is employed to enhance safety and security by actively monitoring potential threats and footage for unusual activities or unauthorized access. Facial recognition technology can also be used for check-ins and to enhance overall security (Access 2023).

Finally, AI communication tools can communicate effectively with international guests in multiple languages to cater to customers worldwide. This ensures a smoother and more pleasant experience for guests from diverse linguistic backgrounds.

Examples of AISA in the Hotel Industry

ChatGPT, Jasper and Writesonic are generative AI tools that can produce written content, generate artwork, paraphrase text and more (ROH 2023).

Cendyn, MindOS and Allora.AI assist properties in refining the booking procedure and on-site guest experience.

Easyway supports hotels to streamline their operations and manage guest relationships more efficiently.

Pegasus aids hospitality teams in improved data tracking and comprehension.

Duetto GameChanger employs predictive analytics to enhance booking revenue.

Recommendations for Business Practices: The Key to Success

With the rapid emergence of AI in the hospitality industry, businesses need to be able to implement AISA effectively. Here are five key recommendations for any business in the hospitality industry to succeed with AI:

Recommendation 1: Identify Existing Service Fail Points

One potent area of AISA implementation is addressing existing service fail points. Accordingly, service managers need to have a clear understanding of these fail points customers are encountering with the hospitality service. Such information can come from feedback from customers, frontline service professionals and observations from service managers themselves. Benchmarking the organization's service performances against records or industry standards can also help highlight service shortcomings which may not necessarily be reported by dissatisfied customers.

Recommendation 2: Educate and Support Whole of Business

Everyone in the organization needs to have a clear understanding of their role and contribution to delivering excellent service to the customer. Accordingly, the introduction of AISA to the service process should be seen by employees as a way to assist their current roles and ultimately enhance the level of hospitality and service quality to the customer. The buy-in from existing employees, as well as proper training and support to them, is crucial for the organization to adjust effectively to the new ecosystem with AISA.

Recommendation 3: Don't Be Afraid of Collaboration

Businesses can look beyond their industry and expertise to collaborate with technological companies to integrate manual labour and automate certain tasks. To be open to this possibility, proper infrastructure and expertise need to be made available for business owners to learn and adapt to new AI technologies. Data scientists and business developers can work together to develop deeper insights to uncover the day-to-day bottlenecks and seek solutions. The data that these AI technologies collect may allow businesses to cater to and personalize their service interactions better.

Recommendation 4: Seek Out Co-Creation Opportunities

Co-creation can occur with customers participating in the service delivery process in the initial design stages, during the early adoption stages and when gathering feedback after a full implementation phase. Customers would be intrigued and excited to try or interact with AI technologies, especially if the AI displays certain appealing characteristics or personality. Customer service interactions and features can be elevated and lead to overall positive experiences. Ultimately, a business's purpose is delivered through value creation. This can be done through harnessing the capabilities of AI and incorporating new and novel ways to entice the customer.

Recommendation 5: Test and Stay Up to Date

AI technologies continue to advance rapidly, and both AI in hospitality research and industry implementation are still in their early stages. Hence, there is much volatility and uncertainty. To navigate these unchartered waters, business managers must be agile and test new AISA initiatives with experts and selected customers to gather feedback. This can include understanding preferences related to anthropomorphic designs on AISA as well as customer preferences of AISA over human service employees in certain service contexts. Organizations can also stay up to date with the latest developments in the emerging AI space by including academics in their boards in order to provide fresh perspectives and the latest insights on AI research.

Conclusion

This chapter has shown the importance of how businesses can leverage AI technologies to improve productivity, efficiency and customer service interactions. Specifically, in the food service and restaurant industry, the only constant is change. There are still ways that the industry can improve. AI can help democratize the industry to provide more access and variety to a wider audience and empower service staff with in-demand skill sets. AI has revolutionized how restaurants and hotels operate and interact with their guests to provide a more seamless experience while improving their profitability and competitiveness in the market. These hospitality sectors will continue to rely significantly on intelligent machines in the future to deliver their services.

Specifically, for the restaurant industry, more can be done to integrate AI. For instance, chefs can monetize their recipes through AI gastronomy collaborations by selling their recipes to 'dark kitchens' – virtual restaurants that can be ordered through meal delivery platforms (Travel and Leisure 2023). AI programming can be used to track fraudulent and inconsistent transactions, especially in cases of internal employee theft (Srivastava 2022). Finally, employee interactions and performance can be analyzed using AI clustering. The data collected can assist in assessing, scoring and improving employee performance (Srivastava 2022).

The adoption of AI does not have to be a rapid and steep process. Future research can uncover how industry players can pilot back-end functions to be managed by AI while focusing on customer-facing interactions. Troubleshooting and testing are important to ensure the quality of food and service provided. Studies on consumers' level of acceptance of AI technologies can help restaurateurs decide the amount of investment to put into AI. Understanding consumers' emotions and well-being when interacting with AI technologies would also give insight to the sophistication the entire industry can strive for.

As for hotels, hotel operators that fail to embrace innovative technologies such as AI and ChatGPT run the risk of falling behind their competitors who leverage these tools to enhance both guest experiences and operational effectiveness. With a growing demand for personalized interactions, hotels that refrain from implementing AI and chatbot technology may miss out on potential guests seeking tailored and efficient communication methods. Moreover, hotels that do not integrate these technologies into their operations may encounter delayed services and inefficient guest interactions, potentially resulting in negative reviews that affect their reputation and eventually losing competitive advantages. Accordingly, the adoption of AI technologies can empower hotels to maintain competitiveness while streamlining their operations, leading to potential revenue growth and increased guest experiences.

References

Access. 2023. "The Rise of AI in Hospitality: Trends, Opportunities and Challenges." Accessed April 25, 2023. www.theaccessgroup.com/en-gb/blog/hos-ai-hospitality/

Alma Çallı, Büşra, Levent Çallı, Didar Sarı Çallı, and Fatih Çallı. 2023. "The Impact of Different Types of Service Robots Usage in Hotels on Guests' Intention to Stay." *Journal of Hospitality and Tourism Technology* 14, no. 1: 53–68. doi: 10.1108/JHTT-09-2021-0266

Arizton. 2023. "Self-Service Kiosk Market -Global Outlook and Forecast 2023–2028" Arizton. www.arizton.com/market-reports/self-service-kiosk-market

Batat, Wided. 2022. "Transformative Luxury Research (TLR): An Agenda to Advance Luxury for Well-Being." *Journal of Macromarketing* 42, no. 4: 609–623. doi: 10.1177/02761467221135547.

Chartier, F. n.d. "The First Recipe Created with the Help of Artificial Intelligence or How to Multiply Culinary Creativity Tenfold." François Chartier. https://francoischartier.ca/en/a-i-first-recipe/

Chen, Yuangao, Yuqing Hu, Shasha Zhou, and Shuiqing Yang. 2023. "Investigating the Determinants of Performance of Artificial Intelligence Adoption in Hospitality Industry during COVID-19." *International Journal of Contemporary Hospitality Management* 35, no. 8: 2868–2889. doi: 10.1108/IJCHM-04-2022-0433.

Collins, Christopher, Denis Dennehy, K. Conboy, and Patrick Mikale. 2021. "Artificial Intelligence in Information Systems Research: A Systematic Literature Review and Research Agenda." *International Journal of Information Management* 60, no. C: 102383. doi: 10.1016/j.ijinfomgt.2021.102383

Cronin Jr, J. Joseph, Michael K. Brady, and G. Tomas M. Hult. 2000. "Assessing the Effects of Quality, Value, and Customer Satisfaction on Consumer Behavioral Intentions in Service Environments." *Journal of Retailing* 76, no. 2: 193–218. doi: 10.1016/S0022-4359(00)00028-2.

Culinary Institute of Barcelona (CIB). 2023. "How Will AI Influence the World of Gastronomy, and What Opportunities and Challenges Will It Pose for Restaurants?" CIB. https://blog.cib.education/en/how-will-ai-influence-the-world-of-gastronomy-and-what-opportunities-and-challenges-will-it-pose-for-restaurants

Diener, Ed. 1984. "Subjective Well-being." *Psychological Bulletin* 95, no. 3: 542–575. doi: 10.1037/0033-2909.95.3.542.

Diener, Ed, Eunkook M. Suh, Richard E. Lucas, and Heidi L. Smith. 1999. "Subjective Well-being: Three Decades of Progress." *Psychological Bulletin* 125, no. 2: 276–302. doi: 10.1037/0033-2909.125.2.276.

Fang, Shujie, Xiaoyun Han, and Shuping Chen. 2023. "The Impact of Tourist – Robot Interaction on Tourist Engagement in the Hospitality Industry: A Mixed-method Study." *Cornell Hospitality Quarterly* 64, no. 2: 246–266. doi: 10.1177/19389655221102383

Field, Joy M., Darima Fotheringham, Mahesh Subramony, Anders Gustafsson, Amy L. Ostrom, Katherine N. Lemon, Ming-Hui Huang, and Janet R. McColl-Kennedy. 2021. "Service Research Priorities: Designing Sustainable Service Ecosystems." *Journal of Service Research* 24, no. 4: 462–479. doi: 10.1177/10946705211031302.

Guszkowski, J. 2023. "ChatGPT Can Now Recommend Restaurants on OpenTable." *Restaurant Business,* March 24, 2023. https://restaurantbusinessonline.com/technology/chatgptcan-now-recommend-restaurants-opentable.

Hollander, J. 2023. "AI in Hospitality: The Impact of Artificial Intelligence on the Hotel Industry." *Hotel Tech Report,* May 10, 2023. https://hoteltechreport.com/news/ai-in-hospitality

Hospitality Net. 2022. "What's the Impact of Artificial Intelligence in the Hotel Industry." *Hospitality Net*, May 5, 2022. www.hospitalitynet.org/news/4110360.html

Horton, Donald, and R. Richard Wohl. 1956. "Mass Communication and Para-social Interaction: Observations on Intimacy at a Distance." *Psychiatry* 19, no. 3: 215–229. doi: 10.1080/00332747.1956.11023049.

Houser, K. 2023. "McDonald's Opens Its First Automated Restaurant in Texas." Free Think. www.freethink.com/robots-ai/automated-restaurant

Hu, Hsin-Hui, Jay Kandampully, and Thanika Devi Juwaheer. 2009. "Relationships and Impacts of Service Quality, Perceived Value, Customer Satisfaction, and Image: An Empirical Study." *The Service Industries Journal* 29, no. 2: 111–125. doi: 10.1080/02642060802292932.

Huang, Ming-Hui, and Roland T. Rust. 2020. "Engaged to a Robot? The Role of AI in Service." *Journal of Service Research* 24, no. 1: 30–41. doi: 10.1177/1094670520902266.

IBM. 2016. "Hilton and IBM Pilot 'Connie', the World's First Watson-enabled Hotel Concierge." *PR Newswire*, March 9, 2016. www.prnewswire.com/news-releases/hilton-and-ibmpilot-connie-the-worlds-first-watson-enabled-hotel-concierge300233140.html#:~:text=Meet%20Hilton's%20Connie%3A%20Pilot%20of,by%20IBM%20Watson%20and%20WayBlazer.

Kang, Sung-Eun, Chulmo Koo, and Namho Chung. 2023. "Creepy vs. Cool: Switching from Human Staff to Service Robots in the Hospitality Industry." *International Journal of Hospitality Management* 111: 103479. doi: 10.1016/j.ijhm.2023.103479

Ladeira, Wagner, Marcelo Gattermann Perin, and Fernando Santini. 2023. "Acceptance of Service Robots: A Meta-Analysis in the Hospitality and Tourism Industry." *Journal of Hospitality Marketing & Management* 32, no. 6: 694–716. doi: 10.1080/19368623.2023.2202168

Ladhari, Riadh. 2009. "A Review of Twenty Years of SERVQUAL Research." *International Journal of Quality and Service Sciences* 1, no. 2: 172–198. doi: 10.1108/17566690910971445.

Lee, Yun Lok, and Nerilee Hing. 1995. "Measuring Quality in Restaurant Operations: An Application of the SERVQUAL Instrument." *International Journal of Hospitality Management* 14, no. 3–4: 293–310. doi: 10.1016/0278-4319(95)00037-2.

Lin, Jiun-Sheng Chris, and Pei-Ling Hsieh. 2011. "Assessing the Self-service Technology Encounters: Development and Validation of SSTQUAL Scale." *Journal of Retailing* 87, no. 2: 194–206. doi: 10.1016/j.jretai.2011.02.006.

Linthwaite, R. 2019. "Prioritize Personalization When Choosing Conversational Chatbot Platforms To Reap Rewards." Forrester. https://info.ada.support/hubfs/Ada%20Content%20Assets/Ada_Forrester%20Opportunity%20Snapshot.pdf?utm_campaign=Forrester%20Ops%20Report&utm_medium=email&_hsmi=102454842&_hsenc=p2ANqtz-__2O1ki-4o880FqIzVjcjXOAtey-Z0EF5gCHXCkPpqBWwIF_WoHNpZJ9bwgly_VF2tKVv_v86tkIlZByKeGyiSfKEV0A&utm_content=102454842&utm_source=hs_automation

Lu, Carol, Celine Berchoux, Michael W. Marek, and Brendan Chen. 2015. "Service Quality and Customer Satisfaction: Qualitative Research Implications for Luxury Hotels." *International Journal of Culture, Tourism and Hospitality Research* 9, no. 2: 168–182. doi: 10.1108/IJCTHR-10-2014-0087.

McEleny, C. 2016. "Mastercard Has Helped SoftBank's Pepper the Robot Get a Job at Pizza Hut." *The Drum*, May 25, 2016. www.thedrum.com/news/2016/05/25/mastercard-has-helped-softbank-s-pepper-robot-get-job-pizza-hut

Mugaritz. 2023. Andoni Luis Aduriz Is the Winner of the Icon Award 2023 by the World's Best 50 Restaurants." Mugaritz. www.mugaritz.com/en/andoni-luis-aduriz-is-d-the-winner-of-the-icon-award-2023-by-the-worlds-50-best-restaurants/co-1684413697/

Nestlé. 2014. "Nestlé to Use Humanoid Robot to Sell Nescafe in Japan." Nestlé. www.nestle.com/media/news/nestle-humanoid-robot-nescafe-japan

Noor, Nurhafihz, Sally Rao Hill, and Indrit Troshani. 2022a. "Artificial Intelligence Service Agents: Role of Parasocial Relationship." *Journal of Computer Information Systems* 62, no. 5: 1009–1023. doi: 10.1080/08874417.2021.1962213.

Noor, Nurhafihz, Sally Rao Hill, and Indrit Troshani. 2022b. "Developing a Service Quality Scale for Artificial Intelligence Service Agents." *European Journal of Marketing* 56, no. 5: 1301–1336. doi: 10.1108/EJM-09-2020-0672.

Ota Insight. 2023. "Artificial Intelligence for the Hotel Industry and Other Key Trends For 2023." *Ota Insight*, March 28, 2023. www.otainsight.com/resources/blog/artificial-intelligence-hotel-industry

Parasuraman, A., Valarie A. Zeithaml, and Leonard L. Berry. 1988. "SERVQUAL: A Multiple-item Scale for Measuring Consumer Perceptions of Service Quality." *Journal of Retailing* 64, no. 1: 12.

Parasuraman, A., Valarie A. Zeithaml, and Arvind Malhotra. 2005. "E-S-QUAL: A Multiple-item Scale for Assessing Electronic Service Quality." *Journal of Service Research* 7, no. 3: 213–233. doi: 10.1177/1094670504271156.

Park, Jinsoo, and EuiBeom Jeong. 2019. "Service Quality in Tourism: A Systematic Literature Review and Keyword Network Analysis." *Sustainability* 11, no. 13: 3665.

PR News Wire. 2023. "Appetronix (formerly SJW Robotics) Partners with Iconic Donatos Pizza to Pioneer Fully Autonomous Restaurant Experience." *PR News Wire*, July 13, 2023. www.prnewswire.com/news-releases/appetronix-formerly-sjw-robotics-partners-with-iconic-donatos-pizza-to-pioneer-fully-autonomous-restaurant-experience-301876809.html

Revfine. 2021. "How to Use Artificial Intelligence in the Hospitality Industry." Revfine. www.revfine.com/artificial-intelligence-hospitality-industry/#why-artificial-intelligence-becoming-important-hospitality-industry

Riaz, Umar. 2023. "Hospitality Industry Looks Strong for 2023 – Despite Recession Fears." EY. Accessed August 16. www.ey.com/en_us/real-estate-hospitality-construction/hospitality-industry-looks-strong-for-2023-despite-recession-fears.

ROH. 2023. "AI in Hotels: A Complete Guide for the Hospitality Industry." *ROH*, May 16, 2023. https://roh.co/proptech-articles/ai-in-hotels-hospitality-ai

Rust, Roland T., and Richard L. Oliver. 1994. *Service Quality: New Directions in Theory and Practice*. Sage Publications.

Santiago, E. 2023. "How AI Perceptions Have Changed in the Last Decade [Comparing New & Old Consumer Data]." *Hub Spot,* July 11, 2023. https://blog.hubspot.com/marketing/artificial-intelligence-is-here#:~:text=Furthermore%2C%2062%25%20agree%20AI%20tools%20can%20help%20them,can%20help%20them%20improve%20the%20overall%20customer%20experience.

Sennaar, K. 2019. "Examples of AI in Restaurants and Food Services". Emerj. https://emerj.com/ai-sector-overviews/ai-in-restaurants-food-services/

Srivastava, S. 2022. "10 Ways AI Is Transforming The Restaurant Industry." *Forbes*, September 22, 2022. www.forbes.com/sites/forbestechcouncil/2022/09/22/10-ways-ai-is-transforming-the-restaurant-industry/

Statista, 2023. "Artificial Intelligence – Worldwide." Statista. www.statista.com/outlook/tmo/artificial-intelligence/worldwide

Stevens, Pete, Bonnie Knutson, and Mark Patton. 1995. "Dineserv: A Tool for Measuring Service Quality in Restaurants." *Cornell Hotel and Restaurant Administration Quarterly* 36, no. 2: 56–60. doi: 10.1177/001088049503600226.

Su, Lujun, Scott R. Swanson, and Xiaohong Chen. 2016. "The Effects of Perceived Service Quality on Repurchase Intentions and Subjective Well-being of Chinese Tourists: The Mediating Role of Relationship Quality." *Tourism Management* 52: 82–95. doi: 10.1016/j.tourman.2015.06.012.

Sweeney, B. n.d. "AI in Restaurants: 9 Ways Artificial Intelligence Is Shaping the Food Industry". PopMenu. https://get.popmenu.com/post/ai-in-restaurants

Travel and Leisure. 2023. "How AI Could Bring the Dishes of the World's Great Chefs to Your Doorstep." *Travel and Leisure*, February 24, 2023. www.travelandleisureasia.com/global/dining/food/ai-could-bring-the-dishes-of-the-worlds-great-chefs-to-your-doorstep/

Trejos, N. 2016. "Introducing Connie, Hilton's New Robot Concierge." *USA Today*, March 9, 2016. www.usatoday.com/story/travel/roadwarriorvoices/2016/03/09/introducing-connie-hiltons-new-robot-concierge/81525924/.

Van Hooijdonk, R. 2023. "Fully Autonomous Restaurants with AI-powered Menus: The Future of Eating Out?" Richard Van Hooijdonk. https://blog.richardvanhooijdonk.com/en/fully-autonomous-restaurants-with-ai-powered-menus-the-future-of-eating-out/

Wadhwa, R. 2023. "Is Artificial Intelligence the Future of the Hospitality Industry?" *Press Reader*, February 23, 2023. https://blog.pressreader.com/hotels/is-artificial-intelligence-the-future-of-the-hospitality-industry

Walker, J. 2019. 'Fast Food Robots, Kiosk and AI Use Cases from 6 Restaurant Chain Giants." Emerj. https://emerj.com/ai-sector-overviews/fast-food-robots-kiosks-and-ai-use-cases/

Xu, Jingjing, Aaron Hsiao, Sacha Reid, and Emily Ma. 2023. "Working with Service Robots? A Systematic Literature Review of Hospitality Employees' Perspectives." *International Journal of Hospitality Management* 113: 103523. doi: 10.1016/j.ijhm.2023.103523

Zeithaml, Valarie A. 1988. "Consumer Perceptions of Price, Quality, and Value: A Means-end Model and Synthesis of Evidence." *Journal of Marketing* 52, no. 3: 2–22. doi: 10.1177/002224298805200302.

14 AI in the Hospitality Industry

Revolutionizing Guest Experience

Dr. Malla Jogarao

1. Introduction

The hospitality industry is no stranger to change. Over the years, it has adapted to shifting customer preferences, technological advancements, and global economic trends. However, the current era is witnessing a transformation that surpasses anything the industry has seen before. This transformation is driven by the integration of artificial intelligence (AI) technology, which is revolutionizing the way hospitality establishments cater to their guests. In the words of Xiang, "The adoption of AI technology in the hospitality sector represents a fundamental shift in how guest experiences are curated, services are delivered, and operational processes are optimized" (Xiang et al., 2017). This shift is not limited to a single aspect of the industry; it touches upon nearly every facet, from the initial guest interaction to post-departure feedback.

The hospitality industry plays a pivotal role in the global economy. It encompasses a wide range of businesses, from hotels and resorts to restaurants, travel agencies, and event management companies. According to the World Travel and Tourism Council, the industry contributed 10.4% of global GDP and supported over 300 million jobs in 2019. However, the industry's dynamism also presents unique challenges. In the digital age, guest expectations have evolved. Modern travellers, armed with smartphones and an abundance of information, seek more than just a place to stay or dine. They desire experiences that resonate with their preferences, reflect their individuality, and align with their values. This confluence of evolving guest expectations and AI capabilities is the catalyst for change.

AI in Hospitality: A Strategic Imperative

AI in the hospitality industry has the potential to revolutionize guest experience by increasing guest satisfaction, streamlining operations, and enhancing convenience and comfort (Al-Hyari et al., 2023). AI technologies such as personalized guest experience, chatbots and virtual assistants, revenue management, operational efficiency, fraud detection and security, and predictive maintenance have been found to positively impact guest satisfaction in luxury hotels. However, it is important to balance the use of AI with human interaction, as many guests still value the

DOI: 10.4324/9781003488248-14

personal touch and human connection that comes with traditional hospitality. The integration of AI in the hospitality sector is not merely a response to a passing trend; it is a strategic imperative. AI aligns with the industry's core principles of guest-centricity, operational excellence, and the relentless pursuit of elevated guest experiences. It empowers hospitality establishments, from small boutique hotels to multinational chains, to meet and exceed these expectations. AI's role in hospitality extends far beyond chatbots and virtual assistants. From the moment a guest contemplates a stay, AI is involved in shaping every touchpoint of the guest journey. It automates routine tasks, predicts guest preferences, and facilitates seamless communication between guests and hotel staff.

As we embark on this exploration of AI's profound impact on the hospitality industry, we will delve into its various dimensions. From AI-enabled guest services to AI's role in revenue management, operational efficiency, and safety and security, this chapter aims to provide a comprehensive understanding of how AI is redefining the hospitality landscape.

2. Understanding Artificial Intelligence (AI)

Artificial intelligence (AI) refers to the development of computer systems that can perform tasks typically requiring human intelligence. AI systems are designed to simulate human-like cognitive functions such as learning, problem-solving, reasoning, and decision-making. In the context of the hospitality industry, AI encompasses a wide range of technologies, including machine learning, natural language processing, computer vision, and robotics (Russell & Norvig, 2010). The evolution of AI has been marked by significant milestones. It began with rule-based systems and expert systems, which relied on predefined rules and knowledge bases. However, recent advancements, particularly in machine learning, have propelled AI into a new era. Machine learning models, such as deep neural networks, have enabled AI systems to learn from data and improve their performance over time. Currently, AI is in a state of rapid development, with ongoing research and applications across various industries (Peretz-Andersson et al., 2021).

Latest Trends in AI Relevant to Hospitality

The hospitality industry is witnessing the integration of cutting-edge AI technologies to enhance guest experiences and operational efficiency. Some of the latest trends in AI relevant to hospitality include:

Voice Assistants: AI-powered voice assistants like Amazon's Alexa and Google Assistant are being integrated into hotel rooms, allowing guests to control room settings, request services, and access information using voice commands. Using AI-powered voice assistants leads to lower satisfaction levels due to a perceived deficiency in control, particularly among consumers with independent self-construal tendencies and with perceived control influencing service evaluation and future behavioural intentions such as consumption preference and word-of-mouth recommendations. It contributes to the growing literature on AI-powered voice assistants by shedding light on consumer responses and providing practical implications (Alei et al., 2021).

Chatbots and Virtual Concierges: AI-driven chatbots and virtual concierges are providing real-time responses to guest inquiries, streamlining the booking process, and offering personalized recommendations for dining and activities (Xiang et al., 2017).

Personalization Engines: AI algorithms are analyzing guest data to create highly personalized experiences, from room preferences to dining recommendations, resulting in increased guest satisfaction and loyalty (Mastertej, 2021).

Predictive Analytics: AI is being used for demand forecasting, allowing hotels to optimize pricing strategies, allocate resources efficiently, and maximize revenue (Močarníková & Greguš, 2020).

Robotic Assistance: Robots equipped with AI capabilities are assisting with tasks such as room service delivery, cleaning, and concierge services, reducing operational costs and enhancing guest experiences (Sigala, 2020).

The Increasing Adoption of AI in the Industry

The adoption of AI in the hospitality industry is on the rise. Hotels, resorts, and restaurants are investing in AI technologies to stay competitive and meet the evolving expectations of tech-savvy guests. AI is not limited to large hotel chains; even smaller establishments are integrating AI solutions to improve guest services and streamline operations ("The Rise of Service Robots in the Hospitality Industry: Some Actionable Insights, Boston Hospitality Review," 2021)

3. Benefits of AI Implementation in Hospitality

The integration of artificial intelligence (AI) in the hospitality industry brings forth a myriad of benefits, touching upon various aspects of both guest experiences and operational excellence.

Improved Operational Efficiency Through Automation and Optimization

AI-powered automation streamlines numerous operational tasks in the hospitality sector. This includes:

Check-In and Check-Out Processes: AI-driven systems enable seamless and contactless check-in and check-out experiences through facial recognition or mobile apps. Facial recognition check-in services at hotels have gained popularity, but there is a lack of academic studies on this area (Feng et al., 2021). This technology allows hotel guests to adopt facial recognition as a means of identification, eliminating the need for manual processes. Similarly, in vehicle checkpoints, automatic check-in and check-out systems are being implemented using automatic number plate recognition (ANPR) technology (Sangay et al., 2020). This system captures the vehicle number plate through CCTV cameras, recognizes it using image processing, and stores the information in a database for registration and surveillance purposes. Additionally, self-service check-in and check-out systems are being developed, where guests can use mobile apps to scan information and receive a random password for room access (Guo, 2017). These advancements in AI-driven systems have not only improved efficiency but also enhanced security and reduced human errors in the check-in and check-out processes.

Housekeeping and Maintenance: Robots equipped with AI algorithms can autonomously clean and maintain guest rooms, optimizing staff resources (Sigala, 2020). The robots use a combination of imitation learning and model predictive control (MPC) for intelligent and efficient motion planning. This is used to generate multiple optimal actions for different initial conditions of the robots, obstacles, and target locations. Imitation learning is then used to learn a policy network from the optimal policies generated by MPC. The concept of data aggregation (DAgger) is also adopted to further improve the learning performance. Experimental results confirm the effectiveness of the algorithms used in the design of the autonomous housekeeping robots (Zhu & Wu, 2022).

Inventory Management: AI-driven systems can forecast demand for supplies, reducing overstocking or understocking of essential items. Forecasting is important for supply chain management to minimize costs and improve productivity and profits. Excessive inventory and stock outs can lead to financial losses and customer dissatisfaction. The use of neural networks for seasonal time series forecasting and proposes a new form of transfer function to improve the quality of the forecast (Zhu & Wu, 2022).

Staff Scheduling: AI can optimize staff schedules based on historical data and current demand, reducing labor costs while ensuring adequate staffing levels (Lawless, 2015). These automations not only cut costs but also free up staff to focus on more personalized guest interactions.

Enhanced Guest Services and Personalization

In the realm of AI's impact on the hospitality sector, one of its most profound effects lies in the realm of personalization. AI empowers hotels and establishments to offer highly personalized guest experiences. Through AI-driven guest preferences analysis, including room types, dining choices, and activities, establishments can provide tailored recommendations based on individual preferences (Mastertej, 2021). AI-powered recommendation engines further enhance personalization by suggesting activities, dining options, and services that align precisely with each guest's unique tastes (Xiang et al., 2017). Additionally, AI-driven chatbots and virtual assistants offer instant responses to guest inquiries, provide assistance, and even anticipate guest needs based on historical data, creating a seamless and personalized interaction (Zhu & Wu, 2022). Voice recognition technology, integrated into guest rooms, elevates convenience by allowing guests to control room settings through voice commands, ensuring a personalized and effortless experience ("The Rise of Service Robots in the Hospitality Industry: Some Actionable InsightsBoston Hospitality Review," 2021). This heightened personalization not only leads to increased guest satisfaction but also fosters guest loyalty and garners positive reviews, solidifying AI's role in shaping exceptional guest experiences.

Revenue Management and Pricing Strategies

AI assumes a pivotal role in revolutionizing revenue management within the hospitality sector. Leveraging advanced algorithms, it conducts meticulous demand forecasting by analyzing historical data and real-time information, thus enabling hotels to dynamically adapt pricing and inventory to accurately meet demand and leveraging business intelligence and analytic insights to have a bottom-line impact on the business (Malla, 2018). The implementation of AI-driven dynamic pricing strategies becomes paramount, as they continuously optimize room rates in real time based on variables such as demand and occupancy, thereby maximizing revenue potential (Močarníková & Greguš, 2020). Furthermore, AI facilitates precise customer segmentation, categorizing guests according to their unique preferences and behaviours, thereby facilitating targeted marketing initiatives and personalized offers that serve to further augment revenue generation (Mastertej, 2021). In essence, these AI-driven strategies not only fine-tune revenue but also ensure competitive pricing strategies in the ever-evolving hospitality landscape.

Heightened Safety and Security Measures

AI enhances safety and security in the hospitality sector by utilizing AI-powered surveillance systems to monitor public spaces for potential threats, detecting fraudulent activities such as credit card fraud and identity theft through AI algorithms, and promoting contactless technologies like check-in/check-out and keyless entry systems to reduce physical contact and bolster hygiene measures. These multifaceted measures collectively contribute to a safer and more secure environment for both guests and establishments ("The Rise of Service Robots in the Hospitality Industry: Some Actionable Insights | Boston Hospitality Review," 2021). These safety and security measures are crucial for guest well-being and peace of mind. The benefits of AI implementation in the hospitality industry extend from improving operational efficiency and enhancing guest services to optimizing revenue management and ensuring heightened safety and security measures. These advantages position AI as a transformative force in revolutionizing the guest experience.

4. Challenges and Ethical Considerations

The integration of AI in the hospitality industry, while transformative, brings forth a set of complex challenges and ethical considerations that require thoughtful navigation.

Privacy Concerns and Data Protection

As AI systems collect and analyze vast amounts of guest data to personalize experiences, privacy concerns and data protection become paramount. Guests entrust establishments with their personal information, necessitating robust data privacy policies and practices to safeguard this sensitive data. Adherence to regulations such as the GDPR (general data protection regulation) is essential to maintain guest trust and comply with legal requirements (Ojino et al., 2022; Al-Hyari et al., 2023)

Security Challenges and Cyberthreats

The reliance on AI systems for guest services and operational processes exposes establishments to new security challenges and cyberthreats. AI-driven systems are potential targets for cyberattacks, and vulnerabilities can lead to data breaches or service disruptions. Establishments must invest in robust cybersecurity measures to protect both guest data and the integrity of their operations (Rauf et al., 2023).

Ethical Implications of AI in Hospitality

The ethical implications of AI adoption in hospitality require careful consideration. These implications include issues related to bias in AI algorithms, potential discrimination in personalized services, and the responsible use of guest data. Establishments must proactively address these ethical concerns to ensure fairness, transparency, and accountability in their AI-driven practices (Buhalis & Sinarta, 2019).

Workforce Adaptation and Skills Development

The introduction of AI technologies necessitates workforce adaptation and skills development. Employees must be trained to work alongside AI systems and leverage their capabilities effectively. Upskilling and reskilling initiatives are essential to empower the workforce to embrace AI-driven tools and contribute to enhanced guest experiences (Sigala, 2020).

These challenges and ethical considerations are crucial for hospitality establishments to harness the full potential of AI while maintaining guest trust, ensuring data security, upholding ethical standards, and fostering a skilled and adaptable workforce.

5. AI-Enabled Guest Services

AI is revolutionizing guest services in the hospitality industry, enhancing guest interactions and delivering personalized experiences in unprecedented ways (Morosan & Dursun-Cengizci, 2024).

Virtual Assistants and Chatbots in Guest Interactions

AI-driven virtual assistants and chatbots have become indispensable in guest interactions. These intelligent systems offer real-time responses to guest inquiries, provide information about services and facilities, and assist with tasks such as making reservations or requesting room service. They ensure efficient and round-the-clock support, enhancing guest satisfaction. Virtual assistants and chatbots are being used in guest interactions in various domains such as hotels and organizations. These assistants aim to provide information and assistance to guests. They utilize technologies like face recognition and natural language understanding to identify guests and interact with them (Michaud, 2018).

Personalized Recommendations for Elevated Guest Experiences

AI algorithms analyze guest data, including preferences and past behaviours, to provide highly personalized recommendations. From suggesting dining options that align with individual tastes to proposing activities tailored to guest interests, these recommendations elevate the guest experience, making it memorable and unique (Mastertej, 2021).

Voice Recognition and Natural Language Processing Technologies

Voice recognition and natural language processing technologies are reshaping guest interactions. Voice-controlled devices in guest rooms allow guests to adjust room settings, request services, or obtain information simply by speaking, enhancing convenience and personalization. These technologies enable seamless communication between guests and the establishment, making guest requests and inquiries more intuitive (Buhalis & Moldavska, 2021).

Streamlining Communication and Guest Requests

AI streamlines communication and guest requests, ensuring prompt and efficient service. Chatbots, for example, can anticipate guest needs based on historical data, enabling proactive assistance. Additionally, AI-driven systems prioritize and route guest requests to the appropriate departments, reducing response times and enhancing overall guest satisfaction (Xiang et al., 2017).

Incorporating these AI-enabled guest services not only improves operational efficiency but also ensures that every guest interaction is personalized, efficient, and memorable, contributing to the overall enhancement of the guest experience.

6. Enhancing Security and Customization

AI takes center stage in the hospitality sector by simultaneously fortifying security measures and enhancing guest customization. Facial recognition and biometric authentication, propelled by AI, ensure secure yet seamless guest check-in and access while personalizing their experiences. AI's surveillance prowess, driven by advanced computer vision algorithms, actively monitors public areas, detecting unusual activities and potential threats, prioritizing guest safety (Sigala, 2020). In tandem, AI acts as a sentinel against fraud, scrutinizing transaction data and guest behaviour to spot anomalies like credit card fraud, thereby safeguarding both guests and establishments ("The Rise of Service Robots in the Hospitality Industry: Some Actionable Insights| Boston Hospitality Review," 2021). Moreover,

AI-fueled contactless technologies, encompassing check-in/check-out and keyless entry systems, not only augment guest convenience but also align seamlessly with hygiene protocols, vital in today's health-conscious climate. Through these innovations, AI revolutionizes security and personalization, elevating guest experiences while ensuring their safety and well-being.

7. Future Trends and Opportunities

The future of AI in the hospitality sector is poised to be characterized by dynamic and interconnected innovations. AI's integration with the Internet of Things (IoT) and smart technologies promises intelligent ecosystems within hotels, optimizing energy usage and offering unprecedented guest control over room settings and IoT significantly impacts the decision-making in HR practices (Thirupurasundari et al., 2021). Augmented and virtual reality applications are set to redefine guest experiences, offering real-time information, interactive guides, and immersive entertainment options that transport guests to virtual destinations (Xiang et al., 2017). Further, AI will fuel hyper-personalization and context-aware services, going beyond personalized recommendations to adapt to guests' immediate needs and preferences in real time (Mastertej, 2021). This ongoing wave of AI-driven innovation, from robotic concierges to emotionally responsive art installations, will continuously elevate guest experiences, setting new industry standards (Sigala, 2020). As the hospitality sector embraces these trends, it will usher in a new era of guest-centricity and operational efficiency, solidifying AI's pivotal role in shaping its future.

8. Case Studies and Success Stories

Several leading hospitality brands have harnessed the power of AI to transform guest experiences and operations. These case studies and success stories offer practical insights into AI's real-world impact in the industry.

Marriott International: AI-Driven Guest Services

Marriott International has been at the forefront of implementing AI-driven guest services. They have integrated AI-powered chatbots and virtual assistants into their guest interactions, allowing guests to make reservations, request services, and receive personalized recommendations effortlessly. Marriott's use of AI demonstrates how technology can enhance guest experiences by providing convenient and responsive services (Marriott International, 2021).

Hilton Worldwide: AI-Powered Guest Interactions

Hilton Worldwide has embraced AI to enhance guest interactions. Its AI-powered concierge service provides guests with valuable information about local attractions, dining options, and hotel services. This not only improves guest satisfaction but also streamlines the guest experience by offering quick and accurate responses to inquiries. Hilton's success story highlights how AI can elevate guest engagement and convenience (Hilton, 2021).

Alibaba's Fly Zoo Hotel: The Future of AI in Hospitality

Alibaba's Fly Zoo Hotel in China offers a glimpse into the future of AI in hospitality. This futuristic hotel is staffed by robots that handle tasks such as check-in, room service, and concierge services. Guests can use facial recognition for seamless access to their rooms. The entire guest experience is underpinned by AI and automation, showcasing the potential for technology to redefine the industry ("Alibaba Group Official Website," n.d.).

These case studies and success stories from Marriott International, Hilton Worldwide, and Alibaba's Fly Zoo Hotel provide valuable insights into how AI is being effectively leveraged to enhance guest experiences, streamline operations, and shape the future of the hospitality industry. They serve as practical examples of AI's transformative power in the field and inspire other establishments to embrace innovation.

9. Recommendations for Business Practices: The Key to Success

The integration of AI into the hospitality industry represents a profound and ongoing transformation. As we navigate the dynamic landscape where technology converges with the art of hospitality, it becomes increasingly clear that the path to success lies in strategic and agile business practices. Here, we share a set of recommendations that encapsulate the essence of thriving in an era defined by AI's pervasive impact on the hospitality sector.

Embrace a Culture of Innovation

In a world where technological advancements occur at an unprecedented pace, a culture of innovation is the linchpin of success. Hospitality businesses must invest in research and development, keeping a finger on the pulse of AI trends and emerging technologies. Innovation should not be confined to the IT department but should permeate every aspect of the organization. It entails a mindset that constantly seeks ways to enhance guest experiences, streamline operations, and adapt to changing guest expectations.

Prioritize Data Privacy and Security

AI's transformative power in the hospitality industry hinges on the vast amount of guest data it leverages. Consequently, businesses must prioritize data privacy and security. Guest data should be treated with the utmost care and responsibility. Compliance with data protection regulations, such as GDPR, is non-negotiable. Data encryption, access controls, and robust cybersecurity measures are essential components of any AI-driven operation. Building and maintaining trust through secure data handling is paramount.

Invest in Workforce Adaptation

AI is not a substitute for the human touch in hospitality; it's a powerful tool that can augment and empower the workforce. Therefore, investing in workforce adaptation and skills development is crucial. Employees need to be proficient in working alongside AI systems, understanding their capabilities, and using them to enhance guest experiences. Training programmes and upskilling initiatives should be integral to human resources strategies, ensuring that staff can seamlessly collaborate with AI and provide a seamless, empathetic, and highly personalized service.

Unleash AI's Personalization Potential

The true magic of AI lies in its capacity to deliver hyper-personalized, context-aware services. To harness this potential, hospitality businesses should implement AI systems that not only collect data but also analyze it in real time. This analysis should inform every guest interaction, providing guests with recommendations, services, and experiences tailored to their immediate needs and preferences. Personalization is not a luxury but an expectation in today's hospitality landscape, and AI is the vehicle to deliver it.

Evolve With the Technology

The digital transformation of the hospitality industry is an ongoing journey. Businesses should continually evolve with the technology, adopting and adapting to innovations as they emerge. Augmented and virtual reality, the integration of AI with the Internet of Things, and the exploration of immersive experiences are all on the horizon. Staying at the forefront of these developments ensures that an establishment remains competitive and continues to deliver exceptional guest experiences.

The success of hospitality businesses in an AI-driven world hinges on their ability to embrace innovation, safeguard guest data, empower their workforce, utilize AI for personalization, and evolve with emerging technologies. These recommendations represent the key to not just surviving but thriving in the ever-evolving landscape where AI and hospitality intersect. By adopting these practices, businesses can ensure they consistently exceed guest expectations and remain pioneers in this dynamic and innovative future.

10. Conclusion

The integration of AI into the hospitality industry has brought about a profound transformation, redefining guest experiences and operational excellence. AI's ability to deliver highly personalized services, optimize revenue management, enhance security, and streamline guest interactions has revolutionized the way hotels and resorts operate. From virtual assistants and chatbots providing instant responses to AI-driven recommendation engines shaping guest choices, AI has become a cornerstone of modern hospitality.

However, the journey is far from over. The importance of ongoing research and innovation cannot be overstated. As technology evolves, new opportunities and challenges will emerge. Continuous exploration and adaptation are essential to unlocking the full potential of AI in delivering exceptional guest experiences.

Looking forward, the potential for AI in the hospitality sector is boundless. With the integration of AI with IoT, augmented reality, and virtual reality, hyper-personalization, and context-aware services, the industry stands on the precipice of a new era. These innovations promise to elevate guest experiences to unprecedented heights, ensuring that each guest feels not only welcomed but also truly understood. In this dynamic landscape, AI is not just a tool; it is a catalyst for change. It empowers the hospitality industry to not only meet but exceed guest expectations, fostering loyalty, positive reviews, and a renewed sense of wonder in the world of hospitality.

As we reflect on AI's transformative journey in hospitality, we recognize that the horizon is limitless, and the path forward is illuminated by innovation. The future of hospitality belongs to those who embrace the possibilities of AI, and it is a future in which exceptional guest experiences are not just the goal but the expectation. As the hospitality industry continues to evolve, it does so hand in hand with AI, working tirelessly to deliver extraordinary moments and memories to every guest, every time.

References

Alei, F., Zhi, L., & Zhenxing (Eddie), M. (2022). To talk or to touch: Unraveling consumer responses to two types of hotel in-room technology. *International Journal of Hospitality Management*, 101, 103112. https://doi.org/10.1016/J.IJHM.2021.103112

Al-Hyari, H. S., Al-Smadi, H. M., & Weshah, S. (2023). The impact of artificial intelligence (AI) on guest satisfaction in hotel management: An empirical study of luxury hotels. *Geojournal of Tourism and Geosites*, 48(2 supplement), 810–819. https://doi.org/10.30892/gtg.482spl15-1081

Alibaba Group official website. (n.d.). Retrieved from www.alibabagroup.com/en/news/press_pdf/p210127.pdf

Buhalis, D., & Moldavska, I. (2021). In-room voice-based AI digital assistants transforming on-site hotel services and guests' experiences. In *Springer eBooks* (pp. 30–44). https://doi.org/10.1007/978-3-030-65785-7_3

Buhalis, D., & Sinarta, Y. (2019). Real-time co-creation and nowness service: Lessons from tourism and hospitality. *Journal of Travel & Tourism Marketing*, 36(5), 563–582. https://doi.org/10.1080/10548408.2019.1592059

Bulchand-Gidumal, J., William Secin, E., O'Connor, P., & Buhalis, D. (2023). Artificial intelligence's impact on hospitality and tourism marketing: Exploring key themes and addressing challenges. *Current Issues in Tourism*, 1–18. https://doi.org/10.1080/13683500.2023.2229480

Peretz-Andersson, Einav, Niklas Lavesson, Albert Bifet, and Patrick Mikalef. (2021). "AI Transformation in the Public Sector: Ongoing Research." In *2021 Swedish Artificial Intelligence Society Workshop (SAIS)*, pp. 1–4. IEEE, 2021.

Feng, Z. X., Yun, Z., Tingting, Z., & Jing, W. (2021). Facial recognition check-in services at hotels. *Journal of Hospitality Marketing & Management*, 30(3), 373–393. https://doi.org/10.1080/19368623.2020.1813670

Hilton. (2021, March 30). Hilton: Many pandemic safety innovations to remain. Stories from Hilton. Retrieved January 9, 2024, from https://stories.hilton.com/corporate-news/hilton-many-pandemic-safety-innovations-to-remain

Lawless, M. (2015). Predictive analytics: An opportunity for better demand planning and forecasting. *The Journal of Business Forecasting*, 33(4), 44–46.
Malla, J. (2018). HR analytics center of excellence. *International Journal of Business, Management and Allied Sciences*, 5, 282–284. http://ijbmas.in/5.S2.18/282-284.pdf
Marriott International. (2021). *How Marriott is using artificial intelligence*. Retrieved from https://marriott.gcs-web.com/financial-information/fact-sheet
Mastertej, T. (2021, August 30). *How artificial intelligence is reshaping the hospitality sector*. Retrieved from https://automatonai.com/how-artificial-intelligence-is-reshaping-the-hospitality-sector
Michaud, L. N. (2018). Observations of a new chatbot: Drawing conclusions from early interactions with users. *IT Professional*, 20(5), 40–47. https://doi.org/10.1109/mitp.2018.053891336
Močarníková, K., & Greguš, M. (2020). Conceptualization of predictive analytics by literature review. In N. Kryvinska, & M. Greguš (Eds.), *Data-centric business and applications. Lecture notes on data engineering and communications technologies*, vol 30. Cham. https://doi.org/10.1007/978-3-030-19069-9_8
Morosan, C., & Dursun-Cengizci, A. (2024). Letting AI make decisions for me: An empirical examination of hotel guests' acceptance of technology agency. *International Journal of Contemporary Hospitality Management*, 36(3), 946–974. https://doi.org/10.1108/IJCHM-08-2022-1041
Ojino, R., Mich, L., & Mvungi, N. H. (2022). Hotel room personalization via ontology and rule-based reasoning. *International Journal of Web Information Systems*, 18(5/6), 369–387. https://doi.org/10.1108/ijwis-02-2022-0045
Rauf, U., Mohsen, F., & Wei, Z. (2023). A taxonomic classification of insider threats: Existing techniques, future directions & recommendations. *Journal of Cyber Security and Mobility*, 12(02), 221–252. https://doi.org/10.13052/jcsm2245-1439.1225
Russell, S. J., & Norvig, P. (2010). *Artificial intelligence a modern approach*. London.
Sangay, T., Pema, D., Bevek, S., & Thinley, T. (2020). *Smart check-in check-out system for vehicles using automatic number plate recognition*. https://doi.org/10.1109/ICCCNT49239.2020.9225555
Sigala, M. (2020). Tourism and COVID-19: Impacts and implications for advancing and resetting industry and research. *Journal of Business Research*, 117, 312–321. https://doi.org/10.1016/j.jbusres.2020.06.015
The rise of service robots in the hospitality industry: Some actionable insights | Boston Hospitality Review. (2021, October 4). Retrieved from www.bu.edu/bhr/2021/10/04/the-rise-of-service-robots-in-the-hospitality-industry-some-actionable-insights
Thirupurasundari, D. R., Jogarao, M., Prakash, O., & Raj, K. B. (2021). Investigating the Impact of IoT on Business Performance. *Turkish Online Journal of Qualitative Inquiry*, 12(6). Retrieved from www.tojqi.net/index.php/journal/article/view/3311/2246
Xiang, Z., Du, Q., Ma, Y., & Fan, W. (2017). A comparative analysis of major online review platforms: Implications for social media analytics in hospitality and tourism. *Tourism Management*, 58, 51–65. https://doi.org/10.1016/j.tourman.2016.10.001
Zhu, F., & Wu, Z. (2022). Algorithmic design of autonomous housekeeping robots through imitation learning and model predictive control. *2022 Asia Conference on Algorithms, Computing and Machine Learning (CACML)*. https://doi.org/10.1109/cacml55074.2022.00024

15 Artificial Intelligence (AI)–Powered Chatbots

Providing Instant Support and Personalized Recommendations to Guests 24/7

Dr. Tarun Kumar Vashishth, Vikas Sharma, Dr. Kewal Krishan Sharma, Dr. Bhupendra Kumar, Atul Kumar, Rajneesh Panwar

1. Introduction

1.1 Background and Significance of AI-Powered Chatbots in Customer Service

In recent years, the landscape of customer service has witnessed a significant transformation, primarily driven by advancements in artificial intelligence (AI) and natural language processing (NLP) technologies. As businesses across various industries strive to enhance customer experiences and streamline their support operations, AI-powered chatbots have emerged as a groundbreaking solution.

Chatbot powered metrics provides insights into the challenges that businesses face when attempting to deliver prompt, personalized, and efficient support to their customers. These challenges include:

a Scale and Availability: Businesses, especially those operating globally, often struggle to provide round-the-clock customer support due to human limitations. This section highlights how AI chatbots can fill this gap by being available 24/7, ensuring customers receive assistance when they need it, regardless of time zones.
b Personalization: Tailoring support to individual customer needs and preferences is a critical aspect of customer service. AI-powered chatbots are discussed as tools that can analyze customer data in real time to provide personalized recommendations and solutions.
c Efficiency: Customer service operations can be resource intensive. This section explores how chatbots can significantly improve the efficiency of customer interactions, reducing response times and enabling human agents to focus on more complex issues.
d Cost Savings: Businesses are under constant pressure to optimize their operational costs. AI chatbots are presented as cost-effective solutions that can reduce the need for large customer support teams while maintaining service quality.

DOI: 10.4324/9781003488248-15

1.2 Research Objectives and Scope

Research Objectives:

a To Examine the Evolution of AI-Powered Chatbots: The primary objective is to trace the development of AI-powered chatbots, from their inception to the present, highlighting key milestones and technological advancements.
b To Explore Use Cases Across Industries: This chapter will delve into diverse industry verticals, showcasing how AI chatbots have been deployed effectively to provide instant support and personalized recommendations. Case studies from sectors such as hospitality, e-commerce, finance, healthcare, and more will be analyzed.
c To Discuss the Technological Underpinnings: Understanding the core technologies behind AI chatbots is essential. This section will elucidate the role of natural language processing (NLP), machine learning, and conversational design in creating intelligent chatbot solutions.

Scope:

a Industry Diversity: The scope of this chapter encompasses a wide range of industries, providing a comprehensive overview of AI chatbot applications. From hotels and online retail to financial institutions and healthcare providers, the chapter will explore how chatbots are tailored to suit diverse customer service needs.
b Global Perspective: While focusing on the global landscape, regional differences and preferences in AI chatbot adoption will also be considered.
c Technological Aspects: The technological aspects will be explained in a manner accessible to both technical and non-technical readers, shedding light on the AI and NLP techniques that empower chatbots.

By exploring these objectives and within this defined scope, this chapter aims to provide a valuable resource for readers seeking a deeper understanding of the pivotal role AI-powered chatbots play in modern customer service.

2. Literature Review

Al-Hyari et al. (2023) suggest a strategic focus for hotels on delivering personalized experiences, optimizing operations, and improving convenience and comfort to elevate guest satisfaction.

Gupta et al. (2023) present a model that interconnects various critical components, integrating AI with ethical considerations and privacy concerns to deliver customized customer services.

Kaplan and Haenlein (2019) introduce a framework known as the Three C Model of Confidence, Change, and Control, which assists organizations in considering both the internal and external impacts of AI.

Kim et al. (2021) investigate how regulatory focus and privacy concerns influence consumer responses to highly personalized chatbot advertising.

Zhu et al. (2022) investigate the impact of the certainty of consumer needs on consumers' acceptance of artificial intelligence (AI) chatbots during the online pre-purchase stage.

Khan et al. (2023) explore the relationship between artificial intelligence (AI) and customer loyalty within the realm of advanced digital marketing, with a particular emphasis on the mediating role of chatbots.

Gupta et al. (2022) propose the use of AI-enabled robots by practicing managers in the hospitality industry to automate and enhance processes, ultimately delivering a more personalized and enjoyable guest experience in the context of a smart city.

Lee, Sae Bom (2020) demonstrates that chatbots enhance the efficiency and productivity of current business operations, with a specific focus on enhancing the convenience of customer interactions related to shopping, ordering, and payments.

Lukanova and Ilieva (2019) offer a comprehensive review of the present status and prospective applications of robots, artificial intelligence, and automated services (RAISA) within hotel enterprises.

Calvaresi et al. (2021) argue that the rapid technological and financial developments necessitate ongoing investments, skills enhancement, and innovative system approaches to address the evolving dimensions of e-tourism challenges.

Dash and Bakshi (2019) investigate customer perceptions of chatbot usage in the hospitality sector, particularly in chain hotels where chatbots are integrated with CRM solutions, streamlining information access for both hotels and customers from a unified source.

Kumar, Gupta, and Bapat (2023) highlight that while ChatGPT is a potent tool for retailers, challenges such as comprehending non-standard accents and unconventional language can lead to customer frustration. They recommend that retail managers should strategically integrate ChatGPT to enhance the overall customer experience.

Krishnan et al. (2022) offer an in-depth exploration of the impact of AI chatbots on user interactions, their applications in marketing and customer service, and the underlying factors that drive customer engagement with augmented agents like chatbots. Critical examination is needed to assess the practical implications and potential limitations of this technology in the context of user experiences and brand strategies.

Selamat and Windasari (2021) make a significant contribution to the growing service literature regarding chatbot interactions, focusing on their relevance for small and medium-sized enterprises (SMEs). Their research provides valuable insights from the viewpoints of both SME owners and customers. A critical review is essential to discern the practical implications and potential challenges of integrating chatbot services in SME contexts.

Pillai and Sivathanu (2020) undertake a study to scrutinize customers' behavioural intentions and actual usage (AUE) of AI-powered chatbots in the context of hospitality and tourism in India. They extend the technology adoption model (TAM) with context-specific variables, but a critical examination is essential to

Table 15.1 Literature review of the enablers of AI in hospitality

Reference	*Focus*	*Key Contributions*	*Critical Evaluation*
Al-Hyari et al. (2023)	Personalized hotel experiences	Strategic focus on personalization in hotels for elevated guest satisfaction	Effectiveness in practice and implementation challenges?
Gupta et al. (2023)	AI with ethical considerations	Model connecting AI with ethics for customized customer services	Ethical model, practical application, and privacy concerns?
Kaplan and Haenlein (2019)	Three C Model framework	Framework for considering internal and external impacts of AI	Usefulness in assessing AI impacts and potential limitations?
Kim et al. (2021)	Regulatory focus and privacy	Investigation of regulatory focus and privacy on consumer responses to personalized chatbot advertising	Impact of regulatory focus and privacy on chatbot advertising?
Zhu et al. (2022)	Consumer needs during online shopping	Study on the impact of consumer needs certainty on AI chatbot acceptance during online pre-purchase interactions	Influence of consumer needs certainty on AI chatbot acceptance?
Khan et al. (2023)	AI and customer loyalty in digital marketing	Exploration of AI's role in customer loyalty within advanced digital marketing, with a focus on chatbots	Relationship between AI, chatbots, and customer loyalty?
Gupta et al. (2022)	AI-enabled robots in hospitality	Proposal to use AI robots in hospitality for automation and enhancing guest experience	Practical implications and guest experience improvements?
Lee, Sae Bom (2020)	Chatbots in business operations	Demonstration of chatbots enhancing efficiency and customer convenience in shopping, ordering, and payments	Effectiveness of chatbots in improving business operations?
Lukanova and Ilieva (2019)	RAISA in hotel enterprises	Comprehensive review of robots, AI, and automated services in hotels (RAISA)	Practical applications and impact on hotel enterprises?

Calvaresi et al. (2021)	E-tourism developments and challenges	Argument for investments, skills enhancement, and innovative approaches to address e-tourism challenges	Applicability of proposed solutions for e-tourism challenges?
Dash and Bakshi (2019)	Chatbots in chain hotels with CRM integration	Investigation of customer perceptions of CRM-integrated chatbots in chain hotels	Impact of CRM-integrated chatbots on information access for hotels and customers?
Kumar et al. (2023)	Use of ChatGPT in retail	Highlights ChatGPT's potential in retail and suggests strategic integration for improved customer experiences	Effectiveness of ChatGPT integration in the retail sector and challenges?
Krishnan et al. (2022)	AI chatbots in marketing and customer service	Exploration of AI chatbots' impact on user interactions, applications in marketing, and factors driving engagement with chatbots	Practical implications and limitations in user experiences and brand strategies?
Selamat and Windasari (2021)	Chatbots in SME contexts	Contribution to the service literature on chatbot interactions in small and medium-sized enterprises (SMEs)	Practical relevance and challenges of integrating chatbots in SMEs?
Pillai and Sivathanu (2020)	AI chatbots in Indian hospitality and tourism with extended TAM model	Study of customer behavioural intentions and actual usage of AI chatbots in Indian hospitality and tourism	Model effectiveness and relevance to the Indian market conditions?
Chan et al. (2022)	AI enabling technologies in tourism and hospitality	Introduction of various AI technologies in the tourism and hospitality sector	Practical applications and effectiveness in improving customer experiences?

Source: By authors

assess the model's effectiveness and relevance to the specific market conditions in India.

Chan et al. (2022) introduce various enabling technologies for AI in the tourism and hospitality sector, such as expert systems, voice chatbots, artificial neural networks, and more. However, a critical evaluation of their practical applications and effectiveness in improving the customer experience within the industry is warranted.

3. Understanding AI-Powered Chatbots

3.1 Basics of Chatbots and Their Evolution

Chatbots Defined

Chatbots, short for "chat robots," are computer programmes designed to engage in conversations with users, typically through text- or voice-based interactions. They serve as virtual assistants capable of understanding and responding to user queries, requests, or commands in a conversational manner (Figure 15.1).

Historical Perspective

- Early Chatbots: The origins of chatbots can be traced back to the mid-20th century, when computer scientists and engineers began experimenting with simple programmes that could simulate human-like conversations. Early chatbots, such as ELIZA, developed in the 1960s, used pattern recognition and scripted responses to mimic human conversation.
- Turing Test: The Turing Test, proposed by mathematician and computer scientist Alan Turing in 1950, became a benchmark for evaluating a machine's ability to exhibit intelligent behaviour indistinguishable from that of a human. It laid the conceptual foundation for chatbot development.
- Rule-Based Systems: In the 1970s and 1980s, rule-based systems were employed to create chatbots capable of following predefined sets of rules and decision trees. While limited in their capabilities, these chatbots found applications in specific domains.

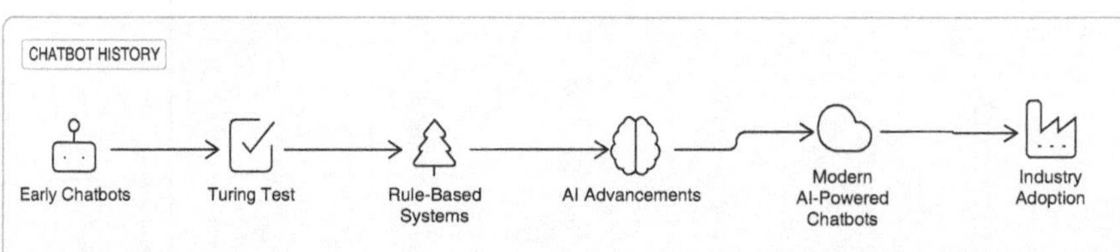

Figure 15.1 Chatbot history

Source: By authors

- AI Advancements: The advent of artificial intelligence (AI) and natural language processing (NLP) in the late 20th century ushered in a new era of chatbot development. Machine learning algorithms enabled chatbots to learn and adapt from user interactions, improving their conversational abilities.

This overview of the basics and evolution of chatbots sets the stage for a deeper exploration of AI-powered chatbots in the context of the hospitality industry. It highlights the transformative impact of technology on customer service and guest interactions.

3.2 How AI Powers Chatbots

Artificial intelligence (AI) plays a pivotal role in powering modern chatbots, enabling them to deliver intelligent and context-aware responses. In this section, we delve into the mechanisms through which AI empowers chatbots, enhancing their conversational capabilities.

Natural Language Processing (NLP)

NLP is a foundational AI technology that equips chatbots with the ability to understand and generate human language. NLP encompasses various subfields, including:

- Text Analysis: AI-powered chatbots utilize text analysis techniques to parse and comprehend user input. They break down sentences into tokens, identify keywords, and extract entities (such as names, dates, and locations).
- Sentiment Analysis: NLP allows chatbots to discern the sentiment and emotion behind user messages. By gauging sentiment, chatbots can tailor responses to be more empathetic or upbeat when necessary.
- Language Understanding: NLP models, like recurrent neural networks (RNNs) and transformers, enable chatbots to understand the context of a conversation. They consider previous messages to provide relevant and coherent responses.

Machine Learning and Deep Learning

Machine learning (ML) and deep learning are at the heart of AI-powered chatbots. These techniques enable chatbots to learn from data and improve their performance over time (Figure 15.2). Key aspects include:

- Training Data: Chatbots are trained on vast datasets containing examples of human conversations. They learn language patterns, common phrases, and contextual cues from this data.
- Model Architectures: Deep learning models, such as neural networks and transformers, are employed to process and generate text. Transformers, in particular, have revolutionized NLP tasks, enabling chatbots to handle complex language understanding tasks.

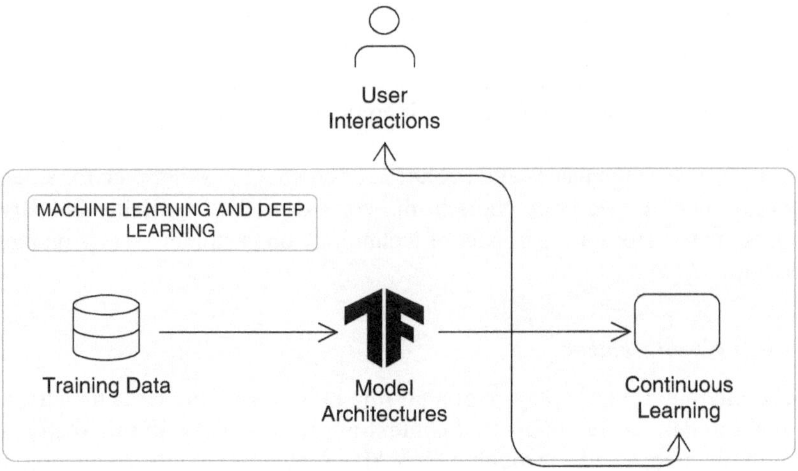

Figure 15.2 Chatbots with machine learning and deep learning

Source: By authors

- Continuous Learning: Chatbots can continuously learn from user interactions. Reinforcement learning techniques enable them to adapt and refine their responses based on feedback.

Speech Recognition

In addition to text-based interactions, AI-powered chatbots can support voice-based conversations. Speech recognition technology converts spoken words into text, allowing chatbots to understand and respond to spoken queries.

Natural Language Generation (NLG)

NLG is another component of AI that enables chatbots to generate human-like text. This is crucial for chatbots to provide coherent and contextually relevant responses. NLG models can generate personalized messages and recommendations.

Context Awareness

AI empowers chatbots to maintain context throughout a conversation. They remember previous messages, user preferences, and session history. This contextual awareness allows chatbots to provide more meaningful responses and handle multi-turn conversations effectively.

Personalization

AI-driven chatbots leverage data about users to personalize interactions. They can recommend products, services, or content based on user behaviour and preferences, enhancing the user experience.

Integration With Data Sources

AI-powered chatbots can access and integrate with databases, APIs, and external systems. This capability allows them to retrieve real-time information, such as room availability, pricing, or order status, and provide accurate responses.

3.3 Types of Chatbots

Chatbots come in various types, each designed for specific purposes and levels of complexity. In the context of the hospitality industry and beyond, understanding these types is essential for selecting the most suitable chatbot for a particular use case (Figure 15.3). Here are the common types of chatbots:

3.3.1 Rule-Based Chatbots

Simple Rule-Based Chatbots: These chatbots operate based on predefined rules and decision trees. They can provide responses to specific user inputs but lack the ability to understand natural language or context beyond the programmed rules. They are commonly used for basic customer support tasks.

Menu-Driven Chatbots: Menu-driven chatbots guide users through a series of pre-defined options, similar to an interactive menu. Users select options by clicking or typing numbers, making them suitable for tasks like ordering food or booking services.

3.3.2 AI-Powered Chatbots

NLP-Powered Chatbots: These chatbots utilize natural language processing (NLP) and machine learning to understand and generate human language. They can engage in more natural and context-aware conversations, making them suitable for a wide range of applications, including customer support, information retrieval, and recommendation systems.

Contextual Chatbots: Contextual chatbots excel at maintaining conversation context. They remember previous user inputs and provide responses that consider the ongoing conversation. This ability makes them valuable for handling multi-turn interactions and complex queries.

3.3.3 AI Assistants

Virtual Personal Assistants: These advanced chatbots act as virtual personal assistants. They can perform tasks beyond chat-based interactions, such as setting reminders, checking emails, or managing calendars. Examples include Apple's Siri and Amazon's Alexa.

Enterprise AI Assistants: Designed for businesses, enterprise AI assistants can handle a range of tasks, including scheduling meetings, accessing company data, and assisting employees with various work-related tasks. They enhance productivity and streamline operations.

3.3.4 Voice-Activated Chatbots

Voice-Activated Chatbots: These chatbots respond to voice commands and are often integrated into smart speakers and voice-enabled devices. They provide hands-free interactions and are valuable in scenarios in which users prefer vocal communication.

3.3.5 Social Media Chatbots

Social Media Chatbots: These chatbots operate on social media platforms and messaging apps. They facilitate customer engagement, answer frequently asked questions, and provide support. Facebook Messenger and WhatsApp are common platforms for social media chatbots.

Understanding these chatbot types is crucial for businesses in selecting the right chatbot solution to enhance customer service, streamline operations, and improve overall guest experiences in the hospitality industry.

3.4 Benefits of AI-Powered Chatbots in the Hospitality Industry

AI-powered chatbots offer a wide range of benefits for the hospitality industry, transforming the way hotels and resorts interact with guests and manage operations. These benefits extend to both guests and hotel staff, creating a more efficient and enjoyable experience for everyone involved (Figure 15.4). Here are some key advantages:

3.4.1 24/7 Availability

AI-powered chatbots are available round the clock, providing instant responses to guest inquiries and requests, regardless of the time of day. This ensures that guests receive timely assistance and information whenever they need it.

3.4.2 Enhanced Guest Experience

Chatbots offer personalized recommendations, room service, and local activity suggestions, enhancing the overall guest experience. Guests can receive tailored information and services based on their preferences.

3.4.3 Efficient Customer Support

Chatbots handle routine guest inquiries and requests, freeing up human staff to focus on more complex tasks and guest interactions. This efficiency reduces response times and improves customer support.

3.4.4 Multilingual Support

AI chatbots can communicate with guests in multiple languages, eliminating language barriers and making international travellers feel more at home. This feature is especially valuable in the global hospitality industry.

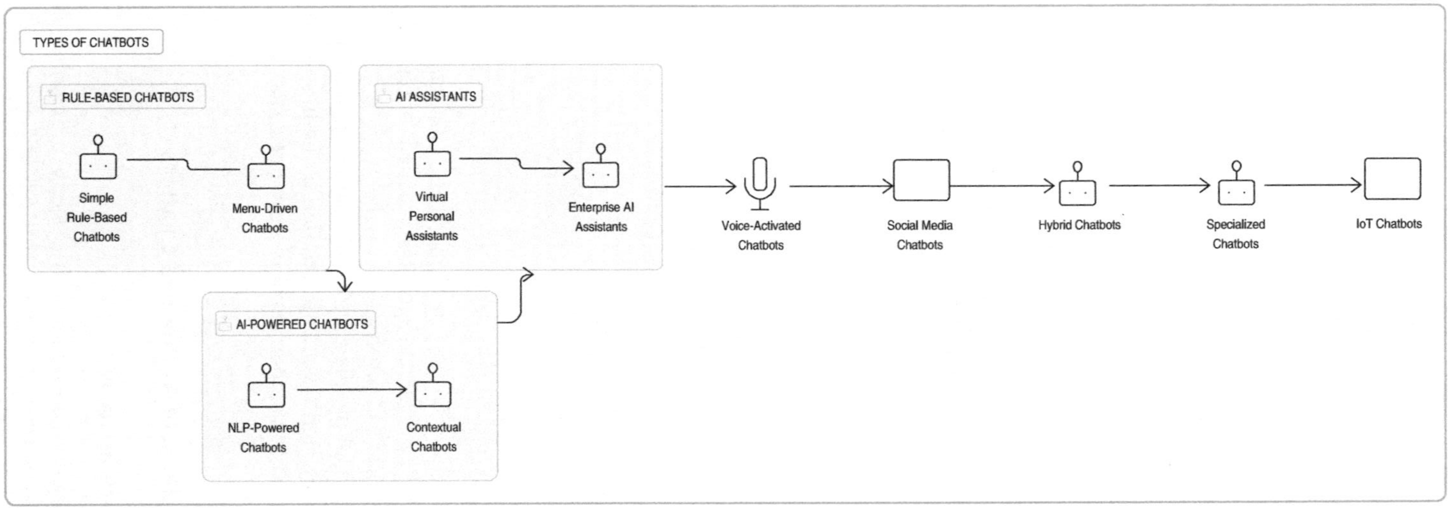

Figure 15.3 Types of chatbots

Source: By authors

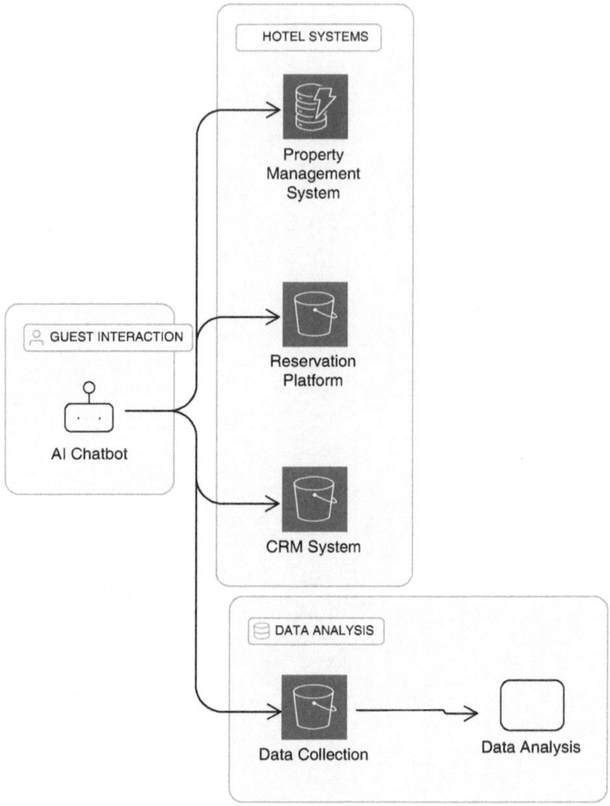

Figure 15.4 Block diagram of AI in healthcare
Source: By authors

3.4.5 Cost Savings

By automating various guest services and inquiries, chatbots can significantly reduce operational costs. Fewer human agents are needed for repetitive tasks, leading to cost savings for hotels and resorts.

Overall, AI-powered chatbots play a pivotal role in improving guest satisfaction, operational efficiency, and revenue generation in the hospitality industry. As technology continues to advance, their capabilities will expand, further enhancing the guest experience.

4. Design and Development of AI-Powered Chatbots

4.1 Planning Chatbot Implementation

In this section, we dive into the essential initial steps of planning chatbot implementation within the hospitality industry. Figure 15.5 underscores the importance of Chatbots Implementation Planning. Effective planning is the foundation for a

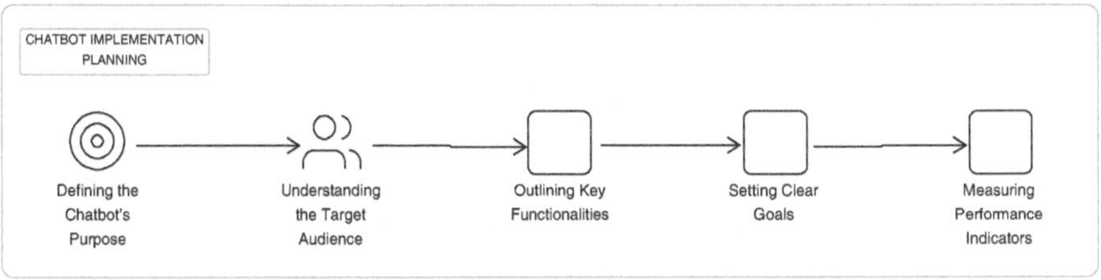

Figure 15.5 Chatbot implementation planning

Source: By authors

successful AI-powered chatbot deployment. It involves defining the chatbot's purpose, understanding its target audience, and outlining key functionalities. Additionally, it discusses the importance of setting clear goals and measuring performance indicators to ensure the chatbot aligns with the hotel's objectives.

Defining the Chatbot's Purpose

Before embarking on the chatbot implementation journey, it's crucial to define the chatbot's purpose. Is it aimed at streamlining booking processes, providing guest services, or offering recommendations? Establishing a clear purpose guides the entire development process.

Understanding the Target Audience

Knowing your audience is essential. Are you developing the chatbot for hotel guests, potential customers, or both? Understanding your target audience's preferences and expectations will shape the chatbot's design and content.

Outlining Key Functionalities

What tasks or functions should the chatbot be able to perform? These functionalities can range from answering frequently asked questions to handling room reservations, providing local recommendations, and offering real-time support.

Setting Clear Goals

Establishing specific, measurable, achievable, relevant, and time-bound (SMART) goals is critical. Whether it's improving guest satisfaction scores, increasing booking rates, or reducing response times, well-defined objectives guide development efforts.

Measuring Performance Indicators

To ensure the chatbot's effectiveness, you'll need to identify key performance indicators (KPIs). These may include user engagement metrics, conversion rates, or customer satisfaction scores. Regularly monitoring these KPIs helps in assessing and optimizing the chatbot's performance.

By focusing on these aspects during the planning phase, hotels can lay the groundwork for a chatbot that not only meets guest needs but also aligns with the broader goals of the establishment. It ensures that the chatbot's implementation is purpose driven, audience centric, and outcome focused.

4.2 Selecting the Right AI Technologies

The success of an AI-powered chatbot greatly depends on choosing the right tools and technologies that align with the chatbot's objectives and functionalities.

Assessing Natural Language Processing (NLP) Capabilities

Natural language processing is the backbone of conversational AI. Evaluate NLP capabilities such as language understanding, sentiment analysis, and multilingual support. Choose an NLP framework or API that suits your chatbot's language requirements and complexity.

Chatbot Development Platforms

Consider leveraging chatbot development platforms that offer pre-built frameworks and tools for chatbot creation. These platforms often include AI components like intent recognition, entity extraction, and dialogue management, streamlining development efforts.

Machine Learning and Training Data

Determine if your chatbot will employ machine learning techniques for tasks like user intent recognition and recommendation generation. Select machine learning libraries and frameworks, and ensure access to high-quality training data.

Voice Recognition and Text-to-Speech (TTS)

If your chatbot will offer voice interactions, explore voice recognition and text-to-speech (TTS) technologies. Choose providers or APIs that provide accurate voice recognition and natural-sounding TTS for a seamless user experience.

Integration Capabilities

Assess how well your chosen AI technologies can integrate with your existing systems, such as reservation databases, customer relationship management (CRM) tools, and website platforms. Integration is vital for accessing and updating guest information.

4.3 Integrating With Existing Systems

The successful integration of your AI-powered chatbot with existing systems is a pivotal factor in providing seamless and efficient guest services in the hospitality industry. This section delves into the key considerations and steps for achieving this integration.

Assessing System Compatibility

Begin by conducting a thorough assessment of your hotel's current technology infrastructure. Identify the systems and platforms that the chatbot needs to interact with, such as reservation systems, customer databases, room management systems, and loyalty programmes.

API and Middleware Utilization

Determine whether your existing systems offer application programming interfaces (APIs) or middleware solutions that enable external access. APIs facilitate data exchange and communication between the chatbot and other systems. If such interfaces are available, evaluate their capabilities and limitations.

Custom Integration Development

In cases in which APIs or middleware are not readily available, consider developing custom integration solutions. This involves creating connectors or adapters that enable data flow between the chatbot and existing systems. Custom development offers flexibility but requires careful planning and resources.

Data Synchronization and Security

Address data synchronization issues to ensure that guest information remains consistent across systems. Implement secure data transmission protocols, encryption, and access controls to protect sensitive guest data during integration.

Real-Time Updates

Assess the need for real-time updates. Certain systems, like room availability or reservation changes, require immediate synchronization between the chatbot and relevant databases. Plan for real-time integration where necessary to prevent discrepancies.

A well-executed integration strategy enables your AI-powered chatbot to function as a valuable extension of your hotel's existing services. It streamlines operations, enhances guest interactions, and contributes to an overall superior guest experience. Figure 15.6 highlights the utilization of Chatbots in Hospitality Services.

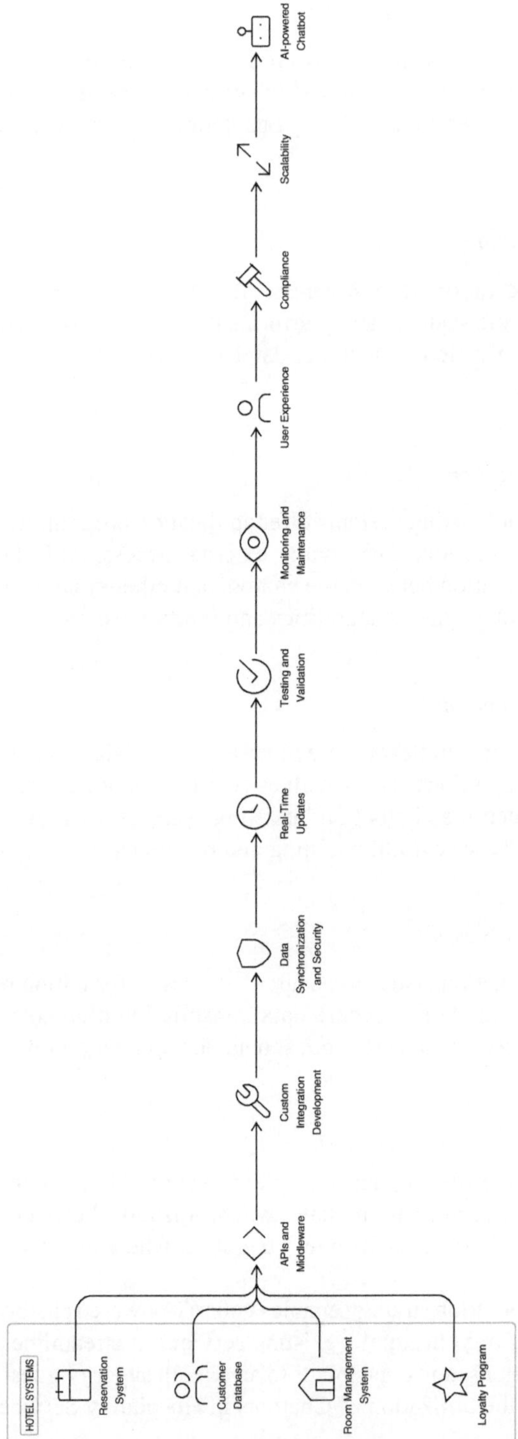

Figure 15.6 Real-time updates integration strategy

Source: By authors

5. 24/7 Guest Support With Chatbots

5.1 Eliminating Time Zone and Language Barriers

The elimination of time zone and language barriers is a crucial aspect of AI-powered chatbots in the hospitality industry. AI chatbots excel in providing round-the-clock guest support and transcending language limitations, ensuring that guests receive assistance at any hour and in their preferred language. This feature significantly enhances accessibility and guest satisfaction, particularly in international hotels catering to a diverse clientele.

24/7 Accessibility

AI chatbots are operational 24/7, which means guests can seek assistance or information at any time, regardless of their time zone or the hotel's operating hours. This accessibility aligns with the modern expectation of instant and convenient service.

Multilingual Capabilities

Many AI chatbots are equipped with natural language processing capabilities, allowing them to understand and respond in multiple languages. This feature is invaluable for hotels with international guests who may not be proficient in the local language. Guests can communicate in their preferred language, breaking down language barriers and ensuring effective communication.

Enhanced Guest Experience

The ability to provide support and information in multiple languages enhances the overall guest experience. It demonstrates the hotel's commitment to accommodating diverse guest needs and preferences. Guests feel more comfortable and valued when they can interact with the hotel in their native language.

Consistency in Service

Regardless of the time or language in which a guest interacts with a chatbot, the service remains consistent. The information provided, reservation processes, and assistance offered maintain a uniform standard, ensuring that guests receive the same high-quality service, regardless of when or how they engage with the chatbot.

5.2 Handling Common Guest Queries and Issues

Handling common guest queries and issues is a fundamental function of AI-powered chatbots in the hospitality industry. These chatbots are designed to efficiently address a wide range of guest concerns, inquiries, and requests, contributing significantly to guest satisfaction and operational efficiency. Here are key aspects of how chatbots excel in this role:

a Instant Responses: AI chatbots provide instant responses to frequently asked questions and common issues. Guests no longer need to wait in line or on hold to get information or resolve minor problems. This immediacy enhances the overall guest experience.
b 24/7 Availability: Chatbots are available round the clock, ensuring that guests can seek assistance or answers to their queries at any time, day or night. This feature is particularly valuable when guests encounter issues outside of regular business hours.
c Multilingual Support: Many AI chatbots have multilingual capabilities, enabling them to interact with guests in their preferred language. This is especially crucial in hotels serving diverse international clientele.
d Booking and Reservation Assistance: Chatbots can assist guests with booking rooms, making reservations at on-site restaurants, and reserving amenities such as spa treatments or gym sessions. This functionality simplifies the booking process and increases the likelihood of upselling.

5.3 Maintaining Consistency in Guest Interactions

Maintaining consistency in guest interactions is a vital aspect of AI-powered chatbots' role in the hospitality industry. Here's how chatbots excel in this regard:

a Uniform Responses: AI chatbots provide guests with uniform responses to commonly asked questions and issues. Regardless of when or how a guest asks a question, they receive the same information. This consistency ensures that guests get accurate and reliable answers, reinforcing trust in the hotel's services.
b Adherence to Hotel Policies: Chatbots are programmed to adhere strictly to hotel policies and guidelines. They don't deviate from established procedures, ensuring that every guest interaction aligns with the hotel's standards and regulations.
c Elimination of Human Error: Unlike human staff, chatbots don't make errors due to fatigue or forgetfulness. They consistently follow predefined scripts and protocols, reducing the likelihood of misunderstandings or misinformation.
d 24/7 Availability: Chatbots are available around the clock, including during late-night or early-morning shifts when human staff might be less alert. This ensures that guests consistently receive assistance at any time.

6. Measuring Chatbot Performance

Measuring chatbot performance is essential to ensure they meet the desired standards of efficiency and effectiveness in the hospitality industry. Here are the key aspects of evaluating chatbot performance:

Key Performance Indicators (KPIs) for Chatbots:

- Response Time: The time taken by the chatbot to respond to guest inquiries is a critical KPI. Quick response times contribute to guest satisfaction.
- Accuracy: The accuracy of responses provided by the chatbot is crucial. Measuring the percentage of correct responses helps assess the bot's performance.
- Resolution Rate: This metric calculates the percentage of guest issues or questions that the chatbot successfully resolves without escalating to a human agent.
- User Satisfaction: Gathering user feedback through surveys or ratings helps gauge guest satisfaction with chatbot interactions.

Gathering and Analyzing User Feedback:

- Surveys: Periodic surveys can collect guests' feedback on their chatbot experiences. Questions should focus on usability, accuracy, and overall satisfaction.
- Ratings: Guests can rate their chatbot interactions, providing a quick indicator of their experience's quality.
- User Reviews: Monitoring online reviews and comments related to chatbot interactions can provide insights into user sentiment.
- Chat Logs: Analyzing chat logs can reveal common guest queries, areas of improvement, and frequently encountered issues.

Continuous Improvement and Adaptation:

- Machine Learning: Implementing machine learning algorithms allows chatbots to learn from previous interactions and improve over time.
- Regular Updates: Chatbots should receive regular updates to stay aligned with changing guest needs, hotel policies, and industry trends.
- A/B Testing: Testing variations of chatbot responses or interface elements can help identify more effective strategies.
- User-Centered Design: Involving guests in the chatbot design process and considering their feedback ensures that it meets their needs.
- Feedback Loop: Establishing a feedback loop between chatbot performance analytics and development teams ensures that issues are addressed promptly.

In summary, measuring chatbot performance in the hospitality industry involves tracking key metrics, gathering user feedback, and continuously improving the chatbot's capabilities. By focusing on KPIs, user feedback, and adaptive strategies, hotels can ensure that their AI-powered chatbots provide efficient and valuable support to guests, ultimately enhancing the overall guest experience.

7. Case Studies and Success Stories

Case studies and success stories illustrate the practical applications and positive outcomes of AI-powered chatbots in the hospitality industry (Figure 15.7). Here are some examples:

a Marriott International's ChatBot: Marriott International implemented a chatbot named "ChatBotlr" across its various hotel brands. Guests can use the chatbot to check availability, make reservations, inquire about amenities, and request services. The chatbot's success is attributed to its ability to provide quick responses and personalized recommendations based on guest preferences.
b Hilton's Connie: Hilton introduced an AI-powered robot concierge named Connie in partnership with IBM's Watson. Connie assists guests with information about hotel facilities, local attractions, and dining options. Its success lies in its ability to enhance the guest experience by providing tailored recommendations and directions.
c Accor Hotels' AccorBot: Accor Hotels implemented an AI-powered chatbot, AccorBot, to engage with guests through Facebook Messenger. The chatbot assists with booking inquiries, provides information about hotel services, and offers personalized travel recommendations. It has contributed to increased direct bookings and improved guest satisfaction.
d InterContinental Hotels Group (IHG): IHG adopted an AI-driven chatbot for its Crowne Plaza brand. The chatbot, accessible through various messaging platforms, assists guests with information on hotel services and local attractions. It has streamlined guest interactions and improved efficiency in handling guest inquiries.

These case studies demonstrate how AI-powered chatbots have enhanced guest experiences, streamlined operations, and increased revenue for hotels and resorts. By providing instant support, personalized recommendations, and efficient service, these chatbots have become valuable assets in the hospitality industry, offering guests a seamless and memorable stay.

8. Future Trends and Innovations

As the hospitality industry continues to evolve, so do the capabilities and possibilities of AI-powered chatbots. Here are some future trends and innovations to look out for:

- AI-Powered Personalization: AI chatbots will become even more adept at personalizing guest experiences. They will analyze guest preferences and behaviours to offer tailored recommendations for dining, activities, and room customizations.
- Voice and Multimodal Interfaces: Chatbots will incorporate voice recognition and multimodal interfaces, enabling guests to interact naturally through speech and gestures. This will make communication more intuitive and accessible.

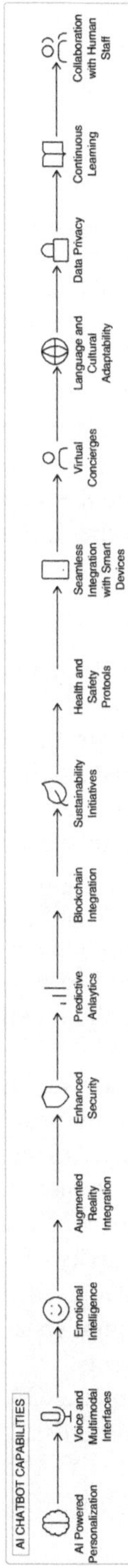

Figure 15.7 Future trends of AI chatbots

Source: By authors

- Emotional Intelligence: Future chatbots will be equipped with emotional intelligence algorithms, allowing them to detect and respond to guests' emotions. They can provide empathy and support when guests are stressed or unhappy.
- Augmented Reality (AR) Integration: Chatbots may integrate with AR applications, offering guests virtual tours of hotel rooms, facilities, and nearby attractions. Guests can visualize their experiences before arrival.
- Enhanced Security: Security features in chatbots will become more robust, ensuring the protection of guests' personal data and payment information. Chatbots will also assist in fraud detection and prevention.

The future of AI-powered chatbots in the hospitality industry is exciting, with advancements that promise to enhance guest services, improve operational efficiency, and provide memorable experiences. As these innovations unfold, hotels and resorts will need to adapt and integrate them into their guest service strategies to stay competitive in the evolving landscape of hospitality.

9. Recommendations for Business Practices: The Key to Success

In the age of digital transformation, the hospitality industry is experiencing a profound shift in the way it serves and interacts with guests. AI-powered chatbots have emerged as indispensable tools for hoteliers seeking to provide exceptional guest experiences. While we've discussed the capabilities and benefits of AI-powered chatbots in detail, it's essential to outline key recommendations for business practices that will pave the way to success in implementing these intelligent systems.

Define Clear Objectives: The first step in integrating AI-powered chatbots is to set clear objectives. Whether it's enhancing guest services, improving operational efficiency, or increasing revenue, well-defined objectives provide direction and a benchmark for success. A chatbot strategy should align with broader business goals to ensure it contributes meaningfully.

Understand Guest Needs: In-depth understanding of your guests' needs and preferences is paramount. Chatbots can only provide personalized recommendations and support when armed with comprehensive guest data. Leverage data analytics and guest insights to tailor chatbot interactions effectively.

Choose the Right Chatbot Solution: Selecting the most suitable chatbot solution is pivotal. Consider factors like the complexity of your guests' needs, budget constraints, and scalability. Whether it's a rule-based chatbot for basic interactions or a sophisticated AI-driven chatbot that can understand natural language, the choice should align with your business requirements.

Provide Seamless Integration: To maximize the benefits of chatbots, ensure seamless integration with your existing systems. Whether it's your property management system, CRM software, or the hotel's website, chatbots should seamlessly communicate and access data across platforms.

Maintain Human Touchpoints: While chatbots provide instant support, don't forget the importance of human touchpoints. There are situations where guests prefer human interactions. Your staff should be ready to seamlessly take over from chatbots when required. Striking a balance between automation and personal interactions is keys.

Continuous Learning and Improvement: AI chatbots are not static solutions. They learn and adapt over time. Regularly analyze performance data and gather user feedback to refine the chatbot's capabilities. This iterative approach ensures that the chatbot remains aligned with evolving guest needs.

Data Privacy and Security: Guests entrust you with their data, and it's your responsibility to safeguard it. Implement robust data privacy and security measures to protect guest information. Compliance with data protection regulations is non-negotiable.

Multilingual Capabilities: If your property caters to international guests, multilingual capabilities are a must. Ensure that your chatbot can effectively communicate in multiple languages, providing a seamless experience for all guests.

24/7 Availability: Guests appreciate instant support around the clock. Ensure that your chatbot is available 24/7 to address inquiries and requests and provide recommendations regardless of the time zone.

Training and Support: Provide adequate training and support for your staff in managing chatbot interactions. They should be well versed in when to escalate to human agents and how to handle unique guest scenarios.

Incorporating AI-powered chatbots into your hospitality business is a forward-looking strategy that can significantly enhance guest experiences and operational efficiency. By following these recommendations, you'll be better equipped to harness the power of chatbots effectively.

AI-powered chatbots have become integral to the modern hospitality landscape, providing instant support and personalized recommendations to guests 24/7. However, their success is contingent on strategic implementation and adherence to best business practices. By setting clear objectives, understanding guest needs, choosing the right chatbot solution, and ensuring seamless integration, hoteliers can unlock the full potential of these intelligent systems. Maintaining a human touch, continuous learning, data privacy, multilingual capabilities, and 24/7 availability are essential factors for success. Moreover, providing comprehensive training and support to staff ensures the effective management of chatbot interactions. Embracing these recommendations will not only delight guests but also drive success in the competitive world of hospitality.

10. Conclusion

In conclusion, AI-powered chatbots have emerged as invaluable tools for modern hospitality providers, revolutionizing guest services and reshaping the way hotels and resorts interact with their guests. This chapter explored the significant role of AI-powered chatbots in the hospitality industry, revealing key findings that underscore their importance and impact.

Recap of Key Findings:

- AI-powered chatbots offer 24/7 guest support, eliminating time zone and language barriers and handling common guest queries efficiently.
- They enhance guest experiences by providing personalized recommendations, helping with bookings, and offering real-time assistance.
- Chatbots contribute to operational efficiency by automating routine tasks like check-ins, check-outs, and room service requests.
- The integration of AI and data analytics enables chatbots to gather valuable insights about guest preferences and behaviours.
- Continuous improvement through user feedback and performance metrics is essential for optimizing chatbot interactions.

The Role of AI-Powered Chatbots in Modern Hospitality: AI-powered chatbots have become indispensable in providing guests with instant support and personalized recommendations. They serve as virtual concierges, assisting guests with information, bookings, and requests. Moreover, they enhance operational efficiency, reduce costs, and gather data to improve services further. Chatbots are not a replacement for human staff but rather valuable assistants that free up human resources for more complex and personalized guest interactions.

Final Thoughts and Recommendations for Hospitality Providers:

- Embrace AI-powered chatbots as a core component of guest services.
- Invest in chatbot design, development, and integration to ensure seamless interactions.
- Prioritize data privacy and security to build and maintain guest trust.
- Stay updated on emerging technologies and trends to remain competitive in the evolving hospitality landscape.

As AI continues to advance, AI-powered chatbots will only become more sophisticated, enabling even more personalized and efficient guest experiences. Hospitality providers that leverage these technologies effectively will not only meet but exceed guest expectations, driving customer satisfaction, loyalty, and ultimately, business success in the ever-competitive hospitality industry.

Key Terms

1 **Artificial Intelligence (AI)** – refers to the development of computer systems that can perform tasks that typically require human intelligence, such as learning, problem-solving, decision-making, and natural language understanding.
2 **Natural Language Processing (NLP)** – is a field of artificial intelligence that focuses on enabling computers to understand, interpret, and generate human language in a way that is both meaningful and contextually relevant.
3 **Virtual Reality (VR)** – is a technology that creates a computer-generated immersive environment, allowing users to interact with and experience a three-dimensional digital world as if it were real.

4 **Augmented Reality (AR)** – is a technology that overlays computer-generated content, such as images, videos, or information, onto the real-world environment, enhancing the user's perception of their surroundings by blending digital and physical elements.
5 **Customer Relationship Manager (CRM)** – is a software tool that helps businesses manage and improve their interactions and relationships with customers by centralizing customer data, automating tasks, and providing insights to enhance customer satisfaction and loyalty.

References

Al-Hyari, H. S. A., Al-Smadi, H. M., & Weshah, S. R. (2023). The impact of artificial intelligence (AI) on guest satisfaction in hotel management: An empirical study of luxury hotels. *Geo Journal of Tourism and Geosites*, 48, 810–819. https://doi.org/10.30892/gtg.482spl15–1081

Calvaresi, D., Ibrahim, A., Calbimonte, J. P., Schegg, R., Fragniere, E., & Schumacher, M. (2021). The evolution of chatbots in tourism: A systematic literature review. In *Information and communication technologies in tourism 2021: Proceedings of the ENTER 2021 eTourism Conference, January 19–22, 2021* (pp. 3–16). Springer International Publishing. https://doi.org/10.1007/978-3-030-65785-7_1

Chan, L., Hogaboam, L., & Cao, R. (2022). Artificial intelligence in tourism and hospitality. In *Applied artificial intelligence in business: Concepts and cases* (pp. 213–229). Springer International Publishing. https://doi.org/10.1007/978-3-031-05740-3_14

Dash, M., & Bakshi, S. (2019). An exploratory study of customer perceptions of usage of chatbots in the hospitality industry. *International Journal on Customer Relations*, 7(2), 27–33.

Gupta, D. G., Jain, V., & Shin, H. (2023). Luxury experience and consumer behavior: A systematic literature review and future research agenda: An abstract. In B. Jochims, & J. Allen (Eds.), *Optimistic marketing in challenging times: Serving ever-shifting customer needs. AMSAC 2022. Developments in marketing science: Proceedings of the academy of marketing science*. Springer. https://doi.org/10.1007/978-3-031-24687-6_97

Gupta, S., Modgil, S., Lee, C. K., Cho, M., & Park, Y. (2022). Artificial intelligence enabled robots for stay experience in the hospitality industry in a smart city. *Industrial Management & Data Systems*, 122(10), 2331–2350. https://doi.org/10.1108/IMDS-10-2021-0621

Kaplan, A., & Haenlein, M. (2019). Siri, Siri, in my hand: Who's the fairest in the land? On the interpretations, illustrations, and implications of artificial intelligence. *Business Horizons*, 62(1), 15–25. https://doi.org/10.1016/j.bushor.2018.08.004

Khan, A., Hamid, A. B. A., Saad, N. M., Hussain, Z., & Arif, A. R. (2023). Effectiveness of artificial intelligence in building customer loyalty: Investigating the mediating role of chatbot in the tourism sector of Pakistan. *International Journal of Academic Research in Business and Social Sciences*, 13(9), 657–671. http://dx.doi.org/10.6007/IJARBSS/v13-i9/18422

Kim, W., Ryoo, Y., Lee, S., & Lee, J. A. (2021). Chatbot advertising as a double-edged sword: The roles of regulatory focus, Ad personalization, and privacy concern. *In American academy of advertising. Conference. Proceedings* (Online) (pp. 11–11). American Academy of Advertising.

Krishnan, C., Gupta, A., Gupta, A., & Singh, G. (2022). Impact of artificial intelligence-based chatbots on customer engagement and business growth. In *Deep learning for social media data analytics* (pp. 195–210). Springer International Publishing. https://doi.org/10.1007/978-3-031-10869-3_11

Kumar, A., Gupta, N., & Bapat, G. (2023). Who is making the decisions? How retail managers can use the power of ChatGPT. Journal of Business Strategy. https://doi.org/10.1108/JBS-04-2023-0067

Lee, S. B. (2020). Chatbots and communication: The growing role of artificial intelligence in addressing and shaping customer needs. *Business Communication Research and Practice*, 3(2), 103–111. https://doi.org/10.22682/bcrp.2020.3.2.103
Lukanova, G., & Ilieva, G. (2019). Robots, artificial intelligence, and service automation in hotels. In *Robots, artificial intelligence, and service automation in travel, tourism and hospitality* (pp. 157–183). Emerald Publishing Limited. https://doi.org/10.1108/978-1-78756-687-320191009
Pillai, R., & Sivathanu, B. (2020). Adoption of AI-based chatbots for hospitality and tourism. *International Journal of Contemporary Hospitality Management*, 32(10), 3199–3226. https://doi.org/10.1108/IJCHM-04-2020-0259
Selamat, M. A., & Windasari, N. A. (2021). Chatbot for SMEs: Integrating customer and business owner perspectives. *Technology in Society,* 66, 101685.https://doi.org/10.1016/j.techsoc.2021.101685
Zhu, Y., Zhang, J., Wu, J., & Liu, Y. (2022). AI is better when I'm sure: The influence of certainty of needs on consumers' acceptance of AI chatbots. *Journal of Business Research*, 150, 642–652. https://doi.org/10.1016/j.jbusres.2022.06.044

16 Charting New Realms

Metaverse Analytics in the Hospitality Landscape

Zahid Hussain and Dr. Arman Khan

1. Introduction

The hospitality sector is poised for a significant evolution in a time of technological advancement and digital transformation. Terms like "big data," "metaverse," and "business analytics" have gained popularity as a result of the explosion in data produced by the numerous systems unique to the hotel industry (Rejeb et al., 2023). The metaverse, a virtual space where the lines between the physical and digital worlds are blurred, represents a new frontier. The use of metaverse analytics in this fully immersive digital environment has the potential to revolutionize the hospitality industry by providing unmatched opportunities to advance business knowledge and improve decision-making (Monaco & Sacchi, 2023). The hospitality industry has seen a rise in the popularity of the metaverse, a virtual world made by the fusion of physical and digital spaces, especially during the COVID-19 pandemic, when opportunities for face-to-face interaction were scarce (Mittal & Bansal, 2023). Before purchasing a travel experience or making a hotel reservation, customers can now test it out with virtual reality in the hospitality industry (Lin et al., 2023). By providing new opportunities for immersive experiences and catering to changing customer needs, the metaverse is revolutionizing the hospitality and tourism sectors (Adel, 2023). Virtual tours are used by 50% of customers to make decisions, increasing reservations for restaurants' and hotels' services (Baggio et al., 2023). The metaverse might end up being an intriguing new way for the hospitality sector to interact with customers. By introducing virtual guest experiences to satisfy changing consumer needs, the 3D internet transforms the hospitality sector (Cha, 2022). The opportunity to develop memorable virtual experiences that are on par with or better than their physical offerings is now available to hotels that have traditionally focused on physical service (Go et al., 2023). Customers and travellers now have new opportunities to visit attractions, attend events, shop around, and interact with the hospitality sector thanks to the metaverse (Koo et al., 2023). By enabling hoteliers to deliver exceptional experiences in a novel way, the metaverse puts hotels on a fast track to exceeding guests' expectations (Chen et al., 2023).

DOI: 10.4324/9781003488248-16

Now, visitors can get a feel for the hotel even before they check in. If the booking office is moved to the metaverse, labor costs may also be reduced. The front office is only required at specific points during the guest's journey as bookings become more automated (Abass et al., 2022). In essence, the metaverse encourages automation to lessen the workload for hotel staff, a great strategy for addressing the staffing crisis (Hsu et al., 2022). To meet changing customer needs, the metaverse is revolutionizing the hospitality sector by introducing virtual guest experiences (Gursoy et al., 2023). Although the metaverse is not yet widely used in the hospitality sector, preparing for the changes now could put hotels ahead of the competition in terms of offering a better guest experience (Kumar et al., 2023).

As we move through this environment, we examine the various aspects of metaverse analytics, highlighting not only how it differs from traditional analytics but also how it has the potential to transform how hospitality businesses run in the digital era (Buhalis et al., 2022). So the hospitality industry is experiencing a transformative shift with the emergence of the metaverse generating an abundance of data. This transformation presents several challenges such as understanding the key themes that have been explored in metaverse analytics within the hospitality industry over the past two decades, identifying what sets metaverse analytics apart from traditional business analytics, assessing the current trends in metaverse analytics and their impact on the hospitality sector, and recognizing the potential for metaverse analytics to transform business knowledge and decision-making in hospitality management. This literature review aims to provide a thorough overview of the status and potential of metaverse analytics in the hospitality industry, shedding light on its research themes, distinct characteristics, and current trends shaping its evolution

2. Material and Methods

In August 2023, a systematic search of online scientific databases was started using the well-known research tool EBSCOhost to conduct a thorough and in-depth investigation of the landscape of metaverse analytics' in the hospitality industry. This study's objective was to find, collect, and assess academic articles related to this developing field. Carefully crafted search queries with the terms "metaverse," "data analytics," and "hospitality" were used in several cases (Gursoy et al., 2023). This step made sure the search was thorough and focused on locating relevant articles within the specified scope. The initial search turned up a sizeable 414 articles, highlighting the growing research activity and interest in the nexus between metaverse analytics and the hospitality sector. A temporal constraint was used, focusing on articles published between 2022 and 2023, to focus the selection on the most recent and pertinent research. The study's goal, to evaluate current field development, is consistent with this time frame. To emphasize the value of thorough and methodical examinations of the subject matter, the search was further refined by focusing on "scientific reviews." A thorough review procedure was started to choose articles that reported accurate empirical data and followed scientific methodology; this exacting standard ensured the inclusion of top-notch research that could offer helpful insights into the field. Following this meticulous curation process, 127 articles in total were chosen for additional in-depth analysis because they met the strict criteria outlined earlier (see Figure 16.1).

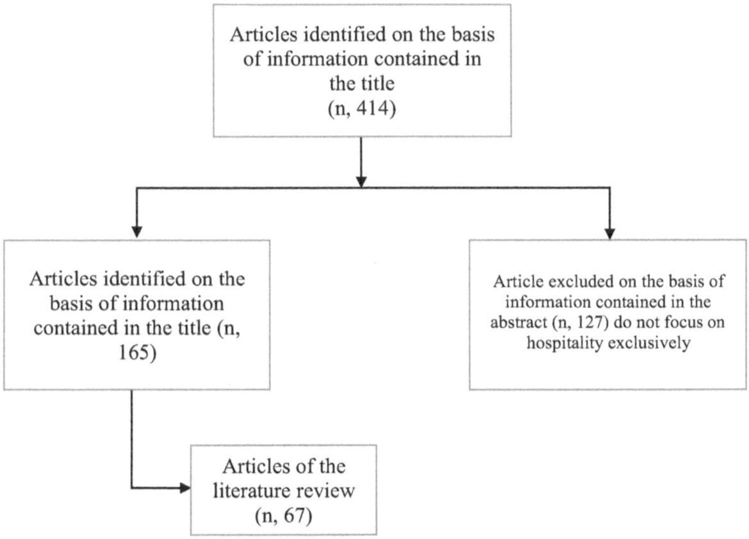

Figure 16.1 Flowchart outlining the literature review

Table 16.1 Research Attributes

Research Attributes	*N*
Big data	37
Metaverse	57
Business analytics	107
Immersive experience	65
Data-driven insights	33
Virtual assets	12
Virtual land	08
Visual and spatial analytics	13
Multi-source data insights	11
Virtual economy insights	11
AI and automation	23

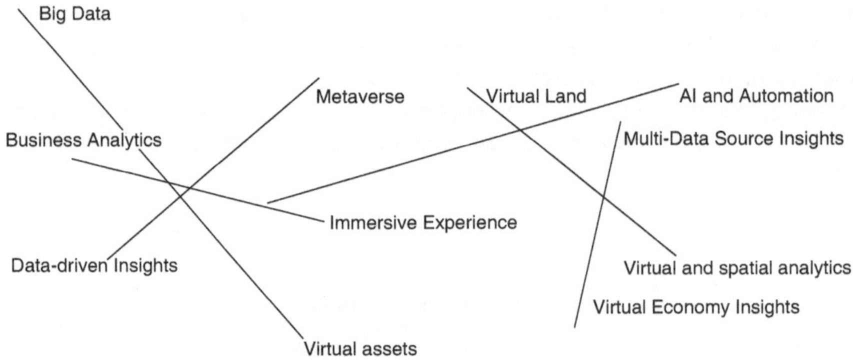

Figure 16.2 Network of the research attributes

3. Theoretical Background

3.1 Metaverse

The metaverse is described as a virtual universe or collective virtual space where users can interact with each other, digital environments, and objects. It's an expensive interconnected virtual world that can encompass a wide range of digital experiences from social interactions to gaming, education, commerce, and more (Adel, 2023). In this definition, it's often likened to a digital parallel to our physical world. The metaverse emphasizes the convergence of physical and virtual reality. It's seen as a space where digital and physical elements merge, allowing users to seamlessly transition between the real world and digital realms (Buhalis et al., 2023a). Augmented reality (AR) and virtual reality (VR) technologies play a significant role in creating this mixed-reality metaverse (Go & Kang, 2023).

Another perspective on the metaverse defines it as a decentralized user-created virtual world where users have control and ownership over their digital assets, including avatars, property, and digital currencies. This definition emphasizes user-generated content, virtual economies, and open standards for interoperability (Jafar & Ahmad, 2023). The metaverse is a global, persistent, and shared virtual environment. It's a place where users from all power the world can connect, communicate, and collaborate in a way that mirrors real-world interactions (Lee & Jo, 2023). It often incorporates the idea of a "Single universe" with various interconnected spaces. Principles of game design, interaction, and player engagement are essential for creating compelling metaverse experiences (Rejeb et al., 2023). While digital interactions in the metaverse are becoming more immersive, it's essential to balance these with real-world connections to maintain healthy social relationships (Wei, 2023). Digital currencies like Bitcoin and in-game virtual currencies impact both virtual and real-world economies (Wider et al., 2023). The metaverse's success largely depends on user contributions and creativity, including the development of virtual products, experiences, and economics (Zhang & Wang, 2023). The chapter cautions against proprietary ecosystems locking users into closed platforms and advocates for open, cross-platform standards to ensure a more open and accessible metaverse (Lee & Jo, 2023). Individual ownership and control of personal data in the metaverse, as well as addressing issues related to privacy, digital rights, and fair compensation for digital contributions, are crucial considerations highlighted by Koo et al. (2023). The chapter raises concerns about the potential impact of the metaverse on human relationships and argues for the need to balance digital interactions with real-world, face-to-face connections (Lee & Jo, 2023). The chapter believes in user-generated content and virtual economies playing a significant role in shaping the metaverse as the next major computing platform focused on social interactions and virtual reality (Monaco & Sacchi, 2023). Lin et al. (2023) envision the metaverse as interconnected virtual worlds and emphasize the importance of open standards for ensuring interoperability between these realms.

3.2 Metaverse Analytics and Business Analytics

Business analytics and metaverse analytics are two separate but related fields that use data to fuel insights and judgement. Gathering, analyzing, and interpreting data from the metaverse are the main objectives of the specialized field of study known as metaverse analytics (Buhalis et al., 2023b). Analytics for the metaverse can offer perceptions of user behaviour, market trends, and business performance (Cheah & Shimul, 2023). To give users the ability to fully immerse themselves in a setting where the virtual and real worlds collide, metaverse analytics combines elements of social media, online gaming, AR, VR, and cryptocurrencies (Chen, 2023). A network of shared, immersive virtual worlds without the need to log in allows users to connect with friends, create and play games, work, and shop (Lee & Jo, 2023). Data collection, analysis, and interpretation within the metaverse are the main objectives of the specialized field of study known as metaverse analytics (Lin et al., 2023). It can shed light on the immersive experience the metaverse offers as well as the metaverse's potential effects on society, culture, and the economy (Jafar & Ahmad, 2023). The identification of ethical use cases and potential applications in the areas of education, sustainable consumption, and other areas can be aided by metaverse analytics (Filimonau et al., 2022). Analytics for the metaverse track user behaviour, interactions, and experiences in virtual worlds and other immersive digital environments. These analytics gather information from virtual worlds such as user movements, social interactions, virtual goods transactions, and more (Jauhiainen et al., 2022). Based on user profiles, metaverse analytics creates customized virtual experiences (Dwivedi et al., 2022). To comprehend social interactions within the metaverse, metrics like chat logs, social group dynamics, and communication patterns are examined (Dwivedi et al., 2023). The effectiveness of virtual environments can be evaluated using performance metrics such as server load, latency, and user experience (Queiroz et al., 2023). A thorough and multidisciplinary approach to research is necessary because the metaverse is a complicated and multidimensional environment. Insights into user behaviour can be obtained from metaverse analytics. Business performance and market trends are analyzed for forecasting and strategic decision-making.

For live shopping in the metaverse, techniques and algorithms from cognitive artificial intelligence, visual and spatial analytics, and immersive digital simulations can be used (Wider et al., 2023). In the areas of education, sustainable consumption, and other industries, metaverse analytics can be used to find ethical use cases and potential applications (Zhang & Wang, 2023). The relationships between the key ideas and potential future trends in metaverse analytics can be represented visually using bibliometric analysis (Wei, 2023). Content analysis can reveal a research field's history as well as the connections between fundamental ideas in metaverse analytics (Rejeb et al., 2023). Analytics for the metaverse can be used to better understand the immersive experience it offers (Wong et al., 2023). Blockchain technology can facilitate secure exchanges and ownership of virtual assets, such as digital parcels of land that can be analyzed using metaverse analytics (Mohanty et al., 2022). For tech and other uses, metaverse analytics can be used to pinpoint the metaverse's difficulties. To help with decision-making regarding the metaverse, metaverse analytics can offer data-driven insights (Koohsari et al., 2023).

Future metaverse research topics in education and other fields can be found with the aid of metaverse analytics. Analytics for the metaverse can be used to assess how well metaverse systems are being adopted in education (Fitriani et al., 2023). Understanding the fundamental properties and conceptual framework for metaverse research can be aided by metaverse analytics. Understanding the potential uses of the metaverse in education, such as learner-centered constructivist education, medical education, and more, is made easier with the aid of metaverse analytics (Jafar & Ahmad, 2023).

Analyses of the metaverse can be used to better comprehend how the metaverse and sustainable consumption interact. The use of blockchain technology to enable secure transactions and the ownership of virtual assets, such as virtual land (parcels), can be better understood with the aid of metaverse analytics (Jafar & Ahmad, 2023). The vast array of use cases and application scenarios supported by the metaverse, from gaming to education to e-commerce, can be better understood with the aid of metaverse analytics (Mohanty et al., 2022). Understanding the traits of an open metaverse, such as interoperability, decentralization, persistency, spatiality, community-driven structure, and self-sovereignty, is made possible by metaverse analytics (Ozdemir et al., 2023). Visual and spatial analytics, cognitive artificial intelligence techniques and algorithms, and immersive digital simulations for in-person shopping in the metaverse can all be better understood with the aid of metaverse analytics (Gursoy et al., 2023). Analytics for the metaverse can be used to better understand the possible effects of the metaverse on culture, society, and the economy (Hsu et al., 2022).

Business analytics cover a wider range of topics while concentrating on data-driven decision-making in conventional business settings. Business analytics improves financial performance, strategic planning, and operational efficiency

(Mariani & Baggio, 2022). Structured data from sources like sales, financial records, and customer databases is frequently the focus of these analytics (Mariani & Baggio, 2022). Business analytics frequently uses business intelligence tools to create reports, dashboards, and predictive models. Organizations aim to gain a competitive edge and identify market trends through the effective use of business analytics tools and techniques (Mirzaalian & Halpenny, 2019). Organizations can use business analytics to support data-driven decision-making to boost productivity and competitiveness (Rodrigues et al., 2020). Business analytics can reveal information about consumer behaviour, industry trends, and company performance. Data transformation into insights for better business decisions is known as business analytics (Mariani, 2020). Data management, data visualization, predictive modeling, data mining, forecasting simulation, and optimization are all used to extract insights from data (Siti-Nabiha et al., 2021). Data analysis, statistical models, and other quantitative techniques are used in business analytics, a set of disciplines and technologies. It involves descriptive analytics, diagnostic analytics, predictive analytics, and prescriptive analytics. Analyzing and interpreting data to understand how businesses perform and locate areas for improvement is known as business analytics (Webb & Legg, 2021). For quick and simple data analysis, it uses data aggregation, data mining, and data visualization. Analytics is a branch of computer science that looks for significant patterns in data using machine learning, math, and statistics (Ogbeide et al., 2021). Analytics is used to analyze business data with a focus on the implications for the business and the decisions and actions that should be taken as a result (Mariani et al., 2018). Data analysis, statistical models, and other quantitative techniques are used in a variety of business analytics disciplines and technologies to address business issues (Siti-Nabiha et al., 2021). It also uses a variety of analytics, including diagnostic, predictive, descriptive, and prescriptive. By maximizing resources, enhancing customer experiences, and lowering operating expenses, business analytics can assist organizations in becoming more productive and competitive (Webb & Legg, 2021). Business analytics can be used to find areas for development and innovation. Business analytics can aid in streamlining operations and processes (Ting et al., 2017). Risk identification and mitigation are made possible by business analytics. Customer loyalty and satisfaction can be increased with the aid of business analytics (Mariani & Baggio, 2022). Businesses that use business analytics can maintain their competitiveness in a market that is changing quickly (Siti-Nabiha et al., 2021). Organizations can use business analytics to make wise resource and investment decisions (Rita et al., 2018). Businesses can enhance their marketing and sales strategies with the aid of business analytics (Zhan et al., 2023). Organizations can enhance their supply chain management by using business analytics. Businesses can enhance their financial performance with the aid of business analytics. Business analytics can assist organizations in enhancing their human resource management as well as their product and service offerings (Webb & Legg, 2021). Organizations can enhance their risk management tactics by using business analytics. Businesses can enhance their decision-making processes with the aid of business analytics (Mariani et al., 2018). Businesses can enhance their customer experiences with the aid of business analytics. Organizations can increase the effectiveness of their operations with the aid of business analytics. Organizations can enhance their planning and forecasting by using business analytics (Rita et al., 2018). Organizations can enhance their data governance and quality with the aid of business analytics. Organizations can increase their overall performance and competitiveness with the aid of business analytics (Zhan et al., 2023). Metaverse analytics can help virtual businesses customize their offerings by revealing user preferences. Personalized user targeting through metaverse analytics has the potential to improve virtual advertising (Gursoy et al., 2022). For content producers in the metaverse, user engagement metrics like event attendance and content consumption are essential. Within virtual ecosystems, metaverse analytics can be used to monitor security and detect fraud (Filimonau et al., 2022). Analyzing the metaverse can help us comprehend virtual economies and the factors that affect the prices of virtual goods (Buhalis et al., 2022). Inventory management and supply chain operations are optimized by business analytics. The financial sector extensively utilizes business analytics for risk assessment and management to mitigate potential losses and ensure regulatory compliance (Buhalis et al., 2023c; Fitriani et al., 2023). Predictive analytics forecasts market demand and improves pricing strategies. Employer retention and talent acquisition are two areas where business analytics are used in HR management (Zhan et al., 2023). Combining business analytics with IoT data enables real-time decision-making in logistics and manufacturing. Although they are two distinct fields of study, metaverse analytics and business analytics have some things in common when it comes to giving data-driven insights to make decisions about the metaverse and, separately, business operations (Mittal & Bansal, 2023).

3.3 Metaverse Analytics Trends

The field of metaverse analytics is still in its infancy, but it already demonstrates several trends that will shape its development and influence in the digital sphere. A development in user-centric metaverse analytics that emphasizes individualized user experiences, behaviour analysis, and the creation of virtual profiles (Hsu, 2023) is gaining traction. Understanding user interactions and journeys in virtual environments can improve user satisfaction and engagement.

An increasingly popular topic is virtual economies (Jafar et al., 2023). Analyses of the metaverse are increasingly being used to examine virtual trade, price movement, and economic models in online environments. The implications of virtual currencies and their influence on virtual economies show that this aspect of metaverse analytics is becoming more and more important (Fitriani et al., 2023). Within the metaverse, social interaction metrics are becoming more important. The study of chat logs, group dynamics, and communication patterns facilitates comprehension of virtual community dynamics (Cheah & Shimul, 2023). A key component of metaverse analytics is sentiment analysis, which involves evaluating the emotions and attitudes expressed by users through their interactions within virtual environments. Additionally, security and privacy are crucial considerations in metaverse analytics, particularly with regard to data security and user privacy in these virtual environments (Buhalis et al., 2023c). Usage of metaverse analytics for fraud prevention and detection in virtual ecosystems is on the rise. There is a discernible trend in metaverse analytics toward the integration of automation and AI (Hsu et al., 2022). Automation and AI-driven insights are speeding up data processing and improving decision-making. In the metaverse, customer interactions are increasingly reliant on AI-powered chatbots and virtual assistants, and analytics are helping to make them better (Lee & Jo, 2023). Multimodal data analysis is becoming more popular. To fully understand virtual experiences, this trend involves integrating data from different sources, including audio, visual, and textual (Mariani & Baggio, 2022). Analyzing user-generated content in the metaverse using natural language processing (NLP) shows a growing interest in textual data (Mirzaalian & Halpenny, 2019). Metaverse analytics are increasingly combining information from various virtual platforms to give a comprehensive picture of user behaviour and trends in various digital spheres (Xiang et al., 2017).

The metaverse's emergence represents a brand-new digital battlefield. The metaverse has the potential to change how people communicate, shop, work, and consume content (Webb & Legg, 2021). The metaverse may have potential effects on inclusivity, privacy, safety, and the future of work. There is potential for consumers in the food service sector to be drawn to the metaverse (Ting et al., 2017). Metaverse analytics can be applied to understand user behaviour, preferences, and trends in the virtual world. Metaverse analytics enables finding new trends and opportunities in the metaverse (Webb & Legg, 2021). Metaverse analytics facilitates making data-driven decisions about the metaverse. Metaverse analytics has the capacity to shed light on metaverse market trends and company performance (Lee et al., 2020). Metaverse analytics has the capacity to aid in resource optimization and reduce overhead. Metaverse analytics can enhance customer loyalty and experience (Xiang et al., 2017). Metaverse analytics offers the potential for businesses to remain competitive in a rapidly changing market. Metaverse analytics makes it easier to make data-driven decisions about the metaverse (Mariani, 2020). Some of the key trends boosting the expansion of the metaverse market include the incorporation of blockchain technology, the use of NFTs, and the creation of DeFi applications (Lee et al., 2020).

Tech behemoths are pouring billions of dollars into the development of the metaverse, which is evolving quickly. By 2040, at least 500 million people are anticipated to value the metaverse (Webb & Legg, 2021). Analytics for the metaverse can offer information on user behaviour, market trends, and business performance. Blockchain technology integration is anticipated to make it possible for virtual asset ownership and transactions to be secure (Fitriani et al., 2023). Non-fungible tokens (NFTs) are increasingly used in digital asset trading. Tech behemoths are creating metaverse platforms for a range of uses (Go & Kang, 2023). Application development for DeFi is accelerating in the metaverse. Virtual assets are becoming more and more in demand. The metaverse uses virtual events more and more frequently (Hsu, 2023). By 2030, consumer and business use cases for the metaverse could generate up to $5 trillion in revenue (Jauhiainen et al., 2022). The number of searches for the term "metaverse" on the internet increased by 7,200% in 2021, indicating the metaverse's current popularity. Consumers in the food service sector are predicted to be interested in the metaverse (Zhang & Wang, 2023). The development of cross-platform insights is made possible by the aggregation of data from various sources by metaverse analytics ecosystems (Webb & Legg, 2021). Metaverse analytics is becoming more and more dependent on real-time monitoring and feedback mechanisms (Lee et al., 2020). Due to this trend, businesses can quickly respond to user behaviour and instantly modify their online services (Mariani, 2020). The function of real-time analytics dashboards is to give quick insights to guide decision-making in virtual environments (Lee et al., 2020). Analytics for engagement and gamification components are becoming more popular. These trends involve using game mechanics to increase user engagement and using analytics to assess their efficacy (Ruel & Njoku, 2021). Data analysis can be used to optimize gamified elements in virtual environments to increase user engagement. Metaverse analytics are increasingly incorporating ethical issues (Ting et al., 2017). In line with this trend, we're talking about ethical conundrums in virtual spaces, like bias and data privacy (Zhan et al., 2023). Metaverse analytics practices are guided by ethical principles and frameworks to ensure fair and responsible data use (Lee et al., 2021). The ever-changing nature of this field, as it responds to the opportunities and challenges brought by immersive digital environments, is reflected in the metaverse analytics landscape's dynamic trends (Rita et al., 2018).

3.4 Perceptions and Beliefs in Metaverse Analytics

When it comes to the adoption, comprehension, and development of metaverse analytics, perceptions and beliefs are crucial. The metaverse is an intricate and multidimensional space that prompts several philosophical inquiries about the nature of reality (Cheah & Shimul, 2023). Analytics for the metaverse can be used to better understand user behaviour, preferences, and trends in the virtual world (Jauhiainen et al., 2022). Many parties are vying for control over the definition of the metaverse. The way people work, shop, communicate, and consume content may change as a result of the metaverse (Jafar & Ahmad, 2023). Identifying ethical use cases and potential applications in fields like education, sustainable consumption, and others is made easier with the aid of metaverse analytics. Analytics for the metaverse can offer data-driven insights to help with metaverse decision-making. Resources can be more efficiently used and expenses can be cut with the aid of metaverse analytics (Cheah & Shimul, 2023). Analytics for the metaverse can enhance customer satisfaction and loyalty. There are many unanswered questions regarding the future of the metaverse, which is still just a collection of hypothetical possibilities (Buhalis et al., 2023c). The metaverse has the potential to improve our lives by granting us access to experiences we could not otherwise have.

Skeptics of the metaverse see it as merely an enhancement of the current state of our digital culture rather than a revolutionary development (Gursoy et al., 2023). The current social media problems, such as misinformation campaigns, could be made worse by the metaverse (Hsu, 2023). Violence-prone tendencies and addictive behaviour (Go & Kang, 2023). Because different stakeholders have varying opinions and perceptions about the metaverse's potential, its impact by 2040 is still uncertain. The ethical and privacy-related ramifications of using metaverse data can be determined with the aid of metaverse analytics (Buhalis et al., 2023b). Analytics for the metaverse can be used to better understand how the metaverse affects user preferences, decision-making, and emotional responses (Cheah & Shimul, 2023). Marketing strategies that make the most of the peculiarities of the metaverse can be found with the aid of metaverse analytics (Buhalis et al., 2022). Understanding how metaverse data can be used for marketing purposes is made easier with the aid of metaverse analytics (Trunfio & Rossi, 2022). The potential for the metaverse to produce significant economic value for both consumer and business use cases is great (Koo et al., 2023). The most important researchers and works in the metaverse field can be found with the aid of metaverse analytics. The academic institutions and researchers who have collaborated most extensively within the metaverse domain can be found with the aid of metaverse analytics (Kumar et al., 2023). Analytics for the metaverse can identify responsible use cases and potential applications in fields like education, sustainable consumption, and other areas, as well as enhance customer satisfaction and loyalty (Go & Kang, 2023). However, there are additional moral and privacy-related ramifications to take into account, in addition to various viewpoints and ideologies regarding the metaverse's potential (Hsu, 2023). Experts believe that metaverse analytics have the power to completely change how businesses interact with customers in virtual spaces and can establish entirely new paradigms for data-driven decision-making with implications that go beyond the virtual world (Cheah & Shimul, 2023). Metaverse analytics are seen as a way to improve user interactions. Analytics are viewed as a tool by businesses to customize virtual experiences based on customer preferences (Go & Kang, 2023). Metaverse analytics are more and more recognized as being essential for developing personalized content and services that increase user engagement. Metaverse analytics are primarily perceived as providing monetization opportunities (Gursoy et al., 2023). Data insights and virtual economies are viewed as potential revenue sources (Lee & Jo, 2023). The idea is that companies see metaverse analytics as helpful in figuring out pricing plans for virtual goods and services, maximizing monetization (Jafar & Ahmad, 2023). Security and privacy concerns are widely held beliefs (Lee & Jo, 2023). The protection of user information in virtual environments is seen as being of utmost importance (Koo et al., 2023). There is a growing consensus among stakeholders that strong security controls should be included in metaverse analytics to guard against potential breaches (Lin et al., 2023). In perceptions and beliefs, ethical issues are very important. Stakeholders voice concerns about the moral application of data in metaverse analytics and the requirement for ethical conduct (Lee & Jo, 2023). Metaverse analytics should be guided by moral principles to ensure fairness, transparency, and equitable data handling (Monaco & Sacchi, 2023). The two fields of metaverse analytics and artificial intelligence (AI) are frequently seen as being mutually beneficial. Many people think AI improves analytics' abilities to drive insights and automation (Mittal & Bansal, 2023). According to stakeholders, intelligent chatbots and virtual assistants in the metaverse are shaped by AI, which is a key enabler. Real-time decision-making is essential, according to perceptions (Zhang & Wang, 2023).

There is a notion that metaverse analytics enables companies to quickly adapt to changing user behaviour (Queiroz et al., 2023). Real-time analytics dashboards are becoming more and more recognized as essential tools for quick, informed decisions in virtual environments (Mittal et al., 2023). Some participants see metaverse analytics as a way to connect the virtual and real worlds (Lin et al., 2023). According to this theory, analytics can produce seamless, integrated experiences (Ozdemir et al., 2023). The idea is that metaverse analytics can improve interactions and business processes outside of virtual environments (Trunfio & Rossi, 2022). Perceptions place a high value on user trust and engagement, and beliefs abound that analytics can help build trust by providing unique, worthwhile experiences (Rejeb et al., 2023). The idea is that businesses can tailor interactions to keep customers' trust by using metaverse analytics to measure user sentiment and engagement (Wider et al., 2023). There is a strong belief, according to perceptions, in the contribution of metaverse analytics to the advancement of innovation and the preservation of competitiveness (Wong et al., 2023). Analytics are seen by stakeholders as being crucial to advancing in the digital sphere (Wei, 2023). The idea is that using metaverse analytics early on can give companies a competitive edge, allowing them to try out novel ideas and maintain their position as market leaders (Zhang & Wang, 2023).

Conclusion

The nexus of hospitality management and metaverse analytics emerges as a dynamic area with enormous potential in the ever-evolving digital landscape. This study has delved into the complexities of metaverse analytics, shedding light on its key characteristics, trends, perceptions, and beliefs through a systematic search of online scientific databases and a thorough analysis of chosen research articles. The research characteristics examined over the previous two decades in the context of metaverse analytics in the hospitality industry show a complex picture. These characteristics paint a complete picture of the diversity of data within the metaverse, from immersive data sources to virtual economies and social interactions. Metaverse analytics is a field that is constantly changing due to the need to better understand user behaviour, improve virtual economies, and protect the security and privacy of data in virtual environments. The incorporation of AI, the analysis of data from multiple media, and the emphasis on real-time monitoring highlight how dynamic this field is. Perceptions and beliefs about metaverse analytics show a wide range of perspectives, from the potential for transformation to worries about data security and ethics. According to stakeholders, metaverse analytics can improve user experiences, monetize virtual goods, and bridge the gap between the virtual and real worlds. Metaverse analytics serves as an essential link between data-driven insights and immersive virtual environments as the metaverse expands and changes how we interact with digital spaces. Businesses in the hospitality industry can navigate the metaverse landscape by using data to their advantage, personalizing customer experiences, maximizing virtual economies, and ensuring data security and ethical practices. This study provides important insights into the metaverse analytics landscape as a foundational investigation. But it's important to recognize that the metaverse and its analytics are constantly changing. Continuous research and adjusting to new trends and technologies will be essential to stay at the forefront of this transformative field. With the potential to transform the hospitality sector and more, metaverse analytics opens the door to a new era of data-driven decision-making within virtual environments.

Conflict of Interest Statement

The authors declare that there are no conflicts of interest related to this study.

References

Abass, M. N., & Zohry, M. A. F. (2022). Mixed reality drama towards metaverse technology in smart hotels: An exploratory study on Egyptian hotels evidence from guests' perspectives. *Journal of Association of Arab Universities for Tourism and Hospitality*, 23(2), 130–154.

Adel, M. (2023). The role of metaverse to create an interactive experience for tourists. *Journal of Association of Arab Universities for Tourism and Hospitality*, 24(1), 242–269.

Baggio, R., & Ruggieri, G. (2023). Metaverse in the tourism domain – introduction to the special issue. *Information Technology & Tourism*, 3(4), 1–2.

Buhalis, D., Leung, D., & Lin, M. (2023a). Metaverse as a disruptive technology revolutionizing tourism management and marketing. *Tourism Management*, 97(2), 104–124.

Buhalis, D., Lin, M. S., & Leung, D. (2022). Metaverse as a driver for customer experience and value co-creation: Implications for hospitality and tourism management and marketing. *International Journal of Contemporary Hospitality Management*, 35(2), 701–716.

Buhalis, D., Lin, M. S., & Leung, D. (2023b). Metaverse as a driver for hospitality customer experience and value co-creation: Implications for hotel and tourism management and marketing. *International Journal of Contemporary Hospitality Management*, 35(2). 33–44.

Buhalis, D., O'Connor, P., & Leung, R. (2023c). Smart hospitality: From smart cities and smart tourism towards agile business ecosystems in networked destinations. International *Journal of Contemporary Hospitality Management*, 35(1), 369–393.

Cha, S. S. (2022). Metaverse and the evolution of food and retail industry. *The Korean Journal of Food & Health Convergence*, 8(2), 1–6.

Cheah, I., & Shimul, A. S. (2023). Marketing in the metaverse: Moving forward – What's next?. *Journal of Global Scholars of Marketing Science*, 33(1), 1–10.

Chen, Z. (2023). Beyond reality: Examining the opportunities and challenges of cross-border integration between metaverse and hospitality industries. *Journal of Hospitality Marketing & Management*, 3(2), 1–14.

Dwivedi, Y. K., Hughes, L., Baabdullah, A. M., Ribeiro-Navarrete, S., Giannakis, M., Al-Debei, M. M., & Wamba, S. F. (2022). Metaverse beyond the hype: Multidisciplinary perspectives on emerging challenges, opportunities, and agenda for research, practice and policy. *International Journal of Information Management*, 66(5), 102–142.

Dwivedi, Y. K., Hughes, L., Wang, Y., Alalwan, A. A., Ahn, S. J., Balakrishnan, J., . . . Wirtz, J. (2023). Metaverse marketing: How the metaverse will shape the future of consumer research and practice. *Psychology & Marketing*, 40(4), 750–776.

Filimonau, V., Ashton, M., & Stankov, U. (2022). Virtual spaces as the future of consumption in tourism, hospitality and events. *Journal of Tourism Futures*, 2(3), 22–34.

Fitriani, D., Azzahra, F. F., Putra, R. A., Setiawan, R., Dyantika, R., Sukowati, S., & Nugraha, R. N. (2023). Analysis Kemampuan Metaverse Untuk Inovasi Hospitality Industry Pariwisata di Masa Yang Akan Datang. *Jurnal Ilmiah Wahana Pendidikan*, 9(7), 133–137.

Go, H., & Kang, M. (2023). Metaverse tourism for sustainable tourism development: Tourism agenda 2030. *Tourism Review*, 78(2), 381–394.
Gursoy, D., Malodia, S., & Dhir, A. (2022). The metaverse in the hospitality and tourism industry: An overview of current trends and future research directions. *Journal of Hospitality Marketing & Management,* 31(5), 527–534.
Gursoy, I. T., Aktas, E., Tecim, V., & Kurgun, O. A. (2023). Beta tourist world: A conceptual framework for organizing an event in the metaverse. *Information Technology & Tourism*, 3(3), 1–20.
Hsu, H. (2023). Facing the era of smartness – delivering excellent smart hospitality experiences through cloud computing. *Journal of Hospitality Marketing & Management*, 3(3), 1–27.
Hsu, M. J., Ting, H., Lui, T. W., Chen, S. C., & Cheah, J. H. (2022). Guest editorial: Challenges and prospects of AIoT application in hospitality and tourism marketing. *Journal of Hospitality and Tourism Technology*, 13(3), 349–355.
Jafar, R. M. S., & Ahmad, W. (2023). Tourist loyalty in the metaverse: The role of immersive tourism experience and cognitive perceptions. *Tourism Review*, 33(4), 23–36.
Jauhiainen, J. S., Krohn, C., & Junnila, J. (2022). Metaverse and sustainability: Systematic review of scientific publications until 2022 and beyond. *Sustainability*, 15(1), 346–365.
Koo, C., Kwon, J., Chung, N., & Kim, J. (2023). Metaverse tourism: Conceptual framework and research propositions. *Current Issues in Tourism,* 26(20), 3268–3274.
Koohsari, M. J., McCormack, G. R., Nakaya, T., Yasunaga, A., Fuller, D., Nagai, Y., & Oka, K. (2023). The metaverse, the built environment, and public health: Opportunities and uncertainties. *Journal of Medical Internet Research*, 25(3), 43–49.
Kumar, S., Dhiraj, A., Shah, M. A., & Rani, D. (2023). Application of metaverse in the hospitality industry. In *Influencer marketing applications within the metaverse* (pp. 178–194). Hershey, PA: IGI Global.
Lee, M., Cai, Y. M., DeFranco, A., & Lee, J. (2020). Exploring influential factors affecting guest satisfaction: Big data and business analytics in consumer-generated reviews. *Journal of Hospitality and Tourism Technology*, 11(1), 137–153.
Lee, M., Kwon, W., & Back, K. J. (2021). Artificial intelligence for hospitality big data analytics: Developing a prediction model of restaurant review helpfulness for customer decision-making. *International Journal of Contemporary Hospitality Management*, 33(6), 2117–2136.
Lee, N., & Jo, M. (2023). Exploring problem-based learning curricula in the metaverse: The hospitality students' perspective. *Journal of Hospitality, Leisure, Sport & Tourism Education*, 32(2), 100–127.
Lin, K. J., Ye, H., & Law, R. (2023). Understanding the development of blockchain-empowered metaverse tourism: An institutional perspective. *Information Technology & Tourism*, 2(3), 1–19.
Mariani, M. (2020). Big data and analytics in tourism and hospitality: A perspective article. *Tourism Review*, 75(1), 299–303.
Mariani, M., & Baggio, R. (2022). Big data and analytics in hospitality and tourism: A systematic literature review. *International Journal of Contemporary Hospitality Management*, 34(1), 231–278.
Mariani, M., Baggio, R., Fuchs, M., & Hopkin, W. (2018). Business intelligence and big data in hospitality and tourism: A systematic literature review. *International Journal of Contemporary Hospitality Management*, 30(12), 3514–3554.
Mirzaalian, F., & Halpenny, E. (2019). Social media analytics in hospitality and tourism: A systematic literature review and future trends. *Journal of Hospitality and Tourism Technology*, 10(4), 764–790.
Mittal, G., & Bansal, R. (2023). Driving force behind consumer brand engagement: The metaverse. In *Cultural marketing and metaverse for consumer engagement* (pp. 164–181), edited by Amandeep Singh et al. Hershey, PA: IGI Global. https://doi.org/10.4018/978-1-6684-8312-1.ch012

Mohanty, M. K., Mohapatra, A. K., Samanta, P. K., Agrawal, G., & Agrawal, G. (2022). Exploring metaverse: A virtual ecosystem from management perspective. *Journal of Commerce*, 43(4), 1–11.

Monaco, S., & Sacchi, G. (2023). Travelling the metaverse: Potential benefits and main challenges for tourism sectors and research applications. *Sustainability*, 15(4), 33–48.

Ogbeide, G. C., Fu, Y. Y., & Cecil, A. K. (2021). Are hospitality/tourism curricula ready for big data? *Journal of Hospitality and Tourism Technology*, 12(1), 112–123.

Ozdemir Uçgun, G., & Şahin, S. Z. (2023). How does Metaverse affect the tourism industry? Current practices and future forecasts. *Current Issues in Tourism*, 3(4), 1–15.

Queiroz, M. M., Fosso Wamba, S., Pereira, S. C. F., & Chiappetta Jabbour, C. J. (2023). The metaverse as a breakthrough for operations and supply chain management: Implications and call for action. *International Journal of Operations & Production Management*, 4(4), 55–68.

Rejeb, A., Rejeb, K., & Treiblmaier, H. (2023). Mapping metaverse research: Identifying future research areas based on bibliometric and topic modeling techniques. *Information*, 14(7), 356–368.

Rita, P., Rita, N., & Oliveira, C. (2018). Data science for hospitality and tourism. *Worldwide Hospitality and Tourism Themes*, 10(6), 717–725.

Rodrigues, J. P., Sousa, M. J., & Brochado, A. (2020). A systematic literature review on hospitality analytics. *International Journal of Business Intelligence Research (IJBIR)*, 11(2), 47–55.

Ruel, H., & Njoku, E. (2021). AI redefining the hospitality industry. *Journal of Tourism Futures*, 7(1), 53–66.

Siti-Nabiha, A. K., Nordin, N., & Poh, B. K. (2021). Social media usage in business decision-making: The case of Malaysian small hospitality organizations. *Asia-Pacific Journal of Business Administration*, 13(2), 272–289.

Ting, P. J. L., Chen, S. L., Chen, H., & Fang, W. C. (2017). Using big data and text analytics to understand how customer experiences posted on yelp. Com impact the hospitality industry. *Contemporary Management Research*, 13(2). 34–44.

Trunfio, M., & Rossi, S. (2022). Advances in metaverse investigation: Streams of research and future agenda. In *Virtual worlds*, 1(2), 103–129. MDPI.

Webb, T., & Legg, M. (2021). The emerging need for hospitality students with analytical skills. *Journal of Hospitality & Tourism Research*, 45(5), 892–894.

Wei, W. (2023). A buzzword, a phase or the next chapter for the Internet? The status and possibilities of the metaverse for tourism. *Journal of Hospitality and Tourism Insights*, 33(3), 34–44.

Wider, W., Jiang, L., Lin, J., Fauzi, M. A., Li, J., & Chan, C. K. (2023). Metaverse chronicles: A bibliometric analysis of its evolving landscape. *International Journal of Human – Computer Interaction*, 3(4), 1–14.

Wong, L. W., Tan, G. W. H., Ooi, K. B., & Dwivedi, Y. K. (2023). Metaverse in hospitality and tourism: A critical reflection. *International Journal of Contemporary Hospitality Management*, 33(3), 23–34.

Xiang, Z., Du, Q., Ma, Y., & Fan, W. (2017). A comparative analysis of major online review platforms: Implications for social media analytics in hospitality and tourism. *Tourism Management*, 58 (2), 51–65.

Zhan, L., Cheng, M., & Zhu, J. (2023). Progress on image analytics: Implications for tourism and hospitality research. *Tourism Management*, 100(3), 104–198.

Zhang, W., & Wang, Y. (2023). An empirical study of the impact of metaverse storytelling on intentions to visit. *Information Technology & Tourism*, 2(3), 1–22.

17 Role of Digitalization in the Luxury Hospitality Industry

A Bibliometric and Content Analysis

Pratim Chatterjee, José Vargas-Hernández, and Namrata Chakraborty

1. Introduction

The increasing importance of digital technology is considered common in many industries, and hospitality and tourism are no exception (Buhalis *et al.*, 2019; Camilleri, 2018). For a long time, hotels have digitalized core and supporting services to achieve convenient, efficient, and memorable guest experiences (Brochado *et al.*, 2016). The hotel industry has progressively increased its investment in the digitalization process to upgrade operational efficiency and productivity, decrease cost, and increase hotel guests' satisfaction to offer better service quality (Kim & Qu, 2014). Luxury can be defined as more of an experience than a mere product. A luxury hotel possesses high standard hotel accommodation and fine dining experience, round-the-clock room service, valet parking, laundry arrangements, business provisions, and competent and educated staff. These hotels provide highly customized contact services and provide personalized service which sets them apart from nonluxury hotels (Kucukusta *et al.*, 2014). Traditionally, luxury hotel managers have a skeptical mind about digitalization and, therefore, do not consider it as an acceptable tool in the service delivery process. Today, this viewpoint needs to be changed because of increased competition, rising operating costs, labor shortages, and modern trends (Connolly, 2000). Technological advancement in the hospitality industry is increasingly recognized as valuable assets for obtaining a competitive edge, yet hospitality digitalization faces challenges, as this service industry traditionally prioritizes human interaction and personalized experiences. Moreover, in luxury hotels, the practice of digitalization is hard to implement because of the highly personalized service acceptance mentality of the guests in those type of hotels. Despite existing research examining the adoption of technology in the hospitality industry, there remains a gap in understanding their impact on the luxury segment of the hotel industry. This chapter aims to present a comprehensive review and bibliometric analysis about the role of digitalization of luxury hotels considering all topics in this area focusing on the specific gaps in the current literature and providing scopes for future research.

DOI: 10.4324/9781003488248-17

2. Theoretical Background

2.1. Hospitality Digitalization

Digitalization in the hotel industry has been established as a current trend with respect to hotel industry guests' requirement for smart technology, digital convenience, and experiencing contactless check-in and -out. This finding is especially true for millennial guests equipped with smartphones, wireless connectivity, and digital literacy. In the hospitality industry, technology has been proved to be a significant factor due to the ability to redesign hospitality, from the booking phase to check-out, leveraging benefits to both the guests and the hotel (Stamboulis & Skayannis, 2003). Guests have been steadily using the internet to search for accommodation and other information on hotel websites (Law & Hsu, 2006). Despite the initial hesitancy of hotels to adopt digitalization, in recent times, efforts have been made by the hospitality industry to adopt modern technology to materialize the opportunity of hotels for online promotion and to concentrate on customized marketing messages (Morosan & Jeong, 2008). Thus, investment in technology will create customers to perceive values and utilities as found in the hotels' websites, which will periodically enhance customer purchase intentions (Sharma, 2016; Pham *et al.*, 2020). Romero-Martínez and García-Muina (2021) illustrated the use of digitalization in the hotel industry as an anti-corruption tool and to stop other unethical behaviours. Successful hotels will be those that effectively implement technology, focusing on positive application and quality of their services as a differentiation strategy from competitors (Šeric *et al.*, 2016).

2.2. IT and Robotics in Hotels

Implementation of IT systems in the hospitality industry has caused decreased costs, improved productivity, and increased revenues, enhancing customer service and business operations (Huo, 1998; Siguaw *et al.*, 2000). Smart technological features in rooms help hotels to improve the tangible guest experience; for example, with technology, guests can modify the room's physical attributes like colour, sound, and theme (Melián-González & Bulchand-Gidumal, 2016). Such technological attributes could seriously impact a hotel guest's overall satisfaction, which will significantly affect revisit intention (Cobanoglu *et al.*, 2011).

The hotel industry encompasses various services like front office, concierge, restaurant service, housekeeping, and room service. While most hotels still primarily employ human staff, some hotels have started experimenting with using robots for certain tasks. The Henn-na hotel in Japan was one of the first hotels to be fully staffed by robots for tasks like check-in, luggage handling, and room service. Following this, some hotel chains like Aloft Hotels (in 2014) and Hilton Hotels (in 2016) introduced robots at select properties to assist with concierge services, providing tourist information to guests. However, these major chains have not fully replaced their human workforce with robots across all their hotel locations (Papathanassis, 2017; Zhong *et al.*, 2020). With the invention of IT in the systems, hotel managers anticipate that profit margins and financial expertise will increase (Law & Jogaratnam, 2005; Wynn & Jones, 2022). The robotic practices in both Aloft and Hilton Hotels are machinelike robots which do not possess any humanoid characteristics. Human–robot systems are considered as more rational than complete service robots replacing human labor in present times (Reis *et al.*, 2020).

2.3. Digitalization in Pandemic/Epidemic

Amidst or after COVID-19, the adoption of digital technologies, such as contactless digital payment, advanced cleaning systems, digital menus accessible via QR codes, service robots, touchless elevators, food delivery apps, etc. has been started in the hospitality industry as an innovative tool to execute risk-reduction strategies (Esposito *et al.*, 2022). The hospitality industry across the globe was compelled to accept digital transformation during the pandemic to maintain social distance (António & Rita, 2021). During or after the COVID-19 pandemic, hotels around the globe categorically made investments in contactless guest experience, such as improved practices of sanitation with hands-free technology and high-tech service (Ivasciuc, 2020; Sujood *et al.*, 2023). Cheng *et al* (2023) explored nine digital technologies applied after the pandemic in the hospitality industry, such as artificial intelligence a robotics, big data, cloud computing, blockchain, virtual reality and augmented reality, mobile terminals and applications, the Internet of Things, short-distance wireless communication technology, and collaboration technology. Supplementary accommodation establishments like homestays and budget hotels are building confidence in the mindset of guests compared to mainstream accommodation in the post-pandemic era (Batabyal *et al.*, 2021).

2.4. Luxury Hospitality Digitalization

The introduction of high-quality components, modern technologies, and evergrowing desire in hotels have boosted luxury experiences by consistently improving the hotel stay experience in the hospitality industry. Ms. Barbara Talbott, former chief marketing officer of the Four Seasons Hotels and Resorts, identified style, comfort, service, and pampering as the four key factors contributing to a luxury hotel experience. Any hotel, whether chain property or independently owned, rated or non-rated, can be considered a luxury hotel if it meets the four requirements mentioned earlier (Talbott, 2004). Four- and five-star hotels can be considered luxury hotels if they provide a high-quality experience beyond minimum basic needs. The government of India identified luxury hotels as five-star deluxe, five-star, and four-star hotels (Ekiz *et al.*, 2012). Vigneron and Johnson (2004), Wiedmann *et al.* (2009), Amatulli and Guido (2012), and Guido *et al.* (2020) focus on the role of status consumption, portraying luxury hotels as more luxurious, introducing modern technologies in their operations that could contribute to increase both guests' satisfaction and their intention to use up-to-date technologies as they consider benefits for their status. Over the past decade, hotels have digitalized their operation to deliver convenient, efficient, and unique guest experiences (Brochado *et al.*, 2016). Hilton Worldwide Holdings, Inc. lately started a digitalized hotel service system called Digital Key and launched it in almost 4,000 properties. Similarly, other global luxury hotel chains of hotels (e.g., Marriott International and Hyatt Hotels Corporation) have initiated smart technology for online booking, room reservation systems, food and beverage service, and concierge service. Luxury hotels, being high-end hospitality, initiated encouraging guests to use smartphone apps and other appliances for greater convenience and customization of their services (Jeong *et al.*, 2016; Han *et al.*, 2021). Luxury hotels contain the most significant area of services – that is, both "high touch" and "high tech" – as the expectation of the guests are always rising regarding the variety of hotel services like accommodation, food and beverage, fitness centers. etc. Compared to other ranges of hotels, luxury hotels fight for market share based more on creativity in services offered and innovation than on price (Ordanini & Parasuraman, 2011; Han *et al.*, 2021). Kim and Ham (2006) opined that property management systems, restaurant management systems, and guest–service interface solutions impact significantly on increasing the overall service quality of luxury hotels. Tom Dieck *et al.* (2017) identified the needs of an effective alternative promotional social media channel for satisfying guests' needs and wants. Smart technologies develop a competitive advantage in the luxury segment and are extensively used by luxury hotels for guests' retention and repeat visits. Concerning the environmental issues, luxury and upscale hotels are investing in smart technologies that contribute to sustainability with the purpose of diminishing energy expenditures in the long run (Triantafyllou *et al.*, 2022).

2.5. Criticality of Digitalization in Hospitality Industry

As a part of the service industry, notable hospitality professionals and guests have remarked that the essence of hospitality is personal care – by people, not by any means of non-humans. Kuo *et al.*, 2016 depict that robots can perform similar services without off days, sick days, and various other human resource issues. Hotel managers' lack of knowledge about information technologies made them reluctant to consider and adopt new technologies in their operations (Law *et al.*, 2014; Mihalic & Buhalis, 2013). The use of artificial intelligence and digital technologies in the tourism and hospitality industry has potential risks and ethical concerns regarding implementation. For instance, it is hard to use such technologies in tourism and hospitality businesses where guests from different nationalities may find it hard to adopt or accept these technologies due to demographic and ethnographic differences such as culture, age, and traditional orientation. Moreover, non-acceptance of technologies by staff, as they think these technologies as their replacement, are challenges hotels will face in the coming years (Alrawadieh *et al.*, 2021; Sun *et al.*, 2020; Jayawardena *et al.*, 2023). Communication of these technologies through sensors among different devices may lead the artificial intelligence programmes being out of control. Lastly, the biggest challenge of digitalization is the cybersecurity problem (Kilichan &Yilmaz, 2020). Managers of the hotels have high hopes for digitalization. A fair return on investment (ROI) is anticipated by management because profit is necessary for the survival and growth of any business. The initial major investment for the digitalization and the payback period for the same is apparently the major concern of management. Another concern is frequent updates and upgrades of technology from the company, so it is difficult to determine the best purchase timing before it gets outdated and an updated version comes onto the market (Cizˇmar *et al.*, 2010; Leung, 2019). Due to the intangible nature of the service industry, the human touch is essential in a hotel. So hospitality managers need to use both technology and human resources because this industry is profoundly related to the attitudes, skills, and service of the employees (Montargot & Lahouel, 2018).

Despite these numerous scholarly attempts to explore, acknowledge, and elaborate on the digitalization in hotel industry literature, there were no extensive literature reviews and bibliometric analysis observed on the role of digitalization of luxury hotels. The best that we can tell, the present literature is the first of its kind that tries to use a bibliometric approach and content analysis to shed light on the conceptual framework of the role of digitalization of luxury hotels in academic literature.

3. Methodology

The research was done through the analysis of 71 research articles where only journal articles were taken into consideration, with the objective of obtaining information on the role of digitalization in the luxury hospitality industry. This systematic review process assumes designing the plan of research, exploring the study through a systematic process, screening out applicable articles, and incorporating the selected literatures (Pickering *et al.*, 2015). The chapter has taken on bibliometric and content analyses of all the significant research areas of almost the last three decades using the Google Scholar search engine (Chatterjee & Datta, 2023). Keyword searches were performed using "(Digitalization OR Technology OR Luxury) AND (Hotel OR Hospitality OR Tourism)." The authors initiated the research project by designing the plan of research, which was established by formulating questions that the authors wished to answer in the research, which involved searching existing literature on digitalization in luxury hotels and related topics included in the existing literature. Step 2 was determining the criteria that were used to establish the effectiveness of the articles that would be reviewed to obtain a vast assortment of opinions and viewpoints on the topic. References from only the last three decades were considered as the time frame of the study. The third step was to search on Google Scholar for all articles as per the key words, which resulted in 55,400 articles. Then filters were applied by the authors, such as timeline of "1989–2023," which led to 16,500 results. At this point, the authors only considered those articles that included "digitalization of hospitality industry" within the title to arrive at a narrower scope of information, which yielded 71 results.

4. Findings and Discussion

The role of digitalization in the luxury hospitality industry has gained prominence only in recent times. The recent establishment of digital technology has ushered in its wide-scale application in the hotel industry. Investment in technology will spur customers to perceive values and utilities as found in the hotels' websites that will periodically enhance customer purchase intentions (Sharma, 2016; Pham *et al.*, 2020). Romero-Martínez & García-Muiña (2021) illustrated the use of digitalization in the hotel industry as an anti-corruption tool and to stop other unethical behaviours. Successful hotels will be those that effectively implement technology, focusing on positive application and quality of their services, as a differentiation strategy from competitors (Šeric *et al.*, 2016). It is expected for luxury hotels to provide best-quality personalized experiences, and their guests typically do not allow any room for error.

Five articles in the study were published between 1989 and 2001, and 66 were published between 2002 and 2023. The anticipated grounds behind the growth in digitalization in hospitality industry literature may be the smart demand of the guests and flexibility of the management of the hotel to satisfy those needs. The objective of the study is to explore the latest theoretical advancement and exciting research ideas. Digitalization in the hospitality industry with special emphasis on luxury hotels is observed separately in Section 4.1., where models related to the study are explored separately. Similarly, the citation analysis, context, methods of study and source of contribution of the literature are discussed individually in Sections 4.2., 4.3., 4.4., and 4.5.

4.1. Review of Theories/Models/Paradigms

The most prevailing theories or models applied in digitalization in the hospitality industry literature are considered as follows:

4.1.1. *Technology acceptance model* is the most influential theoretical framework about the study of utilization of information technology (TAM, Davis, 1989). According to TAM, the decision of the guest to work on a contemporary technical device or software package is decided by his/her behavioural intention to use the system. The model is based on two theoretical constructs, perceived usefulness (PU) and perceived ease of use (PEOU), which are the fundamental factors of technology acceptance. However, research has also explored that there are consequences of user characteristics, like demographic variables (age and gender) on PEOU and PU, as the main factors that have an impact on the behavioural intention to utilize the system (Lee, 2016; Chu & Chu, 2011)

4.1.2. *Extended technology acceptance model* was developed to explore the acceptance of the luxury hotels' guest about the use of service robots (Zhong *et al.*, 2020). This study also has taken into consideration the possible adjustment variables including demographic variables (gender, age, education, income, etc.) and guest feedback on robot services (number of stays in hotel, experience with hotel robot services, experience of other robot services). As per the model among all variables, attitude, usefulness, and perceived value are the factors that have the greatest impact on the guest's acceptance of the technology in a hotel.

4.1.3. *Anti-corruption digitalization model* (Romero-Martínez & García-Muina, 2021) is a distinctive model which was developed to use the digitalization practices in different departments of the hotel industry as an anti-corruption policy. As per this model, a higher digitalization level significantly reduces corruptive practice, which makes that hotel and host country more attractive for foreign investors.

4.1.4. *Perceived job performance model* (Jeong *et al.*, 2016) is a conceptual framework for measuring employees' perceived job performance using mobile technology in operation. Key factors of the model, i.e., self-efficacy, job relevance, facilitating conditions, and perceived job performance, which is related to job satisfaction and employee retention, can be used as a competitive strategy in the hospitality industry.

4.1.5. *Luxury hotel technology readiness model* (Huy *et al.*, 2019) is a technology readiness model which reflects the common characteristics of people when using new technology. As per the technology readiness index built by Parasuraman (2000), optimism and innovativeness are considered to promote people's use of technology, whereas discomfort and insecurity are considered to hinder people's use of technology. In this model the relation of perceived ease of use and perceived usefulness with the technology readiness are considered to determine their impact on customer satisfaction in a luxury hotel.

4.1.6. *ICT technology employees' performance enhancement model* (Vogiatzi, 2015) deduces that independent factors such as self-efficacy (SEF) and personal characteristics notably impact the perceived it beliefs (PIB) of the employees in a hotel. Attitude is influenced by perceived IT beliefs and task–technology fit. Lastly, acquisition of modern technology by the employees depends on the attitude and subjective norm.

4.2. Citation Analysis

To point out the most impactful articles on the role of digitalization in the hospitality industry, we have conducted citation analysis. The total number of citations (Ctotal) and weighted average number of citations (C-total = Ctotal/# of years after article publication) were calculated. The most cited articles were Davis (1989) with 79,937 citations, Parasuraman (2000) with 4,204 citations, Vigneron and Johnson (2004) with 2,399 citations, Wiedmann *et al.* (2009) with 1,424 citations etc. (see Table 17.1).

4.3. Context

The United States, Hong Kong, South Korea, and China can be established as the most researched primary developed countries, and Vietnam, India, Jordan, and Taiwan can be considered as the most researched primary developing countries. Table 17.2 ranks the primary developed and developing countries studied in digitalization in luxury hospitality research.

Table 17.1 Most Cited Articles and Authors on Digitalization in Luxury Hospitality Research Literature (as on August 31, 2023)

Rank	*Author(s) and Published Year*	*Citations Total (Ctotal)*	*Citations Weighted Average Number (C-Total)*
1	Davis (1989)	79,937	2,351
2	Parasuraman (2000)	4,204	192
3	Vigneron and Johnson (2004)	2,399	126
4	Wiedmann *et al.* (2009)	1,424	102
5	Stamboulis and Skayannis (2003)	1,402	176
6	Ordanini and Parasuraman (2011)	1,283	71
7	Law *et al.* (2014)	943	79
8	Buhalis *et al.* (2019)	866	92
9	Law and Jogaratnam (2005)	511	28

Source: By authors

Table 17.2 Primary Country Studied in Digitalization in Luxury Hospitality Research

Rank	*Primary Country (Developed)*	*Rank*	*Primary Country (Developing)*
1	United States	1	Vietnam
2	Hong Kong	2	India
3	South Korea	3	Jordan
4	China	4	Taiwan
5	United Kingdom	5	Thailand
6	Spain	6	Iran
7	France	7	Brazil
8	Italy	8	Turkey

Source: By authors

4.4. Review of Study Method

Statistical measures are essential in research mainly to analyze the quantitative information as received in the study. It was observed that the most used statistical measure used in digitalization in hospitality industry study was confirmatory factor analysis. Besides that, the other frequently used statistical methods were multiple regression, one-way ANOVA, and correlation coefficient. Table 17.3 lists the main statistical methods with notable reference.

Table 17.3 Main Statistical Methods Used in Digitalization in Luxury Hospitality Research

Rank	*Statistical Method*	*Reference*
1	Confirmatory factor analysis	Kim *et al.* (2008); Morosan and Jeong (2008); Chu and Chu (2011); Aluri and Palakurthi (2011); Sun *et al.* (2020)
2	Multiple regression	Ham *et al.* (2005); Zhong *et al.* (2020); Esposito *et al.* (2022)
3	One-way ANOVA	Bilgihan *et al.* (2016); Choi *et al.* (2020)
4	Correlation coefficient	Yu (2020); Memarzadeh and Anand (2020); Romero-Martínez and García-Muina (2021)

Source: By authors

4.5. Source of Contributions

Among the 71 journal articles, 55 were published in hospitality and tourism journals, whereas the other 16 were published in journals of other disciplines (e.g., social science, management, technology, marketing, human resources, etc.). The articles published journal-wise are furnished in Table 17.4. Among all journals, *International Journal of Contemporary Hospitality Management* published six articles, followed by *Journal of Hospitality and Tourism Technology* and *International Journal of Hospitality Management* – four articles each; *Journal of Hospitality and Tourism Research and Sustainability* – three articles; *Acta Turistica, International Journal of Management and Decision Making, Tourism Management, Technology in Society, International Journal of Economics, Finance and Management Sciences* etc. published two articles each.

5. Recommendations for Business Practices: The Key to Success

Digitalization in the hospitality industry is recommended in order to be competitive and successful in the industry. Without technological innovation, the hospitality industry, especially the luxury sector, could not survive in extremely difficult times like an epidemic or pandemic (Farías & Cancino, 2021). Nazir *et al.* (2023), in their study, mentioned that artificial intelligence and technological advancement in the hospitality industry positively affect the customer engagement in social sites, which finally leads to increased customer satisfaction and revisit intention. Besides the main services like luxurious rooms and memorable food and beverages, the technology practiced by the luxury hotel is recommended to be convenient, user-friendly, and consistent with the brand image of the hotel to gain competitive advantage (Furunes & Mkono, 2019). With the continuous effect of sustainable digital transformation in the hospitality industry, hotels bank on their innovative capabilities to enhance or upgrade their existing services for their survival and growth. Amidst or following a pandemic, a lot of innovative digitalization has happened in the business practices and operations of the hospitality industry to increase the confidence level of the customers (Fainshtein, 2023).

Table 17.4 Number of Articles Published in Journals

Journal Name	*Number*
International Journal of Contemporary Hospitality Management	6
Journal of Hospitality and Tourism Technology	4
International Journal of Hospitality Management	4
Journal of Hospitality and Tourism Research	3
Sustainability	3
Acta Turistica	2
International Journal of Management and Decision Making	2
Tourism Management	2
Technology in Society	2
International Journal of Economics, Finance and Management Sciences	2
Journal of Service Research	2
Tourism and hospitality Management	2
The International Review of Retail, Distribution and Consumer Research	1
Tourism Economies	1
Tourism & Management Studies	1
Journal of Contemporary Issues in Business and Government	1
Journal of Service Management	1
Tourism Planning & Development	1
The International Journal of Human Resource Management	1
Journal of Quality Assurance in Hospitality & Tourism	1
Journal of Hospitality & Leisure Marketing	1
MIS Quarterly	1
The TQM Journal	1
Italian Journal of Marketing	1
Tourism Management Perspectives	1
Information Technology in Hospitality	1
Journal of Travel & Tourism Marketing	1
The Consortium Journal of Hospitality and Tourism	1
Tourism Review	1
Economic and Business Review	1
Journal of Organizational Change Management	1
Studies in Higher Education	1
Journal of Business Research	1
Journal of Service theory and Practice	1
Worldwide Hospitality and Tourism Themes	1
Journal of Travel Research	1
Journal of Hospitality and Tourism Management	1
Journal of Tourism Quarterly	1
Journal of Brand Management	1
Psychology and Marketing	1
International Journal of Tourism and Hospitality Management in the Digital Age	1
Industrial Management & Data Systems	1
Journal of Hospitality Marketing & Management	

Source: By authors

Experts (i.e., managers, investors, and academicians) in the hotel industry, especially in the luxury segment, need to focus and work on the literature discussed in the study to gain a competitive edge in a highly competitive and sensitive market. Damnjanović *et al.* (2020) explored the digital marketing strategy of Accord Hotel in a case study where they have emphasized the customers' digital journey in the hotel as a success factor, from customer acquisition through customer retention. Digital practices in the hospitality industry are highly recommended to achieve success. Practices like designing a gamelike digitalized customer experience, developing care as a unique source of digital value creation, providing digital training to the staff for their technological improvement, and creating an optimal environment for enhanced digital experiences of the customers are desirable (Youssofi *et al.*, 2023).

6. Conclusion

The objective of the present study is to undertake a comprehensive review and bibliometric analysis of the role of digitalization of luxury hotels. The authors have explored the most used theories/models, statistical methods, most cited articles, source of contributions, and primary countries/regions in the research literature on digitalization of hospitality industry. This study describes the significance of adopting digitalization in the hospitality sector to make an inclusive environment and offer memorable experiences to guests. The present study also focuses on the impact of digitalization on luxury hotels, the role of digitalization in hospitality industry amidst and after a pandemic, and criticality of digital transformation in the hospitality industry.

6.1. Theoretical Implication

The present study has several implications. First, digital technology has built numerous opportunities for hotels to upgrade their performances by minimizing errors and performing work faster and consequently delivering quality service to guests. The significant theoretical implication of the current study is observed in the exploration and inspection of the models, context, methods of study, and contributions that analyzed the role of digitalization in the hospitality industry. The chapter points out many critical enhancements from the viewpoint of different stakeholders that need to be taken into consideration while employing technology in the hotel industry. The chapter focuses on the impact of digitalization on the mindset of the luxury hotel guests as the basic feature of luxury hotels can be overruled by the basic concept of digital transformation.

6.2. Practical Implication

This study has significant practical implications for the key players in the hospitality and tourism sector. Through a systematic literature review and bibliometric analysis, the present study explored the impact of digitalization on the hospitality industry with special emphasis on luxury hotels. Our results imply that guests in luxury and business hotels assess the decisions to stay in smart hotels as wise and fascinating. Undoubtedly, this present study will enrich the innovative business model, which will efficiently manage the probable cons and improve hospitality services and guest satisfaction by capturing real-time data. Hence, we firmly recommend that academicians and industry practitioners concentrate on the findings of the study to upgrade, intimate, and enlighten the internal as well as the external customers of the hospitality and tourism industry about the positive impact of digitalization in the field.

7. Limitations and Directions of Future Research

Though the study included a modest number of articles, few limitations can be observed. First, it involved only articles written in English – articles in other languages were not taken into consideration. Another limitation can be found in the literature – to explore the digitalization in the hospitality industry, mostly luxury and star-category hotels were considered in the study, whereas budget hotels and alternate accommodation are left out in the present study.

There is enormous scope for future research to explore the role of digitalization in the alternate and supplementary accommodation industry like budget hotels, hostels, and homestays, etc. So further study is highly recommended for these type of accommodation establishments to adapt digitalization. It can be established from the literature that hospitality digitalization research is found mostly in developed countries, whereas studies are scarce in developing countries, so those demand further study. Lastly, there is an enormous scope for future research opportunities to explore the role of digitalization in the hospitality industry in both the luxury and budget segments as a source of foreign exchange earnings from inbound tourists.

References

Alrawadieh, Z., Alrawadieh, Z., & Cetin, G. (2021). Digital transformation and revenue management: Evidence from the hotel industry. *Tourism Economics*, 27(2), 328–345. https://doi.org/10.1177/1354816620901928

Aluri, A., & Palakurthi, R. (2011). The influence of demographic factors on consumer attitudes and intentions to use RFID technologies in the US hotel industry. *Journal of Hospitality and Tourism Technology*, 2(3), 188–203.

Amatulli, C., & Guido, G. (2012). Externalised vs. internalised consumption of luxury goods: Propositions and implications for luxury retail marketing. *The International Review of Retail, Distribution and Consumer Research*, 22(2), 189–207. https://doi.org/10.1080/09593969.2011.652647

António, N., & Rita, P. (2021). COVID-19: The catalyst for digital transformation in the hospitality industry? *Tourism & Management Studies*, 17(2), 41–46.

Batabyal, D., Chatterjee, P., Pandit, A., Goswami, S., & Kumar, D. (2021). Assessing the choice of supplementary accommodation for the new normal urban areas in West Bengal, India, *Journal of Contemporary Issues in Business and Government*, 27(2), 1413–1420. https://doi.org/10.47750/cibg.2021.27.02.153

Bilgihan, A., Smith, S., Ricci, P., & Bujisic, M. (2016). Hotel guest preferences of in-room technology amenities. *Journal of Hospitality and Tourism Technology*, 7(2), 118–134. https://doi.org/10.1108/JHTT-02-2016-0008

Brochado, A., Rita, P., & Margarido, A. (2016). High tech meets high touch in upscale hotels. *Journal of Hospitality and Tourism Technology*, 7(4), 347–365.

Buhalis, D., Harwood, T., & Bogicevic, V. (2019). Technological disruptions in services: Lessons from tourism and hospitality, *Journal of Service Management*, 30(4), 484–506.

Camilleri, M. A. (2018). The promotion of responsible tourism management through digital media. *Tourism Planning & Development,* 15(6), 653–671.
Chatterjee, P., & Datta, S. (2023). Bibliometric and content analysis of literature on role of healthcare hotel in medical and wellness tourism. *Acta Turistica*, 35(1), 7–42. https://doi.org/10.22598/at/2023.35.1.7
Cheng, X., Xue, T., Yang, B., & Ma, B. (2023). A digital transformation approach in hospitality and tourism research. *International Journal of Contemporary Hospitality Management*, 35(8), 2944–2967. https://doi.org/10.1108/IJCHM-06-2022-0679
Choi, Y., Mehraliyev, F., & Kim, S. (2020). Role of virtual avatars in digitalized hotel service. *International Journal of Contemporary Hospitality Management*, 32(3), 977–997.
Chu, A. Z. C., & Chu, R. J. C. (2011). The intranet's role in newcomer socialization in the hotel industry in Taiwan – technology acceptance model analysis. *The International Journal of Human Resource Management*, 22(05), 1163–1179. https://doi.org/10.1080/09585192.2011.556795
Ciz˘mar, S., Bartoluci, M., & Vusic, M. (2010). Planning and development of investment projects in Croatia's hotel industry, *Acta Turistica*, 22(1), 69–96.
Cobanoglu, C., Berezina, K., Kasavana, M. L., & Erdem, M. (2011). The impact of technology amenities on hotel guest overall satisfaction. *Journal of Quality Assurance in Hospitality & Tourism*, 12(4), 272–288.
Connolly, D. J. (2000). Shifting paradigms: Using information technology to enhance service dyads in luxury hotels. *Journal of Hospitality & Leisure Marketing*, 7(2), 3–38.
Damnjanović, V., Lončarić, D., & Dlačić, J. (2020). Digital marketing strategy of Accor Hotels: Shaping the future of hospitality. *Tourism and Hospitality Management*, 26(1), 233–244.
Davis, F. D. (1989). Perceived usefulness, perceived ease of use, and user acceptance of information technology. *MIS Quarterly*, 13, 319–340.
Ekiz, E., Khoo-Lattimore, C., & Memarzadeh, F. (2012). Air the anger: Investigating online complaints on luxury hotels. *Journal of Hospitality and Tourism Technology*, 3(2), 96–106. https://doi.org/10.1108/17579881211248817
Esposito, B., Sessa, M. R., Sica, D., & Malandrino, O. (2022). Service innovation in the restaurant sector during COVID-19: Digital technologies to reduce customers' risk perception. *The TQM Journal*, 34(7), 134–164.
Fainshtein, E., Chkoniya, V., Serova, E., & Vorobyev, P. (2023). Sustainable social systems: Innovative service implications in the restaurant business in the post-COVID era with digital transformation strategies. *Sustainability*, 15(19), 14539. https://doi.org/10.3390/su151914539
Farías, A., & Cancino, C. A. (2021). Digital transformation in the Chilean lodging sector: Opportunities for sustainable businesses. *Sustainability*, 13(14), 8097. https://doi.org/10.3390/su13148097
Furunes, T., & Mkono, M. (2019). Service-delivery success and failure under the sharing economy. *International Journal of Contemporary Hospitality Management*, 31(8), 3352–3370. https://doi.org/10.1108/IJCHM-06-2018-0532
Guido, G., Amatulli, C., Peluso, A. M., De Matteis, C., Piper, L., & Pino, G. (2020). Measuring internalized versus externalized luxury consumption motivations and consumers' segmentation. *Italian Journal of Marketing*, 2020(1), 25–47. https://doi.org/10.1007/s43039-020-00002-9
Ham, S., Kim, W. G., & Jeong, S. (2005). Effect of information technology on performance in upscale hotels. *International Journal of Hospitality Management*, 24(2), 281–294. https://doi.org/10.1016/j.ijhm.2004.06.010
Han, S. H., Lee, J., Edvardsson, B., & Verma, R. (2021). Mobile technology adoption among hotels: Managerial issues and opportunities. *Tourism Management Perspectives*, 38, 100811. https://doi.org/10.1016/j.tmp.2021.100811
Huo, Y. (1998). Information technology and the performance of the restaurant firms. *Journal of Hospitality and Tourism Research*, 22(3), 239–251.

Huy, L. V., Nguyen, P. T. H., Pham, L., & Berry, R. (2019). Technology readiness and satisfaction in Vietnam's luxury hotels. *International Journal of Management and Decision Making*, 18(2), 183–208. https://doi.org/10.1504/IJMDM.2019.098648

Ivasciuc, I. S. (2020). Augmented reality and facial recognition technologies. Building bridges between the hospitality industry and tourists during pandemic. *Bulletin of the Transilvania University of Brasov*. Series V: Economic Sciences, 13(62), 2, 75–92. https://doi.org/10.31926/but.es.2020.13.62.2.8

Jayawardena, C., Ahmad, A., Valeri, M., & Jaharadak, A. A. (2023). Technology acceptance antecedents in digital transformation in hospitality industry. *International Journal of Hospitality Management*, 108, 103350. https://doi.org/10.1016/j.ijhm.2022.103350

Jeong, M., Lee, M., & Nagesvaran, B. (2016). Employees' use of mobile devices and their perceived outcomes in the workplace: A case of luxury hotel. *International Journal of Hospitality Management*, 57, 40–51. https://doi.org/10.1016/j.ijhm.2016.05.003

Kilichan, R., & Yilmaz, M. (2020). Artificial intelligence and robotic technologies in tourism and hospitality industry. *Erciyes Üniversitesi Sosyal Bilimler Enstitüsü Dergisi*, 50, 353–380. https://doi.org/10.48070/erusosbilder.838193

Kim, M., & Qu, H. (2014). Travelers' behavioral intention toward hotel self-service kiosks usage. *International Journal of Contemporary Hospitality Management*, 26(2), 225–245.

Kim, T. G., Lee, J. H., & Law, R. (2008). An empirical examination of the acceptance behaviour of hotel front office systems: An extended technology acceptance model. *Tourism Management*, 29(3), 500–513. https://doi.org/10.1016/j.tourman.2007.05.016

Kim, W. G., & Ham, S. (2006). The impact of information technology implementation on service quality in the hotel industry. *Information Technology in Hospitality*, 4(4), 143–51. https://doi.org/10.3727/154595306779868430

Kucukusta, D., Heung, V. C., & Hui, S. (2014). Deploying self-service technology in luxury hotel brands: Perceptions of business travelers. *Journal of Travel & Tourism Marketing*, 31(1), 55–70. http://dx.doi.org/10.1080/10548408.2014.861707

Kuo, C. M., Chen, L. C., Tseng, C. Y., & Boger, E. P. (2016). SMART SWOT strategic planning analysis: For service robot utilization in the hospitality industry. *The Consortium Journal of Hospitality and Tourism*, 20(2), 60–72.

Law, R., Buhalis, D., & Cobanoglu, C. (2014). Progress on information and communication technologies in hospitality and tourism. *International Journal of Contemporary Hospitality Management*, 26(5), 727–750.

Law, R., & Hsu, C. H. (2006). Importance of hotel website dimensions and attributes: Perceptions of online browsers and online purchasers. *Journal of Hospitality & Tourism Research*, 30(3), 295–312. https://doi.org/10.1177/1096348006287161

Law, R., & Jogaratnam, G. (2005). A study of hotel information technology applications. *International Journal of Contemporary Hospitality Management*, 17(2), 170–180. https://doi.org/10.1108/09596110510582369

Lee, L. Y. S. (2016). Hospitality industry web-based self-service technology adoption model: A cross-cultural perspective. *Journal of Hospitality & Tourism Research*, 40(2), 162–197. https://doi.org/10.1177/1096348013495695

Leung, R. (2019). Smart hospitality: Taiwan hotel stakeholder perspectives. *Tourism Review*, 74(1), 50–62. https://doi.org/10.1108/TR-09-2017-0149

Melián-González, S., & Bulchand-Gidumal, J. (2016). A model that connects information technology and hotel performance. *Tourism Management*, 53, 30–37.

Memarzadeh, F., & Anand, S. (2020). Hotel guests' perceptions of green technology applications, and practices in the hotel industry. *International Journal of Tourism and Hospitality Management in the Digital Age*, 4(1), 1–9.

Mihalic, T., & Buhalis, D. (2013). ICT as a new competitive advantage factor-case of small transitional hotel sector. *Economic and Business Review*, 15 (1), 33–56.

Montargot, N., & Lahouel, B. B. (2018). The acceptance of technological change in the hospitality industry from the perspective of front-line employees. *Journal of Organizational Change Management*, 31(3), 637–655. https://doi.org/10.1108/JOCM-10-2016-0192

Morosan, C., & Jeong, M. (2008). Users' perceptions of two types of hotel reservation Web sites. *International Journal of Hospitality Management*, 27(2), 284–292. https://doi.org/10.1016/j.ijhm.2007.07.023
Nazir, S., Khadim, S., Asadullah, M. A., & Syed, N. (2023). Exploring the influence of artificial intelligence technology on consumer repurchase intention: The mediation and moderation approach. *Technology in Society*, 72, 102190. https://doi.org/10.1016/j.techsoc.2022.102190
Ordanini, A., & Parasuraman, A. (2011). Service innovation viewed through a service dominant logic Lens: A conceptual framework and empirical analysis. *Journal of Service Research*, 14(1), 3–23. https://doi.org/10.1177/1094670510385332.
Papathanassis, A. (2017). R-tourism: Introducing the potential impact of robotics and service automation in tourism. *Ovidius University Annals, Series Economic Sciences*, 17(1), 211–216.
Parasuraman, A. (2000). Technology Readiness Index (TRI) a multiple-item scale to measure readiness to embrace new technologies. *Journal of Service Research*, 2(4), 307–320.
Pham, L., Williamson, S., Lane, P., Limbu, Y., Nguyen, P. T. H., & Coomer, T. (2020). Technology readiness and purchase intention: Role of perceived value and online satisfaction in the context of luxury hotels. *International Journal of Management and Decision Making*, 19(1), 91–117. https://doi.org/10.1504/IJMDM.2020.104208
Pickering, C., Grignon, J., Steven, R., Guitart, D., & Byrne, J. (2015). Publishing not perishing: How research students transition from novice to knowledgeable using systematic quantitative literature reviews. *Studies in Higher Education*, 40(10), 1756–1769. https://doi.org/10.1080/03075079.2014.914907
Reis, J., Melão, N., Salvadorinho, J., Soares, B., & Rosete, A. (2020). Service robots in the hospitality industry: The case of Henn-na hotel, *Japan. Technology in Society*, 63, 101423. https://doi.org/10.1016/j.techsoc.2020.101423
Romero-Martínez, A. M., & García-Muiña, F. E. (2021). Digitalization level, corruptive practices, and location choice in the hotel industry. *Journal of Business Research*, 136, 176–185. https://doi.org/10.1016/j.jbusres.2021.07.032
Šeric, M., Gil-Saura, I., & Mollá-Descals, A. (2016). Can advanced technology affect customer-based brand equity in service firms? An empirical study in upscale hotels. *Journal of Service theory and Practice*, 26(1), 2–27. https://doi.org/10.1108/JSTP-10-2014-0239
Sharma, D. (2016). Enhancing customer experience using technological innovations: A study of the Indian hotel industry". *Worldwide Hospitality and Tourism Themes*, 8(4), 469–480. https://doi.org/10.1108/WHATT-04-2016-0018
Siguaw, J., Enz, C., & Namasivayam, K. (2000). Adaptation of information technology in US Hotels: Strategically driven objectives. *Journal of Travel Research*, 39(2), 192–201.
Stamboulis, Y., & Skayannis, P. (2003). Innovation strategies and technology for experience – based tourism. *Tourism Management*, 24(1), 35–43. https://doi.org/10.1016/S0261–5177(02)00047–X
Sujood, S., Ali, R., Arwab, M., & Hamid, S. (2023). Post-Pandemic intention of the tourism and hospitality (t&h) industry employees towards the use of information technology. *Tourism and Hospitality Management*, 29(2), 279–295
Sun, S., Lee, P. C., Law, R., & Zhong, L. (2020). The impact of cultural values on the acceptance of hotel technology adoption from the perspective of hotel employees. *Journal of Hospitality and Tourism Management*, 44, 61–69. https://doi.org/10.1016/j.jhtm.2020.04.012
Talbott, B. (2004). Looking ahead: Marketing luxury hotels in the 21st century. In B. Dickinson, & A. Vladimir (Eds.), *The complete 21st century travel & hospitality marketing handbook* (pp. 555–568). Upper Saddle River, NJ: Pearson Custom Publishing.
Tom Dieck, M. C., Jung, T. H., Kim, W. G., & Moon, Y. (2017). Hotel guests' social media acceptance in luxury hotels. *International Journal of Contemporary Hospitality Management*, 29(1), 530–550.
Triantafyllou, G., Toanoglou, M., & Strataki, E. (2022). The implementation of smart technologies in luxury hotels. *Journal of Tourism Quarterly*, 4(1–2), 11–20.

Vigneron, F., & Johnson, L. W. (2004). Measuring perceptions of brand luxury. *Journal of Brand Management*, 11(6), 484–506.
Vogiatzi, M. (2015). The use of ICT technologies enhances employees' performance in the Greek hotel industry. *International Journal of Economics, Finance and Management Sciences*, 3(1), 43–56.
Wiedmann, K. P., Hennigs, N., & Siebels, A. (2009). Value-based segmentation of luxury consumption behavior. *Psychology and Marketing*, 26(7), 625–651.
Wynn, M., & Jones, P. (2022). IT strategy in the hotel industry in the digital era. *Sustainability*, 14(17), 10705.
Youssofi, A., Jeannot, F., Jongmans, E., & Dampérat, M. (2023). Designing the digitalized guest experience: A comprehensive framework and research agenda. *Psychology & Marketing*. https://doi.org/10.1002/mar.21929
Yu, C. E. (2020). Humanlike robots as employees in the hotel industry: Thematic content analysis of online reviews. *Journal of Hospitality Marketing & Management*, 29(1), 22–38. https://doi.org/10.1080/19368623.2019.1592733
Zhong, L., Zhang, X., Rong, J., Chan, H. K., Xiao, J., & Kong, H. (2020). Construction and empirical research on acceptance model of service robots applied in hotel industry. *Industrial Management & Data Systems*, 121(6), 1325–1352. https://doi.org/10.1108/IMDS-11-2019-0603

18 Evaluation of Consumer Experiences by Extended AIDUA Framework in the World of the Metaverse – the Future of Next-Gen Hospitality

Dr. Subbulakshmi Somu, Prof. K. Asha, and Dr. Roopashree Raghavendra Rao

Introduction

A platform that lets players make and play games in a virtual world is called Roblox. It is already making progress in the metaverse and has a sizable user base. The well-known online game *Fortnite* has gained popularity in the metaverse, which allows users to explore its virtual events and concerts. Conversely, *Second Life* is a virtual world where people can design and explore virtual spaces. Decentraland is a decentralized 3D virtual platform where individuals can buy virtual plots through cryptocurrency with the help of the Ethereum blockchain. It is basically the platform to produce and monetize virtual content. A New York-based company named Ennead Architects uses virtual reality to help clients with three-dimensional visualization of both space and data. For instance, in its virtual reality projections, architects used different-coloured blocks to project the areas of the Shanghai Planetarium where it receives the most lighting and used redder blocks to project the places where there is increase in light exposure.

Mahindra Lifespace Developers Limited (MLDL), the real estate and infrastructure development arm of the Mahindra Group, unveiled India's first home-buying experience on the metaverse with the launch of Bastion at Mahindra Citadel, which is Phase 2 of the project. This milestone was revealed via a first-of-its-kind drone show, which culminated in a QR code in the skies of Pune, which led the audience to the metaverse experience. These platforms represent only a small portion of the metaverse's present state of development. Virtual and augmented reality are becoming more and more popular, and it's obvious that the metaverse is where online content is headed.

Evolution of technology is necessary in the digital world. It is important to enhance our experiences in extended reality and improve various parts of the digital world (Purdy, 2023). The metaverse provides the rapid advancement in technology which gives the user an immersive, 3D social experience of a virtual world. It uses technologies like virtual reality and augmented reality, which helps bridge the gap between the real and the virtual worlds. It is a 3D universal space which offers a virtual platform in which the user moves around as a digital avatar, communicates with other avatars, and performs various activities like playing games, hanging

DOI: 10.4324/9781003488248-18

out, attending various social events, shopping, or making virtual real estate deals just like the user would do in the real world. It gives the feel of reality inside the virtual world. This is possible with the use of modern technologies like artificial intelligence, machine learning, and blockchain, etc.

Literature Support

Societal progress in the direction of electronic channels is owing to upgraded technologies (Purdy, 2023). The ease of adapting upcoming technologies, such as the metaverse, can benefit the tourism industry by enabling more efficient marketing and enhanced customer experiences. The metaverse offers the tourism industry an opportunity to leverage emerging technologies and provide more engaging and immersive experiences for customers. This can result in increased efficiency in marketing and promotion, as well as improvements in the overall quality of customer experiences (Rancati & d'Agata, 2022; Roy et al., 2022). The increased wider usage of the metaverse owing to the distinct characteristics and predictability was identified by a bibliometric analyses of studies conducted during the time frame 2021–2022 (Celik et al., 2022). The importance of experience enhancement to the consumer by using various technology advancements like the metaverse has been highlighted (Dwivedi et al., 2023). The efficient usage of the metaverse enables businesses to uplift the consumer experiences, thereby reducing cost and increasing revenue (Gursoy et al., 2023; Kelly et al., 2023; Lola Pedro, 2013).

The influence of performance and effort of expectancy on the emotions of the customers was studied with respect to 210 guests of luxury hotels of New Delhi and Chandigarh, which validated how the customer's acceptance or non-acceptance of usage of AI devices is characterized by the decision-making process, which is in three stages (Kelly et al., 2023 and Roy et al., 2020). It is also observed that the applicable usefulness is a result of a positive effect of compatibility, enjoyment, and trust. AI-supplemented, AI-generated, AI-mediated, and AI-facilitated encounters were highlighted as the different modes of service encounters, and a model was formulated to identify the different factors which govern both the service encounters and the outcomes in relation to AI technology based on the literature review (Dwivedi et al., 2023).

What Is the Metaverse?

Evolution of technology is necessary in the digital world, and the metaverse provides rapid advancement by offering an immersive, 3D social experience of a virtual world that bridges the gap between the real and virtual realms through technologies like virtual reality and augmented reality, thereby enhancing user experiences in extended reality and improving various aspects of the digital world (Roy et al., 2020). It is a 3D universal space which offers a virtual platform to the user in which the user moves around as an digital avatar, communicate with other avatars and perform various activities like playing games, hanging out, attending various social events, shopping, virtual real estate deals just like user would do in the real world. It gives the feel of reality inside the virtual world. This is possible with the use of modern technologies like artificial intelligence, machine learning and blockchain etc.

The metaverse offers no restrictions in the number of users experiences this virtual ecosystems. Utilizing the features of the metaverse allows various businesses to leverage the user experiences, unlock major revenue streams by cutting down the cost, makes business operations efficient, and delivers more value to the customers (Yang & Wang, 2023). It is an ecosystem as shown in Figure 18.1 in which multiple virtual worlds combine with technologies that are shared among different layers to create smart virtual experiences. It takes different form when interlinked with cloud technologies, IoT, and 5G. It is used to accomplish the unimaginable things (Rancati & d'Agata, 2022). The real world can be replicated exactly in the virtual world by using 3D reconstruction technologies. A user can move from one virtual environment to another as effortlessly as switching between different websites over the internet.

The Metaverse in the Hospitality Industry

The metaverse is a game changer for the hospitality industry. It supports many businesses with enormous opportunities to connect with customers, strengthen the relationships, increase business profits by driving up the sales, and improve advertising. Industries can use virtual reality headsets and high-speed internet to give the illusion of the real world to customers for exploring the virtual space recreated by the technologies (Kelly et al., 2023 and Chen, 2023). The metaverse is increasingly being seen as a feasible idea for individuals in the hospitality sector (Rather, 2023) to investigate for room and amenities booking, and several facilities have begun offering virtual areas for attending social events like DJ night, music concerts, and online gatherings or celebrations. In the meantime, the metaverse can offer opportunities for clients to try out goods or services before shopping through e-commerce.

Metaverse for Room and Amenities Booking

A cost-effective way to bring the hotel to life for potential visitors and reach audiences is possible through metaverse technology. By developing a metaverse presence, a hotel can show the customers that it is a modern and technologically updated place to stay. The metaverse presents fresh opportunities for the hospitality industry by upselling the business to increase revenue. The metaverse is able to visualize a digital representation of a hotel property within a virtual environment and allow visitors to explore upgraded rooms and other lodging options, get a sense of the experiences at the hotel, and discover the services the hotel offers. Offering virtual reality tours of the rooms allows guests to interact with virtual staff avatars and complete a booking with an avatar (a representative of the hotel). It gives visitors a chance to imagine several choices and frequently convinces them that the extra cost is justified. For instance, visitors can look around a posh suite in the metaverse or even view menu items (Li et al., 2021). Options become less abstract and are more likely to be purchased when guests visualize them.

3D model recreation of the hotel's rooms, lobbies, amenities, and outdoor spaces needs to have details such as textures, lighting, and scale to make the virtual hotel as realistic as possible. Virtual reality (VR) and augmented reality (AR) technology can be utilized to create a metaverse for providing a soothing and engaging virtual spa and sauna environment. Hotels can create a metaverse platform or virtual environment where they offer spa and sauna booking services. Visitors can create personalized avatars to represent themselves in the metaverse and can book the services directly with the available time slots within these virtual spaces and undergo treatments. A hotel can also create digital avatars to serve as concierges who may lead visitors through the metaverse spa and sauna experience (Li et al., 2021). These avatars can help with appointment scheduling, provide information, and guarantee a smooth visit. Hotels can also create virtual treatment menus on which visitors can view detailed descriptions, pricing, and availability of services before making a reservation. Hosting virtual spa- and sauna-related events, such as wellness workshops, guided meditations, or fitness classes, within the metaverse provides visitors a deeper sense of relaxation and also reduces overall stress. Some popular metaverse platform options like Decentraland, The Sandbox, or Somnium Space can be used to create virtual representations of spa and sauna.

Metaverse for In-House Events Booking (DJ Night, Music Concert, and Fashion)

Hotels can provide a great hospitality by utilizing metaverse technology to offer guests a virtual space for attending in-house events like DJ nights, music concerts, and fashion shows. It is a big, challenging task to create virtual event spaces or venues within a popular metaverse to suit the theme and ambiance of the event, whether it's a nightclub for a DJ night or a virtual runway for a fashion show. It is a great idea to host event listings within the metaverse, providing details about upcoming DJ nights, music concerts, and fashion shows. Using mixed reality (MR) technology, the metaverse environment allows attendees to purchase tickets or reserve spots directly within the metaverse using cryptocurrencies or other virtual currencies. Virtual hospitality managers can promote the events through immersive marketing campaigns within the metaverse using virtual posters, billboards, or interactive teasers, which helps to reach a wider audience. Guests can buy virtual tickets or NFT (non-fungible token) collectibles as event access passes, and these digital collectibles can serve as exclusive, limited-edition event tickets and memorabilia.

Within the metaverse, hotels can offer interactive event schedules that let visitors view setlists, performer biographs, and lineups for fashion shows. It gives a still wider view by including links to artist and fashion designer profiles for further information. The metaverse propels a range of innovations which drive the technology-illusive experience like virtual dressing rooms and avatars. Enabling guests to create and customize avatars that can interact within the metaverse event and setting up virtual dressing rooms for fashion events and enabling visitors to try on digital outfits or accessories related to the fashion show provides the spectator experiences and a higher level of immersion to the guests. Also providing the option to switch between different vantage points or camera angles during live DJ performances, music concerts, and fashion shows within the metaverse enhances the visitors viewing experience. The reality can be enhanced or reproduced by incorporating social features like chat rooms, voice chat, and virtual meet-and-greets, which encourages networking and interactions among guests (Lin et al., 2020).

Metaverse for Virtual City Tours

The metaverse propels a range of innovations by creating virtual city tours to improve hospitality for visitors who might not be in the city physically. The metaverse is a boon to the people whose travel is constrained by geographical, economic, or political restrictions (Lin et al., 2020). It helps people learn about the globe through digital means, which transforms their perspectives. Travellers on business and vacation, as well as event planners, are drawn to the option to "try before you buy" because it allows them to research potential destinations ahead of time without having to spend the time, money, or aggravation. The metaverse supports the design of virtual cityscapes by recreating key landmarks, popular streets, and iconic locations of the city. The designer ensures a high level of detail to make the virtual city as realistic as possible.

A virtual presence can be enhanced by using virtual avatars to serve as tour guides who may take visitors around the city. These avatars can offer historical information on famous tourist places and give commentary and intriguing information about each place. Also, visitors get a unique immersive experience by using the option of self-guided exploration. The metaverse can provide the opportunity to have an elusive experience through multilingual support. To accommodate a wide spectrum of visitors, it is a good idea to provide tours in a variety of languages and also offer translation services to improve approachability. Hosting various types of special events within the virtual city, such as virtual food festivals, art exhibitions, or cultural performances helps to enhance the visitors' satisfaction. Promoting these events will help to fascinate more visitors. Offering rewards or virtual souvenirs for those who complete challenges makes the platform still more interesting. Enabling access to metaverse tours for people with disabilities, including those with visual or hearing impairments, provides new innovation model in the hospitality business.

Extended AIDUA Model for Consumer Experience

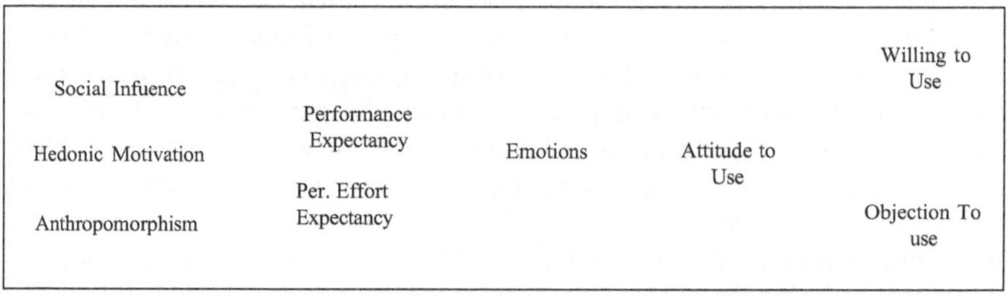

Figure 18.1 Extended AIDUA model

Source: Rather, 2023

Social Influence, Hedonic Motivation, and Anthropomorphism in Virtual Room Tours

In the context of virtual room tours using the metaverse, social influence factors can significantly shape participants' perceptions and attitudes toward this emerging technology. Customers assess the relevance of virtual room tours based on the opinions and norms of their social network. Positive feedback from friends, family, or online communities can make such tours seem important and appealing. Compliance, identification, and internalization processes can impact the adoption of virtual tours (Roy et al., 2020). Participants may conform to group preferences, identify with trends, or internalize the positive opinions of their social network. Participants seek novelty and immersive experiences in virtual room tours, valuing them as a source of entertainment. Emotional fulfillment and enjoyment are key drivers. Hedonically motivated participants aim to satisfy their desires for enjoyable and sensorially rich experiences. Those seeking hedonic value prioritize emotional benefits over practical utility, leading to positive attitudes. Anthropomorphism involves attributing human-like qualities to virtual tour guides or AI-driven characters in the metaverse. Virtual tour guides are personified with human-like traits, appearance, and behaviour. Highly anthropomorphic guides increase engagement and emotional connection with the tour, making it more immersive.

Metaverse Facilities for Customers	*Services Provided Through Metaverse*	*Social Influence*	*Hedonic Motivation*	*Anthropomorphism*
Room and Amenities Booking	Virtual room tour	Relevance and importance assessment	Immersive experience	Virtual tour guide personification
		Social norms and group opinions congruency	Emotional fulfilment	Enhanced engagement
	Spa booking	Compliance, conforming to their social group	Relaxation and enjoyment	Enhanced personalization
		Lack of knowledge and information	Sensorial gratification	Augmented booking
In-House Events	DJ night	Customer evaluation	Sensory delight	Authentic musical experience
		Identification with social network	Virtual socialization	Increased participation
	Music concert and fashion	Internalization	Unique experiences	Model personification
		Reliance on social network	Emotional engagement	Increased attendance
Virtual Tours	City tour	Social network exploration	Novel virtual worlds	Virtual tour guide personification
		Shared expectation and anticipation	Visual and auditory pleasure	Enhanced engagement

Source: By authors

Social Influence, Hedonic Motivation, and Anthropomorphism in Spa Booking

Customers assess whether spa bookings align with the norms and opinions of their social circle. If their social group expresses positive attitudes toward spa visits as a form of relaxation and self- care, customers are more likely to find it relevant and important. When customers lack comprehensive knowledge about spa services, it becomes unavoidable for them to rely on the experiences and recommendations of the social network to guide their decisions. Customers seeking hedonic motivation view the spa as a sanctuary for tranquility and pleasurable experiences. Hedonically motivated spa-goers appreciate the sensory aspects of spa treatments, including tactile sensations, soothing scents, and calming sounds, which contribute to their overall enjoyment. Highly anthropomorphic virtual spa attendants enhance personalization and emotional connection with the spa experience, resulting in a more immersive and enjoyable session. The presence of highly anthropomorphic virtual spa attendants positively influences customers' intentions to book spa sessions and perceive them as friendly, caring, and understanding.

Social Influence, Hedonic Motivation, and Anthropomorphism in Metaverse DJ Nights

The opinions and norms within their virtual or real-world social circles can significantly impact guests' decision to attend such events (Kumar et al., 2023). Positive sentiments and excitement within their social network about virtual DJ nights can make attendees view them as relevant and important. Individuals may attend to conform to group preferences, identify with the virtual nightlife community, or internalize the enthusiasm of their social network. Sensory delight through immersive music and entertainment is a primary driver for attendees. Attendees seek pleasure and enjoyment from the diverse musical experiences and captivating visuals offered in metaverse DJ nights. Attendees anticipate positive emotional experiences, such as euphoria and joy, as they immerse themselves in the music and engage with the virtual crowd during metaverse DJ nights. Highly anthropomorphic virtual DJs enhance engagement and authenticity, creating a more immersive and enjoyable DJ night atmosphere.

Social Influence, Hedonic Motivation, and Anthropomorphism in Music Concerts and Fashion Shows

Social influence extends to participants' perceptions of the metaverse event experience, impacting their expectations regarding performance and effort involved in attending and enjoying the event (Roy et al., 2020). Participants are drawn to the captivating audiovisual experiences, where music and fashion come to life in a dynamic virtual environment. Hedonically motivated attendees perceive metaverse events as novel and creatively stimulating. Higher levels of anthropomorphism in virtual performers and models can enhance participants' engagement and emotional connection with the event. When virtual entities exhibit human-like qualities, participants feel more connected to the music and fashion presentations.

Social Influence, Hedonic Motivation in Metaverse City Tours

Participants use virtual communication tools to share their experiences in real time with their external social networks, acting as personal recommendations for others to consider similar metaverse adventures (Roy et al., 2020). The mental getaway provided by city tours offers a form of relaxation and escapism, contributing to their hedonic appeal. Anthropomorphism leads to an immersive and enjoyable tour experience. Anthropomorphism influences engagement and potential concerns related to AI.

Performance Expectancy, Effort Expectancy, Emotions, and Attitude to Use

Performance expectancy refers to users' expectations of how well a metaverse application or experience will perform and meet their needs. In the metaverse, users expect smooth, immersive, and technically reliable experiences. This expectation affects their overall satisfaction and the likelihood of future use. Effort expectancy reflects the perceived ease of using a metaverse application. Users prefer metaverse experiences that are intuitive and user-friendly and require minimal effort to navigate. Emotions play a significant role in adopting metaverse applications. Users seek positive emotions like excitement, joy, and wonder when exploring virtual environments. Negative emotions, such as frustration or confusion due to technical issues or complex interfaces, can deter users (Wong et al., 2023). Positive attitudes that result from enjoyable, immersive, and user-friendly metaverse applications lead to adoption of the metaverse. Users with positive attitudes are more likely to engage with metaverse experiences, recommend them to others, and become loyal participants, whereas negative attitudes lead to unwillingness to use the technology.

Recommendations for Business Practices: The Key to Success

The metaverse, a transformative technology, merges the real world with the virtual world. The metaverse affects the entire industrial scenario, not just one particular sector. Concentrating on the manufacturing sector owing to the boundaryless advantage of the metaverse, the different stages of the transformation processes can be pushed ahead, and organizations can take a first-mover advantage.

Businesses can tap the transformative impact of the metaverse in hospitality, particularly in room and amenity booking, attending in-house events, and virtual tours. The metaverse empowers guests to optimize in-house event participation and seamlessly navigate their stay through virtual walkthroughs to explore a higher-end suite and tour the city virtually. The metaverse can offer a plethora of opportunities for clients to try out goods or services before shopping through e-commerce, which would result in exceeding customer expectations. By tapping the benefits of the metaverse, and owing to the amalgamation of both the worlds, the service industry, which relies on customer satisfaction, can increase the effectiveness of employee motivation programmes in tandem with business demands.

The metaverse may aid the hospitality industry to improve its competitive advantage, as stated previously. By enabling customers to virtually visualize amenities and reaffirm their decisions, the businesses in the industry may be able to achieve and maintain resilience in their supply chains. By tapping the benefits of the metaverse, businesses may increase the effectiveness of marketing. By strategically integrating the demands of the industry, customer expectations, and developments in the technological domain, the players in the hospitality industry can upscale their competitive advantage. The metaverse would also volunteer players to be open to changes in the external environment and tap the opportunities. Every coin has two faces, which is true of the metaverse also, owing to this disruptive technology and automation of processes. So industries should work towards developing infrastructure, aid in fostering digital learning, and aid in economic growth by bringing together innovation and technological transformation.

Conclusion and Future Scope of Research

The findings highlight the transformative impact of the metaverse in hospitality, particularly in room and amenity booking, attending in-house events, and virtual tours. The metaverse empowers guests to optimize in-house event participation and seamlessly navigate their stay through virtual walkthroughs to explore a higher-end suite and tour the city virtually. The present model is based on secondary data and applicable only to some of the services offered by the hospitality sector, which is a limitation of this study. Future research prospects in the domain of the metaverse, encompassing the complex interplay of social influence, hedonic motivation, anthropomorphism, performance expectancy, effort expectancy, emotions, and attitudes, offer exciting avenues for exploration and development. Investigating methods for dynamic user modelling within the metaverse can offer insights into how these psychological factors evolve over time. Longitudinal studies tracking users' attitudes, emotions, and behaviours in virtual environments could reveal patterns and stages of metaverse engagement, helping developers tailor experiences accordingly. Encouraging interdisciplinary research that combines psychology, sociology, computer science, and ethics is crucial. Collaborative efforts can provide a holistic understanding of the metaverse's impact on individuals and society, enabling the development of more responsible and user-centric virtual environments.

In conclusion, the metaverse is a dynamic and immersive digital realm in which various psychological and sociocultural factors come into play to shape user experiences and behaviours. Social networks within and outside the metaverse significantly impact users' decisions, shared expectations, and engagement levels. Hedonic motivation is a driving force in the metaverse, as users seek pleasure, novelty, and emotional engagement. It fuels exploration, creative expression, and a sense of community within virtual environments. The degree to which virtual entities exhibit human-like characteristics can enhance engagement and emotional connection. However, it also introduces considerations of authenticity and user comfort. Users have high expectations for metaverse applications, favouring seamless, reliable, and immersive experiences. User-friendly interfaces and intuitive navigation are essential in reducing users' perceived effort in the metaverse. Positive emotions like excitement, joy, and wonder drive user satisfaction. Users' overall attitudes toward metaverse applications are shaped by their experiences.

Positive attitudes lead to continued engagement, recommendations, and loyalty to virtual environments.

References

Celik, Z., Dülek, B., Aydin, İ., & Saydan, R. (2022). Metaverse: Bibliometric analysis, a conceptual model proposal, and a marketing-oriented approach. *Bingöl Üniversitesi Sosyal Bilimler Enstitüsü Dergisi*, *24*, 383–394. https://doi.org/10.29029/busbed.1114777

Chen, Z. (2023). Beyond reality: Examining the opportunities and challenges of cross-border integration between metaverse and hospitality industries. *Journal of Hospitality Marketing & Management*, 1–14.

Dwivedi, Y. K., Hughes, L., Wang, Y., Alalwan, A. A., Ahn, S. J., Balakrishnan, J., & Wirtz, J. (2023). Metaverse marketing: How the metaverse will shape the future of consumer research and practice. *Psychology and Marketing*, *40*(4), 750–776. https://doi.org/10.1002/mar.21767

Gursoy, D., Li, Y., & Song, H. (2023). ChatGPT and the hospitality and tourism industry: An overview of current trends and future research directions. *Journal of Hospitality Marketing and Management*, *32*(5), 579–592. https://doi.org/10.1080/19368623.2023.2211993

Kelly, S., Kaye, S. A., & Oviedo-Trespalacios, O. (2023). What factors contribute to the acceptance of artificial intelligence? A systematic review. *Telematics and Informatics*, *77*(November 2022), 101925. https://doi.org/10.1016/j.tele.2022.101925

Kumar, S., Dhiraj, A., Shah, M. A., & Rani, D. (2023). Application of metaverse in the hospitality industry. In *Influencer marketing applications within the metaverse* (pp. 178–194). IGI Global.

Li, M., Yin, D., Qiu, H., & Bai, B. (2021). A systematic review of AI technology-based service encounters: Implications for hospitality and tourism operations. *International Journal of Hospitality Management*, *95*(March), 102930. https://doi.org/10.1016/j.ijhm.2021.102930

Lin, H., Chi, O. H., & Gursoy, D. (2020). Antecedents of customers' acceptance of artificially intelligent robotic device use in hospitality services. *Journal of Hospitality Marketing and Management*, *29*(5), 530–549. https://doi.org/10.1080/19368623.2020.1685053

Lola Pedro. (2013). *The future of customer experience in Africa*. Retrieved from https://trendwatching.com/quarterly/2017-06/future-customer-experience-africa/

Purdy, M. (2023). Building a great customer experience in the metaverse. *Harvard Business Review*. Retrieved from https://hbr.org/2023/04/building-a-great-customer-experience-in-the-metaverse

Rancati, E., & d'Agata, A. (2022). Metaverse in tourism and hospitality: Empirical evidence on generation Z from Italy. *European Scientific Journal ESJ*, *10*, 800–810. https://doi.org/10.19044/esipreprint.10.2022.p800

Rather, R. A. (2023). Metaverse marketing and consumer research: Theoretical framework and future research agenda in tourism and hospitality industry. *Tourism Recreation Research*, 1–9. https://doi.org/10.1080/02508281.2023.2216525

Roy, D., Spiliotopoulou, E., & de Vries, J. (2022). Restaurant analytics: Emerging practice and research opportunities. *Production and Operations Management*, *31*(10), 3687–3709. https://doi.org/10.1111/poms.13809

Roy, P., Ramaprasad, B. S., Chakraborty, M., Prabhu, N., & Rao, S. (2020). Customer acceptance of use of artificial intelligence in hospitality services: An Indian hospitality sector perspective. *Global Business Review*, *0*(0). https://doi.org/10.1177/0972150920939753

Wong, L.-W., Tan, G. W.-H., Ooi, K.-B., & Dwivedi, Y. (2023). The role of institutional and self in the formation of trust in artificial intelligence technologies. *Internet Research*, ahead-of-print. https://doi.org/10.1108/INTR-07-2021-0446.

Yang, F. X., & Wang, Y. (2023). Rethinking metaverse tourism: A taxonomy and an agenda for future research. *Journal of Hospitality & Tourism Research*, *0*(0). https://doi.org/10.1177/10963480231163509

19 Exploring the Role of Artificial Intelligence for Luxury Hotel Brands

A Case Study in Europe

Udgam Mishra, Dr. Nirma Sadamali Jayawardena, and Dr. Park Thaichon

1. Introduction

Luxury hotel brands are experiencing a similar growth trend as the luxury travel market, which contributes to nearly 7% of all international travel (Shin and Jeong, 2022). Luxury consumption refers to the consumption of products and services that are relatively scarce in society and go beyond basic needs, often serving as a form of exhibition (Wu and Yang, 2018; Shin and Jeong, 2022). The visitors to luxury hotels anticipate various benefits from luxury consumption, leading to emotions and a strong affinity for a particular hotel brand (Wu and Yang, 2018). There is a rich history of luxury hotel brands, and many Western consumers consider the experience gained in a luxury hotel to be an integral part of their lifestyle (Wu and Yang, 2018).

According to Kucukusta et al. (2014), luxury hotel brands are often classified as five-star city hotels and are referred to as "high tariff" hotels in certain parts of Europe. These luxury hotel brands are renowned for providing exceptional and personalized services tailored to the requirements of the consumers (Shin and Jeong, 2022). Compared to budget and independent hotels, luxury hotel brands provide superior service due to their technological advantages, strong brand recognition, and skilled management teams (Yang and Mao, 2017). The adoption of technology in luxury hotel brands has become a tradition that satisfies the target audience and enhances customer experiences by providing reliable, guest-centric, and innovative services through the use of machines and AI (Shin and Jeong, 2022). In sectors such as hotels and airlines, the hospitality and tourism industry has been at the forefront of VR advertising experiments (Shin and Jeong, 2022).

Key Takeaways

- Luxury industries have recognized that consumption patterns are changing and that consumers have an increased disposable income.
- Luxury goods have evolved from the traditional orientation of possessing them to the orientation of experiencing them.
- There has been a long and storied history of luxury hotel brands, making them an integral part of the lifestyle industry.

DOI: 10.4324/9781003488248-19

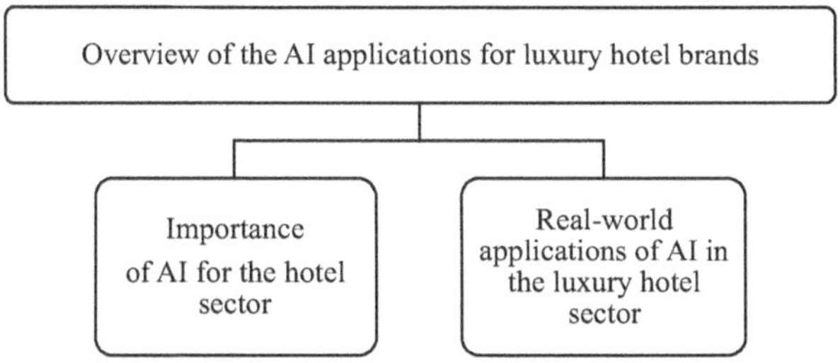

Figure 19.1 Overview of the AI applications for luxury hotel brands

Source: Developed by authors

Figure 19.1 further illustrates the overview of the next three sections as follows.

1.1 Importance of AI for the hotel sector

The application of technology and innovation in the hotel sector attracts customers (Citak et al., 2021), and the hotel industry must recognize the potential benefits of AI and its application in an industrial setting (Zeng et al., 2020). The use of AI was initially prevalent in manufacturing industries, where human-like AI was adopted to replace repetitive human work. This trend spread to other sectors, including transportation, medical, education, and supply chain management (Mustafa, 2022; Citak et al., 2021). The first recorded introduction of AI in the hotel sector was at Henn-na Hotel, inaugurated in Japan in 2015, followed by Wynn Las Vegas in the United States in December 2016 (Yang et al., 2020). Hotel operations have been transformed fundamentally and significantly by AI and robotics technologies. Self-service kiosks are now used at customer service desks to allow guests to check in and check out on their own, thereby reducing waiting times and ensuring prompt service (Kim and Qu, 2014).

As AI is increasingly used in the hotel sector, it helps to meet customer expectations and analyze bookings and transactions (Kim and Qu, 2014). Using artificial intelligence, hotels can generate new customer experiences by learning from customer-related data (Ivanov et al., 2017). The application of AI in the hotel sector is becoming more common, from chatbots to smart gatekeepers, leading to an enhanced in-house guest experience (Kim and Qu, 2014). Currently, numerous AI tools have been established and implemented in various sectors, most notably in the tourism and hospitality industry with language translation facilities, voice recognition facilities, booking cancellation, and network processing facilities (Mustafa, 2022). AI has changed the pattern of communication, capturing the needs of visitors, improving customer service, and increasing customer preference (Jayawardena et al., 2022). Additionally, AI benefits hotel employees because it reduces monotonous tasks such as taking orders, checking in, and checking out, as well as answering the same questions repeatedly (Zeng et al., 2020). Therefore, it is important to explore the role of AI in the luxury hotel sector because providing top-notch, personalized service is the goal of luxury hotels (Jayawardena et al., 2023a; Jayawardena et al., 2023b). Data collected by AI can be analyzed to create a customized experience for guests, ranging from room customization to personalized amenities. Luxury hotels place a great deal of emphasis on personalization (Mustafa, 2022; Citak et al., 2021).

Key Takeaways

- As one of the most competitive markets, the hotel industry should assess the potential benefits of AI.
- AI is widely used in various fields, including manufacturing, transportation, medicine, and education.
- AI can function like a human, recognizing the current needs of the customer, providing a solution, and making timely decisions.
- There is a need to explore AI's role in the luxury hotel sector, because luxury hotels strive to provide top-notch, personalized service.

1.2 Real-World Applications of AI in the Luxury Hotel Sector

Hospitality is one of the industries in which AI is gaining more attention. The Hilton Group, for example, employs an AI robot named Connie, which provides visitor information to customers and, importantly, learns from human voice interactions, improving its performance with each new conversation (Konstantinova, 2019). Many luxury hotels are applying AI tools for hotel operations. For instance, Caesar's Palace was the first hotel to introduce data-driven analytics, which had a customer database that had been stored for approximately two decades from its total rewards loyalty programme (Boulton, 2016). Another example is Starwood Hotels, which utilizes AI analytics to personalize services based on customer needs, especially to optimize energy and water consumption (Boulton, 2016).

It is very common to use AI-powered chatbot services in Europe. The Edwardian Hotel, owned by Radisson, utilizes AI-powered chatbot services. These AI-powered tools help customers find their required restaurants, bars, or information simply by listening to their voice (Prentice et al., 2020a). Radisson Blu Edward's chatbot provides service in London and Manchester and seamlessly connects customers to a human operator if it cannot fulfill their needs. Similarly, Aloft Hotels uses delivery robots to deliver food, amenities, and luggage to hotel rooms, and Flyzoo Hotel, owned by Alibaba, employs a face recognition system for guest check-ins and check-outs (Jayawardena et al., 2022).

In 2023, Zurich's The Dolder Grand introduced an AI-based robotic housekeeper (Frank et al., 2020). This robotic housekeeper uses a positioning system and operates autonomously, without requiring commands from an authorized person. It performs four essential functions namely excellent floor surface cleaning, autonomous navigation in all directions, automatic water refilling, and returning to its charging station when needed. This development signifies a significant leap toward a digital future (Mishra et al., 2023; Frank et al., 2020).

Key Takeaways

- Many luxury hotels have incorporated AI into their operations, revenue management, and marketing.
- Caesar's Palace is the first hotel to introduce data-driven analytics, which had a customer database that had been stored for approximately two decades from its total rewards loyalty program.
- It is very common to use AI-powered chatbot services in Europe such as The Edwardian Hotel, owned by Radisson and Radisson Blu Edward Hotels.
- When considering the face recognition systems, the Flyzoo Hotel, owned by Alibaba, employs a face recognition system for guest check-ins and check-outs.

2. Summary of Recent Research Studies

When considering the recent research, it was identified that social media engagement and conversion rate optimization are positively influenced by AI within the hotel and tourism sector (Nazir et al., 2023). Furthermore, Li and Khan (2023) found that in Chinese hotels, perceived value of AI has a positive and significant influence on turnover intention among employees. For organizational activities, AI directly affects determining the return on investment, improving sustainability, and controlling legal and ethical issues related to the use of data (Bulchand-Gidumal et al., 2023). The advantages of hybrid intelligence in marketing include enhancing customer service and personalization, analyzing customer data, preferences, and behaviour, and using human judgement to create engaging content, offers, and interactions (Petrescu and Krishen, 2023).

It is possible to improve hotels' resilience and sustainability by addressing guests' growing concerns and turning adversity into an opportunity (Gaur et al., 2021; Robinson et al., 2020). Another important contribution is that employees and customers must be trained to work with and around their robotic support staff, to use their AI, and to continuously enhance guest experience through the advancement of AI and robotic devices (Cain et al., 2019; Gursoy and Chi, 2020; Loureiro et al., 2021). In terms of AI replacement, it would be better suited for food and beverage services than wellness (Rauf et al., 2022) for millennial guests (Rauf et al., 2022). A summary of ten recent research studies on AI applications in the hotel sector is presented in this section. Table 19.1 shows the summary of the studies as follows;

Key Takeaways

- Recent research identified that social media engagement and conversion rate optimization are positively influenced by AI within the hotel and tourism sector.
- For organizational activities, AI directly affects operations by determining the return on investment, improving sustainability, and controlling legal and ethical issues related to the use of data.
- Hybrid intelligence provides many marketing benefits, including improving customer experience and personalization; analyzing customer data, preferences,

Table 19.1 Summary of the Recent Research Studies on AI Applications for the Hotel Sector

Source	*Key Constructs*	*Methodology*	*Key Findings*
Nazir et al. (2023)	AI and repurchase intention	Surveys	Social media engagement and conversion rate optimization are positively influenced by AI. Engagement on social media and conversion rate positively influence consumer satisfaction, increasing repurchase intentions.
Li and Khan (2023)	Organizational support and turnover intention based on employee perceptions of AI's value	Surveys	The perceived value of AI has a positive and significant influence on turnover intention among employees.
Bulchand-Gidumal et al. (2023)	Impact of AI on organizational functions and stakeholder relationships within the hospitality sector	Focus groups/ interviews/surveys	A key component of the implementation of AI is determining the return on investment, improving sustainability, and controlling legal and ethical issues related to the use of data.
Petrescu and Krishen (2023)	The current state of knowledge regarding hybrid intelligence in marketing	Bibliometric analysis	Hybrid intelligence can bring numerous benefits including enhancing customer experience and personalization; analyzing customer data, preferences, and behaviour to provide insights; as well as utilizing human judgement to create relevant and engaging content, offers, and interactions.
Gaur et al. (2021)	The role of AI and robotics in facilitating touchless travel during pandemics	Literature review	Hotels' resilience and sustainability can be improved by addressing guests' growing concerns and turning adversity into opportunity. Compelling strategies are needed to boost guests' confidence and help hospitality businesses recover quickly from a crisis.

Robinson et al. (2020)	Developed a framework for delineating encounter types in which human or artificial actors can take part (customers or frontline encounters)	Literature review	Traditionally, interhuman service encounters may not share much with interspecific, and interAI service encounters as AI replaces the role of the customer or the frontline encounters and premise.
Cain et al. (2019)	Literature review on the state of robotics and AI in the service industry	Literature review	People must be trained to work with and around their robotic support staff, to use their AI, and to continuously enhance guest experience through the advancement of AI and robotic devices.
Gursoy and Chi (2020)	An analysis of the effects of the COVID-19 pandemic on the hospitality industry	Literature review	Among the most important safety precautions customers expect are hand sanitizers at the entry, masks for staff, social distancing, limiting the number of customers served, and health and safety training for employees.
Loureiro et al. (2021)	Research on AI in the business context and future research agenda	Literature review	Based on the findings, 18 topics were classified into four main clusters: societal impact of AI, organizational impact of AI, AI systems, and AI methodologies.
Rauf et al. (2022)	Assessed the reactions of millennial guests toward AI-based hotel applications	Surveys	In total, four service encounter categories were studied: (i) check-in, (ii) reception services (excluding check-in), (iii) wellness, and (iv) food and beverage services. In terms of AI replacement, it would be better suited for food and beverage services than wellness.

Source: Developed by authors

and behaviour to provide insights; and utilizing human judgement to create relevant and engaging offers, content, and interactions.

- For millennial guests, four service encounter categories were studied: (i) check-in, (ii) reception services (excluding check-in), (iii) wellness, and (iv) food and beverage services. in terms of ai replacement, it would be better suited for food and beverage services than wellness.

3. Methodology

The primary data was collected using semi-structured interviews conducted through telephone conversations with five members of the senior management team at two highly reputed luxury hotels in Europe, representing the United Kingdom and Germany. Additionally, secondary data was utilized to validate the thematic findings, including annual reports, recent research studies, and website data (Jayawardena et al., 2022). This study employed the non-probability sampling method of snowball sampling. One significant reason for selecting participants through snowball sampling is that participants were recruited through a social network, specifically through friends of friends (Jayawardena et al., 2022).

Thematic analysis was carried out by the researchers using note cards and manual coding (Jayawardena et al., 2022). Researchers manually coded the data by reading through it, assigning codes and themes, and reviewing the results (Basit, 2003; Bogdan and Bilken, 2003). This method is considered suitable for small sample sizes, and a few authors who have described manual coding methods and techniques, such as cut-and-paste and note cards, include Basit (2003) and Bogdan and Bilken (2003). The interview questions covered five areas, including AI applications and their impact on employee performance in the hotel sector. How AI can tools provide 24-hour service and improve convenience for customers? How AI can tools provide 24-hour service and enhance the operational efficiency of the hotel? Perceptions of consumers regarding human intelligence versus AI as machine intelligence? Adoption techniques of AI and robotics in the hotel industry?

4. Qualitative Thematic Analysis

The main themes indicated four categories: (1) emotional intelligence (EI) training for employees; (2) service encounters; (3) hotel cancellation, and (4) reliability and safety factors.

4.1 EI training for Employees

Training employees in EI can improve guest satisfaction, employee well-being, and overall efficiency in European hotels (Prentice et al., 2020a). Housekeeping staff with a strong understanding of EI comprehend the importance of respecting guest privacy and comfort (Budhwar et al., 2022). As part of their efforts to make guests feel welcome and appreciated, they may leave personal notes in the rooms to demonstrate their concern for the guests' well-being beyond just cleaning the room (Jayawardena et al., 2022). It is common for hotel managers and staff to encounter conflicts, either among their employees or between their employees and guests (Jayawardena et al., 2022). EI can be employed to mediate and resolve these conflicts more effectively than before. For example, a manager might utilize active listening skills and empathy to understand the root cause of a dispute and find a mutually beneficial resolution (Budhwar et al., 2022; Jayawardena et al., 2022; Kim et al., 2021). This can be further justified based on the following interview quotes, such as:

> "I always know my friends' emotions from their behavior. I treat my staff as friends and highly encourage direct communication. I always prefer and allow them to speak directly to me if they encounter any problem with the guests."
>
> (Participant 1)

AND

> "Hotels often have high-stress situations, especially during peak seasons. Emotional intelligence helps employees deal with stress, remain calm under pressure, and provide great service even when there are a lot of guests. So, I would prefer to leave feedback or complaints with the help of the voice assistant."
>
> (Participant 5)

Hotel staff members with high EI are trained to recognize repeat guests by name when they return to the hotel (Prentice et al., 2020b). This personal touch not only makes guests feel valued and appreciated but also encourages them to return to the hotel in the future (Budhwar et al., 2022; Prentice et al., 2020b).

4.2 Service Encounters

Although AI adoption is still in its infancy (Romero and Lado, 2021; Ivanov et al., 2017), hotel managers anticipate that AI and machines will assume various responsibilities, including critical service interactions (Budhwar et al., 2022). However, due to the potential drawbacks of AI, no studies have determined which service interactions are best suited for AI and robotics (Jayawardena et al., 2022). Consequently, it is challenging to determine when AI and robots should replace employees in service encounters (Kim et al., 2021; Jayawardena et al., 2022). For example, customer service inquiries in a call center, where most conversations are relatively straightforward and repetitive, may be better suited for AI and robots than more complex customer service inquiries requiring problem-solving or EI (Jayawardena et al., 2022).

In general, there are two interpretations of what a "service encounter" entails. A service encounter is defined as any time a consumer interacts with a service, regardless of whether a human is present (Rauf et al., 2022; Buhalis and Moldavska, 2022). Tussyadiah and Park (2018) found that hotel service robot adoption is influenced by human–robot interaction: anthropomorphism, perceived intelligence, and perceived safety. Robots will manage the front desk and deliver items to guestrooms, replacing human staff and interacting socially with guests (i.e., direct interaction during check-in and indirect interaction during room delivery). Consequently, robots are attributed human characteristics and behaviour (Li et al., 2022; Li et al., 2021). Hotel guests showed a more positive attitude toward robotic staff during COVID-19 (Rauf et al., 2022; Kim et al., 2021). This can be further justified based on the following interview quotes, such as:

> "It's important to understand what service encounters mean since they include check-in and check-out, information provision, wellness, and various restaurant-related service encounters. For example, sometimes 'restaurant encounters' are 'greeting' and 'order taking.'"
>
> (Participant 4)

4.3 Hotel Cancellation

Due to the fact that cancellations directly affect income, they are considered crucial in hotel and lodging revenue management (Rauf et al., 2022). Cancellations made close to the service time are particularly damaging to hotels due to the lack of time for management to react. Hotel and lodging companies need to be aware of potential cancellations to minimize their idle capacity (Sánchez et al., 2020). Booking data assists hoteliers in predicting cancellations and improving their booking schedules by aiding in the forecasting of cancellations (Kim et al., 2021; Sánchez et al., 2020). With the help of AI, hotel cancellation issues are likely to be addressed efficiently and effectively (Sánchez et al., 2020).

To predict which reservations are more likely to be canceled, AI algorithms can analyze historical booking data and external factors (e.g., weather events or local events) from historical booking data (Tussyadiah and Park, 2018; Li et al., 2022). In such cases, hotels can take proactive measures such as overbooking, offering special promotions, or contacting guests to confirm their bookings to avoid cancellations (Rauf et al., 2022). This can be further justified based on the following interview quotes, such as:

> "As a person who has been working in the hotel industry for 15 years, I think using artificial intelligence-powered chatbots or automated messaging systems will help send personalized reminders to guests before their scheduled check-in dates. It is also possible to include cancellation policies and penalties in these reminders to encourage guests to make timely decisions regarding their reservations."
>
> (Participant 2)

AND

> "Normally the facilities include the swimming pool, sports complex, food services, spa, business centers, and a lot of complementary services. So, the cancellation is a loss when considering all these aspects as we need to think about it as an overall expense."
>
> (Participant 4)

4.4 Reliability and Safety Factors

Although there are many benefits to using AI in hotels, it also poses several difficult questions regarding its reliability and safety (Hussein et al., 2022). For instance, questions arise around data security, particularly considering the sensitivity of customer information that is gathered and stored by AI systems (Kim et al., 2023). There is a great deal of sensitive data held by hotels about their guests, including payment details as well as personal information (Thaichon and Quach, 2023). AI systems must be designed with robust security measures to keep this data safe from breaches or being accessed by unauthorized individuals (Kim et al., 2023).

> "AI systems should be designed to include features such as encryption, multi-factor authentication, and secure storage to protect the data from potential cyber-attacks. Additionally, access to the data should be restricted to only those with the required authorization."
>
> (Participant 3)

Hotel operations are continuous, and any downtime in AI systems, such as reservation systems or self-check-in kiosks, can impact the guest experience (Kim et al., 2023). To minimize service interruptions, it is essential to ensure high availability and redundancy.

> "Any downtime in AI systems, like reservation systems or self-check-in kiosks, can affect hotel operations. To minimize service interruptions, you need high availability and redundancy. Suppose a hotel has multiple data centers for its reservation system, so if one goes down, the other takes over and keeps things running."
>
> (Participant 5)

Key Takeaways

- Two highly reputed luxury hotels in Europe representing the United Kingdom and Germany were interviewed using semi-structured interviews with five members of their senior management teams.
- Additionally, secondary data sources such as annual reports, research studies, and website data were used to validate the thematic findings. The non-probability sampling method of snowball sampling was used.
- The main themes indicated four categories: (1) EI training for employees; (2) service encounters; (3) hotel cancellation; and (4) reliability and safety factors.

5. Discussion of the Findings

This study proposes several new insights into the current AI applications in the hotel sector. One of the most challenging issues hotel managers face is balancing capacity with demand (Sánchez et al., 2020). A hotelier has to manage demand and the limited number of rooms within a specified timeframe without losing revenue per unused room because the product cannot be stored in the hospitality industry (Hussein et al., 2022; Sánchez et al., 2020). In order to maximize revenue, hotels try to maximize occupancy, which involves dealing with future demand (Sánchez et al., 2020). Pricing strategies are used by hoteliers based on predicted demand. By adjusting the price of rooms, hoteliers can attract more customers when demand is low and reduce costs when demand is high (Jayawardena et al., 2022).

In the hospitality industry, where guest satisfaction and interpersonal relationships are paramount, EI plays a significant role (Rauf et al., 2022; Kim et al., 2021). Conflicts can be effectively mediated and resolved with EI. To resolve a dispute, a manager might use active listening skills and empathy (Kim et al., 2023; Sánchez et al., 2020). Hotels with high EI train their staff to recognize repeat guests by name as a new strategy. When guests feel valued and appreciated, they are more likely to return to the hotel in the future (Rauf et al., 2022). Hotels in Europe often host guests from a variety of countries, so cultural sensitivity is essential (Jayawardena et al., 2022). Staff trained in EI are more likely to understand and respect the cultural differences of guests, avoiding misunderstandings and ensuring a welcoming atmosphere for everyone (Thaichon and Quach, 2023).

The most common definition of a service encounter is that it occurs whenever a customer interacts with the service, regardless of whether a human is present (Rauf et al., 2022; Buhalis and Moldavska, 2022). As a result of the potential negative consequences of AI, limited research focused on the suitability of service encounters in replacing employees with AI and robots (Jayawardena et al., 2022). Thus, it is difficult to determine when AI and robots should replace employees in service encounters (Jayawardena et al., 2022). A customer service inquiry in a call center, where most conversations are straightforward and repetitive, may be better suited to AI and robots than more complex inquiries, such as those requiring problem-solving or EI (Jayawardena et al., 2022).

In the hospitality industry, research has been conducted on the effects of AI contactless service encounters on psychological safety needs during the COVID-19 pandemic (Kim et al., 2021; Li et al., 2022; Romero and Lado, 2021). With the help of AI, hotel cancellation issues are likely to be addressed more efficiently and effectively in the future (Rauf et al., 2022; Sánchez et al., 2020). AI systems can learn from past customer data and develop algorithms to anticipate customer needs, allowing hotels to anticipate and respond to customer needs quickly and accurately (Thaichon and Quach, 2023). Customers are significantly less likely to be dissatisfied due to cancellation issues (Sánchez et al., 2020). AI algorithms can predict which reservations are more likely to be canceled by analyzing historical booking data and external factors (e.g., weather events) (Sánchez et al., 2020).

In such cases, hotels can take proactive measures such as overbooking, offering special promotions, or contacting guests to confirm their reservations (Thaichon and Quach, 2023). There is no doubt that the use of AI in hotels will bring many benefits, but it will also pose several challenging questions regarding the dependability and safety of this technology (Jayawardena et al., 2022). Considering the sensitivity of consumer information gathered and stored by AI systems, there are concerns regarding data security as hotels hold a great deal of sensitive information about their visitors, including payment information and personal details (Jayawardena et al., 2022). AI systems must be built with robust security measures to prevent data breaches and unauthorized access (Jayawardena et al., 2022). Any downtime in hotel AI systems, such as reservation systems or self-check-in kiosks, can negatively impact the visitor experience (Rauf et al., 2022; Buhalis and Moldavska, 2022). It is imperative to ensure high availability and redundancy to minimize service interruptions (Kim et al., 2021; Li et al., 2022).

Key Takeaways

- By adjusting accommodation rates, hoteliers can attract more customers during periods of low demand and reduce expenses during periods of high demand.
- Conflicts can be effectively mediated and resolved with EI.
- It is difficult to determine when AI and robots should be used to replace employees in service encounters.
- Research has been conducted on the effects of AI contactless service encounters on customer psychological safety needs in the hospitality industry during the COVID-19 pandemic.

6. Managerial Implications

Researchers, policymakers, and administrative bodies can benefit from the authors' identification of two broad practical implications. Firstly, it is necessary to conduct specific research studies that have identified which service encounters are more conducive to replacing employees with AI and robots, given the potential negative consequences of AI (Kim and Qu, 2014; Ivanov et al., 2017). It is often the case that service encounters that are more conducive to replacing employees with AI and robots involve repetitive tasks and routines and do not require a high level of human empathy, creativity, or adaptability (Ivanov et al., 2017; Mustafa, 2022). For example, call center employees and restaurant waiters are more likely to be replaced by AI and robots than personal trainers, artists, or therapists (Cain et al., 2019).

Secondly, the implementation of AI in hotels has several managerial implications that can affect a variety of hotel operations, guest experiences, and employee responsibilities (Cain et al., 2019). Managers must devise a strategic plan for integrating AI into their hotels' operations (Gursoy and Chi, 2020; Loureiro et al., 2021). This involves evaluating the prospective benefits, costs, and risks of adopting AI (Gursoy and Chi, 2020; Loureiro et al., 2021). For AI implementation, decision-makers must allocate funds for technology, staff training, and ongoing maintenance (Thaichon and Quach, 2023). Hotel administrators must invest in training programmes to prepare employees to work alongside AI systems (Yang and Mao, 2017; Shin and Jeong, 2022). Training should focus on assisting employees in comprehending AI technologies, operating AI systems, and interacting with AI-enabled devices (Kim and Qu, 2014). AI can improve customer service, inventory control, resource allocation, and revenue management in hospitality, as well as other operational aspects (Cain et al., 2019). Businesses can maximize profitability by using AI-powered analytics to make data-driven decisions (Li et al., 2022), optimize pricing strategies, and allocate resources efficiently (Thaichon and Quach, 2023).

Key Takeaways

- Given the potential negative consequences of AI, specific research studies are required to determine which service encounters lend themselves to replacing employees with robots and AI.
- To implement AI, decision-makers must allocate funds for technology, staff training, and maintenance.

7. Recommendations for Business Practices: The Key to Success

Brand managers are facing a variety of challenges because of the increasing demand for luxury brands, which is adding complexity to the luxury market (Hennigs et al., 2013). In order to succeed in brand management, it is important to understand what consumers expect from brands and to be able to respond accordingly in order to increase profitability (Pelet et al., 2019; Nam et al., 2021). Luxury hotel management is gaining increasing interest from scholars and practitioners in both the field of brand management and the field of tourism management literature as a whole (Loureiro, 2022; Nozawa et al., 2022; Giglio et al., 2020).

The hospitality industry has rapidly embraced AI, and luxury hotel brands are no exception. Luxury hotels can benefit from the use of artificial intelligence by enhancing guest experiences, streamlining operations, and gaining a competitive edge (Loureiro, 2022; Nozawa et al., 2022; Giglio et al., 2020). Developing a strategic plan should include an evaluation of current technology, the scope of AI implementation, and the resources required for its implementation. It is also important to consider the legal and ethical implications of implementing AI in the hotel's operations (Nozawa et al., 2022).

The application of artificial intelligence in the restaurant industry is showing promise (Berezina et al., 2019). It has been shown that artificial intelligence can be helpful in reducing errors and in portion control and cost control in the restaurant industry (Berezina et al., 2019). There is no doubt that the role of artificial intelligence and robots will expand in the restaurant industry over the coming years, including kitchen preparation, quality checking in the kitchen, training staff, serving guests, seating guests, etc. (Garcia-Haro et al., 2020). Currently, robot chefs are an emerging reality in the restaurant industry (Berezina et al., 2019).

Another AI tool is to demonstrate the way around the hotel. Delegates can use interactive touchscreens mounted on the walls of the reception or the outside of conference rooms, which are used to direct them in the right direction, provide them with flight or rail information, or advertise special spa treatment rates (Loureiro, 2022; Pelet et al., 2019; Nam et al., 2021). There is a possibility that such touchscreens (visual and tactile senses) may also include sound effects (auditory sense) and even emit the scent of the hotel's signature scent (olfactory sense), which can be purchased at the hotel's reception desk (Nozawa et al., 2022; Giglio et al., 2020). If the touchscreen invites the viewer to a local wine tasting, it indirectly stimulates the viewer's gustatory sense in an indirect manner (Nozawa et al., 2022; Giglio et al., 2020).

Key Takeaways

- Increasing demand for luxury brands is adding complexity to the luxury market, giving brand managers a variety of challenges.
- Developing a strategic plan should include an evaluation of current technology and the scope of AI implementation.
- It has been shown that artificial intelligence can be helpful in reducing errors and in portion control and cost control in the restaurant industry.
- Employee resistance and job replacement are serious challenges to overcome.
- It is also possible to use interactive touchscreens that are mounted on the walls of the reception and outside of the conference rooms in order to show the way around the hotel. These touchscreens can be used to direct visitors in the right direction, provide flight or rail information to travellers, or advertise special spa treatment rates.

8. Conclusion

The objective of this study is to present the results of a qualitative case study conducted in Europe that investigates the factors influencing AI in luxury hotel brands. The first section of this chapter provided an overview of luxury hotel brands and the significance of AI for these brands. The second section provided a concise literature review of how luxury brands are utilizing AI and the real-world implementations of technology in the luxury hotel sector in several European countries. Since this is a qualitative analysis based on case studies of two European luxury hotels, Section 3 discusses the research methodology. In addition, Sections 4 and 5 presented thematic findings and managerial implications, respectively. The findings of this study provide marketers and policymakers with important insights into various AI-based business strategies for promoting luxury hotels.

References

Basit, T. (2003). Manual or electronic? The role of coding in qualitative data analysis. *Educational Research, 45*(2), 143–154.

Berezina, K., Ciftci, O., & Cobanoglu, C. (2019). Robots, artificial intelligence, and service automation in restaurants. In *Robots, artificial intelligence, and service automation in travel, tourism and hospitality* (pp. 185–219). Emerald Publishing Limited.

Bogdan, R. C., & Biklen, S. K. (2003). *Qualitative research for education: An introduction to theories and methods*. Chestnut Hill Enterprises.

Boulton, C. (2016). Starwood taps machine learning to dynamically price hotel rooms. *CIO*. Retrieved from: www.cio.com/article/3070384/starwood-taps-machine-learning-to-dynamically-pricehotel-rooms.html. Accessed on 19th of July 2023.

Budhwar, P., Malik, A., De Silva, M. T., & Thevisuthan, P. (2022). Artificial intelligence – challenges and opportunities for international HRM: A review and research agenda. *The International Journal of Human Resource Management, 33*(6), 1065–1097.

Buhalis, D., & Moldavska, I. (2022). Voice assistants in hospitality: Using artificial intelligence for customer service. *Journal of Hospitality and Tourism Technology, 13*(3), 386–403.

Bulchand-Gidumal, J., William Secin, E., O'Connor, P., & Buhalis, D. (2023). Artificial intelligence's impact on hospitality and tourism marketing: Exploring key themes and addressing challenges. *Current Issues in Tourism*, 1–18.

Cain, L. N., Thomas, J. H., & Alonso Jr, M. (2019). From sci-fi to sci-fact: The state of robotics and AI in the hospitality industry. *Journal of Hospitality and Tourism Technology, 10*(4), 624–650.

Citak, J., Owoc, M. L., & Weichbroth, P. (2021). A note on the applications of artificial intelligence in the hospitality industry: Preliminary results of a survey. *Procedia Computer Science, 192*, 4552–4559.

Frank, P., Fischer, D., & Wamsler, C. (2020). Mindfulness, education, and sustainable development goals. *Quality Education*, 545–555.

Garcia-Haro, J. M., Oña, E. D., Hernandez-Vicen, J., Martinez, S., & Balaguer, C. (2020). Service robots in catering applications: A review and future challenges. *Electronics*, *10*(1), 47.

Gaur, L., Afaq, A., Singh, G., & Dwivedi, Y. K. (2021). Role of artificial intelligence and robotics to foster the touchless travel during a pandemic: A review and research agenda. *International Journal of Contemporary Hospitality Management, 33*(11), 4079–4098.

Giglio, S., Pantano, E., Bilotta, E., & Melewar, T. C. (2020). Branding luxury hotels: Evidence from the analysis of consumers' "big" visual data on TripAdvisor. *Journal of Business Research, 119*, 495–501.

Gursoy, D., & Chi, C. G. (2020). Effects of COVID-19 pandemic on hospitality industry: A review of the current situations and a research agenda. *Journal of Hospitality Marketing & Management, 29*(5), 527–529.

Hennigs, N., Wiedmann, K. P., Behrens, S., & Klarmann, C. (2013). Unleashing the power of luxury: Antecedents of luxury brand perception and effects on luxury brand strength. *Journal of Brand Management, 20*, 705–715.

Hussein, A., Elsawah, S., Petraki, E., & Abbass, H. A. (2022). A machine education approach to swarm decision-making in best-of-n problems. *Swarm Intelligence, 16*(1), 59–90.

Ivanov, S. H., Webster, C., & Berezina, K. (2017). Adoption of robots and service automation by tourism and hospitality companies. *Revista Turismo & Desenvolvimento, 27*(28), 1501–1517.

Jayawardena, N. S., Behl, A., Thaichon, P., & Quach, S. (2022). Artificial intelligence (AI)-based market intelligence and customer insights. *Artificial Intelligence for Marketing Management*, 120–141.

Jayawardena, Nirma Sadamali, Sara Quach, Charitha Harshani Perera, Park Thaichon, and Narayanage Jayantha Dewasiri. (2023a). "Luxury marketing and sustainability in the South Asian context." In *Luxury Marketing, Sustainability and Technology*, pp. 1–14. Routledge.

Jayawardena, Nirma Sadamali, Park Thaichon, Sara Quach, Ali Razzaq, and Abhishek Behl. (2023b). "The Persuasion Effects of Virtual Reality (VR) and Augmented Reality (AR) Video Advertisements: A Conceptual Review." *Journal of Business Research, 160*(2023): 113739. https://doi.org/10.1016/j.jbusres.2023.113739.

Kim, J., Erdem, M., & Kim, B. (2023). Hi Alexa, do hotel guests have privacy concerns with you?: A cross-cultural study. *Journal of Hospitality Marketing & Management*, 1–24.

Kim, M., & Qu, H. (2014). Travelers' behavioral intention toward hotel self-service kiosks usage. *International Journal of Contemporary Hospitality Management, 26*(2), 225–245.
Kim, S. S., Kim, J., Badu-Baiden, F., Giroux, M., & Choi, Y. (2021). Preference for robot service or human service in hotels? Impacts of the COVID-19 pandemic. *International Journal of Hospitality Management, 93*, 102795.
Konstantinova, S. (2019). Digital transformation in tourism. *Knowledge -International Journal, 35*(1), 188–193.
Kucukusta, D., Heung, V. C., & Hui, S. (2014). Deploying self-service technology in luxury hotel brands: Perceptions of business travelers. *Journal of Travel & Tourism Marketing, 31*(1), 55–70.
Li, M., Yin, D., Qiu, H., & Bai, B. (2022). Examining the effects of AI contactless services on customer psychological safety, perceived value, and hospitality service quality during the COVID-19 pandemic. *Journal of Hospitality Marketing & Management, 31*(1), 24–48.
Li, Y., & Khan, M. S. (2023). Impact of perceived organizational support on turnover intention in luxury hotels: The mediating role of the perceived value of artificial intelligence. *Vision*, 1–10.
Loureiro, S. M. C. (2022). Technology and luxury in tourism and hospitality. In *The Emerald handbook of luxury management for hospitality and tourism* (pp. 273–284). Emerald Publishing Limited.
Loureiro, S. M. C., Guerreiro, J., & Tussyadiah, I. (2021). Artificial intelligence in business: State of the art and future research agenda. *Journal of Business Research, 129*, 911–926.
Mishra, U., Jayawardena, N. S., & Thaichon, P. (2023). Exploring the role of sustainable organic food consumption and the role of organic food as a luxury product: A case study in Nepal. In *Luxury marketing, sustainability and technology* (pp. 92–115). Routledge.
Mustafa, E. (2022). Technology in the hotel sector. In *Technology application in aviation, tourism and hospitality: Recent developments and emerging issues* (pp. 73–87). Springer Nature Singapore.
Nam, K., Dutt, C. S., Chathoth, P., Daghfous, A., & Khan, M. S. (2021). The adoption of artificial intelligence and robotics in the hotel industry: Prospects and challenges. *Electronic Markets, 31*, 553–574.
Nazir, S., Khadim, S., Asadullah, M. A., & Syed, N. (2023). Exploring the influence of artificial intelligence technology on consumer repurchase intention: The mediation and moderation approach. *Technology in Society, 72*, 102190.
Nozawa, C., Togawa, T., Velasco, C., & Motoki, K. (2022). Consumer responses to the use of artificial intelligence in luxury and non-luxury restaurants. *Food Quality and Preference, 96*, 104436.
Pelet, J. E., Lick, E., & Taieb, B. (2019). Internet of Things and artificial intelligence in the hotel industry: Which opportunities and threats for sensory marketing? In *Advances in national brand and private label marketing: Sixth international conference, 2019* (pp. 154–164). Springer International Publishing.
Petrescu, M., & Krishen, A. S. (2023). Hybrid intelligence: Human – AI collaboration in marketing analytics. *Journal of Marketing Analytics*, 1–12.
Prentice, C., Dominique Lopes, S., & Wang, X. (2020a). Emotional intelligence or artificial intelligence – an employee perspective. *Journal of Hospitality Marketing & Management, 29*(4), 377–403
Prentice, C., Dominique Lopes, S., & Wang, X. (2020b). The impact of artificial intelligence and employee service quality on customer satisfaction and loyalty. *Journal of Hospitality Marketing & Management, 29*(7), 739–756.
Rauf, A., Zurcher, M., Pantelidis, I., & Winbladh, J. (2022). Millennials' perceptions of artificial intelligence in hotel service encounters. *Consumer Behavior in Tourism and Hospitality, 17*(1), 3–16.

Robinson, S., Orsingher, C., Alkire, L., De Keyser, A., Giebelhausen, M., Papamichail, K. N., Shams, P., & Temerak, M. S. (2020). Frontline encounters of the AI kind: An evolved service encounter framework. *Journal of Business Research, 116*, 366–376.

Romero, J., & Lado, N. (2021). Service robots and COVID-19: Exploring perceptions of prevention efficacy at hotels in Generation Z, *International Journal of Contemporary Hospitality Management*, *33*(11), 4057–4078.

Sánchez, E. C., Sánchez-Medina, A. J., & Pellejero, M. (2020). Identifying critical hotel cancellations using artificial intelligence. *Tourism Management Perspectives, 35*, 100718.

Shin, H. H., & Jeong, M. (2022). Redefining luxury service with technology implementation: The impact of technology on guest satisfaction and loyalty in a luxury hotel. *International Journal of Contemporary Hospitality Management, 34*(4), 1491–1514.

Thaichon, P., & Quach, S. (Eds.). (2023). *Luxury marketing, sustainability, and technology: The future of luxury management*. Taylor & Francis.

Tussyadiah, I. P., & Park, S. (2018). Consumer evaluation of hotel service robots. In *Information and communication technologies in tourism 2018: Proceedings of the International Conference in Jönköping, Sweden, January 24–26, 2018* (pp. 308–320). *Springer International Publishing.*

Wu, B., & Yang, W. (2018). What do Chinese consumers want? A value framework for luxury hotels in China. *International Journal of Contemporary Hospitality Management, 30*(4), 2037–2055.

Yang, L., Henthorne, T. L., & George, B. (2020). Artificial intelligence and robotics technology in the hospitality industry: Current applications and future trends. *Digital Transformation in Business and Society: Theory and Cases*, 211–228.

Yang, Y., & Mao, Z. E. (2017). Do independent hotels benefit from the presence of branded ones? *Journal of Business Research, 76*, 108–117.

Zeng, Z., Chen, P. J., & Lew, A. A. (2020). From high-touch to high-tech: COVID-19 drives robotics adoption, *Tourism Geographies*, *22*(3), 724–734.

20 Transforming Workplace Wellness in the Next-Generation Hospitality Industry by Leveraging Transformational Digital Technologies and Tools

Namita Priya, Dr. Ipseeta Satpathy, Dr. B.C.M. Patnaik, and Dr. Park Thaichon

Introduction

"Change is the only constant" has perhaps not been more relevant than in the present days, especially due to the rapid advancement in technology such as the Internet, AI, and automation; globalization, leading to a more interconnected economy, where a small change in one part has a far-reaching effect on the economy of the world; evolving societal shifts promoting changes in laws, policies, and practices; and environmental challenges prompting adaptation to climatic changes and depleting resources, and mitigation responses that prevent and reduce the harmful effects. Certainly, being adaptable to this fast-paced change is the mantra for thriving in this dynamic environment, but it does bring its own challenges and drawbacks. It creates disruption in the routine and established workflow and processes, leading to uncertainty, discomfort, and resistance; inequality and burnout due to continuous and varied extent of learning and adaptation, affecting the mental and physical well-being; and mistakes and loss of expertise due to insufficient time, and knowledge getting obsolete more quickly. The constant change in the world and environment has impacted the nature of work, employee expectations, and employee motivation and has brought in high anxiety, low morale, and low self-esteem (Britto et al., 2018). Lack of effective and supportive structure at work can lead to absenteeism, low performance and productivity, elevated health risk, and high healthcare costs. In times when anxiety is high and employee morale is low, workplace wellness isn't a luxury; it's a necessity.

Definition, Historical Perspective, and Evolution of Workplace Wellness

Workplace wellness programmes (WWP), also known as corporate well-being programmes, are health promotion activities and organization policies designed to support positive health and behaviour among employees (Mattke et al., 2013). It's a dynamic process that aims at teaching new life skills, spreading awareness, and providing guidance in making conscious decisions for a balanced and healthy lifestyle.

DOI: 10.4324/9781003488248-20

As per WHO, by balancing the seven dimensions – mental, physical, social, intellectual, emotional, environmental, and spiritual – individuals can develop their own resources and capacity that can help them to live a healthy lifestyle and allow them to be positively engaged in different facets of life, i.e. personal, social, and work life.

The concept of workplace welfare can be traced back to the 1900s, when labor unions and social reformers highlighted the poor working conditions of industrial workers. During the 1920s and 1930s, employers affirmed the role of workers in the foundation of businesses and a democratic society. The importance of worker loyalty and its effect on turnover, absenteeism, and productivity led to a focus on employee well-being through the practice of welfare capitalism. In the early 20th century, employers focused on providing basic health and safety measures like safety shoes, eye goggles, and heavy machinery guards. By the end of World War II, in the 1940s and 1950s, there was a shift towards basic healthcare facilities as part of the employee benefit package. The growing awareness of the linkage between working habits, lifestyle choices, and chronic diseases led to the next decade of the 1960s to 1970s offering preventive healthcare like health screening, onsite clinics, vaccination programmes and campaigns against addictive habits like smoking and alcoholism. The surge of interest in fitness and health-related activities in the 1980s, saw the inclusion of fitness centers, exercise classes, and emphasis on ergonomics and nutritional education programmes. As employers understood and started recognizing the potential of cost-saving associated with healthy and well-looked-after employees, the 21st century witnessed the evolution of workplace wellness programmes to include a broader range of services and initiatives (Rucker, n.d.). The health perspective of wellness expanded to include social, emotional, and even spiritual well-being. Safe and healthy working environments have become the fundamental rights of employees, but to attract and retain the scarce talent pool and to improve work performance and productivity, employers are looking at workplace wellness programmes as an attractive tool. They have realized that a lack of effective structure and support at the workplace can be detrimental to achieving an employee's full potential.

The significance and importance led to governments around the globe enacting and enforcing provisions to encourage workplace wellness programmes. These programmes also introduced regulations to ensure that such programmes do not discriminate against employees based on their health and wellness and promote diversity, equity, and inclusion. Different countries have taken holistic approaches to these regulations, reflecting the global concern for employees' mental, physical, emotional, financial, and social well-being.

Like all other fields, technology has played a significant role in enabling workplace wellness programmes in modern days. The data-driven approach of collecting, comparing, and analyzing the historical data has allowed for more personalized and individualistic interventions, leading to enhanced effectiveness of such programmes.

The drastic change in the workplace realm driven by the pandemic brought about a radical change in work models, forcing employers to realign their strategies to include remote and hybrid workers (Santos et al., 2023). In these turbulent economic and sociopolitical times, companies are moving away from their old approach of employee support to well-being strategies that are interconnected with employees' needs to help build a resilient workforce. As digital technology becomes more commonplace, it is being used by employers to automate, expedite, improve, and make workplace wellness programmes tools more accessible to dispersed employees.

Challenges in the Hospitality Industry and the Importance of Workplace Wellness

The hospitality industry is a varied and unique industry that calls for high interaction with customers. It is attention seeking as it grows by serving and satisfying guests. Building and sustaining long-lasting relationships by maximizing benefits at optimal cost is integral to repeat business and maintaining brand loyalty. With the change in the living patterns in society and the globalization of the workplace, the industry has witnessed a tremendous rise in business. This has led to fierce competition from the existing verticals and new options like homestays and other seasonal options. The pandemic and digitalization have not only amplified the inherent challenges like shortage of trained and talented manpower, rising operational costs, changes in regulatory compliances, and supply chain disruptions but have also posed new and unpredictable issues. The hospitality industry was the worst affected during the pandemic due to lockdowns, travel restrictions, and health concerns. Although the industry is recovering, it faces new challenges related to public health measures and changes in consumer behaviour. The shift towards technology-driven platforms calls for adapting to digital trends and maintaining a strong online presence, which has led to increasing operating costs due to investments in technology, statutory compliance, cybersecurity, and hiring of trained and experienced manpower. To overcome these challenges, the industry needs to revisit its strategies, encourage innovation, and ensure a strong commitment to the safety and well-being of its customers and employees. (He et al., 2019). The challenges faced by the industry are coupled with the change in the workforce, their expectations from employers, the joining of millennials, and the stress on their personal and professional lives. By promoting a culture of well-being, companies can attract, retain, and enhance the productivity and loyalty of their employees. Improving well-being and happiness calls for a new view and perspective of strengthening optimism, hope, resilience, and gratitude instead of focusing on reducing deficits and disorders (Kun & Gadanecz, 2019). There are several pieces of evidence that confirm that employee well-being cultivates a feeling of belongingness and makes team members feel valuable, creating a positive work culture. The positive culture of the organization leads to increased job satisfaction and task performance and decreased turnover and burnout. In addition to the high-stress due to lengthy working hours, work–life conflicts, and desire for continuous respect, recognition, and development, service-based industries like the hospitality industry face a unique and growing problem of customer mistreatment when the service employees fail to gratify their needs (Riches et al., 2023). Such low-quality interpersonal treatment, with high frequency of appearance and violation of social norms of mutual respect received by the employees has a negative impact on services of the employees, due to high absenteeism, higher turnover, and low morale (Varga et al., 2021). Hence, employers should feel responsible for mitigating and diminishing such occupational perils, enhancing the trait resilience, and recovering self-efficacy, for better handling of stressful experiences and avoiding dysfunctional outcomes by service employees. Well-thought-out and tailor-made workplace wellness programmes that provide relaxation opportunities, break rooms, meditation areas, stress relief, and healthy-eating educational programmes and perks help improve mental health, reduce stress, and instill a sense of responsibility.

Digital Transformation in the Hospitality Industry

Technology has changed the world by seeping into every aspect of our lives. It has revolutionized the world by creating amazing tools and resources that are multifunctional, faster, portable, and high powered. Technology has developed in leaps and bounds since the advent of the internet, which led to other technological advancements. We are still experiencing a lot of changes on a regular basis. Innumerable technology gadgets have been introduced, which were unimaginable at the turn of the century. It has changed the way we connect and communicate in social life, from telephone to cellular phone and from keyboard phones to touch phones and in business from emails to online chats to chatbots, video calling, and virtual interactions (Van Der Schaft et al., 2022). Due to the tremendous advancement in technology, we are now living in the information era, which is nothing like the world we have seen before. It has led to better information access by a couple of clicks or by asking a smart home assistant. Humans have now become reliant on technology; homes, educational institutes, and offices have all been taken over by technology and made more accessible and fast paced. It has changed the way we work, giving flexibility of work and benefits of remote workplace, access to global talent, distance education, e-learning, and augmented and virtual reality. By its contribution to improved efficiency, enhanced customer service, fostering a culture of innovation, and agility to adapt quickly to customer demands and changing market conditions, technology has brought about a paradigm shift in the operations, strategies, and customer interactions of the organizations (Gutierriz et al., 2023). Digital transformation is not only investing in new technology tools, but it refers to the organization's ability to change its approach while managing these technologies and the people and processes related to them (Jayawardena et al., 2023). It calls for restructuring of the organization to build a more empowering corporate culture, change in leadership style, and adoption of new business models that can drive operational and personnel changes necessary to be successful. Digital transformations begin with adopting a digital-first mindset, where the industry needs to take a leap of interest to transform to improve guest experience, operational efficiency, and bottom-line performance. The hotel, restaurants, and travel-related businesses have made several changes in the way they operate and interact with customers. Some key areas of change are:

Online Booking and Reservations: Online booking platforms and mobile apps are being conveniently used by customers to book accommodations, travel tickets by air or land, cruise booking, and restaurant reservations. This has forced hospitality companies to increase and optimize their online presence. Consumers expect companies to have intuitive, frictionless, and user-friendly solutions for booking, payment, cancellation, and refunds. As per some market research data, the reservation and booking software market is poised to grow at the rate of 12.50% up to the year 2027. Online booking software is improving customer experience by sending confirmation messages, reminders, and follow-ups. With continued automation and digitalization, guests' behaviour has also changed, and they have become more tech savvy. The various touchpoints are now embracing smart technologies to make the customer experience seamless. Automations are now taking the form of bots, which can provide real-time support by answering simple and anticipated questions no matter what the time of day is (Ristova & Dimitrov, 2019). AI-powered chatbots and virtual assistants can handle guest inquiries, provide information, and even process reservations, improving efficiency and reducing labor costs. These chatbots are available 24/7 and thus provide flexibility to the customers by being available day and night.

Personalized Experience: The new technology saves the customer's history from previous visits, their preferences, and their behaviour, enabling businesses to offer personalized experiences and treat them as unique individuals. Harnessing the power of data and artificial intelligence businesses are delivering highly targeted, relevant, and captivating experiences by making well-informed decisions regarding customer engagement strategies (Lei et al., 2020). The use of data and advanced technology is a point of competitive differentiation that helps a business to outperform the competitors and gain market share. Brands are striving to meet customer expectations by optimizing their customers' journey and converting them into longer-term satisfaction, loyalty, and retention (Dwivedi et al., 2023).

Guest Experience: Guest-facing modern technology tools provide more customer-centric experiences. The tools can be used to control the environment, like contactless check-in and check-out, enhancing the safety of staff and customers. Mobile phones are used as keys and for the convenience of adjusting room temperature, controlling the blinds, televisions, and lighting, and using a mobile app to contact hotel staff. Hilton Hotel has introduced a mobile app as part of its "connected room" through which guests can control the features of their rooms by the touchscreen of their smartphone, helping them to adjust the lights, control the room temperature, and manage the television and sound system (Imtiaz & Kim, 2019). Similarly, Hotel Marriott provides apps to keep in touch with the hotel staff for any extra help on cleanliness, sleeping arrangements, pool facility access, and local travel information on their Marriott mobile app. They also provide an automated payment feature, integrated invoicing systems, and a digitalized maintenance schedule. Digital advancements have also improved security measures in the hospitality industry. For example, facial recognition technology can enhance access control and verify guest identities.

Robotic Appliances: Programmed robots are being used for mundane and repetitive work like housekeeping, lobby assistants, bellboys, and now as waiters in many restaurants. It is seen as an opportunity to save costs. The Henn na Hotel in Tokyo, Japan, is using programmed robots to manage low-cost hotels by reducing human interactions and thus expenses to a minimum (Drexler & Lapré, 2020). These robots can interact with the environment, express emotions, and work for extended hours without being tired or suffering reductions in efficiency.

Employee Engagement and Digital Platforms

Digital transformation has modernized the world, characterized by data supremacy. It has impacted almost every aspect of society, life, business, and work. Among the various technological developments like big data, AI, quantum computing, 3D printing, and VR, AI has made a spectacular difference in IT applications (Mitchell et al., 2020). By leveraging these digital advancements, organizations are creating personalized and engaging wellness experiences for their employees. Processes that were manual and time-consuming are being replaced by quick and efficient digital tools and applications. Here are some ways in which these digital changes are improving employee engagement.

Remote Work Support: Communication in this world of technology remains a crucial aspect. Digital platforms are helping remote and hybrid workers to stay connected with their peers and managers. Online platforms like videoconferencing, virtual meetings, project management, and instant messaging tools aid employees to remain connected and share information in real time on their personal as well as professional milestones, regardless of their location. The right technology use has aided increased productivity as it provides flexibility to work at one's own convenience without distraction and interruptions. It also promotes work–life balance as employees schedule their work to fit work around other aspects of life like family and personal hobbies and interests. Companies are implementing regular check-ins and virtual and physical meetings to ensure everyone stays connected and there is a smooth flow of information. As technology evolves, we can expect more attractive options to enhance remote working conditions.

Recognition and Feedback: Employee recognition is essential to create employee engagement as it boosts morale, increases performance, and helps in employee retention. Many software platforms and apps allow us to create, manage, and track employees' efforts and achievements. It helps to automate the process of recognition and appreciation and make it visible and accessible to create more equity. It can be used to send e-cards, badges, and certificates to employees for their achievements and conduct. Social recognition tools like Yammer, Slack, and Microsoft Teams help to set up peer-to-peer recognition, team spirit, and social recognition. Employees can use the platform to nominate, praise or send thank-you notes. If aligned to company values, it serves a dual purpose. The value-based recognition and rewards system makes the employee feel happy due to receipt of rewards and helps the company to propagate its value system amongst the employees.

Learning and Development: Technology has impacted every aspect of our work life, and so has it changed the training and development process. Acquiring knowledge and its application in improving performance has become more engaging and accessible. Online learning platforms and e-learning modules provide access to training materials from anywhere and at any time. Hence, it gives the employees the convenience to learn from anywhere and at their own pace. To keep the viewer's attention, such technologies are aiming to be more engaging and interactive. By providing custom-made modules catering to individual needs and preferences, technology is helping to provide a personalized learning experience. The AI algorithms store and analyze the employee's data to monitor their progress and provide individual feedback and recommendations (Wijayati et al., 2022). The learner also gets a virtual environment to apply their learning in a safe and controlled space. It helps retention and boosts their confidence as they are able to apply their newly learned skills to simulated real-life scenarios, where their mistakes do not have real-life consequences. Companies are using these platforms to teach the importance, benefits, and best practices in their respective functions. Adding gamification tools has increased employees' interest and attention.

Employee Survey and Feedback: Using technology and tools is not a one-time event; it should be monitored and evaluated at frequent intervals to assess its impact and alignment (Berry et al., 2020). Digital survey tools, polls, and feedback platforms make it easier for the organization to collect data and metrics. These data, when analyzed, give a pulse of the employees' sentiments and emotions. It helps in evaluating the continuation of an old practice and process and the usefulness of the newly introduced technology and tools. A continuous assessment of whether the processes are meeting their objectives and expectations of enhancing communication, collaboration, retention, learning, and well-being is a must to bring about desired adjustments and modifications. It helps in identifying the areas of addition, change, or removal of some features, settings, or options. For effective use of this technology, it should be made a two-way conversation process. Employers are using technology to move to online feedback tools like online suggestion boxes, exit interviews, structured feedback interviews, and surveys. However, the success of any feedback scheme depends on the acknowledgement and response to the received inputs. Hence, a two-way dialogue needs to be ensured.

Some Examples of Digital Transformation in the Hospitality Industry

Starbucks: The coffee chain company, with a presence in 80 countries, adopted digital transformation way back in 2017 and introduced Digital Flywheel. The company focused on reward, personalization, payment, and order to drive superior business results. Mobile-order and pay-with-augmented-AI features enabled personalized offerings and discounts based on the customer's historical data of unique preferences and spending habits (Azriuddin et al., 2020). Starbucks has a unique offering in providing Aira, which helps visually impaired people to navigate the closest Starbucks store with ease.

Airbnb: Its digital interface helps identify unique and affordable accommodation with a few clicks. It provides a platform for anonymous hosts to share their space and stories through transparent and real user reviews and the guests with a universe of one-of-a-kind accommodations like treehouses, castles, farms, and orchard retreats (Busulwa et al., 2022). It also secures the payment system, providing peace of mind to the guest and host alike.

Domino's Pizza: The company introduced user-friendly mobile apps and websites for ordering pizza with just a few clicks. Features like online payment, real-time order tracking, and pizza customization gave a significant boost to sales and customer satisfaction. The Hero app provides a gaming experience (Sigala & Nilsson, 2021) by which customers can customize their own pizza by kneading the dough, applying sauce, and adding cheese.

Delta Airlines: Delta Airlines is recognized for its digital transformation. It has launched a first-of-its-kind digital platform, Delta Sync Exclusive, for entertainment and discovery to personalize the onboard experience of its customers. The online mobile app enables passengers to check in, get boarding passes, make changes to their trip, track their flights, and other flight-related real-time details. It provides exclusive informational and entertainment content and other offers by connecting to onboard Wi-Fi and logging in with SkyMiles credentials (Avi et al., 2021). The company has also introduced Delta Discover Map, which helps plan the trip and serve as a deal finder. The use of data analytics has also helped Delta take up preventive maintenance, reducing flight delays and improving services with declining incidences of cancellation.

Royal Caribbean Cruises: Living up to its mission of delivering the best vacation experience to its guests, Royal Caribbean Cruises has rolled out new technology updates to keep up with the ever-changing expectations of its customers. It includes the use of smartphones and other wearable technology such as RFID wristbands. These technologies can be used as keys to guests' cabins, make onboard purchases, and plan entertainment and gaming activities during the cruise. The mobile apps also assist the decision-making of its clients by including virtual reality videos and destination information. The smart device helps enhance the onboarding experience of the guests through a preboarding process of uploading selfies, which then displays as a digital boarding pass and allows guests to simply walk through by use of facial recognition technology. It also helps them to track their luggage and other itinerary details in real time.

TripAdvisor: TripAdvisor, the largest travel guidance platform in the world, has changed the way people plan their travel. Its crowdsourcing process gathers information regarding various services like stay, food, and travel from real visitors through their online reviews (Gegenhuber et al., 2020). TripAdvisor aggregates the reviews and provides more relative content suited to the requirements of the customer. For instance, a query of a European traveller regarding a family trip is answered by a another family traveller's review rather than solo travellers. The company has recently launched virtual voice technology to boost business. In the words of the GM/VP-Global Media Business at Tripadvisor, "Conversational interfaces like voice technology can help travellers find the most sustainable forms of travel suited to their needs, while also providing tips and educational resources on how to travel more sustainably." With more than 1 billion reviews, TripAdvisor now operates websites in 48 countries and 28 languages, finding deals on accommodations, travel, restaurants, and travel destinations.

Ungerboeck: This is the world's leading event technology platform, which provides industry-leading event and venue management software in more than 50 countries. Ungerboeck's livestreaming technology has changed the way events are planned and managed. Its wider reach, allowing the audience to watch the event from the comfort and safety of their home, increased the attendance and broadened the audience base. It made event management efficient, cost-effective, and convenient. It has the most comprehensive and fully integrated event management module to make customized events by mixing and matching available options of space management, event planning, catering, exhibition, attendee management, registration, billing, and payment.

Sony Interactive Entertainment LLC: Sony is a multinational video game and digital entertainment company that pushed the boundaries of entertainment with the launch of its PlayStation, a console primarily used to play games. Even today, Sony continues to deliver innovative and thrilling experiences to audiences around the world through the advancement of its technology and the inclusion of 3D graphics, VR, and AI (Mehta, 2021). With the evolving technology of big data, cloud, blockchain, and IoT, players are getting a premium experience of fully immersive simulations, giving a more realistic feel. Sony has focused on enhancing operational efficiency and product offerings and have become the dominating player in the virtual reality market of Europe.

The Role of Technology in Workplace Wellness Programmes

Companies have now understood the role of wellness programmes for their employees because it has a direct effect on their productivity and profitability. They are now rapidly adopting technology to enhance the effectiveness, accessibility, and efficiency of such programmes. Technological tools are now playing a ubiquitous role in creating holistic employee wellness strategies to cater to the ever-changing work landscape (Johnson et al., 2020). Workplace wellness programmes provide a helping hand in creating a feeling of belongingness and understanding to enhance organizational performance. With remote working here to stay, it is difficult to bring the widespread workforce to a common platform all at one time to conduct such programmes. Hence, companies are now using technology to meet online to create an environment of oneness and also personalize the programmes for individualistic comforts. Some of the key ways in which technology is being used to improve and accelerate wellness programmes are:

Wearable Devices and Apps: Wearable fitness trackers like wristwatches, VR headsets, smart jewelry, and Bluetooth handsets are becoming popular tools for monitoring health and fitness (Souza et al., 2017). The built-in sensors in these wearable devices track bodily movements, heart rates, sleep quality, and anxiety pangs. Digital apps are also used to collect data through various surveys, and the analysis can give interesting insights into emotional and mental health and day-to-day mood during work. With the help of these tools, organizations can understand the emotional state of employees regarding their work and colleagues (Mejia et al., 2021). Other interventions like happiness meters, surveys and polls, and psychological tests on these tech tools are helping in understanding dissatisfaction, anxiety triggers, and emotional well-being. The data gathered are synced with the wellness programmes to set goals and offer personalized recommendations.

Wellness Portals and Programmes: Many companies are coming up with wellness portals or platforms for easy access to available resources and programme offerings. Portals like the Wellsteps online portal help in simplifying the overall process of wellness programmes (Wagner, 2020). All information related to the workplace wellness programmes can be accessed in one place, including the facilities available, the procedure to access such facilities, simple and time-saving methods to evaluate personal requirements, and recommendations on personal action plans based on employee data. It assists employees in understanding the significance of wellness and provides instructions in an innovative and motivational way. Employees can also get information on how their own colleagues have benefitted by using the wellness programmes, which motivates other employees and gives a sense of achievement to those who follow the procedure rigorously. Customized wellness programmes on the portals provide team challenges, leaderboards, and other activities to keep them engaged and motivated. It serves as social connectivity among co-workers. The appreciation and credit points for achieving every milestone encourage employees to go the extra mile to stay fit. The videos, articles, and online webinars are all available on these portals for easy access and use.

Telemedicine and Virtual Health: Telemedicine has emerged as a game changer in corporate wellness programmes. Based on the assessed employee needs, corporations explore different telemedicine service providers and establish partnerships with healthcare professionals who are qualified, licensed, and experienced. The eligibility, confidentiality, scheduling, and payment procedures are defined for simple and easy access. Telemedicine programmes support fitness programmes and health issues and provide mental health resources and preventive care initiatives (Langlieb et al., 2021). The feedback received from employees is used to identify areas of improvement and refine the telemedicine programme to meet evolving employee needs. The convenience, cost-effectiveness, and improved access to healthcare have proved to be important to increasing employee health, well-being, work–life balance, and engagement, fostering higher productivity.

Wellness Programme Networking Tools: These are software applications that help in connecting and communicating with other wellness programme participants and experts. It gives access to online communities and groups. These groups and forums share best practices, challenges, and remedial measures for relevant fitness programmes (Wenger, 2021). Employees can join such events in their nearby vicinity for social interaction and other community work. Such apps help in finding local communities, mentors, and peers. These social media platforms help in organizing online and offline activities and gatherings for meeting people with similar hobbies or professions.

Wellness Day: Employers are now coming up with well-being days that are designated time off that employees can use to recharge themselves. They understand that overworked employees are detrimental to the company's health because it is more likely to be rushed or mediocre work. The wellness day programme gives its employees a chance to proactively take care of their mental well-being. Staff in management roles are given adequate training to trust their team members and allow their absence on the defined days to take care of themselves. As reported in *Forbes*, fewer working hours have a positive correlation with higher productivity and well-being. Introducing wellness days as part of employee well-being programmes also reflects the "caring" core value of the organization, and employees appreciate the same by being more engaged, productive, and loyal. As employees spend most of their working hours in artificial light, it is important that they take time off for exposure to natural air and sunlight. The evidence of a relationship between direct exposure and better well-being varies in quality and quantity, but exposure to a green environment is associated with better health and less risk of physical health issues like obesity and myopia (White et al., 2019). Apps with options for such parks, greens, and open spaces nearby and the tracking of such leaves ae being used to measure employee involvement.

Gamification: Gamification is adding game mechanics to non-game wellness activities with the goal of engaging with employees and inspiring them to take up health habits. Applying the gaming process creates a goal-oriented framework that helps in setting tasks and then rewarding the employees who achieve their set goals. It can be applied to set targets for various activities like in weight management. It creates competition with self and others on the board, transforming routine tasks into fun activities and friendly competition. The intrinsic and extrinsic rewards associated with the achievement of each activity, whether it be healthy habits or diet management or even a daily exercise regime and yoga, make the gaming process irresistible. The game mechanisms inspire the employees to take an active role and collect points and badges in return to redeem them for goodies. It also involves storytelling and avatars, bringing a fresh dimension to the gamification process. These interactions, although virtual, are bridging the gap between information and understanding, making learning easier and enjoyable.

Examples of Workplace Wellness Transformation in the Hospitality Industry

Wellness programmes have now become an integral part of employee retention strategy. Studies have shown that wellness programmes are strategic imperatives rather than nice extras. Workplace wellness programmes that focus on lifestyle management with interventions to reduce health risk factors like smoking and other nicotine misutilization or alcoholism and support healthy behaviours like physical exercise and activities are clinically meaningful and have created a higher level of belonging and feeling of thriving, helping in controlling absenteeism and attrition. Some real-life examples are:

Kimpton Hotels & Restaurants: The first boutique hotel and company in the U.S. provides customized and individualistic workplace wellness options to its employees. As part of the company's training program, it provides classes related to work to understand key responsibilities, and as part of the wellness program, it has introduced app-based classes such as communication skills, stress management, positive employee relations, and personal finance management (Abdelmoaty & Soliman, 2020). The company serves surprise boxes of cool drinks and desserts to employees working on hot days. Long service awards and online gift cards to loyal employees are part of wellness programmes to keep the employees motivated. All employees and close family are covered under the medical insurance schemes. The employees can opt for insurance for their pets and are eligible for paid leave for their caretaking and in the event of their unfortunate demise. The company provides online yoga and physical activity on the apps, with reminder bells and monitoring facilities.

Marriott's Take Care Program: The Timeless People First value of Marriott International is reflected in Marriott's TakeCare program, which is designed to support the well-being of its employees. It offers digital wellness platforms that include physical activity and fitness challenges, guidance for financial wellness, tips, and accessible help for emotional well-being in addition to online training and community involvement opportunities. The app also provides affordable opportunities to develop skills and use community development platforms to build meaningful relationships (Popely & Uhlir, 2023). The new technology is being used to guide employees in their personal and professional events and help them reorganize their families to return to the workplace. Through this app, employees have also enrolled in their "beloved benefits" that allow them to stay at company properties at substantial discounts.

Westin's Six Pillars of Well-Being in a Programme for Guests and Employees: Westin's Well-being initiative, which it calls Well-Being Movement, has been designed for both guests and employees around its various properties spread across the globe. The programmes under the scheme are based on six pillars – "feel well," "work well," "move well," "eat well," "sleep well," and "play well." It provides open house and online meditation tools for all employees and guests. Employees could also download a 10-minute meditation session and advice on healthy eating for reference at any point in time. The online advisories are focused on health and well-being, as they believe that healthier employees are less likely to be absent due to sickness. It has also introduced the global Associate Enrichment Program by the name Elements of Well-Being to inspire healthy choices and overall well-being at home and at the workplace. Its main components are SuperfoodsRx, WestinWorkout, and Breathe Westin, all driven by the latest technology and overseen by "well ambassadors" who are available for assistance both online and offline.

Hyatt Hotels Wellness Initiatives: Hyatt fosters a culture of the well-being of its employees by realizing who they are and how they are. Hyatt's Colleague Well-Being Council tries to create a workplace in which employees can be their best selves by helping them find out what makes them truly happy, healthy, and fulfilled both in their personal and professional lives. It has a proprietary online employee wellness assessment tool, Hyatt Well-Check, developed with the help of Psychiatrists, which helps in assessing own mental well-being over time and then various help available to address those needs. The company celebrates Global Day of Gratitude. On that day, colleagues, guests, and customers can send personalized gratitude notes digitally. Global Wellness Week offers virtual programmes, discussions, and tools to support wellness strategy. Hyatt has collaborated with HeadSpace, one of the world's leading meditation apps. Through HeadSpace apps and websites, employees can seek guidance on everything from stress to sleep. The downloadable app and websites are loaded with animations, articles, and videos to make employees feel energized, focused, and relaxed for that extra mindfulness. HeadSpace has proven content that helps in decreasing stress levels and improving focus and mental clarity. The hotel giant's employee assistance programme offers virtual counseling and behavioural health guidance through its telemedicine provider.

Accor's Lifeworks Total Well-Being Program: The leading hotel operator in the Asia Pacific region, Accor, is offering assistance to protect the mental and physical well-being of its employees through a range of programmes both offline and online through apps and websites. The Lifeworks Total Wellbeing app provides 24/7 assistance and support through access to counseling sessions and free webinars on emotional well-being. LifeWorks, a mobile-first platform, offers support and guidelines in full confidentiality at the click of a button. Easy and private access encourages employees to seek help in times of need to overcome life issues like depression, addiction, abuse, loneliness, anxiety, and more (Pfaffinger et al., 2020). Their Lift Exercise sessions help members create their own fitness programmes that suit their work life. The Accor employee well-being and assistance programme provides a platform to access experienced and trained counselors to deal with difficulties and provides methods to stay calm under pressure (Franza et al., 2020). The programme also emphasizes physical health, the programme manager sends daily challenges, and the team is encouraged to post their pictures and videos on private social media groups. The posts are linked with winning points for the team and act as an excellent booster for team spirit. The Talent and Culture team has created links to tutorials of free virtual sessions to manage the workday, which includes tips to stay well and safe, smart working, staying active, and staying stress free. Accor's core belief is that prioritizing employee well-being will protect the group for the long term.

Royal Caribbean Wellness Works program: One of the largest cruise companies in the world believes in providing high service and programmes while at work so as to have a motivated and dedicated team that can keep the company afloat. The company is investing in technology-driven programmes and benefits that enable employees to thrive personally and professionally. Employees have been provided with a handheld device to check in for a shift, which allows them to start working immediately after the check-in process instead of walking to the central workstation. The company enhanced its already-robust wellness options for employees to include apps that allow personal communication to seek help at all hours of work and off time and is also creating an environment to break down the stigma related to mental health. The app offers one-on-one counseling via text, audio, and video messages. It also makes available behavioural therapy and mindfulness meditation. Royal Caribbean Group has a unique challenge in that only 10% of its employees are based on land; hence, the new technology has helped keep the shipboard employees eating, sleeping, and working well together to bring down stress levels.

Recommendations for Business Practices: The Key to Success

To bridge the gap between traditional mental health systems and digital health or e-health wellness programmes, the next-generation hospitality industry should focus on the development and implementation of new ways of remote and digital working known as e-mental health (EMH) (Tan et al., 2023). Recommendations for business practice:

1 Provide wellness apps and platforms that can offer a range of features like videos and live sessions on mental, physical, financial, and emotional well-being to track physical fitness, provide stress management and mental and emotional health support, and provide nutritional guidance and financial management to meet current and future financial obligations. Tracking and monitoring the usage is equally important, so apps should be used to set targets, track progress, and personalize the offers.
2 Create general health awareness and its usefulness. Wearable devices like smartwatches can be provided to employees to track their daily physical activity, sleep pattern, heart rate, and stress level and give easy access to online and offline help (Margam, 2023).
3 Easy access to medical advice and treatment through telehealth services, leading to a reduction in absenteeism. Healthcare providers can be available 24/7 in case of emergency and help maintain continuity of healthcare (Serwe & Walmsley, 2023).
4 Well-suited ergonomics help reduce injury and illness. An ergonomically inefficient workplace can lead to musculoskeletal disorders, leading to loss in productivity. Effective ergonomic improvements remove deterrents and maximize

work by limiting fatigue and discomfort. Workplace wellness programmes are ergonomically designed to reduce risk factors of chronic health conditions and create high-impact and cost-effective answers to disturbing work trends for the workforce.

5 Employers need to create an open culture about mental health issues. With the support of technology, employees should be provided meditation apps, online counseling facilities, and tools for stress release.
6 The wellness programmes can be made attractive by the use of technology through introducing games and targets and rewards for achieving milestones. Friendly competition, leaderboards, online tracking, and simple and fun progress-management tools like quizzes, prizes, badges, and incentives can be introduced on computers and mobiles. It helps turn passive employees into active participants by breaking large tasks into engaging and achievable goals.
7 It is not only important to introduce wellness programmes, but they need to be monitored and followed through by continuous communication and engagement. Employers can use social media tools like Facebook, X (formerly called Twitter), and Instagram in wellness programmes to spread bite-sized chunks of wellness information and to send regular emails, texts, and notifications to introduce a new challenge, complete their targets, and preview the new goodies to be won.
8 Technology in wellness programmes can be used to collect and analyze data to test the effectiveness of the wellness program. This data is further used to personalize individual employees' requirements and help them make informed decisions. It helps in identifying employees' goals and preferences, sending reminders and notifications, and also calculating the ROI of the amount spent on wellness programmes versus the amount saved on health expenses and absenteeism.
9 Remote-working employees are also kept engaged and healthy by enabling them to maintain well-being outside the traditional office premises. Their next of kin can also be included and influenced to maintain healthy eating and living habits.

Conclusion

Workplace wellness programmes have been used in different forms by companies the world over. However, current wellness programmes have evolved significantly from health and fitness to a much broader array involving emotional, financial, and even spiritual well-being. Hospitality and service industry employees work in constantly changing environments, which poses tremendous challenges to their wellness. With the changing global landscape, employers need to remodel the wellness programmes to match the requirements of the new normal. In the words of Leah Mello, lead, Wellness Initiatives, Royal Caribbean Group, we need to create "positive disturbance" that can shake things up and improve the quality of life of the employees. Technology has aided in rethinking and curating a new approach in which well-being programmes have moved out of company premises to include remote-working and offshore employees. The advancement of technology has increased accessibility by remote and hybrid workers through online therapy, meditation, and fitness programmes. Technology also helps employers to gather and collate reliable health and wellness resources for consumption by employees at their own convenience. Easy-to-digest digital content breaks down complex lessons into manageable bites so that people can learn, absorb, and retain essential details. Authentic and vetted data on digital repositories also helps clarify concepts and curb misinformation. Technology has helped forward-thinking organizations to evolve from one-size-fits-all to a more personalized approach. Machine learning and AI technology help collect and analyze employees' preferences, activities, and health risk assessments to provide custom-made solutions, leading to more involvement and commitment. However, using technology in wellness programmes has its own drawbacks. It increases costs, leads to the depersonalization of care because the human touch is missing, and, like any other technological intervention, has its own cybersecurity risks. Hence, ensuring data privacy, robust security measures for employee data, and compliance with data protection regulations should be prime concerns when adopting any new tech-led apps or interventions. Companies should take steps to mitigate cyberthreats and ensure secure server and access controls, firewalls, and encryption and implement stringent security protocols with limited, documented, and authorized access to confidential data, because building trust is essential for successful technology-driven well-being initiatives. Technological advances have blurred the line between work and personal life and infringed on employees' private lives and personal time, leading to anxiety and discomfort. Relying too heavily on technology may unintentionally result in workers feeling disconnected and distanced, and employees may feel isolated due to the reduced amount of time of personal interactions. This may lead to the wellness programme not achieving its desired result of enhanced employer–employee relationship. Due to diverse individual needs and preferences, understanding the quality and reliability of individual offers and suggesting personalized tools for employee well-being can be a challenging task, so employers cannot rely only on technology and data-driven solutions.

Even with all its drawbacks, tech remains the competitive differentiator, and employers need to strike a balance between the use of technology and the human aspect of wellness programmes to provide compassionate and personalized employee well-being. By leveraging transformational digital technologies and tools, the next-generation hospitality industry can drive a successful well-being program, leading to a resilient workforce, satisfied workers, and overall organizational excellence. The advent of new technologies provides enhanced potential for ever-growing wellness demands, promising a healthier, happier, and more productive workforce in years to come.

References

Abdelmoaty, G. A., & Soliman, S. A. E. M. (2020). Smart technology applications in tourism and hospitality industry of the new administrative capital, Egypt. *Journal of Association of Arab Universities for Tourism and Hospitality*, *19*(2), 102–129.

Avi, M. A. R., Nasrin, M., & Hassan, A. (2021). Application of innovative technologies in the tourism and hospitality industry of Bangladesh: The present scenario. *Technology Application in the Tourism and Hospitality Industry of Bangladesh*, 81–95.

Azriuddin, M., Kee, D. M. H., Hafizzudin, M., Fitri, M., Zakwan, M. A., AlSanousi, D., . . . Kurniawan, O. (2020). Becoming an international brand: A case study of Starbucks. *Journal of The Community Development in Asia*, *3*(1), 33–43.

Berry, L., Mirabito, A. M., & Baun, W. (2020). What's the hard return on employee wellness programs? In *What's the hard return on employee wellness programs?* [Sl]: SSRN. https://hdl.handle.net/11159/149398

Britto, M., & Rajarathinam, M. (2018). Wellness programs and engagement of information technology workforce. *International Journal of Engineering & Technology*, *7*, 75. https://doi.org/10.14419/ijet.v7i3.1.16802.

Busulwa, R., Pickering, M., & Mao, I. (2022). Digital transformation and hospitality management competencies: Toward an integrative framework. *International Journal of Hospitality Management*, *102*, 103132.

Drexler, N., & Lapré, V. B. (2020, January 14). (PDF) ajol-file-journals 176 articles 223430 submission proof 223430 . . . www.researchgate.net/publication/373119825_ajol-file-journals_176_articles_223430_submission_proof_223430-2101-546010-1-10-20220330

Dwivedi, Y. K., Pandey, N., Currie, W., & Micu, A. (2024). Leveraging ChatGPT and other generative artificial intelligence (AI)-based applications in the hospitality and tourism industry: Practices, challenges and research agenda. *International Journal of Contemporary Hospitality Management*, *36*(1), 1–12.

Franza, F., Basta, R., Pellegrino, F., Solomita, B., & Fasano, V. (2020). The role of fatigue of compassion, burnout and hopelessness in healthcare: Experience in the time of COVID-19 outbreak. *Psychiatria Danubina*, *32*(suppl. 1), 10–14.

Gegenhuber, T., Logue, D., Hinings, C. R., & Barrett, M. (2020). *Digital transformation and institutional theorizing: Consequences, opportunities and challenges*. Research in the Sociology of Organizations.

Gutierriz, I., Ferreira, J. J., & Fernandes, P. O. (2023). Digital transformation and the new combinations in tourism: A systematic literature review. *Tourism and Hospitality Research*, *0*(0). https://doi-org.kiitlibrary.remotexs.in/10.1177/14673584231198414

He, J., Morrison, A. M., & Zhang, H. (2019). Improving millennial employee well-being and task performance in the hospitality industry: The interactive effects of HRM and responsible leadership. *Sustainability*, *11*(16), 4410.

Imtiaz, S., & Kim, D. J. (2019). Digital transformation: Development of new business models in the tourism industry. *Culinary Science & Hospitality Research*, *25*(4), 91–101. https://doi.org/10.20878/cshr.2019.25.4.010

Jayawardena, C., Ahmad, A., Valeri, M., & Jaharadak, A. A. (2023). Technology acceptance antecedents in digital transformation in hospitality industry. *International Journal of Hospitality Management*, *108*, 103350. ISSN: 0278-4319, https://doi.org/10.1016/j.ijhm.2022.103350. www.sciencedirect.com/science/article/pii/S027843192200216X

Johnson, A., Dey, S., Nguyen, H., Groth, M., Joyce, S., Tan, L., Glozier, N., & Harvey, S. B. (2020). A review and agenda for examining how technology-driven changes at work will impact workplace mental health and employee well-being. *Australian Journal of Management*, *45*(3), 402–424. https://doi.org/10.1177/0312896220922292

Kun, A., & Gadanecz, P. (2019). Workplace happiness, well-being and their relationship with psychological capital: A study of Hungarian teachers. *Current Psychology*, 1–15. https://doi.org/10.1007/s12144-019-00550-0

Langlieb, A. M., Langlieb, M. E., & Xiong, W. (2021). EAP 2.0: Reimagining the role of the employee assistance program in the new workplace. *International Review of Psychiatry*, *33*(8), 699–710.

Lei, S. I., Ye, S., Wang, D., & Law, R. (2020). Engaging customers in value co-creation through mobile instant messaging in the tourism and hospitality industry. *Journal of*

Hospitality & Tourism Research, 44(2), 229–251. https://doi-org.kiitlibrary.remotexs.in/10.1177/1096348019893066
Margam, R. (2023). *Importance of wearables to enable employee wellness*. WSR.
Mattke, S., Schnyer, C., & Van Busum, K. R. (2013). A review of the US workplace wellness market. *Rand Health Quarterly, 2*(4).
Mehta, S. (2021). *The 'new screen ecology' in India: A study in digital transformation of media* (Doctoral dissertation, Queensland University of Technology).
Mejia, C., Ciarlante, K., & Chheda, K. (2021). A wearable technology solution and research agenda for housekeeper safety and health. *International Journal of Contemporary Hospitality Management, 33*(10), 3223–3255. https://doi.org/10.1108/IJCHM-01-2021-0102
Mitchell, R., Schuster, L., & Jin, H. S. (2020). Gamification and the impact of extrinsic motivation on needs satisfaction: Making work fun? *Journal of Business Research, 106*, 323–330. https://doi.org/10.1016/j.jbusres.2018.11.022
Pfaffinger, K. F., Reif, J. A. M., Spieß, E. et al. (2020). Anxiety in a digitalised work environment. *Gruppe. Interaktion. Organisation. Zeitschrift fur Angewandte Organisationspsychologie, 51*, 25–35. https://doi.org/10.1007/s11612-020-00502-4
Popely, D., & Uhlir, L. (2023). *Advancing health and well-being in hospitality: Employers respond to new workforce expectations*. Kendall College Research. 3. https://digitalcommons.nl.edu/kc/3
Raja, R. V., Seshasai, S. J., & Selvakumar, A. (2023). 18 impact of employee health and well-being on job performance and future of work. *Commerce, Economics & Management*, 128.
Riches, S., Taylor, L., Jeyarajaguru, P., Veling, W., & Valmaggia, L. (2023). Virtual reality and immersive technologies to promote workplace wellbeing: A systematic review. *Journal of Mental Health*, 1–21.
Ristova, C., & Dimitrov, N. (2019). Digitalisation in the hospitality industry-trends that might shape the next stay of guests. *International Journal of Information, Business and Management, 11*(3), 144–154.
Rucker, M. (n.d.). *The history of workplace wellness*. https://michaelrucker.com/well-being/the-history-of-workplace-wellness/
Santos, S. C., Liguori, E. W., & Garvey, E. (2023). How digitalization reinvented entrepreneurial resilience during COVID-19. *Technological Forecasting and Social Change, 189*, 122398. https://doi.org/10.1016/j.techfore.2023.122398
Serwe, K. M., & Walmsley, A. L. (2023. The effectiveness of telehealth for a caregiver wellness program. *Journal of Telemedicine and Telecare, 29*(7), 504–512. https://doi.org/10.1177/1357633X21994009
Sigala, M., & Nilsson, E. (2021). Innovating the restaurant industry: The gamification of business models and customer experiences. *Gamification for Tourism, 92*, 100.
Souza, M., Miyagawa, T., Melo, P., & Maciel, F. (2017). Wellness programs: Wearable technologies supporting healthy habits and corporate costs reduction. In C. Stephanidis (Ed.), *HCI international 2017 – Posters' extended abstracts. HCI 2017. Communications in Computer and Information Science*, Vol. 714. Springer. https://doi-org.kiitlibrary.remotexs.in/10.1007/978-3-319-58753-0_44
Tan, C. H., Koo, A. C., Rahmat, H., Siew, W. F., Cheang, A. W. O., & Sharji, E. A. (2023). Workplace wellness, mental health literacy, and usage intention of E-mental health amongst digital workers during the COVID-19 pandemic. *International Journal of Mental Health Promotion, 25*(1), 99–126.
Van Der Schaft, A. H. T., Lub, X. D., Van Der Heijden, B., & Solinger, O. N. (2022). How employees experience digital transformation: A dynamic and multi-layered sensemaking perspective. *Journal of Hospitality & Tourism Research, 0*(0). https://doi-org.kiitlibrary.remotexs.in/10.1177/10963480221123098
Varga, S., Mistry, T. G., Ali, F., & Cobanoglu, C. (2021). Employee perceptions of wellness programs in the hospitality industry. *International Journal of Contemporary Hospitality Management, 33*(10), 3331–3354.

Wagner, P. (2020). *Program evaluation: Wellness for life*. Capstone Experience. 106. https://digitalcommons.unmc.edu/coph_slce/106

Wenger, G. C. (2021). *The supportive network: Coping with old age*. Routledge.

White, M. P., Alcock, I., Grellier, J., Wheeler, B. W., Hartig, T., Warber, S. L., . . . Fleming, L. E. (2019). Spending at least 120 minutes a week in nature is associated with good health and wellbeing. *Scientific Reports*, *9*(1), 1–11.

Wijayati, D. T., Rahman, Z., Fahrullah, A., Rahman, M. F. W., Arifah, I. D. C., & Kautsar, A. (2022). A study of artificial intelligence on employee performance and work engagement: The moderating role of change leadership. *International Journal of Manpower*, *43*(2), 486–512. https://doi-org.kiitlibrary.remotexs.in/10.1108/IJM-07-2021-0423

Index